THE PRIVATE LIVES OF THE TUDORS

THE PRIVATE LIVES OF THE TUDORS

Uncovering the Secrets of Britain's Greatest Dynasty

TRACY BORMAN

Grove Press
New York

First published in Great Britain in 2016 by Hodder & Stoughton
An Hachette UK company

Printed in the United States of America

First Grove Atlantic hardcover edition: January 2017
First Grove Atlantic paperback edition: October 2017

Library of Congress Cataloging-in-Publication data available for this title.

ISBN 978-0-8021-2754-9
eISBN 978-0-8021-8980-6

Grove Press
an imprint of Grove Atlantic
154 West 14th Street
New York, NY 10011

Distributed by Publishers Group West

groveatlantic.com

21 22 23 24   10 9 8 7 6 5 4

Also by Tracy Borman

Thomas Cromwell:
The Untold Story of Henry VIII's Most Faithful Servant

Witches: A Tale of Sorcery, Scandal and Seduction

Queen of the Conqueror:
The Life of Matilda, Wife of William I

Elizabeth's Women:
Friends, Rivals, and Foes Who Shaped the Virgin Queen

King's Mistress, Queen's Servant:
The Life and Times of Henrietta Howard

In memory of my childhood friend
Susie Fairhead

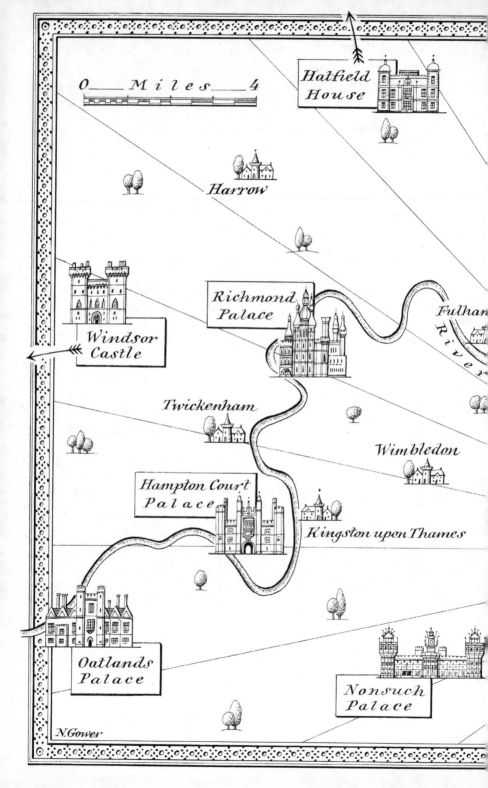

0 ___ Miles ___ 4

Hatfield House

Harrow

Windsor Castle

Richmond Palace

Fulham

River

Twickenham

Wimbledon

Hampton Court Palace

Kingston upon Thames

Oatlands Palace

Nonsuch Palace

N. Gower

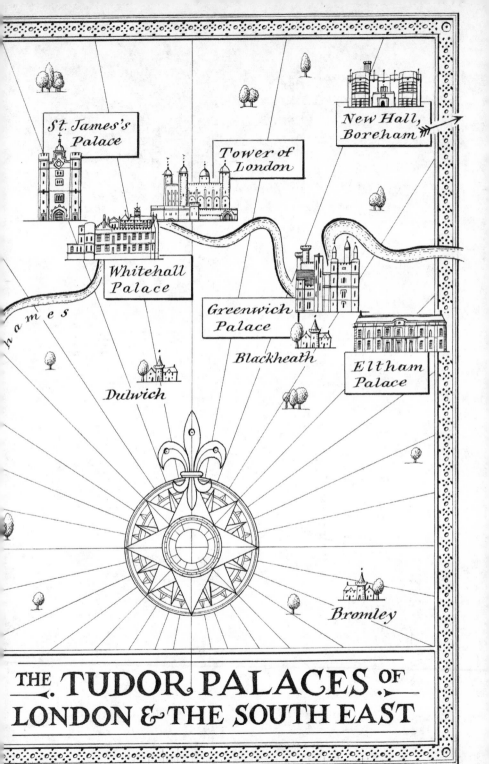

St. James's Palace

Tower of London

New Hall, Boreham

Whitehall Palace

Greenwich Palace

Eltham Palace

Thames

Blackheath

Dulwich

Bromley

THE TUDOR PALACES OF
LONDON & THE SOUTH EAST

The Tudor Dynasty

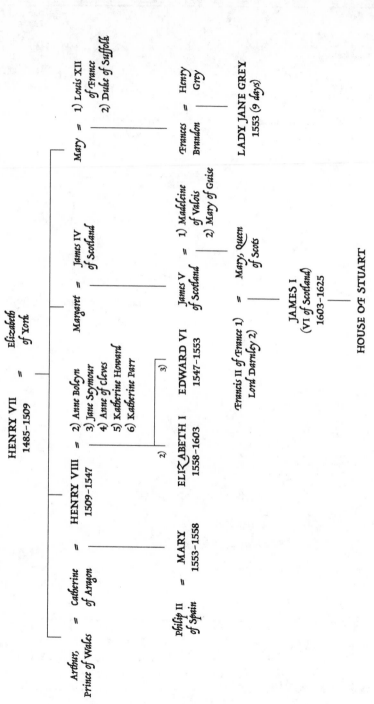

CONTENTS

Preface   I

Introduction: 'The public self and the private'   3

Henry VII

Chapter 1: 'Infinitely suspicious'   5
Chapter 2: 'Not admitting any near approach'   37
Chapter 3: 'Closeted away like a girl'   61

Henry VIII

Chapter 4: 'Their business is in many secrets'   78
Chapter 5: 'Lay hands upon his royal person'   101
Chapter 6: 'She excelled them all'   133
Chapter 7: 'A thin, old, and vicious hack'   158
Chapter 8: 'True carnal copulation'   177
Chapter 9: 'Kings and Emperors all be but mortal'   198

Edward VI

Chapter 10: 'Being yet but a child'   220

Mary I

Chapter 11: 'Thinking myself to be with child'   245

Elizabeth I

Chapter 12: 'We highly commend the single life'   271
Chapter 13: 'She seldom partakes before strangers'   294

Chapter 14: 'A thousand eyes see all I do'   315
Chapter 15: 'I am soft and made of melting snow'   336
Chapter 16: 'The crooked carcass'   350

Epilogue: 'Such lack of good order'   373

Acknowledgements   377
Author's note   379
Bibliography   381
Notes   396
Index   427

PREFACE

Towards the end of Elizabeth I's reign, her face and body ravaged by time, sickness and toxic cosmetics, she was obliged to undergo an increasingly elaborate ritual to preserve the so-called 'mask of youth'. When she emerged, triumphant, in front of the public court, she was Gloriana once more, bedecked in dazzling gowns, bejewelled wigs and thick layers of white make-up, and could just about fool her adoring subjects that she was still the most desirable woman in Europe. A visitor to her court in 1599 was amazed to see the queen, now well into her sixties, looking 'very youthful still in appearance, seeming no more than twenty years of age.'

Only in the privacy of her 'secret lodgings' at court was Elizabeth's true self revealed to the handful of trusted ladies who were permitted to attend her. But on one notorious occasion, her privacy was breached by an irreverent young 'admirer'. Robert Devereux, Earl of Essex, was more than thirty years her junior but paid court to the queen like a lover. A natural showman, Essex was handsome, charismatic and extremely self-confident, and treated his royal mistress with such over-familiarity that he was more than once reprimanded for lacking respect. But Elizabeth loved his exuberance and audacity, and she fell so passionately in love with him that she would fly into a jealous rage if any of her ladies so much as cast an admiring look in his direction.

Believing that his hold over the queen was unshakeable, the earl's behaviour became increasingly shocking. On one notorious occasion, he flouted the strict rules of access to Elizabeth's privy apartments and burst into her bedroom unannounced. He was appalled by the sight of the old woman before him, stripped of her courtly finery, her grey hair and deeply wrinkled face a shocking contrast to the queenly visage that she presented to the world. In great haste, he left his royal mistress's chamber, never to return.

Essex showed little repentance, and secretly mocked his royal mistress as 'an old woman . . . no less crooked in mind than in carcass.'[2] But Elizabeth never forgot the episode, and it was rumoured to have played as great a part in the earl's downfall as his failed rebellion some time later. She had forgiven her favourite many things, but was not prepared to overlook his outrageous intrusion into her private life.

INTRODUCTION:
'THE PUBLIC SELF AND THE PRIVATE'

'I do not live in a corner. A thousand eyes see all I do.' This telling lament by Elizabeth I begs the question: did the Tudors have a private life at all? As monarchs, they were constantly surrounded by an army of attendants, courtiers, ministers and place-seekers. Even in their most private moments, they were accompanied by a servant specifically appointed for the task. A groom of the stool would stand patiently by as Henry VIII performed his daily purges, and when Elizabeth I retired for the evening, one of her female servants would sleep at the end of her bed. Little wonder that in protesting her innocence of any sexual misdemeanour, she called as her witness those 'thousand eyes' that watched her constantly.

But if the Tudors were rarely alone, they did lead a very different life behind closed doors to the one that most of their subjects witnessed. In their private apartments at Hampton Court, Whitehall or the myriad other sumptuous palaces where they spent their days, their more 'human' characteristics and habits could find expression. 'A monarch has at least two selves, the public self and the private,' remarked one recent historian.[1] It was vital for a king or queen to show no vulnerability to the outside world: any sign of frailty, illness or even the natural process of ageing had to be disguised by a mask of invincibility. If this mask slipped, then so might their dynasty. But their closest attendants knew the truth. They saw the tears shed by the seemingly implacable Henry VII upon the death of his son Arthur. They knew the real cause of 'Bloody' Mary's protracted – and, ultimately, fruitless – pregnancies. And they saw the 'crooked carcass' beneath Elizabeth I's carefully applied make-up, gowns and accessories.

It is the accounts of these eyewitnesses, as well as a rich array of other contemporary sources – correspondence, household accounts, architectural and pictorial evidence, ambassadors' reports and the words of the monarchs themselves – that have enabled me to explore the private life of the Tudors. In so doing, I have interwoven familiar tales, such as Henry VIII's turbulent affair with the 'Great Whore', Anne Boleyn, and the endlessly debated question of their daughter Elizabeth I's virginity, with lesser-known episodes such as Henry VII's courtship of his own daughter-in-law, and the lingering, excruciating death of his grandson, Edward VI.

The marital (and extramarital) relations of the Tudors of course form an important theme but, ironically, this was one of the least 'private' aspects of their life at court. The production of heirs was a matter in which their subjects could justifiably take a close interest. This was not the case, or at least not to the same extent, for other aspects of how they lived behind closed doors: their education, what they ate, how they dressed, their hobbies and friends, health and hygiene. Although the monarchs themselves form the main focus, the private lives of their courtiers are introduced at appropriate points in the narrative.

All of this is set against the backdrop of the court itself. I have been privileged to have special access to some of the most important palaces in which the Tudor monarchs and their courtiers lived and died – from the pomp and pageantry of that mighty fortress, the Tower of London, to the labyrinthine corridors and chambers of Hampton Court. Here, sex and power, the ratio of men to women, and the very architecture of the palace created a hothouse atmosphere in which scandals erupted on an almost daily basis. It also created a very deliberate distinction between the public and private worlds of the Tudor monarchs.

By exploring Britain's most famous dynasty through the lens of their private lives, this book aims to shed new light upon an enduringly popular period. It is only when we understand the real people behind the mask of royalty – with all their qualities, defects, tastes and temperaments – that we can truly understand the political, religious and social tumults of this extraordinary period.

I

'Infinitely suspicious'

WHEN THE TUDORS came to power in 1485, it signalled the closing stages of more than thirty years of bitter civil war. The Wars of the Roses, as they subsequently became known, were a series of dynastic conflicts between the rival branches of the royal House of Plantagenet, the Houses of York and Lancaster. Fought in several sporadic episodes rather than a continuous war, they lasted from 1455, when Richard, Duke of York, contested Henry VI's authority as king at the Battle of St Albans, to 1487, when the Lancastrian Henry VII defeated the 'pretender' Lambert Simnel and his Yorkist supporters at the Battle of Stoke.

Henry Tudor's ambitions for the throne had been galvanised by the death of Edward IV in 1483. Edward had left two sons but both were minors and were placed under the protection of their uncle, Richard, Duke of Gloucester. Richard subsequently declared their parents' marriage invalid on the basis that Edward IV was already betrothed at the time of his marriage to Elizabeth Woodville. Their children were therefore declared illegitimate and removed from the line of succession, and Richard was free to seize the throne. His two nephews, who had been lodged in the Tower of London, disappeared in mysterious circumstances shortly afterwards, and it has long been assumed that they were put to death at Richard's orders.

Spying his chance, Henry Tudor launched an invasion in summer 1485, landing off the coast of Pembrokeshire and rapidly marching towards England. Against the odds, his ragtag army of prisoners and mercenaries defeated the superior forces of King Richard at the Battle of Bosworth on 22 August, and Henry was proclaimed king. His coronation took place two months later in 'triumph and glory' at Westminster Abbey. Reunited with the son she had not seen for fourteen years, Lady Margaret Beaufort 'wept marvellously'.[1]

Although Henry VII's victory at Bosworth was seen as a decisive moment in the conflict, he came to the throne with credentials that were at best questionable. His Lancastrian blood flowed from his formidable mother, who was the great-granddaughter of Edward III's son, John of Gaunt and Katherine Swynford. The trouble was, Margaret's grandfather had been born a bastard, the result of a long-standing affair between John and Katherine before their marriage. Henry's father, meanwhile, had been the child of Henry V's queen, Catherine of Valois, by her Welsh page. That Henry Tudor was the best remaining Lancastrian claimant by 1485 is an indication of how desperate their cause had become. Few of his new subjects could have expected him to survive for long: there would surely be other, better claimants to take his place. In short, the Tudors had no business being on the throne of England at all.

Born in 1457, when his mother was just thirteen years old and his father had already been dead for two months, Henry had been separated from the former at an early age. He was raised first by his paternal uncle, Jasper, Earl of Pembroke and then, after Jasper's flight abroad in 1461, by William, Lord Herbert, an ardent Yorkist supporter. It was a dangerous existence for this precious Lancastrian heir, who was obliged to be forever watchful of potential assassins. Confined in Wales for most of his young life, at the age of fourteen he fled into exile to Brittany with Jasper and remained there for the next fourteen years, until the time was right to stake his claim on the throne of England.

When Henry defeated Richard III in 1485, it was just the beginning of a long and bitter struggle to win the loyalty of his new subjects. In their eyes, he was an illegitimate usurper with no right to be king. Henry did himself few favours in this respect. Described by the contemporary Burgundian chronicler Jean Molinet as a 'fine ornament' of the Breton court, he had adopted French manners, worshipped Breton saints and spoke with a marked accent. He also lacked the natural charisma and flamboyance of his Yorkist predecessors. Introverted, paranoid and 'infinitely suspicious', he was arguably the most private of all the Tudor monarchs.[2] He may have had good cause to be watchful – Yorkist rebels and claimants were everywhere – but Henry was of a naturally reticent disposition. He guarded his money and possessions as closely as his secrets and would soon gain a reputation as a miser. The contrast to the charismatic, open-handed Edward IV, whose memory his subjects still revered, could not have been greater.

But Henry Tudor also had a number of attributes that would stand him in good stead as king. He was a patient and sharp observer and, well trained by his uncle, always remained cool under pressure. Conscientious, methodical and shrewd, his 'vast ability' was acknowledged by his contemporaries.

According to the Italian humanist Polydore Vergil, who met the king on many occasions, Henry was 'extremely attractive in appearance, his face was cheerful, especially when he was speaking.'[3] Of a little above average height, Henry had a regal bearing and was slender, strong and blue-eyed, but with a sallow complexion. He had a cast in his left eye, which meant that 'while one eye looked at you, the other searched for you.'[4] This made his gaze even more disconcerting for those upon whom it was fixed.

Despite spending so much time among military men, Henry had lived a relatively chaste life and only had one bastard son, Roland de Velville, who was conceived during his exile in Brittany. Perhaps not surprisingly for the son of Lady Margaret Beaufort, who was renowned for her intense piety, Henry was observed to be 'a most zealous supporter of religion, daily taking part, with great devotion, in divine service.' Although piety was expected of a king, particularly one who needed to erase the stain of usurpation, Henry's faith seems to have been genuine. Vergil revealed: 'To those whom he knew were worthy priests, he often gave alms secretly in order that they might pray for his soul.'[5]

Henry VII has long had the reputation of a dour man, but he had a more light-hearted side. His household accounts reveal that he was fond of playing cards, even though he regularly suffered heavy losses – most notably in June 1492 when he was obliged to raid the royal coffers for £40 (equivalent to almost £20,000 today) in order to pay off his creditor. Physically fit from his years of campaigning, he held regular jousts and liked to play tennis. The latter was a particular favourite with the king and was commended by a contemporary expert on courtly refinement as a 'noble sport which is very suitable for the courtier to play . . . for this shows how well he is built physically, how quick and agile he is in every member.'[6] Later in his reign, Henry employed two professional players to act as coaches. Tudor tennis (or 'real tennis') was very different to the more common lawn tennis that was invented during the Victorian era. It was played in an enclosed court, and the ball could be hit against the walls, as well as over the net. The ball was also harder, heavier and less bouncy than its modern counterpart. It was made from tightly packed wool bound with tape and then covered in another tight layer of wool.

The king also employed a fool called Patch, paid 'the foolish Duke of Lancaster' for entertaining him, and rewarded minstrels, lute players, pipers, dancers and a group of singing children. But if Henry knew how to enjoy himself, he never lost sight of how much the various revelries cost. All of the expenses were carefully noted in his accounts, and he personally checked them, adding his countersignature next to each entry.[7] He also deplored waste and, even though he was fond of the pastime himself, introduced heavy penalties for gambling. Servants and apprentices were specifically banned from playing card games except at Christmas. Few heeded the new legislation, however, and gambling became so commonplace at court and in aristocratic houses across the kingdom that certain officials were given responsibility for the profits that were generated.

Henry inherited an impressive suite of palaces in and around London from his Yorkist predecessors. The easternmost was Greenwich, originally built as 'Bella Court' by Humphrey, Duke of Gloucester, fourth son of Henry IV and regent to the young King Henry VI, in 1453. The duke lost his position and his life following a coup by Henry VI's wife, Margaret of Anjou, who renamed the house 'Placentia' and carried out a number of substantial improvements.

Henry VII later enlarged it, refacing the entire building with red brick and changing its name to Greenwich. It would become one of the favourite palaces of the Tudor monarchs.

Nearby, to the south-east, was another medieval palace, Eltham, set in a spacious park. Originally a rural manor house, it had become a royal residence at the beginning of the fourteenth century and had been frequently rebuilt and expanded thereafter. It was the favourite palace of Edward IV, who in 1480 built a new Great Hall complete with magnificent hammer-beam roof. By the time of Henry VII's accession, it was one of the largest and most visited royal residences in England, but the new king thought the palace more suitable as a hunting lodge or royal nursery than as a venue for full-scale court entertainments.

By far the most imposing, and one of the most ancient of the royal residences of the city, was the Tower of London, originally built by William the Conqueror after 1066. It incorporated the south-east corner of the ancient Roman city walls, and the giant Norman keep that became known as the 'White Tower' dominated the skyline for miles around. A suite of royal lodgings was later built close to the White Tower, and Henry VII extended these to include a residential tower, a gallery and a garden. By the time of his accession, it was a well-established tradition that new monarchs spent the night before their coronation at the Tower.

Close to the west wall of the City of London, Baynard's Castle commanded excellent views from its riverside location, close to where St Paul's Cathedral now stands. The London headquarters of the House of York during the Wars of the Roses, it was more suited for defence than for comfort, so in 1500 Henry set about transforming it from a fortified castle into a 'beautiful and commodious' house.[8] But the site was still rather constricted and soon fell out of favour, being used more as a royal storehouse than a residence.

York Place was the residence of the Archbishop of York and lay close to the centre of royal government at Westminster. It had been significantly extended during the decade before Henry Tudor seized the throne so that it was now an impressive palace, complete with a gatehouse, hall, chapel and private lodgings. During the 1530s, it would be extended further into a huge, sprawling mass of buildings, courtyards and gardens, and became known as Whitehall Palace.

To the west of London lay the manor of Sheen, which had been a royal residence since the early fourteenth century. It was largely rebuilt by Henry V in 1414 and became known as Sheen Palace. Further west was Windsor Castle, founded by William the Conqueror in the eleventh century. Three centuries later, Edward III transformed it from a fortress into a Gothic palace, with lavish new royal apartments and a magnificent new chapel, St George's. As well as being a royal residence, Windsor was the home of the Order of the Garter, and new Garter knights were invested here.

The roads linking each of the principal residences were the best in the kingdom, but most of the palaces were on the river and easily accessed by barge. Transport was an important consideration, given that the court was still a peripatetic institution and moved between the main royal residences up to thirty times a year on average.

The new Tudor king was quick to take possession of these and the other royal residences that were now his by right. Naturally introspective, he preferred the company of a few trusted servants and advisers, but appreciated the need to surround himself with a court that was every bit as magnificent as that of his Yorkist predecessors. In order to create an impression of continuity, and therefore reinforce his rightful place in the succession, Henry retained most of the structure, personnel and traditions that he had inherited.

Having spent most of his adult life in exile in Brittany, Henry must have been staggered by the sheer scale of the court over which he now presided. The royal household was vast and comprised up to a thousand officers and servants. Numbers were swelled still further by the fact that each courtier was allowed to bring their own staff. A duke, for example, might bring twelve servants to court. All needed food, accommodation and the facilities to keep themselves and their apparel clean and presentable.

The spectacles of pageantry and ceremony that were the hallmark of royal court life were only achieved thanks to the immense level of activity and preparation that took place behind closed doors.

Even on an average day – one without a special event – a vast amount of work was undertaken by hundreds of officials, attendants and servants to keep the court looking, and smelling, good.

The royal household was divided into two sections. The household above stairs (the *Domus Magnificence*) comprised the Chamber (including the Guard Chamber), the Presence Chamber and the Privy Chamber. This department was controlled by the Lord Chamberlain, who was usually a trusted and close friend of the monarch. The queen's household was organised along similar lines and was subject to the authority of her Chamberlain. But it was smaller than the king's and was almost entirely staffed by women. The household below stairs (the *Domus Providencie*) was controlled by the Lord Steward, and the stables were under the master of the horse. Outside the jurisdiction of both the Lord Chamberlain and Lord Steward were a number of miscellaneous departments, including the Jewel House, the Office of the Revels, the Office of Works, the Royal Ordnance and the Chapel Royal. The entire royal household was under the nominal direction of the Lord Great Chamberlain.

The *Domus Magnificence* comprised significantly more servants than the *Domus Providencie*, and included footmen (typically seven or eight), henchmen (anywhere between four and fourteen) and yeomen of the guard (who fluctuated between forty and two hundred). The footmen's role was to attend the king while outdoors, such as when hunting or riding, so they would be provided with clothing that was both sumptuous and warm.[9] The henchmen were part of the ceremonial entourage when the king appeared in public, and were members of the gentry and nobility. As such, they were the best dressed of the king's attendants and would be regularly decked out in silks, satins, velvets and furs. The yeomen of the guard, meanwhile, had to be highly visible because their role carried the greatest weight of responsibility, namely 'to watch the king'.[10] A scarlet livery was introduced for them in 1514 and has remained their uniform to this day. Various other servants were counted among the staff of the *Domus Magnificence*, such as the king's barber, musicians and the officers of the Wardrobe.

The Domus Providencie, or household below stairs, was divided into a number of sections such as the scullery, larder, pastry kitchen, buttery, cellar, ewery (which presided over the laundry), and the poultry (which presided over the porters and the carters). The vast majority of the staff who populated these departments were men. The only women below stairs were employed to do the washing, cleaning, and basic household tasks.

The smart, uniform appearance of the *Domus Magnificence* staff conveyed the monarch's ability to provide for them and symbolised his authority and control over his household – and, by extension, his kingdom. By contrast, little was provided for the below-stairs staff because they were not seen by those who mattered. Thus, the kitchen staff would deliver the food to serving areas, from where the liveried staff of the *Domus Magnificence* would take over.[11] There were a few notable exceptions, such as the four 'rockers' whose job it was to rock the royal infant's cradle, and the court laundress and chimney sweep, all of whom were granted livery.

By the dawn of the Tudor period, the private life of the monarchy had long been subject to a strict order of routine, tradition, ceremony and etiquette. This was reflected by the structure of the court and the architecture of the royal palaces. The creation of a private suite of chambers for the king or queen can be traced to as early as the twelfth century. But it was only 300 years later, during the reign of Edward IV, that this development was accelerated when the king transformed all of the royal residences in order to provide himself and his family with separate, private lodgings known as the Chamber. This was a deliberate strategy by Edward to control access to the royal person, and in so doing to centralise power in the hands of the king. Separating the king from his subjects in this way enhanced the mystique of monarchy, and elevated those who were allowed to penetrate the architectural divide and gain access to the royal presence.

By the end of Edward's reign, the Chamber comprised the Great or Guard Chamber, which was the first of the ceremonial rooms *en route* to the king and was staffed by his personal bodyguard; the presence chamber (or throne room), where the king dined in state, received important visitors and met his council; and the privy chamber, which was both the king's bedroom and private lodgings, and the name of the organisation which populated and governed these inner rooms. The privy chamber was not as private as the name suggests but, in common with the more public-facing rooms beyond, it was subject to a great deal of formal ceremony.

In around 1470, the influential lawyer, Sir John Fortescue, penned the political treatise, *The Governance of England*, in which he set out the principles of kingship. One of the most important was that a monarch should not stint upon fine clothes and furnishings: 'It shall need that the king have such treasure, as he may make new buildings when he will, for his pleasure and magnificence; and as he may buy him rich clothes, rich furs . . . convenient to his estate royal. And often times he will buy rich hangings and other apparel for his houses . . . for if a king did not so, nor might do, he lived then not like his estate, but rather in misery, and in more subjection than doth a private person.'[12]

Edward IV had fully embraced the concept of magnificence as being synonymous with power. A visitor to his court in 1466 remarked that the English king had 'the most splendid Court that could be found in all Christendom.'[13] By contrast, Edward's Lancastrian rival, Henry VI, had eschewed such royal trappings – and had paid a heavy price for it. A scornful commentator had described his entry into London after temporarily reclaiming the throne in 1471 as being 'more like a play than the showing of a prince to win men's hearts.' Dressed in a simple long blue velvet gown 'as though he had no more to change with', he had also refused to maintain a great household but instead lived as if in 'great poverty'.[14]

Miserly he may have been, but Henry Tudor was shrewd enough not to repeat this mistake. A man's clothes – far more than those of a woman – were of great symbolic importance. A statute passed in 1483 closely defined the colours and fabrics that a man might wear according to his status. The use of 'cloth of gold' and purple silk was limited to the royal family, and velvet cloth was the preserve of those who enjoyed the rank of knight or above. It was therefore possible to discern, at a glance, a person's status by the clothes that they were wearing.

Henry and his successors invested huge proportions of their wealth in the creation and maintenance of their wardrobe, and took great interest in how they presented themselves. Far from being a vain or frivolous pursuit, dress had enormous symbolic importance, reflecting not just the status of the wearer, but their personality, taste, influences, aspirations and power. Throughout his reign, Henry would spend extravagantly on vestments and livery promoting his personal badges of the Tudor rose and the Beaufort portcullis.

In contrast to the majority of their subjects, how the Tudor monarchs dressed in private was as important as their public apparel. They did not possess what would be defined today as 'casual' clothes. Even their nightwear was crafted from the finest linens and decorated with embroidery. Their sportswear was no less elaborate. Personal comfort was always sacrificed to outward display.

The first man whom Henry appointed to the important role of tailor was George Lovekyn, a Parisian by birth who had worked for both Edward IV and Richard III. This was a deliberate ploy to emphasise the continuity of the royal succession – and thus Henry's rightful place within it. Although he was very much an outsider, having spent fourteen years in exile in Brittany, Henry's style of dress was consistent with that of his Plantagenet predecessors. His coronation followed the same pattern as Edward IV's, and Lovekyn provided a traditional ceremonial robe of crimson satin with white fur and a mantle of purple velvet.[15] None of this escaped the notice of the Venetian ambassador, who observed that the king did 'not change any of the ancient usages of England at his court.'[16] After Lovekyn's death in 1504, Henry promoted the latter's apprentice, Stephen Jasper, to the position of tailor, a post that he kept for the remainder of the reign.

Working closely with the tailors were the embroiderers. At the beginning of his reign, Henry appointed William Moreton and William More to this position. The latter continued in post for the remainder of the reign and also served Henry's successor. Only the most trusted men and women would be appointed to this most private of court departments, and often the positions would pass from one member of the family to another. Elizabeth Langton is a rare example of a female in the royal wardrobe, but she was probably appointed as Henry VII's silkwoman in around 1502 because she was known to be the widow of Thomas Langton, who had supplied silks to the king during the 1490s.[17]

Henry spent the greatest sums on his apparel during the early years of his reign, when he felt most insecure on his newly won throne. Just over a week after defeating Richard III at Bosworth, he ordered a long gown of rich cloth of gold lined with black satin, another of velvet lined with violet satin, four short gowns of purple cloth of gold lined with black satin, a doublet of black and crimson satin, and a quantity of linen for shirts. The total order came to £336, which roughly equates to £180,000 in today's money. During the two years that followed, he spent a total of £5,386 (£3 million) on his wardrobe. His expenditure dropped to around a third of this for the remainder of his reign, by which time he had become more established.[18]

By contrast, the king's mother, Lady Margaret Beaufort, reinforced her pious image by eschewing the ostentatious gowns of court and dressing more like a member of the religious orders than of the royal family. In all of the surviving portraits, she is wearing a white linen gable headdress with a wimple covering her neck and chin, and a sombre black robe. Margaret's intention was to express not only her piety, but her autonomy, since it suggested that she was unencumbered by wifely duties. She had taken two vows of chastity, in 1499 and 1503, and lived alone from 1499. This was quite common for widows, but the king's mother was still married to her second husband, Thomas Stanley. The image she wished to project, however, was as royal mother superior. Although she wore deliberately simple garments to reinforce this, they were made of the most luxurious materials. Her accounts include gowns of black damask furred with ermine and twenty-four lambskins to line her nightgown. She also spent considerable sums on jewellery: gold rings set with rubies, gilded girdles, and jewels of flowers with diamonds and rubies.[19] Lady Margaret's table linen was no less luxurious and included a damask tablecloth and towel woven with roses and a portcullis, her family badge.

Even comparatively simple fabrics such as woollen cloth involved a lengthy production process and were therefore sold at exorbitant prices. Silks and velvets were so eye-wateringly expensive that only those who were permitted to wear them could afford them anyway. Investing in new clothes for a visit to court could bankrupt members of the minor nobility and gentry. The fact that the monarch was able to appear in the finest cloth of gold or velvet as often as they liked reinforced their superiority. If most of their courtiers were unable to compete, then their lowlier subjects did not stand a chance. A yard of cloth of gold would cost six months' wages for a labourer, and he would need to work for three years to afford a fine cloak.[20]

As well as being crafted from the finest, most expensive materials, the monarch's clothes also required specialist care and cleaning. Given the peripatetic nature of Tudor monarchy, it was essential that the garments were portable so that they could be regularly packed up and transported by a team of royal servants, and still appear at their best when worn on the next occasion.

Rich textiles were not just required for the royal wardrobe. They were also used to adorn the palaces in which the monarch and his family lived – as well as to keep out the draughts. And as with the king's clothes, the furnishings that were crafted for behind closed doors were as important as those that would be on public display. Henry was particularly fond of rich tapestries. He was probably inspired by his years in exile in France, where he may have seen the weaving of an enormous set called *The Story of the Trojan War* by Pasquier Grenier. As soon as he was king, he commissioned his own set, which was delivered by Grenier's son in March 1488. Grenier would receive numerous other commissions during the course of the reign.

Contemporary documents reveal that Henry and his officials paid minute attention to the hanging of these tapestries according to their value. The outer chambers of court would be hung with tapestries made from wool alone; the middle chambers with wool and silk, and only the king's private apartments would be decorated with tapestries woven from gold thread. This served to reinforce the strict order of precedence at court, which was also reflected by the architecture of the palaces themselves. The king's private chapel required another suite of bespoke fabrics, such as vestments and napery.

The priceless tapestries, clothes and other material possessions of the monarch were stored in a dedicated department of the royal household known as the Great Wardrobe of Robes and Beds. This had been established in the Middle Ages and had originally been a storehouse for armour, tents and liveries. It was housed in the Tower of London for the first 150 years or so of its existence, but by the mid-fourteenth century, it had grown so large that a new home had to be found for it close to Baynard's Castle, at the western end of the City of London.[21] It resembled an Oxford or Cambridge college, with buildings surrounding gardens and a courtyard, where packhorses and carts could be loaded and unloaded. There were also permanent stores for its stocks and collections at the Tower, Somerset Place and Whitehall Palace. In addition, each palace had a 'removing wardrobe', where clothes would be delivered in coffers and trunks when the king and his court took up residence. This was usually situated beneath the king's and queen's privy chambers with a stair connecting it to the room above.

The queens consort had their own version of the Great Wardrobe based at Baynard's Castle itself. Items of clothing would be delivered directly to the officers of the queen's robes from Baynard's Castle to the palaces where they were required. The structure of the queen's wardrobe was the same as for the Great Wardrobe, with yeoman, groom and page, and most officers transferred from one queen consort to another.

By Tudor times, the Great Wardrobe was under the jurisdiction of the Privy Chamber, reflecting the essentially personal nature of its contents. It was here that all of the royal clothes and furnishings were not only stored, but made, ordered and paid for. The monarch would personally sign all of the orders and accounts for clothes. These tended to be ordered in bulk every six months, but the Great Wardrobe also had to respond at short notice to bulk orders for events such as funerals.

The man who served as Henry VII's first keeper of the wardrobe was selected as much for his loyalty as for continuity with the Yorkist regime. Peter Curteys had first been appointed to the position by Edward IV in April 1481 and had been responsible for preparing the abortive coronation of Edward V two years later, but had lost his office shortly afterwards when Richard III seized the throne. When an invasion by Henry Tudor looked imminent, Curteys stole away into sanctuary at Westminster along with other Tudor sympathisers. After defeating Richard at Bosworth, Henry rewarded Curteys by giving him back his old office 'in consideration of his true heart and service, and of the great persecution, dangers and losses of goods sustained by him in the King's cause, he having kept sanctuary at Westminster long time in sadness, punishment, and fear awaiting the King's arrival.'[22]

Curteys was one of many important links with the past, all of which enabled the first Tudor king to quickly order his household, ceremonies and other trappings of power. But for all its finery, Henry's new court lacked one important adornment: a queen.

Keen to establish his dynasty, the new king needed to enhance his legitimacy by taking a bride of impeccable pedigree. In fact, the perfect candidate had already been selected for him before he even came to the throne. In 1483, while Henry waited in the wings for the right moment to contest Richard III's throne, his mother Margaret made a tacit agreement with Edward IV's widow, Elizabeth Woodville, that if Henry succeeded in taking the crown of England, he would marry her eldest daughter Elizabeth. Henry swore an oath to this effect at Rennes Cathedral on Christmas Day 1483 and applied for the necessary papal dispensation early the following year.

Elizabeth of York held many attractions as a potential bride. Nine years younger than Henry, she was every inch the Plantagenet princess: tall and slender with luscious blonde hair. It was hardly surprising that she should have grown into such a beauty: her mother, Elizabeth Woodville, was so strikingly attractive that her father, Edward IV, had courted scandal across the kingdom in order to marry this commoner. Even disapproving commentators could not help but admire Henry's chosen bride. A Venetian envoy described her as 'a very handsome woman, and of great ability.'[23]

Elizabeth of York's true appeal for Henry lay not in her physical charms, but in her lineage. As the eldest daughter of Edward IV, she was the greatest prize of the House of York – described by Thomas More as 'a king's fare in marriage' – and in making her his wife Henry was signalling an end to the bitter war that had been waged with his own House of Lancaster.[24] 'Everyone considers [the marriage] advantageous to the kingdom,' observed one foreign ambassador, adding that 'all things appear disposed towards peace.'[25] So ideal a bride was Elizabeth in every respect that her late uncle, Richard III, was rumoured to have considered marrying her himself. When Henry had heard of this, he was said to have been 'pinched to the very stomach.'[26]

Henry was quick to claim custody of his intended bride. Shortly after arriving in London, he had her placed in the household of his indomitable mother, Margaret Beaufort, at her residence of Coldharbour. A handsome medieval manor house on the banks of the Thames close to London Bridge, it boasted a great hall over-looking the river. It had previously lodged Alice Perrers, mistress of Edward III. Determined to put his stamp on the capital, Henry had ordered the renovation of the house. It was one of a series of opulent Thames-side houses that the new king would renovate in the latest Burgundian fashions, complete with imported glazing and glittering cupolas, with opulently furnished galleries and chambers within.

It was probably at Coldharbour that Henry and Elizabeth first met, although no record of that meeting survives. During the autumn of 1485, the king sent ten yards of crimson velvet and six yards of russet damask, and sixty-four 'timbers' (bales containing forty skins each) of ermine to his bride-to-be, determined that she should be as finely dressed as he was.[27] How they felt about each other was of little relevance. There was no public pretence of love, only of courtesy and respect. At most, couples brought together by such alliances might hope for harmony and mutual respect. Love, romance and passion were mostly reserved for a king's extramarital affairs.

But did Elizabeth have different expectations? As the daughter of a king she was certainly well versed in the customs of the court. But, unusually, her parents had married for love, and the strong attraction that had existed between them had hardly abated during the nineteen years of their marriage. Elizabeth may have been inspired by their example to hope for a love match herself. But, although she was still only nineteen years old at the time of her marriage to Henry Tudor, she was hardly a political ingénue. Her childhood had been played out against the turbulent backdrop of civil war, the crown rapidly changing hands between Yorkist and Lancastrian claimants. She had been raised to expect not conjugal felicity, but political expediency in her marriage.

While Elizabeth enjoyed the dubious pleasure of sharing a house with her prospective mother-in-law, Henry began laying the legal groundwork for their marriage. On 7 November, parliament formally recognised the legitimacy of his title and annulled the instrument whereby Richard III had claimed the throne, which had asserted the bastardy of Edward IV's children. The following month, Thomas Lovell, Speaker of the House of Commons, urged the new king to fulfil his promise to marry 'that illustrious lady Elizabeth, daughter of King Edward IV' and thus pave the way for 'the propagation of offspring from the stock of kings.' This suggests that, no matter how much Henry might assert his right to the throne, he desperately needed Elizabeth to legitimise his kingship. Four days earlier, Giovanni de' Gigli, prebendary of St Paul's, had shrewdly observed to the Pope: 'It is positively asserted that the king is about to marry her, which everybody considers advantageous for the kingdom.'[28] The House of Lords echoed the Speaker's request and Henry formally agreed to marry the York princess. Parliament approved the match on 10 December, and Elizabeth was treated as Queen of England from that day forward.

First, though, a papal dispensation had to be secured because Henry and Elizabeth were 'joined together in the fourth and fifth degrees of kindred'.[29] It could take many months to get anything from Rome, and Henry was not prepared to wait. Luck was on his side. A papal legate was then in England, and he was persuaded to authorise the marriage on behalf of his pontiff. He duly gave his signed permission on 16 January, and the wedding took place two days later at Westminster Abbey, where the bride had been christened almost twenty years before.[30]

Henry and Elizabeth then processed the short distance from the abbey to Westminster Palace, followed by the Lord Chamberlain, bishops, cardinals, lords, Knights of the Bath, nobles, heralds, officers, trumpeters and minstrels. Like the abbey, it was originally founded by Edward the Confessor and was now the monarch's principal London residence and the heart of government. It was also the birthplace of the new queen, and she had spent a good deal of her childhood there.

Upon arriving at the palace, the king and his bride retired to a private chamber for a brief rest and perhaps a change of clothes. It must have been a welcome moment of privacy in a day of protracted ceremonies and pageantry. A contemporary recorded: 'When he [Henry] had pleasure somewhat rested him, in the same estate, with those nobles, he may return in to the said hall, there royally to be served as is according to the feast.'[31]

There is no record of where the wedding feast took place, but it is likely to have been in the enormous Great Hall. Built by William II at the end of the eleventh century, it was the largest great hall in Europe, measuring 240 feet long and covering 17,000 square feet. It was hardly the most intimate of spaces for the celebration of a wedding but, anxious as he was to impress his new subjects, it would have suited Henry's requirements exactly.

It is interesting to speculate whether the royal cooks would have prepared any of the foods believed to excite lust in the newly married couple. Chestnuts, pistachios and pine nuts had long been used in folk medicine to stimulate the libido. The consumption of meat was believed to strengthen the husband's potency, as well as aiding the wife's fertility. In between each course the royal couple would have been served with a 'subtlety' – a lavish sculpture of marchpane (marzipan) or spun sugar, covered with gold leaf. A popular design for weddings was a model of the new wife shown in the last stages of pregnancy – just in case she was not already aware of what was expected of her. Neither were the Tudors prudish about phallic-shaped foods like asparagus, or those that could inspire sexual puns, such as 'apricock'.[32] The wedding feast was, after all, merely a prelude to the main event: the bedding ceremony.

When the last dishes of this sumptuous and protracted feast had been served, and the royal couple had eaten and drunk their fill, they would have been escorted to the bedchamber. The very public beginning to this essentially private event was for a purpose: even after the wedding ceremony had taken place in church, a marriage was not considered binding until it had been consummated. Sexual failure could have far-reaching consequences for a royal couple, sparking political unrest and even rebellion. It was therefore imperative that members of their court and household be given sufficient reassurance that the act had been satisfactorily performed.

Moreover, to have any hope of securing lasting peace, Henry's marriage to Elizabeth had to produce an heir – and quickly. The king knew that his claim to the throne was weak and that his rivals from the House of York were preparing to challenge it. An undisputed heir born of a Yorkist princess might just silence them – even if only for long enough for Henry to secure a firmer grip on his new kingdom. As the sixteenth-century chronicler Edward Hall remarked, the chief hope of the marriage was that from their 'two bodies one heir might succeed.'[33]

Henry and Elizabeth were well past the age at which consummation might first take place – twelve in girls and fourteen in boys. For a male royal heir to gain sexual experience before marriage was not only expected, but actively encouraged. It would prove his sexual potency and, potentially, his ability to sire children, as Henry had done. By contrast, however, unless she had been married before, the bride must be unquestionably chaste. Despite the rumours about her relationship with her late uncle, Elizabeth almost certainly came to the marriage bed a virgin. One of the most powerful bargaining tools a potential royal wife had was her virtue. It was imperative that the mother of future kings or queens must have morals that were utterly beyond reproach. Elizabeth had been closely guarded during her father's reign, both her parents very conscious of the value of their eldest daughter in the international marriage market.

The royal bedding ceremony was subject to a similarly strict set of rules as the marriage ceremony and wedding feast. At around 8 o'clock in the evening, the bride was escorted to her chamber by her ladies, who undressed her and put her to bed. The groom, meanwhile, was stripped down to just his shirt – an undergarment that would have reached to at least mid-thigh and, in Henry's case, would have been delicately embroidered. Then, accompanied by his gentlemen attendants, musicians, priests and bishops, he joined his wife in the bedchamber. The clerics would pronounce their blessings, and then a concoction of wine and spices would be served. Known as the void or voidee, this was a mixture of expensive sweet and sharp spices such as pepper, saffron, ginger, cloves, cinnamon and nutmeg. It was thought to be beneficial to health and digestion, as well as sweetening the breath and engendering strength and courage.

The onlookers were often slow to leave. Sometimes, they demanded to see the naked legs of the couple touching, which in some cases was accepted as a sign of consummation. Others expected to witness the royal newlyweds kissing or embracing. It was a crude reminder that a royal body was the property of the state; its functions of great interest to the people of the realm. In this, the king and his wife were poorer than the lowliest of their subjects. The latter may not have enjoyed the array of comforts that came with royal blood, but they at least had the luxury of a private life in its true sense.

Even after the throng of courtiers had bidden the couple goodnight and left the chamber, some may have lingered outside the closed door, straining their ears for any sound that might indicate the act of consummation was under way. For Henry and Elizabeth, this lack of privacy for even their most intimate moments was a sign of things to come. It was common for kings and queens to be attended by servants throughout the night. While some had a truckle bed positioned outside the door of the royal bedchamber or in the antechamber, others slept in the same room as their master and his wife or mistress.

The close proximity of servants served a practical, as well as a security function. Having an attendant in or near the room in which one slept meant that they could quickly carry out any commands if required. Moreover, a monarch was at his or her most vulnerable when asleep. Given the turbulent events that had resulted in Henry VII's accession, he may well have required his attendants to stay close by during the night. Little wonder that servants often played a key role in the exposure of adultery or the dissolution of an unsuccessful marriage.

The presence of a thick curtain drawn around the royal bed prevented the couple from being overlooked (if not overheard), but the visible results of their marital consummation were sometimes displayed to the entire court the following morning. The bloodstained bed sheets of Isabella of Castile were shown off as proof of her lost virginity when she married Ferdinand of Aragon in 1469. By contrast, those of her impotent half-brother's bride were kept under wraps.

Although records are scarce, it is likely that Henry and Elizabeth spent their wedding night in the painted chamber at Westminster, the most luxurious apartment in the palace. As the name suggests, it was richly decorated. A mural commissioned by Henry III depicted the coronation of Edward the Confessor, and a fourteenth-century description noted that 'all the warlike stories of the Bible are painted with wonderful skill.'[34] The room was heated by a large fireplace and contained a private chapel for the use of the royal couple. It commanded a view of the river and Lambeth Palace, and also over-looked a series of narrow gardens.

The painted chamber was dominated by a huge ornate bed. This could have been the bed that, more than a hundred years later, was still on display at one of their granddaughters' royal palaces. A German visitor to England in 1599 was impressed by 'a bed of extraordinarily large proportions, very ornate, sixteen of my spans broad, and fourteen long, said to be King Henry VII's bed, and I never saw a bigger in my life.'[35]

Such elaborate beds were used for ceremonial or state occasions, but the rest of the time it was common for the king to sleep on a simpler, smaller bed out of public view. The Tudors invented the four-poster bed, which began to appear from the late fifteenth century. Before then, the more elaborate beds had canopies and curtains suspended from the ceiling beams, but now posts were added at each corner of the bed and fixed to the canopy above. These newly designed beds became a symbol of status, rather than sleep. As well as protecting the occupants from any vermin that might drop onto the canopy overhead, the thick woollen curtains that were drawn around it would create a cosy, peaceful interior, keeping out both draughts and noise. Across the base of the bed would be threaded tightly pulled ropes (the origin of the term 'sleep tight'), on top of which a thick fresh rush mat would be laid. This was surmounted by a layer of straw interspersed with sweet-smelling lavender (to aid sleep), and then a tightly woven sack filled with sheep's wool. Finally, there would be two mattresses laid on top.

While most ordinary people slept on scratchy, sagging wool sacks stuffed with straw, the richest members of society enjoyed the comforts of a feather-filled mattress. These were not only the softest mattresses available, but also retained the heat generated by their sleeping occupants. The best-quality mattresses were filled with small, fluffy down feathers, and the down from eider ducks was the softest of all – although as it was something of a rarity, it would be reserved for members of the royal family and their highest-ranking nobles. The sheets would be of the finest white patterned linen, and blankets were laid over for extra warmth, with an embroidered coverlet completing the ensemble.

A royal bed would be made with a staggering number of different layers during the winter months. The typical sequence was as follows: bedstead, canvas, featherbed and bolster, fustian (a heavy cloth of linen, cotton or occasionally wool), bottom sheet, pillows and pillow-beres (cases), top sheet, fustian, quilts, scarlet (a high-quality woollen cloth from the Netherlands, prized for its softness and vivid colour), damask and a counterpoint. Given that Henry and Elizabeth's wedding took place in the depths of winter, it is safe to assume that their bed would have been similarly arrayed.

The new king was also known to have favoured ermine covers for extra warmth and luxury.

The details of the bed in which Henry and Elizabeth spent their wedding night have not survived, and until 2010 there were thought to be no Tudor royal beds still in existence. However, in that year a chance discovery was made of a bed that may have been created for them later in their marriage. Fashioned from oak, it is covered with ornate carvings featuring biblical scenes of Henry and his queen as Adam and Eve. The intricate lacework of leaves and branches that covers each side of the bed represents the Tree of Knowledge. Other decorative features leave no doubt that this was a royal bed. The front two pillars are each surmounted by a lion, and the royal arms (bearing the lions of England and the fleur-de-lys of France, over which the Tudors held a claim) are carved into the headboard and foot of the bed. The canopy is decorated with an image of Edward the Confessor's coronation. Fragments of paint reveal that the bed would once have been decorated in rich colours.[36]

On the morning after the wedding night, the king presented his new wife with a 'morning gift' – a poem by Giovanni de' Gigli. Elizabeth would then have taken part in a small ceremony of 'uprising'.[37] All of the trouble that her new husband had gone to for their wedding night and its aftermath appeared to be justified. Just days after the wedding, 'Great enjoyment filled the queen.'[38] In other words, she was pregnant. Elizabeth must have conceived either on the wedding night or very shortly afterwards because her first child was born on 20 September – just eight months after the wedding. She had fulfilled her promise as a fertile York princess.

But had Henry left it to chance? The fact that the child was born a month earlier than expected raises the tantalising prospect that Henry had bedded Elizabeth before the wedding. This was unlikely to have been the result of a lack of restraint, no matter how attractive his betrothed was purported to be. Henry was known to be a 'most prudent' king, who did not act impetuously.[39] Indeed, according to the later sixteenth-century commentator, Francis Bacon, he found the prospect of marrying a scion of his enemy house abhorrent: 'His aversion toward the house of York was so predominant in him as it found place not only in his wars and councils, but in his chamber and bed.'[40] Rather, if Henry did have sex with Elizabeth before the wedding, it was because he wanted to make sure that she was fertile. He may have considered that he had too much at stake to risk it all on a barren wife. If he died without an heir, then the Tudor dynasty would be extinguished almost as soon as it had begun.

The fact that Henry and Elizabeth had been betrothed for more than a month before their wedding lends weight to the theory that the bride was already pregnant at the time of their marriage. A verbal promise of marriage or 'handfasting' was seen as a binding agreement. As such, it was sometimes viewed as enough to justify physical relations. It would have been easy enough for Henry to bed his betrothed in the privacy of his mother's house at Coldharbour. Indeed, this could have been the purpose of moving her there in the first place.

Given the vital importance of producing an heir, Henry may have bedded Elizabeth early because he believed she would be more likely to conceive then than on the wedding day itself. According to late fifteenth-century wisdom, a woman must reach orgasm in order to conceive. She would then emit a 'seed' to mix with that of her partner. This view was still pervasive in the seventeenth century, when the influential herbalist Nicholas Culpeper advised that a woman would probably fail to fall pregnant if there was 'very little or no pleasure in the act of copulation'. Another authority went so far as to claim that if a wife hated her husband, her womb would not open.[41] The pressures of the wedding night, with all of its exhausting ceremonies and formalities, were hardly conducive to female pleasure. Henry might therefore have resolved to ensure his betrothed's enjoyment in more relaxed conditions before the wedding night itself.

It is of course possible, though, that all due decorum had been observed and that Elizabeth simply did not carry her first baby to full term. Francis Bacon certainly believed that the child was born 'in the eighth month', but was nevertheless 'strong and able'. Other evidence suggests that the baby was weak and needed careful nursing for the first six months of its life.

After the formal ceremony of bedding that had marked the beginning of her marriage to Henry Tudor, Elizabeth was established in her own chambers, which mirrored the king's. They included a bedchamber, where the king would visit his wife when he wished to have sex with her. These occasions were often preceded by dining together in the queen's apartments. As soon as it was certain that the queen was pregnant, her husband would have abstained altogether from these conjugal visits. It was believed to be detrimental to the health of the child to continue with sexual relations during the pregnancy. This was commonly the time when a royal husband would seek comfort in the arms of a mistress.

Tudor medicine offered an array of different potions – mostly unsavoury – for the relief of the symptoms of early pregnancy. Powders made from the stones found in a swallow's belly or the liver of a kite would be administered to a woman complaining of nausea or dizziness. Alternatively, she might be advised to drink enzymes from a hare's stomach, the juice of cowslip or of 'fine leaved grass'. If the expectant mother was experiencing swelling in her legs, then she could eat elderberries boiled in ale with 'sparrow's grease'. Stomach pains, meanwhile, could be eased by filling a small bag with wormwood, spearmint, vinegar, rose water and a dead chaffinch. Not surprisingly, many of these so-called remedies did more harm than good, and frequent complaints were voiced against the physicians and midwives who prescribed them.

There was no shortage of advice about the best diet to follow when pregnant in order to ensure the birth of a healthy child. The ninth- or tenth-century *Leechbook* ('Leech' being an ancient word for physician) by the physician Bald was still popular in Tudor times. This cautioned pregnant women against eating anything salty, sweet or fatty, and advised that they should avoid pork or else their child would be humpbacked. She should also eschew fruit and vegetables, and should drink wine and ale rather than milk or water. On the whole, a bland diet was recommended for expectant mothers, although they were at least spared the fast days that were a regular fixture of the Catholic calendar.

As well as adjusting her diet, a pregnant woman was expected to undergo all manner of rituals and precautions in order to safeguard her unborn child. It was commonly believed that she nourished her child with her blood and shaped it with her imagination, so she must take care to avoid certain practices and influences. For example, any activities that involved winding or grinding were believed to cause the child to strangulate in the womb. Over-enthusiastic dogs must be restrained in case they jumped up on the mother and caused a deformity. She must avoid looking at a hare because that would give her baby a hare-lip; seeing a snake would give it green eyes, and if she gazed up at the moon her child would become a lunatic or sleepwalker. Worst of all, if she tiptoed through the May dew, she would be sure to miscarry.

More sensibly, pregnant women were advised against running, leaping or rising suddenly. They must avoid lifting heavy burdens, and their stays should not be too tightly laced. Avoiding extremes of temperature, getting plenty of sleep and staying free of emotional upset were also recommended. The latter stipulation was difficult for Elizabeth. The first summer of her marriage, in 1486, was one of turbulence in the kingdom. Rumours of unrest in the north had reached the court and were serious enough for the king to make the long and arduous journey there so that he might quell the resistance to his rule.

Meanwhile, his queen travelled to Winchester to await her confinement or 'lying-in'. This would typically begin a month before the baby was due. As one foreign observer noted with some bemusement: 'This is an ancient custom in England whenever a princess is about to be confined: to remain in retirement forty days before and forty after.'[42] But in the absence of any accurate means of deciphering the likely date of birth, mistakes were often made and confinements could begin any time between seven days and seven weeks before the baby arrived.

Henry gave his wife a generous parting gift of some rich items of clothing. Even though she would not be able to parade these in front of the court, the gift was well chosen. The king knew that Elizabeth loved fine clothes and had previously made her gifts of luxury items, such as nine metres of crimson satin and a pair of fur-lined night boots.[43]

The choice of Winchester for Elizabeth's confinement was symbolic. England's ancient capital was a city rich in royal legend and tradition. Henry's banner at Bosworth had borne the red dragon, King Arthur's heraldic device, and Elizabeth's own father had commissioned a genealogical tree to prove his connection with the mythical hero. There could be no more fitting place for the Tudor king's first child to be born.

Although the obvious choice of residence in Winchester was the castle, built by William the Conqueror and expanded into a huge edifice in the thirteenth century, it was now considered old-fashioned, uncomfortable and draughty. Far more appealing were the Prior's lodgings at St Swithin's Priory. This three-storey stone building, with an arched entrance portico, provided luxurious accommodation for distinguished guests. The priory itself was one of the richest monastic houses in the land, so was well able to accommodate royal guests. The beautiful gardens surrounding the priory provided fresh apples and flowers. The prior may also have arranged a supply of oranges for his royal guest because these were often given to expectant mothers as a treat.

While Elizabeth's hosts did everything they could to ensure her comfort, her mother-in-law had already set down a strict set of rules that must be observed during her confinement. As soon as the child had 'quickened', around Easter 1487, Margaret Beaufort had begun compiling the Book of the Royal Household. Drawing upon centuries of conventions – part-religious, part-medical – this dictated every minute detail for ensuring the successful delivery of an heir. It was reiterated by a set of ordinances drawn up for the government of the household in 1494.

Privacy was paramount. The expectant queen would be secluded in her chamber, which was actually a suite of rooms based upon the privy chamber apartments usually found at court, but with certain modifications. For example, an oratory would be installed so that prayers could be said to help along a difficult labour, together with a font to provide a quick baptism for a sickly baby. The birthing chamber would be furthest from the outside world so that the mother and her child were shielded from its corrupting influence, and no one but her attendants might witness her dishevelment or hear her agonised screams.

The cupboards would be well stocked with wine, food and spices, as well as gold and silver plate upon which to serve them. Fresh supplies would be delivered to the outer door of the apartments, but this would be the only contact with the outside world and would in any case be kept well shielded from the expectant mother.

The staff appointed to the confinement chamber were exclusively female. Once an expectant royal wife had taken her leave of the public court, 'no man [is] to come into the chamber where she shall be delivered, save women.'[44] As Lady Margaret Beaufort's ordinances dictated: 'Women were to be made all manner of officers, as butlers, panters, sewers.'[45] Any provisions or other necessary items would be brought to the door of the great chamber and passed to one of the female attendants within. Even the king and male doctors were barred entry. A troop of 'good sisters' or 'gossips' took over the usual daily ceremonies of service, as well as the maternity duties. Elizabeth was also attended by her mother and two of her sisters, Anne and Cecily, as well as the less welcome presence of her indomitable mother-in-law.

The entire chamber – 'sides, roof, windows and all' – was hung with heavy arras tapestries and 'laid all over with thick carpets'. Even the keyholes would be stuffed with pieces of material. As well as creating a womb-like environment, this served the dual purpose of blocking out fresh air, which was considered unhealthy for a newborn, and natural light, which was believed not only to harm the mother's eyesight but to leave her and her child vulnerable to the attacks of evil spirits. Meanwhile, braziers were lit in each fireplace a few days before the queen entered her chamber, and rich perfumes filled the air from the unstoppered bottles that were scattered around the room.

As might be expected, the centrepiece of the birthing chamber was a specially constructed bed of state, measuring eight feet by ten, upon which the precious infant would be born. Finally, two cradles would be installed in the chamber – one a 'great cradle of estate', richly upholstered with crimson cloth of gold and an ermine-lined counterpane to match that of the queen's bed. This was intended for ceremonial use, while the other – a more modest carved wooden cradle painted with silver gold, with ermine-lined bedding, was reserved for sleep.[46] Even as a tiny baby, the royal heir would experience a 'public' and a 'private' bed.

The prospect of childbirth was terrifying to most first-time mothers. Instances of death – both of mother and child – were high, and even if they survived the birth, one or both could die of infection days later. The rate of mortality remained high during the first few years of a child's life. Medical knowledge was derived more from folklore than science. At the time of Elizabeth's first confinement, physicians still based their ministrations upon the ancient Greek theory that the human body was made up of four humours: blood, sweat, phlegm and bile. Most ailments were therefore ascribed to an excess of one of these humours. The young queen may have been bled before giving birth in order to remove 'bad influences', which would have sapped her much-needed strength instead.

As soon as the queen's labour began, her gossips would set about making the last-minute preparations for the birth. They would remove all of her fastenings, such as rings, bracelets, buckles and laces, because these were thought to risk strangling the child. Similarly, nobody in the chamber was permitted to cross their legs, arms or fingers because this might make the birth difficult. In order to ease the contractions, Elizabeth's belly might be rubbed with creams made from brandy, distilled marjoram and saffron. A 'magic girdle' would be tied around it, along with pieces of paper inscribed with 'charms' to offer protection. She might also have worn a belt hung with cowrie shells, which were thought to bring good luck because of their resemblance to the vulva.

In the absence of effective pain relief, the skin of a wild ox was sometimes tied around a woman's thigh, and snakeskin or hartskin belts pulled around her stomach. Others relied upon herbal potions made from lilies, almonds, roses, cyclamen and wild thyme or, more bizarrely, powdered eel liver, ants' eggs, virgin's hair and red cow milk. Women were also often given special powders to make them sneeze because it was thought to help expel the baby from the body.

As labour wore on, the queen's ladies – and perhaps even Elizabeth herself – would have recited prayers or read from the Gospels. In a highly devout age, the comfort derived from this practice was obvious. But there might also have been something beneficial to be derived from the formulaic, repetitive chants, giving the mother something other than the pain to concentrate upon. The word 'abracadabra', now more associated with stage magic, was part of a popular chant used in childbirth.

There is no record of the midwives who attended Elizabeth during her first labour. It is possible that her mother's favourite midwife, Marjory Cobbe, was present. She had helped Elizabeth Woodville during her final confinement less than six years before. Midwives were usually older women, past childbearing years, who had gained experience from many lyings-in. Certain characteristics were sought among prospective midwives, such as having small hands with nails cut short, an absence of rings or bracelets, and a patient, polite, gentle and cheerful demeanour. They must also be discreet and report nothing that they saw or heard in the birthing chamber, unless it was evidence of moral or sexual transgression.

The more experienced midwives employed methods that were surprisingly modern. They would encourage the labouring mother to walk up and down the chamber until the 'matrice' or womb ruptured. If the waters did not break naturally, however, the midwife would pierce the womb with her fingernail, a sharp knife or even shears. Midwives were advised not to encourage the mother to push until the baby was ready to be born, before which 'all labour is in vain, labour as much as ye list.' If a mother wasted all of her energy too early on in the labour, it could become a 'perilous case'.[47]

A midwife also had various tricks and tools at her disposal to hasten along a protracted labour. As well as encouraging the patient to walk about the chamber or kneel on the bed, some midwives brought along their own 'groaning chair', on which the labouring mother would sit while one midwife pressed down on top of her womb and the other knelt down to receive the baby. Other midwives used rope tourniquets to literally squeeze the baby out of the womb, while some favoured more gentle interventions such as massage, warm towels and applied herbal remedies. Above all, the midwife must be calm, cheerful and encouraging, setting the tone for the other attendants, so that the mother might be as relaxed as possible.

One manual advised that in these final stages a midwife should encourage her patient to hold her breath and push downwards 'as though she would go to the stool'.[48] When it was clear that the baby was ready to emerge, the midwife would stroke and massage the womb, and continually anoint the mother's genitals with butter or grease until the baby's head began to crown. If it was a queen giving birth, only the leading midwife would be permitted such intimate physical contact.

The contemporary sources do not mention how long Elizabeth laboured with her first child. All that mattered to the chroniclers was the fact that, at one o'clock in the morning of 20 September, she gave birth to a longed-for prince. Henry VII's fledgling Tudor dynasty had taken a step closer to security.

As soon as the baby boy had emerged from his mother's womb, the umbilical cord was cut and anointed with powdered frankincense or aloe before being left to dry. Great care was taken over this task because the cord was believed to have magical powers of protection, and some people carried a piece of it around with them as a charm against witches. The child's navel was then closely inspected because it was believed to hold the key to his mother's future fertility: if it was wrinkled, she would bear more children; if smooth, there would be none to follow.

Next, the baby was washed in a mixture of wine, herbs, milk, sweet butter or barley water and rubbed with butter or oil of almond, rose or acorns to prevent harmful vapours entering his pores. He was then swaddled tightly in linen so that his limbs might grow straight, and would typically remain in this uncomfortably restricted state for the first six months of his life. He would then be permitted to wear a 'short coat', which was similar to the ankle-length dresses worn by little girls.

The first sustenance to be administered to the precious infant was not his mother's milk (royal wives were forbidden to breastfeed because it hindered conception and interfered with their royal duties) but a spoonful of wine and sugar. He was then appointed a wet-nurse to suckle him. That woman must have borne a son herself because contemporary medical theory dictated that the sex of her child influenced the type of milk she produced. She must also be of impeccable character because it was thought that 'oftentimes the child sucketh the vice of his nurse with the milk of her pap.'[49] The royal mother, meanwhile, would have her breasts tightly bound so that they would stop producing milk.

Having performed her duty, Elizabeth was briefly washed down with a linen cloth, and herbal ointments were applied to her skin by the women in attendance. Despite her undoubted exhaustion, she was not allowed to sleep until two hours later, as tradition dictated. Her chamber would remain in darkness for at least three days after the birth. Only then would she be washed, dressed and transferred to a state bed by a duchess or countess, who would help her 'sit up' and receive visitors.

But as the bells rang out across Winchester to herald the birth of her son, Elizabeth fell into a fever. The court held its breath. Instances of maternal death from infection in the days following a birth were alarmingly high. To the great relief of everyone – not least her husband – the young queen survived and, shortly after her ordeal, founded a chapel in Winchester Cathedral where her son was christened Arthur. In early October, she was 'churched' – a ceremony of purification from the 'sin' of childbirth – and permitted to re-enter society.

Tradition dictated that a royal baby should be established in his or her own household, separate from their parents, at the age of just three months. Accordingly, Arthur was moved to Farnham in Surrey, where he was to be served by a veritable army of attendants, including his wet-nurse, dry-nurse, yeomen, grooms and, at the head of the nursery, Lady Governess. Deeply suspicious of even his closest courtiers and advisers, the king ensured that only men of proven fidelity were chosen to care for his precious son. Chief among them was his cousin, Sir Richard Pole, who headed up the household as chamberlain. A generous annual allowance of 1,000 marks (equivalent to around £300,000 in modern money) was granted for the upkeep of Arthur's establishment.

Henry and Elizabeth were both ambitious for their son's education, which combined a classical curriculum with physical training and the skills that Arthur would need as king. The queen had far more experience of a royal education than her husband, so it was she who had the greatest influence upon Arthur's schooling, which incorporated many elements from that of her ill-fated brothers, Edward and Richard. The sober-minded, worthy and dependable scholar, John Rede, formerly head of Winchester College, was appointed as tutor.

Although she helped to shape her son's upbringing, Elizabeth's contact with him was at best intermittent. This was the harsh reality of traditional royal motherhood: other women would feed, clothe, comfort and play with her children. By contrast, the parents of royal children tended to be distant figures to whom they were taught to show the utmost respect and deference. Love was an unlooked-for emotion that may or may not be felt by the young prince towards the woman who had brought him into the world.

Meanwhile, as a royal wife Elizabeth knew that her body was the property of the state. And that state was already impatient for the birth of another heir.

'Not admitting any near approach, either to his power or to his secrets'

ON 25 NOVEMBER 1487, fourteen months after giving birth to Prince Arthur, Elizabeth of York was finally crowned. It was as if her production of a healthy son had proved that she was a worthy queen, and she was therefore rewarded with the full pomp and pageantry of a coronation. Elizabeth's famously parsimonious husband did not stint on the lavish ceremonials, which included two full days of feasting and entertainments. As a public relations exercise, it was a triumph. England had a beautiful, fertile and, above all, legitimate queen. She and Henry had a healthy son and there would no doubt soon be more to follow. Within two short years of Bosworth, the Tudors looked set to reign supreme.

But it would not be quite as straightforward as that. For a start, although his wife had conceived either before the wedding or a few days after, there was no sign of another heir yet. Yet, the royal couple were both young and regularly shared the same bed. Tracing Henry and Elizabeth's movements during the year following her coronation proves that they were almost always together. They celebrated Christmas 1487 at Greenwich, were at Windsor for Easter, Woodstock for the summer and Westminster for the autumn. Henry had even summoned his 'dearest wife' to be with him at Kenilworth before riding out to the battle in the summer of 1487. Concern must have been growing that there was some impediment.

Perhaps the anxiety provoked by the numerous plots and rebellions that had surrounded the throne ever since Henry's accession had played a part. Or it is possible that Elizabeth did conceive soon after the birth of her son Arthur. There is some evidence in the sources of a short-lived prince named Edward, although the date of his birth is not certain.[1]

Elizabeth had no recorded physical problems after Arthur's birth. Women who married young typically gave birth to a number of children in rapid succession in the early years of their marriage. The gap between each child subsequently lengthened until the final pregnancy, which was generally when a woman reached her mid-thirties – soon after which she would begin the menopause. Elizabeth's mother had given Edward IV a child almost every year for the first half of their marriage.

Henry's queen must have been watchful for any signs of pregnancy. She had already experienced at least one so would have been more aware of the symptoms. In the absence of modern methods of testing, Tudor women resorted to observing certain physical symptoms, including the cessation of periods, enlarged breasts, vomiting and 'strange desires'. Less reliable advice was given by various contemporary manuals, which claimed that a man would be the first to know if conception had occurred because he would feel 'extraordinary contentment' or a 'sucking or drawing at the end of his yard', which when he withdrew it was not 'over-moist'. The woman, meanwhile, would experience a 'yawning or stretching' in the womb, or a 'shaking and quivering' when she passed water.[2] The Tudor version of a pregnancy test was to mix the woman's urine with wine, or alternatively to make her drink rainwater at night or eat honey with aniseed, both of which would bring pain to her stomach if she was pregnant.

The king and queen spent Christmas 1488 together at Sheen Palace. Despite the anxiety over their failure to produce another heir, there seems to have been a growing affection between the couple. Knowing her love of reading, Henry gave his wife several beautifully illuminated books, including the *Miroir des Dames*, a moral instruction for queens and other high-born ladies. Elizabeth also gave her husband gifts from time to time. She excelled at embroidery, a typical accomplishment for a royal lady, and spent many of her private hours working on tokens of her wifely devotion. They included a Garter robe woven with Venetian gold, which she presented to her husband.

About a month after the Twelfth Night revels concluded the festivities, Elizabeth fell pregnant, and by April 1489 it seems that both she and her husband were aware of her condition. At the Feast of St George, Henry presented his wife with an array of gifts, almost all of which were designed for her comfort. They included cloth of black velvet, squirrel fur, beds of down and feather, and sheets of Holland cloth to furnish her bed.

The velvet cloth in particular would have been greatly appreciated by Elizabeth. As the daughter of a king, she was accustomed to wearing gowns of the richest materials and favoured black in her wardrobe, but also had dresses of crimson, purple and gold.[3] Many of her gowns were made of wool, which would have kept out the chill of the royal palaces, but they were all beautifully decorated with deep borders at the hem. Her possessions also included a range of linen smocks and scarlet petticoats.

Unlike her husband, who spent lavishly on his apparel only when he deemed it necessary, Elizabeth had a love of fine clothes that would last throughout their marriage. Queens consort were expected to pay for their own wardrobes, which they did from the grants of land and offices provided to them by the king. Although she made most purchases from her own privy purse and was far from extravagant, Elizabeth's expenditure was evidently more than her husband expected it should be and she was often in debt, dependent on Henry to pay her creditors for household items and clothing. This must have been irksome to a king who liked to keep the royal purse strings tightly pulled.

For now, though, Elizabeth was high in favour with her husband. As her pregnancy progressed, she was obliged to take more rest, but she still sought the company of her considerable body of female attendants. Her mother had had just five ladies-in-waiting, but according to Rodrigo de Puebla, the Spanish ambassador, 'the Queen has thirty-two ladies, very magnificent and in splendid style.' They attended her in private, as well as in the public court, which meant that her privy chamber must have been somewhat crowded. In the close-knit world of the court, many of her gentlewomen were the wives of Henry's own servants and councillors, who were themselves often to be found in the queen's private apartments, delivering messages and gifts from their royal master. The two households also shared entertainers and musicians. Particularly popular was the marshal of the king's minstrels, Henry Glasebury, who had a talent for composing doggerel verse, which was deliberately irregular in rhythm and rhyme for comic effect.

The atmosphere of Elizabeth's household was convivial, engaging and open, reflecting her own personality. Thomas More remarked that she enjoyed 'plenty of every pleasant thing'.[4] Among the personnel she selected was her illegitimate half-brother, Arthur Plantagenet, who was appointed as a cupbearer. With the characteristic auburn hair, well-built frame and easy-going nature of the Yorkist offspring, Arthur entered into all of the diversions that the court had to offer, and was particularly fond of jousting and fine wine. He was so personable and easy-going that one friend described him as 'the pleasantest man in the world'.[5]

By stark contrast, the household of Elizabeth's indomitable mother-in-law was as sober, strict and pious as Lady Margaret herself. She ruled her attendants with a rod of iron. Even her confessor, John Fisher, admitted that she tended to repeat the same moralising tales 'many a time'.[6] Naturally domineering and keenly aware of her status as the king's mother, Lady Margaret was far more involved in the life of her son and daughter-in-law than was customary. She saw herself as queen in all but name, and demanded as much honour and ceremonial as was due to her – sometimes even more so. At the great events of court and state, she walked a mere half-pace behind Elizabeth, whose rightful precedence as queen was clearly irksome to her mother-in-law.

Henry deferred to his mother in all things. Her apartments were often next to his in the palaces where they took up residence. At the Oxfordshire manor of Woodstock, for example, they shared an interconnecting 'drawing chamber', where they would often confer on the affairs of the day or play cards. Her piercing black eyes were ever watchful of the comings and goings at court, and she even had one of her servants, Sir Reynold Bray, appointed to her son's household so that he might keep her informed of all that passed there.

Lady Margaret also kept a close eye on her daughter-in-law – suspicious, no doubt, of this Yorkist princess and her treacherous relatives. The Spanish envoy observed that she kept Elizabeth 'in subjection'. Another visitor to court claimed that she was the queen's gatekeeper, and begrudged the fact that he would have spoken more to Elizabeth 'had it not been for that strong whore, the king's mother.'[7]

All of this must have been extremely irksome to Elizabeth who, having been raised as a princess in the Yorkist court, was well aware of the status and honour due to her as queen. She was far from politically naïve, eager to submit herself to the direction of her domineering mother-in-law. But she was wise enough to mask any private resentment she might have felt with a public display of family unity. Indeed, far from rebelling against Lady Margaret's authority, Elizabeth realised that the most effective way to best her mother-in-law was to emulate her. The keystone of Lady Margaret's character was her piety, and she never tired of parading her spirituality across the court and kingdom. Not to be outdone, Elizabeth began to observe the daily rituals and devotions with unflinching piety, and also gave regular and generous endowments to the Church. Such was the apparent unity between his wife and mother that Henry often referred to them in the same breath.

Not surprisingly, Lady Margaret was in attendance at her daughter-in-law's latest confinement. It began at the end of October 1489, when the queen entered the rooms that had been assigned to her at the Palace of Westminster, the place of her own birth. Her chamber was adjoined by a chapel and afforded views of the river – although these would have been mostly obscured by the curtains and hangings, which were of blue cloth embroidered with gold fleurs-de-lys. Her bed and birthing pallet were hung with canopy of gold and velvet of many colours, decorated with the red roses of Lancaster. Perhaps Elizabeth had succeeded in charming her mother-in-law into relaxing the strict rules that she had laid down for her confinement, because the latter allowed a visit from Elizabeth Woodville's male cousin, François de Luxembourg, who was staying in London with a group of French ambassadors.

On the evening of 28 November, after almost a month in confinement, Elizabeth gave birth to a daughter. This must have been something of a disappointment to the king, who was eager to secure his throne with another male heir. The London Grey Friars chronicler did not even trouble to record it. But the infant princess might at least be useful for forging a foreign alliance through marriage. She was christened Margaret two days later in honour of her paternal grandmother. The court remained at Westminster for the Christmas celebrations, and the queen's churching was delayed until 27 December because of an outbreak of measles, which claimed the lives of several of her ladies.

Elizabeth made a quick recovery from the birth and soon resumed her royal duties. These included superintending the upbringing of her new daughter. Tradition dictated that while the heir was groomed for kingship by specially appointed tutors and attendants, the other royal children were entrusted to the care of their mother. Having enjoyed such an upbringing herself, Elizabeth would have known exactly what was required.

The queen also resumed her wifely duties shortly after returning to court. This time, there would not be a long wait for another heir: she was pregnant again before the year was out. The place selected for the queen's third confinement was the Palace of Placentia in Greenwich. It was considerably smaller and less symbolic than the first two locations had been. Elizabeth may have chosen it herself because it was said to be her favourite house, and it was quieter and more private than Westminster. It was also an advantage to be away from the heat and bustle of central London for this, her first summer birth.

The queen probably arrived in Greenwich in early June, the usual preparations having been made. On the 28th of that month she was safely delivered of a son, Henry. She and her husband would have been gratified to have another male heir in the royal nursery. But the infant Henry was just the spare, and little official attention was given to his birth – at least compared with that of his elder brother Arthur. All of the focus was on the latter, who, at almost five years old, was growing into a fine boy, as praised for his intellect as for his physical prowess.

Soon after his christening, Prince Henry was sent to join his sister Margaret at Eltham Palace. As he became more aware of the world around him, Henry would have been reminded of his Yorkist forebears by his grandfather Edward IV's *rose en soleil* emblem carved above the entrance to the magnificent Great Hall. He was raised with his sister Margaret in a predominantly female household, superintended by their mother, who doted upon her younger son. The prince was equally attached to her – far more so, it seems, than to his father. Analysis of Henry's childhood scrawl reveals a similarity to Elizabeth of York's handwriting, which suggests that she taught him his letters.

The queen's household was intimately linked to that of her children at Eltham. When Henry was three years old, his mother appointed Elizabeth Denton, one of her own gentlewomen, as head of her children's nursery. 'Lady Mistress' Denton did not relinquish her service to the queen, however, for she continued to draw a salary from her household. That she was able to maintain both roles simultaneously suggests that Elizabeth spent a great deal of her time at Eltham.

The queen also introduced some of her York relatives to her children. They included Arthur Plantagenet, whom she evidently hoped would provide a positive role model for her energetic youngest son. She judged right: Henry's character was far more aligned to his vivacious Yorkist ancestors than to his sober-minded father, who was too weighed down by the cares of state to indulge in most of the sporting and leisure pursuits so adored by Henry. The young prince later reflected that his uncle Arthur had been 'the gentlest heart living'.[8] By contrast, the references he made to his father were in restrained, albeit respectful terms.

Although preoccupied by the upbringing of her youngest son and her daughter Margaret, Elizabeth knew that she was expected to swell the nursery with yet more heirs. Three months after Henry's birth, she fell pregnant once more. According to what had become her custom, the queen chose another new location for her confinement: the Palace of Sheen. But this was the first birth that her own mother, Elizabeth Woodville, had declined to attend. She was gravely ill at Bermondsey Abbey, which had been her home for the previous five years. How the queen felt at being deprived of the comfort of her mother's love and experience in the birthing chamber is not recorded. But this was as nothing to the sorrow she experienced upon hearing the news that Elizabeth had died on 8 June 1492.

When the queen gave birth to a daughter on 2 July, she named her Elizabeth in honour of her late mother. The princess joined her elder sister and brother at Eltham Palace, but her childhood was cut short by the onset of atrophy. The most common causes of this wasting disease are genetic defects, poor nutrition or lack of exercise. As the latter two were unlikely to have applied to the princess, she may have been afflicted with the condition from birth.

Princess Elizabeth was the first of the royal children to die in infancy, and her parents were grief-stricken when they received the news of her death, aged three, on 14 September 1495. Her body was brought from Eltham in state and buried on the north side of St Edward the Confessor's shrine in Westminster Abbey. Her funeral was conducted with great ceremony and cost £318 (equivalent to around £155,000 today). The king commissioned an exquisite tomb for his daughter. Crafted from Purbeck and black marble, it was surmounted by a finely polished slab of black lydian on which were placed inscriptions to the infant princess together with her effigy in copper gilt – neither of which survive.

Infant mortality was alarmingly high in the Tudor period, compared to modern times. Some families lost as many as half of their children to disease, stillbirths and cot deaths. Poor hygiene, malnutrition, complications during birth and accidents contributed to many thousands of deaths. The rates were highest among the poorer classes, but sudden and unpredictable infant death was no respecter of rank, and many aristocratic and royal families shared in the misfortune.

The king and queen may have drawn some comfort from the fact that by the time of their daughter's death, Elizabeth was pregnant once more. On 18 March 1496, she gave birth to another princess, Mary, at Sheen. She would be the last royal infant to be born there, for the palace was razed to the ground by a fire the following year.

Although Henry's dynasty was becoming ever more established, this did not guarantee the safety of his throne. He was constantly plagued by rumours of Yorkist plots and rebellions, each of which deepened his natural suspicion and paranoia. A sign of his unease is revealed by his account books, which, in late 1493, included a payment to a man named Cornish for a 'prophecy'.[9] Henry may have been seeking reassurance about the most dangerous 'pretender' to the throne that he had yet faced. Perkin Warbeck, as he became known, claimed to be Richard, Duke of York, the younger of the queen's brothers, who were presumed murdered by their uncle Richard III. A handsome young man of regal bearing, he had already attracted a great deal of support among Henry's international rivals, including his 'aunt', Margaret of Burgundy, who formally recognised his claim to the English throne in 1490, and James IV of Scotland, who never missed an opportunity to cause trouble for the English king.

A sign of Henry's unease is the fact that during the years 1490–2, when the threat from Warbeck was gaining ground, his expenditure on clothing reverted to the extortionate sums of his early reign. For each of these three years, he lavished an impressive £3,533 (£1.7 million in today's money) on apparel for himself and his family.[10] Yet again, perhaps he was attempting to mask his deep-seated insecurity with a show of outward magnificence.

Even more telling was a set of ordinances drawn up in December 1494 for the regulation of the royal household. These instituted a significant change to the workings of the king's privy chamber. Having discovered that there were conspirators within the household itself, the king was no longer prepared to adhere to the detailed protocols that governed it. These had enabled servants to move between the public and private worlds of the royal court: from the kitchens and laundry to the presence and privy chambers. From now on, however, Henry made the privy chamber an entirely separate, private and closely guarded entity, not subject to the normal rules of the court. Normally, the door of the room in which the king was present was guarded by a gentleman usher, but Henry decreed that this official should cede responsibility 'to such one as he thinketh by his discretion should best content the king's mind and is accustomed thereto.'[11]

Now that it was separate from the rest of the court, the privy or 'secret' chamber expanded into a more luxurious suite of rooms, where the king's every private whim was catered for. First among these rooms was the privy chamber itself – usually a medium-sized apartment richly decorated with tapestries, carpets and a chair of estate. Beyond it lay a small complex of inner chambers or privy lodgings that varied in size and number in each palace. They included at least one bedchamber with a garderobe leading off it, a bathroom, a withdrawing room, a robing chamber, a closet or oratory for the king's private devotions, and a study or library filled with his most precious and well-thumbed books. The rooms were often lined with wooden linenfold panelling, which made them rather gloomy and heightened the feeling of privacy. They were usually linked to the public rooms of court by a short corridor or gallery, and to the queen's apartments by another gallery or privy stair.[12] The galleries were havens of calm and beauty, with pleasing views within and without. Here, the king and his intimates could walk and talk in confidence and comfort, shielded from both the elements and the public world of the court.

The new structure was modelled on the French court and meant that only a handful of the hundreds of royal household servants and attendants were granted close access to the king. This created a new mystique around the monarch by putting a greater distance between him and his courtiers, and by surrounding him with elaborate ceremony. The innovations, as one historian claims, 'had created a Secret Chamber which institutionalised distance.'[13] Henry's first biographer, Francis Bacon, describes how the king was intent upon 'keeping of distance . . . not admitting any near or full approach, either to his power or to his secrets.'[14] As well as making the monarch less accessible, this ritualised his appearances in public. As a result, his courtiers fought more fiercely for the king's attention than they had been obliged to before.

No less fiercely contested were the few places that were on offer in the new inner sanctum. In contrast to the main chamber with its hundreds of officials, the privy chamber staff now comprised just six grooms led by a groom of the stool. And in choosing them,

Henry was guided not by rank or status, but by who he thought would 'best content the king'. Chief among them was Hugh Denys, groom of the stool, a Gloucestershire gentleman who had married into the influential family of Ros (or Roos), whose Lancastrian connections were strong. Born around 1440, Denys was one of the oldest members of Henry's entourage and his loyalty had already been well proved.

The earliest reference to the post is found in a warrant of the Great Wardrobe dated 15 November 1497, which ordered its keeper to supply to 'Hugh Denys, Groom of our Stool . . . first a stool of timber covered with black velvet and fringed with silk', as well as 'two pewter basins and four broad yards of tawny cloth'.[15] Denys was therefore arranging the construction of a close-stool for his royal master. He was also responsible for its maintenance and transport to other palaces as required, and above all for attending the king when he made use of it.

The basic duties of the groom of the stool were set out in John Russell's *Book of Nurture* (c.1452), which includes the following instructions for the office holder:

> See the privy-house for easement be fair, sweet, and clean;
> And that the boards thereupon be covered with cloth fair and
>   green;
> And the hole himself, look there no board be seen;
> Thereon a fair cushion, the ordure no man to vex.
> Look there be blanket, cotton, or linen to wipe the nether end,
> And ever he calls, wait ready and prompt,
> Basin and ewer, and on your shoulder a towel.[16]

It may seem perplexing to modern observers that such an unsavoury position should be so highly sought after. But a number of important administrative tasks also fell to the groom of the stool. He was responsible for those items of the king's jewels and plate that were in daily use, as well as of his linen and the furnishings and equipment of his private apartments in general. The groom was also ex officio keeper of the privy purse, which gave him responsibility for the financial management of the royal household, and he had a number of important secretarial tasks. He would also undertake any other duties that his sovereign required.

Above all, though, the groom of the stool's prestige was enhanced by the fact that he spent more hours alone with the king than anyone else. If he proved his worth and discretion, he could become the most trusted confidante in the kingdom; the man with whom the king shared his innermost thoughts. As such, he had the potential to exert more influence than even the highest-ranking member of the council. The fact that he regulated access to the king also gave him considerable power. He could make it difficult for his rivals or enemies to gain an audience and, equally, could promote his allies by not only facilitating access, but using his many private hours alone with Henry to recommend them.

The official duties of the other privy chamber staff focused upon the body of the king. They dressed and undressed him, bathed him, tested his food for poison, served him at table, arranged his bedtime drink, and took turns to guard their master during the night by sleeping on a pallet mattress on the floor of the privy chamber. They were akin to private security officers, being ever watchful and present. The grooms also carried out the more menial duties of cleaning, making up fires, strewing fresh rushes on the floor of his bedchamber and laying out sleeping pallets. Yet they were also expected to turn their hands to playing cards, singing, playing music, engaging in lively conversation and other pastimes for the king's amusement. In short, as one historian has pointed out, 'They were the nearest thing he had to friends.'[17]

The six grooms, and the groom of the stool, were the only attendants who were allowed to lay hands on their royal master. Because the king had been anointed at his coronation and thus made holy, it was thought that the royal power and charisma would – literally – rub off on his privy chamber servants. This gave them considerable prestige and enabled them to command a great deal of respect at court.

Among the new ordinances was an extraordinarily detailed list of instructions that the king's personal servants had to adhere to in order to ensure that he could sleep safely at night. The seemingly straightforward task of preparing the royal bed each night now became a ritual of several hours' duration.

Henry VII's desire for privacy would have a lasting impact on the layout, functions and personnel of the court, with the privy chamber's prestige becoming ever greater as the Tudor age progressed. Much as he loved the private hours that he spent there, however, Henry knew that he still had to maintain a suitably impressive façade to the rest of the court and kingdom. The Tudor dynasty must look unshakeable even if, underneath, it was dangerously fragile.

In September 1497, after several failed invasion attempts, Warbeck landed off the coast of Cornwall. Having been declared 'Richard IV' on Bodmin Moor, he marched to Exeter with his 6,000-strong army and, after taking the city, advanced towards Taunton. Henry sent a force to attack the Cornish, and when Warbeck heard that the king's scouts were at Glastonbury, he panicked and deserted his army. He was subsequently captured at Beaulieu Abbey in Hampshire. Although Henry showed him clemency once he had been forced to admit publicly that he was an imposter, and even welcomed him to court, Warbeck remained a thorn in his side. When the increasingly paranoid king heard a rumour that the pretender had been conspiring with Edward Plantagenet during their imprisonment in the Tower, he had him tried for treason and hanged.

Partly in response to the Perkin Warbeck controversy, Henry resolved to undertake some very public displays of kingship. Formal crown-wearing ceremonies and regular touchings to heal his scrofulous subjects of the 'king's evil' (scrofula) were held to reinforce his majesty. Meanwhile, the use of his dynastic badges on buildings, charters and the liveries of his servants became widespread, proclaiming his inherited right to rule.

In October 1497, two Italian ambassadors arrived at Woodstock in Oxfordshire, where Henry and his entourage were in residence. One was the secretary of Ludovico Sforza, Duke of Milan, and the other a special envoy from Venice. They were clearly impressed by what they saw. The English king received them 'in a small hall, hung with very handsome tapestry, leaning against a tall gilt chair, covered with cloth of gold.' Henry was richly attired in 'a violet-coloured gown, lined with cloth of gold, and a collar of many jewels, and on his cap was a large diamond and a most beautiful pearl.'

After being granted the privilege of a private audience with the king, the ambassadors concluded that he was 'gracious, grave, and a very worthy person.' They were also introduced to the queen, who was 'dressed in cloth of gold' and flanked by the king's mother on one side and her six-year-old son Henry on the other. Now aged thirty-three, she was still a 'handsome woman' according to the Italians.

But this impressive display of majesty could not altogether disguise the strain under which Henry had laboured in recent years. The ambassadors noted his spare physique and prominent cheekbones, as well as the greying hair around his temples. The more they became acquainted with the king and his court, the more heightened was their awareness that all was not as it seemed. The Milanese envoy, Raimondo da Soncino, reported that although Henry was 'most wise', he was 'suspicious of everything', adding that: 'he has no one he can trust, except his paid men at arms.'[18]

Increasingly private and distant, the king often retreated to his privy chamber. There, far from indulging in pastimes to help him forget the cares of state, he would spend many hours 'writing the accounts of his expenses with his own hand.' He took refuge in a growing obsession with money – an obsession that, ironically, was doing more to spark disloyalty among his people than the plots and rebellions that were constantly swarming about him. Pedro de Ayala, an envoy from Spain, shrewdly observed that although the English king liked to be thought of as a 'great man', nobody believed he was, because his love of money was 'too great'.[19]

The queen was painfully aware that members of her own family were plotting endlessly against her husband. Giving him another heir would be a powerful way of reiterating her loyalty. But just as the first pretender, Lambert Simnel, may have contributed to Elizabeth's failure to conceive for more than two years, the great anxiety occasioned by Warbeck's invasion seemed to have had a similar effect. Now that the pretender was out of the way for good, however, Elizabeth fell pregnant. The date of conception is not certain, but she was certainly pregnant by May 1498. Her husband's accounts include payments to her physician Master Lewis and her surgeon Robert Taylor. This suggests that there may have been cause for concern with her latest pregnancy.

By the time she gave birth in February 1499, the thirty-three-year-old queen was considered to be of an advanced age for childbearing. Moreover, although the child – another son, Edmund – seemed healthy, the Spanish ambassador reported that there had been 'much fear for her life' during the birth. It is possible that the difficult birth also created problems for the baby because Edmund died on 19 June 1500, at the age of just fifteen months. He was buried in Westminster Abbey next to his sister Elizabeth.

Edmund's death was the cause of profound sorrow for the queen, who sought solace by spending a great deal of time at Eltham, where her son Henry and his two sisters, Margaret and Mary, were being raised. Elizabeth had paid particular attention to the education of her favourite son. Assisted by her mother-in-law, she had selected the tutors and companions whom she deemed most suitable for shaping Henry's character and learning. They included his cupbearer, Henry Guildford, son of Elizabeth's gentlewoman Joan and the king's trusted adviser Sir Richard Guildford. Close in age to Henry, Guildford was boisterous and quick-witted and struck up an instant rapport with the young prince. They shared a mutual passion for jousting and sport, and Guildford would serve his royal master for the rest of his life.

By far the most influential of all the men appointed to serve Prince Henry, however, was his tutor, John Skelton, who had joined the Eltham household in the late 1490s. A veritable force of nature, he was bursting with ideas, humour, languages, verse and – above all – self-confidence. As such, he was a highly unconventional and potentially risky choice, but Henry's mother had shrewdly judged that he was far more likely to inspire her wayward younger son with learning than his elder brother's more traditional and sober-minded tutor. Skelton's credentials were certainly impressive. He had first met the king upon the latter's visit to Oxford University in 1488, when Henry had conferred upon him a laureateship in classical Latin rhetoric. This degree had never been awarded before in England, which meant that Skelton was the first English poet laureate. Cambridge followed suit and gave him its own laureate five years later, which brought him to the attention of its benefactor, the king's mother, Lady Margaret Beaufort.

Having served as assistant to Elizabeth Countess of Surrey, wife of the powerful courtier Thomas Howard, Skelton was clearly comfortable in the company of women, and thus ideally suited to the household at Eltham. His position was further strengthened in 1495 when the countess's son, Thomas, was married to the queen's sister, Anne. He was appointed tutor or 'mentor' to Henry in around 1496 and as his chaplain two years later, following his admission to holy orders. This meant that he was responsible for shaping the prince's mind and soul. Although somewhat unconventional, the appointment won praise from some of the greatest intellectuals of the age. In a letter to Henry written in 1499, the renowned Dutch scholar Desiderius Erasmus referred to Skelton as 'a light and glory of English letters'.[20]

Skelton was quick to realise the potential of his position and proceeded to teach Henry not just the classical curriculum of grammar, Latin and religious studies, but manners, courtesy and government. He included many of his own texts in Henry's reading list, such as the *Speculum Principis*, or 'mirror for princes', a guide to behaviour that he presented to the prince in 1501. This text reveals more about Skelton's self-interest than the pedagogical thinking of the day. He urges Henry to 'love poets', insisting: 'Athletes are two a penny but patrons of the art are rare.' He also cautioned against taking 'vain pride in riches' but instead recommended 'the glory of virtue'.[21]

Although Skelton had long hankered after a position at court, he soon grew frustrated by its strictures. With an increasingly flagrant disregard for what his royal patrons might think, he produced a series of controversial satirical texts on sex, society and the nature of court life. In the most famous of these, *The Bowge of Court*, he cast himself as 'Drede', a man of 'virtue' surrounded by thieves, gamblers, pimps and potential murderers, all of whom relentlessly flatter and scheme against each other.

Skelton's influence was in any case already being supplanted by that of another mentor or 'study companion': William Blount, Lord Mountjoy. Henry's mother had selected him as a man of the world: educated, cultured and well rounded. She was determined that Henry should have a positive role model who would help shape him into a prince that her chivalric Yorkist forebears would have been proud of. Mountjoy was ideally suited to the task. His grandfather had been a close attendant of Edward IV and the Woodville family, and Mountjoy himself was the stepson of the Earl of Ormond, who was chamberlain to the queen.

By the time he joined the Eltham household in around 1499, Mountjoy, then in his early twenties, had an exemplary record of service. He had proved his loyalty to Henry VII by fighting against a rebellion, and had subsequently travelled to Paris to immerse himself in classical studies. While there, he had become acquainted with Erasmus, who had been so impressed with the young man that he had vowed himself willing to follow Mountjoy even to the 'lower world' itself. Mountjoy had taken him at his word and invited Erasmus to accompany him when he returned to England in 1499. He arranged for both Erasmus and his friend Thomas More to visit the royal nursery at Eltham. Both men made a profound impression upon the eight-year-old boy, who was replete with learning and accomplishments, but was also rather spoilt.

Erasmus later recalled the visit. All three royal children were assembled in the Great Hall, with Henry at the centre – already a presence to be reckoned with. Writing with the benefit of hindsight, the Dutch scholar claimed that the young prince looked 'somehow like a natural king, displaying a noble spirit combined with peculiar courtesy.'[22] Impressed though he was, Erasmus was also deeply embarrassed by the fact that he had not thought to bring a gift for the prince. This was made all the more obvious when his companion presented Henry with a gift of writing. When they all dined together afterwards, the precocious young prince challenged Erasmus to write him something. Eager to make amends, the scholar raced off a ten-page ode to England entitled *Prosopopoeia Britanniae Maioris*, full of praise for Henry and his family. If he hoped thus to ingratiate himself into a position at court, he was disappointed. A few months later, he left England, still grumbling about 'those wretched courtiers'.[23]

While his wife found comfort in the company of their young children, the king was an increasingly distant figure – both to his family and his court. But there was one person to whom he remained close. In July 1501 he wrote to his mother for the first time in many months, confiding that the anxiety and sorrow of the previous few years had begun to take its toll on his health. 'Verily, madame, my sight is nothing so perfect as it has been, and I know well it will appear daily wherefore I trust that you will not be displeased, though I write not so often with mine own hand, for on my faith I have been three days ere I could make an end of this letter.'[24] Failing eyesight was a source of great frustration to a king who took intense personal interest in all accounts and state papers, so he tried everything to arrest the decline. Lotions and eyebaths made of fennel water, rose water and celandine were employed 'to make bright the sight', but to no avail.[25]

Beset with grief at the loss of his infant son and still plagued by fears for his crown, Henry appeared suddenly vulnerable. Perhaps this is why he had the sudden impulse to write to the woman who was more devoted to him than anyone else – even his own wife. This typically guarded man expressed his filial love with unusual sentiment and affection, assuring Lady Margaret: 'I shall be glad to please you as your heart can desire it, and I know well, that I am as much bounden so to do, as any creature living for the great and singular motherly love and affection that it hath pleased you at all times to bear me.' He concluded: 'Mine own most loving mother, in my most hearty manner I thank you, beseeching you of your good continuance in the same.'[26]

A few months after writing this letter, Henry at last had cause for rejoicing when he secured one of the most sought-after brides in the international marriage market for his son and heir. The idea of marrying Prince Arthur to Catherine, daughter of Ferdinand and Isabella of Spain, had been mooted as early as March 1489, but it wasn't until 1497 that the details had finally been agreed. This included the provision of a handsome dowry (200,000 crowns) for the bride, which appealed as much to her prospective father-in-law as did her pedigree.

Catherine finally arrived in Plymouth in October 1501 and journeyed to Hampshire to meet her betrothed. Despite being unable to understand each other, their first encounter on 4 November proceeded well enough. Arthur wrote to assure his parents-in-law that he was immensely happy to 'behold the face of his lovely bride' and promised to be 'a true and loving husband'. Just shy of her sixteenth birthday, Catherine was indeed a great beauty, with light auburn-coloured hair and fine features. Her clothes presented a stark contrast to those worn by the rest of the ladies at court, but it was not long before the latter began to adopt the Spanish fashions favoured by Catherine. Her fifteen-year-old groom, meanwhile, had grown into a tall, slender young man, rather serious like his father. In the few surviving portraits of the prince, he is shown wearing the sombre-coloured clothes favoured by the king.

The wedding took place on 14 November at St Paul's Cathedral. Thousands of people lined the streets, craning to catch a glimpse of the exotic princess, decked out in 'costly apparel both of goldsmith's work and embroidery, rich jewels [and] massy chains' as she rode on a horse decked with glittering gold bells and spangles.[27] Unusually for the time, both Catherine and her groom were dressed all in white. The bride was led into the church by her soon to be brother-in-law, the ten-year-old Prince Henry. Already, young Henry had the charisma and presence that his elder brother and father notably lacked.

After the ceremony, the newlyweds, along with the king and queen and their guests, made their way to the Bishop's Palace for the wedding feast. Arthur and Catherine seemed delighted with each other, being 'both lusty and amorous'.[28] After they had finished their dinner at about five in the afternoon, the king sent the Lord

Chamberlain to instruct a number of high-ranking ladies to prepare his son and daughter-in-law's bedchamber at nearby Baynard's Castle. This task took three hours, which no doubt heightened the anticipation – and nerves – of the newlyweds. At length, they were conveyed to the castle so that the formal bedding ceremony could begin.

The bed and bedchamber were blessed by the priests and bishops who were present. Arthur climbed into bed next to his wife, and they were both blessed by the officiating prelates, who prayed that they should be protected from 'phantasies and illusions of devils'. Wine and spices were served to the guests, who then departed, leaving the prince and his new wife to 'conclude and consummate' their marriage.[29] What followed has become the most controversial wedding night in history. Although they did not know it, the question of whether Arthur Tudor consummated his marriage to Catherine of Aragon that night, or during the four and a half months that followed, would have far-reaching consequences for the political and religious life of England.

The contemporary accounts for what happened after the guests had departed are scarce. Only when the matter became pivotal during the 1520s and 30s were the attendants present at the wedding called to give their testimonies. These were frustratingly contradictory. Some (including Catherine herself) claimed that nothing had passed between the youthful couple but chaste embraces, both believing that they had plenty of time to consummate their union when they had gained in maturity. Others claimed that the force and regularity of their sexual intercourse fatally weakened the already frail groom, just as Catherine's brother Juan had allegedly been killed by the exertion of satisfying his 'over-passionate' wife Margaret four years earlier.

The chronicler Edward Hall had no doubt that the marriage had been consummated. He recorded that 'this lusty prince and his beautiful bride were brought and joined together in one bed naked and there did that act, which to the performance and full consummation of matrimony was most requisite and expedient.'[30] But he was writing during the early 1540s, when it was politic (to say the least) to affirm that Catherine had lost her virginity to Arthur. By contrast, Catherine's physician, Dr Alcaraz, later testified that her new husband had been unable to perform the sexual act: 'The Prince had been denied the strength necessary to know a woman, as if he was a cold piece of stone, because he was in the final stages of phthisis [consumption].' He went on to claim that Arthur's limbs were weak and that he had 'never seen a man whose legs and other bits of his body were so thin.'[31]

Catherine herself observed the utmost discretion after the wedding night. The following day, Monday 15 November, Baynard's Castle was 'under silence' and the bride kept to her chamber with only her ladies present. 'No access utterly' was permitted, and the only visitor who was admitted to her chambers was the Earl of Oxford, who had come to deliver an affectionate note from Catherine's new father-in-law.[32]

In contrast to his bride's discretion, Arthur emerged from their bedchamber with a 'good and sanguine complexion' and was apparently eager to boast of their exploits. He called upon Anthony Willoughby, one of his body servants, to bring him a cup of ale, 'for I have this night been in the midst of Spain'.[33] The following day, accompanied by his father and younger brother, along with 500 members of the royal household and Catherine's retinue, he processed in great state to St Paul's for a thanksgiving ceremony. His new wife was still kept under wraps, being 'secretly conveyed' to a closet high up in the cathedral, from where she could watch the proceedings.[34]

There followed a week of festivities at Westminster, including tournaments, pageants and dancing. Arthur's fourteen-year-old sister Margaret took part in the latter, accompanied by her younger brother Henry. They performed two slow dances until, impatient with the formality of it all, the ten-year-old prince 'suddenly cast off his gown and danced in his jacket'. The assembled dignitaries were delighted with this show-stealing gesture, and his indulgent parents showed 'right great and singular pleasure'.[35]

The final stage of the festivities took place ten miles west of the city at the king's magnificent new palace of Richmond, which he had ordered to be swiftly completed in time to receive the newly-weds. Built on the site of Sheen Manor (which burned down in 1497) the palace was designed to impress not just the young Spanish princess, but the kingdom as a whole. It was a magnificent, self-confident symbol of the fledgling Tudor dynasty.

Viewed from the river, Richmond was a fairy-tale palace with clusters of domed towers and turrets behind a high curtain wall. It was set within some of the most beautiful gardens in England, with sweet-smelling flowers and herbs, topiaried mythical beasts, and orchards that provided apples, pears, peaches and damsons for the royal kitchens. There were also bowling alleys, butts for archers, tennis courts and 'other goodly and pleasant disports for every person as they would choose and desire.'

The privy lodgings at Richmond were decorated with fourteen turrets and boasted a great number of windows. Fresh water was piped to the royal apartments, and a remarkably advanced heating system kept the occupants warm and cosseted, even in the depths of winter. The palace also had a network of covered passages that linked the various buildings, which meant that it was possible to pass from one part of the palace to another without crossing a draughty open courtyard.

But the cold reality of life in England soon became apparent to Catherine when the festivities were finally concluded and she and her new husband made their way to the castle of Ludlow, the traditional seat of the Prince of Wales. The thick stone walls of this imposing borders castle, built more for defence than for comfort, did little to hold at bay the cold, damp winter. Far from alleviating the conditions, the onset of spring brought a new hazard: a 'great sickness' that broke out in the area surrounding the castle. It has been conjectured that this was the sweating sickness or even the plague, but neither was named in the contemporary sources. More likely is that it was a deadly strain of influenza.

Some sources suggest that both Arthur and his bride fell prey to the disease. If so, then Catherine soon recovered. But the prince had long been of a fragile disposition and his health had been deteriorating since the beginning of February. It seems likely that he had been suffering from tuberculosis. Either this alone proved fatal, or it weakened his immune system so that he was unable to fight off the sickness that swept through the local area. A contemporary record claimed that 'a pitiful disease and sickness' of 'deadly corruption did utterly vanquish and overcome the blood.'[36] Arthur died on 2 April, leaving Catherine a widow after just four and a half months of marriage. His body was disembowelled, embalmed, spiced and wrapped in waxed cloth before being placed in an open coffin and displayed in his chamber at Ludlow Castle. It would remain there for the next three weeks.

That the king's heir had died at so tender an age, and so soon after his marriage to a daughter of one of the most powerful families in Europe, was a catastrophe. The late prince's chamberlain, Sir Richard Pole, wrote at once to the king and council at Greenwich. When the letters arrived late in the evening of 4 April, the council agreed that the unenviable task of breaking the news to Henry should be assigned to his private chaplain. Early the following morning, the king was disturbed by a knock at his chamber door. Surprised to see his chaplain before his usual time, Henry immediately let him in. The chaplain then requested all of the king's other attendants to leave so that he might impart the sad news to his royal master in private.

An anonymous source describes what happened next. 'When his grace understood that sorrowful heavy tidings, he sent for the queen, saying that he and the queen would take the painful sorrows together.' Upon being told that her eldest son was dead, Elizabeth reacted as a steadfast consort rather than a loving mother. 'She with full great and constant comfortable words besought his grace that he would first after God remember the weal of his own noble person, the comfort of his realm and of her.' She then reminded Henry that his own mother 'had never no more children but him only, and that God by His grace had ever preserved him, and brought him where he was.' Moreover, they still had 'a fair prince, two fair princesses' and 'are both young enough' to have more. Henry thanked his wife for her 'good comfort' and she took her leave.

But as soon as Elizabeth was in the privacy of her chamber, her composure crumbled. Now it was her 'natural and motherly remem-brance' that held sway, and the realisation of her 'great loss smote her so sorrowful to the heart' that she wept uncontrollably. Her attendants were so desperate to relieve her suffering that they sent for the king to comfort her. Henry did not hesitate, but 'of true gentle and faithful love, in good haste came and relieved her, and showed her how wise counsel she had given him before, and he for his part would thank God for his son, and would she should do in like wise.'[37] It is an indication of how much closer the royal couple had grown that in this, the greatest tragedy of their reign, they should abandon the customary formality of royal marriages and seek comfort in each other's arms.

Grief-stricken though she was, Elizabeth was solicitous for the welfare of her newly widowed daughter-in-law and sent a litter of black velvet to carry her back to London. Given the princess's fragile condition, however, the cortège was obliged to make painfully slow progress. The queen was undoubtedly concerned for Catherine's health, but another reason for the care she took over her transport was the very real prospect (at least as she understood it) that Catherine might be pregnant.

It soon became obvious that the princess was not carrying a future heir to the English throne. Instead, it was Elizabeth herself who fell pregnant just one month after Arthur's death. Her reminder to Henry that they were still young enough to produce another heir had proved prescient.

3

'Closeted away like a girl'

As ARTHUR'S WIDOW, aided by his mother, tried to adjust to her changed circumstances, his brother Henry – now 'my lord prince' – had been suddenly thrust into the spotlight. This had an immediate impact upon the household at Eltham. The prince's Lady Mistress, Elizabeth Denton, was transferred to the household of Lady Margaret Beaufort, and in her place the king appointed several new male attendants. Although most of these new men were in their late teens or early twenties, they had already proven their loyalty to the crown. They included William Thomas, a devout Welshman who had previously attended Henry's brother Arthur. Ralph Pudsey had been a groom of the king's privy chamber and now became the prince's sewer and keeper of his jewellery. Another appointee was William Compton, son of a Warwickshire landowner, who had been brought up among the menial servants of the royal household. The hard-bitten and ambitious royal councillor, Sir Henry Marney, was put in overall charge of the household.

With Eltham no longer a female-dominated household, the prince's mother seldom visited. This was not for want of care. Still grieving over the loss of her eldest son, she had other, private, troubles. Her latest pregnancy was not progressing well. She fell sick while staying at Woodstock in July 1502, and in September her apothecary received payment for delivering 'certain stuff for the use of the queen'. On 14 November, she was visited by Mistress Harcourt at Westminster, and twelve days later another (French) nurse attended her at Baynard's Castle. This may have been part of the preparations for her confinement, but there is no record of any such visits on previous occasions.

Even though she was still seven weeks from giving birth, Elizabeth had the girdle of Our Lady of Westminster delivered to her in mid-December. This hints at the anxiety that a difficult pregnancy had engendered. But she put on a characteristically brave face during the Christmas celebrations at Richmond, where there was the usual feasting and revelry. Perhaps to take her mind off her worries about the child she carried, Elizabeth played games of cards for hours on end, gambling away the princely sum of one hundred shillings. Among the gifts that she and Henry received that New Year was a horoscope by the renowned Italian astrologer, William Parron. The predictions made in his *Book of the Excellent Fortunes of Henry Duke of York and his Parents'* included the assertion that the queen would live to the age of eighty. The inaccuracy of his forecast would be proved all too soon.

At the end of January, the queen made her way from Richmond to the Tower of London so that she could spend Candlemas with her husband before entering her confinement. Reclining heavily on cushions and carpets in her barge, and kept warm by burning braziers filled with sweet herbs, she was conveyed along the freezing Thames with the utmost care. Upon reaching the Tower, she attended a ceremonial mass in the chapel of St John the Evangelist, after which wine and sweetmeats were served. Then, accompanied by an entourage of ladies headed by her mother-in-law Lady Margaret Beaufort, Elizabeth entered the chambers that had been appointed for her in the medieval Queen's Lodgings.

However, either the royal physicians had miscalculated the date of conception or the baby was premature, because just a few days later, on 2 February 1503, the queen was delivered 'suddenly' of a girl. This was in marked contrast to most of her other labours and adds weight to the theory that all was not well. Even though her favourite midwife, Alice Massy, had been present, it seems the labour was badly handled.

The baby was named Katherine, perhaps as a compliment to her parents' grieving daughter-in-law. But neither mother nor daughter thrived. Soon after the birth, a messenger was dispatched to Kent to find a doctor named 'Aylsworth' or 'Hallysworth'. The queen's symptoms are not clear, but it is possible that she had succumbed to a post-partum infection such as puerperal fever, or that she was suffering the consequences of iron-deficiency anaemia. The more babies a woman bore, the greater the risk of sickness or death due to the increased physical toll on her body, coupled with her advancing age. The infant princess also began to wane, and on 10 February she died. Elizabeth followed her to the grave the following day, her thirty-seventh birthday.

Her husband was prostrate with grief. According to one account, he 'privily departed to a solitary place and would no man should resort unto him.'[1] His last act before retreating to the seclusion of his privy chamber at Richmond Palace was to send Sir Richard Guildford and Sir Charles Somerset to the household of his late wife the day after her death. They were to convey his assurances to the staff that he would find them places elsewhere.

Only Lady Margaret Beaufort was permitted to visit the grieving king, but even she was unable to offer any comfort. Devastated by the loss of the wife whom he had grown to love dearly, Henry became gravely ill. For this intensely private king to show both infirmity and emotion was highly unusual, and members of his entourage became alarmed.

Henry did not grieve alone. Elizabeth was idolised by her children, particularly her adored favourite son Henry. The family's grief is vividly illustrated in an illuminated manuscript once belonging to Henry VII that was recently discovered in the National Library of Wales. The king is shown in mourning robes with a doleful expression on his face. In the background, behind their father, are the late queen's daughters, Mary and Margaret, both wearing black veils. The eleven-year-old Henry, Elizabeth's 'loving son', is weeping into the sheets of his mother's empty bed.[2] His face, buried in his hands, is obscured, but his trademark red hair can clearly be seen. The manuscript is believed to have been in Prince Henry's own library when he became king.

Henry had probably been told the news of his mother's death not by the king, but by Guildford and Somerset. This was typical of the man who had always been a distant and rather cold father, certainly by contrast to the prince's loving and indulgent mother, and Henry may have resented him for it. The pain of his loss was still raw four years later, when the precocious young prince wrote to Erasmus, lamenting the death of Philip 'the Handsome', King of Castile: 'Never, since the death of my dearest mother, hath there come to me more hateful intelligence,' he confided. He went on to upbraid the scholar for telling him about Philip's death 'because it seemed to tear open again the wound to which time had brought insensibility.'[3]

Meanwhile, the young Henry's grieving father emerged from his seclusion only long enough to arrange his wife's funeral. Their daughter Katherine had been quietly interred next to her two infant siblings, Elizabeth and Edmund, in the vault at Westminster Abbey. But there would be no stinting on the pomp and pageantry surrounding Elizabeth's burial. Thomas More penned a 'Rueful Lamentation', which was painted on a board and hung next to her tomb. Written as a farewell address from Elizabeth to her grieving family, it reserved the most tender words for 'mine own dear spouse, my worthy lord', urging him:

Erst were you father, and now must you supply
The mother's part also, for lo now here I lie.

More – who by this time was rapidly rising in influence with Prince Henry – wrote this with him in mind. He would have known how greatly the prince had revered his mother, and the fact that he felt compelled to urge the king to fill her place suggests that he was well aware of how lacking he had been as a father.

But the king seemed not to heed this advice. For six long weeks he remained shut away from the rest of the court, with only his privy chamber servants for company. There is no record of how he passed the long hours of seclusion, but any of the usual diversions that he might have sought, such as card games or reading, were soon overtaken by sickness. Weakened by the turmoil of his wife's death, Henry fell prey to the tubercular condition that had afflicted him during previous winters. He also developed a quinsy and an acute, pustular tonsillitis. His lungs infected and his breathing laboured, he was unable to swallow or even open his mouth. As he lay like this for several days, his closest attendants began to fear for his life. Coming so soon after the death of the queen and their eldest son Arthur, if news of the king's sickness had leaked out to the wider court and country, it could have spelt disaster for the fledgling Tudor dynasty, which was still beset by rival claimants and rebellion.

The ever-dependable and discreet groom of the stool, Hugh Denys, duly tightened the security around his royal master. Only Henry's most intimate body servants, Piers Barbour, James Braybroke, Francis Marzen (an old Breton attendant), William Smith (page of the wardrobe) and Richard Weston, were permitted access. Also present, of course, was the king's mother, who had taken up residence at Richmond. For once, her domineering presence must have been welcome to the anxious servants who knew the king's secret. She busied herself with ordering medicines and supplies for her son, as well as liberal quantities of sweet wine for herself.

The only other visitor to the ailing king's bedchamber was his wife's half-brother, Arthur Plantagenet. As well as providing a much-needed genial presence in the oppressive atmosphere of the privy chamber, he may also have relayed confidential messages to his young royal master at Eltham, who was no doubt anxious for news of his father.

The days turned into weeks and still the king fared no better, but continued to slip in and out of delirium. Only towards the end of March 1503, as the daylight hours grew longer and the biting winter chill gave way to the milder air of spring, did he finally begin to show signs of recovery. But in a secret conversation that was betrayed to the authorities, Sir Hugh Conway, treasurer of Calais, described his king as 'a weak man and a sickly, not likely to be a long-lived man.'[4]

When, at last, Henry re-emerged into the world of the court, he looked noticeably older. His hair had turned white and his face was marked with the lines of grief. He continued to wear mourning robes, and a seventeenth-century ballad about Elizabeth's death described the king as 'possess'd with grief', claiming that he spent 'many Months in Moan'.[5]

There was another difference in the king who reappeared before his subjects that spring. Always somewhat cold and distant, he was now utterly implacable. Without the benevolent influence of his wife, and with just one heir left to safeguard the future of his fragile dynasty, he was consumed by paranoia and suspicion. As a result, as one recent historian has shrewdly observed: 'Few around him, including his closest counsellors, would see or hear anything of the private man ever again.'[6]

For all Henry's private grief at the loss of his beloved spouse, just two months after her death, he was already considering a new bride. 'All these sovereigns after being once married are unable to remain single,' Philip the Fair, Catherine of Aragon's brother-in-law, remarked on the matter.[7] This was neither unusual nor frowned upon: every king needed a consort, and every court a queen. Moreover, the brevity of life in Tudor times meant that one's first marriage was rarely for the lifetime of both partners.

But if the notion of Henry's remarriage was widely accepted – indeed, expected – his choice of bride was not. At forty-six, the king was moving into what the Tudors considered old age. Prematurely aged by grief and stress, he had also lost most of his teeth and those that remained were 'black-stained'.[8] By contrast, his prospective bride was just seventeen and in the full bloom of youth. Many men before him had taken wives who were considerably younger than themselves. But what made Henry's choice so shocking (not least to the lady concerned) was that it was his own daughter-in-law.

Upon hearing the news in April 1503, Catherine's mother was horrified. She wrote at once to Henry, upbraiding him for contemplating 'a very evil thing; one never before seen . . . which offends the ears'. She demanded that he send her daughter home so that she might escape his lecherous clutches. But the wily English king was attracted by more than just Catherine's youthful beauty. The untimely death of his son Arthur had sparked diplomatic wranglings between the two countries about the long-overdue payment of Catherine's dowry.[9] All the while, the notoriously frugal Henry had been obliged to keep the widowed princess and her household in the considerable style that her status demanded.

Catherine evidently confided to her family in Spain the distaste that she felt at the prospect of marrying her ageing father-in-law. Her mother, Isabella, decided to take action by diverting Henry's attention to another potential bride. Joanna, Queen of Naples, was twenty-six and by all accounts something of a beauty. She had been widowed at seventeen, just a few months after marrying her nephew Ferdinand, and had not remarried. Henry took the bait, and two years later the Venetian ambassador, Vicenzo Quirini, reported that he had received 'true and certain intelligence that the King of England had concluded a marriage with the young Queen of Naples, the niece of the King of Spain; and that he had already sent a deputation to her at Valentia; the only doubtful point being whether she would accept him.'[10]

The extraordinarily detailed instructions that Henry gave to his ambassadors were published 250 years later. They suggest that this was rather more than a diplomatic arrangement for the ageing king. He told his ambassadors to find out about every aspect of Joanna's appearance: the colour of her hair, the condition of her teeth, the size and shape of her nose, the smoothness of her complexion, even whether she had hair on her upper lip. They should also pay particular attention to 'her breasts . . . whether they be big or small'. The ambassadors duly informed their king that Joanna's breasts 'be somewhat great & fully, and in as much as that they were trussed somewhat high after the manner of [the] country, which causes her Grace for to seem much the fuller and her neck to be the shorter.'[11]

Henry was greatly pleased by the answers he received, but he was never to have this buxom bride. The marriage negotiations failed for political and financial reasons. But by then, he was already attracting interest from other quarters. Margaret of Savoy, daughter of the powerful Holy Roman Emperor Maximilian I, was put forward as a rival candidate. Of a similar age to Joanna, she had been twice widowed already and had sworn never to marry again. The Venetian ambassador reported in December 1505 that she was 'rather averse' to the idea of marrying the English king.[12]

Undeterred, Henry commissioned a portrait to be sent to his prospective bride. It would become the most famous likeness of the ageing king, who was forty-eight when it was painted. If it flatters Henry's regality, bedecked as he is in rich silks and furs, and adopting a coolly appraising stare, it is far from a flattering portrayal aimed at seducing a potential wife. The king's hair is flecked with grey and his sharp cheekbones hint at the anxiety and poor health from which he has suffered for many years. There is only the ghost of a smile on his thin lips, which are pressed tightly together. The few teeth that he had left are therefore concealed, which is a mercy.[13]

Despite considering various candidates to replace his late wife, Henry never remarried. Increasingly plagued by ill health, he evidently resigned himself to life as a widower. It was left to his youngest son Henry to woo his brother's widow – with dramatic consequences. According to Nicholas Fox, an expert in matrimonial law who was present when the king summoned his son from Eltham to discuss the matter, his royal master began rather bluntly: 'Son Henry, I have agreed with the King of Aragon that you should marry Catherine, your brother's widow, in order that the peace between us might be continued.' He then demanded to know whether the prince acquiesced. Aware of the answer expected of him, the prince assented, dutiful and compliant – for now at least. The betrothal was duly agreed, but many months of diplomatic wrangling lay ahead.

As her future continued to hang in the balance, Catherine began to suffer ever more frequent bouts of ill health. A devout Roman Catholic, Catherine followed the strict observances of her faith, including regular fast days. It may have been stress, malnourishment or a combination of the two that contributed to what in August 1504 was described as an 'ague and derangement of the stomach'.[14] A doctor was dispatched to attend the princess at Greenwich and twice tried to bleed her. This suggests that one of her symptoms was that she had stopped menstruating. It was believed that if a woman missed a period then her womb would 'choke' from an excess of blood, which therefore needed to be let out from some other part of the body. In fact, this would have exacerbated the problem. The attempts failed, however, and the doctor noted in some alarm that 'no blood' would come.[15] He concluded that Catherine's ill health was caused by her lack of sexual activity. The cure for all manner of ailments suffered by maidens, with their 'cold, damp' wombs, was the 'hot, dry' seed of a man. For Catherine, it seemed, her only hope of recovery was to marry as soon as possible.

On 23 February 1504 Henry was formally created Prince of Wales – almost two years after the death of his brother Arthur. The following June, four days before the prince's thirteenth birthday, he left Eltham to join the royal household. The timing was significant: thirteen was the age at which boys were thought to become adults. When he arrived at Richmond on a warm midsummer night, the prospect of living with a father whom he hardly knew must have been a daunting one.

Upon his arrival at court, the prince's staff and council were absorbed into the king's own. He was delighted that his uncle, Arthur Plantagenet, was allowed to remain with him, along with the more recent appointee, Sir Henry Marney, and various other servants. The king was also keen, though, for his own trusted attendants to serve (or more precisely, to keep an eye on) his son and heir. They included Sir Richard Empson, a rising star at court, who now joined the prince's council.

Henry himself was very watchful of his son, and a good deal more attentive to his upbringing than was usual for a royal father. 'Nothing escapes his attention,' remarked one observer.[16] Although it was understandable that this paranoid and insecure king should wish to keep his only surviving son close, this was the opposite of what was recommended for a royal heir. Rather than encouraging his son's independence, the king kept him cosseted and restricted, closely scrutinising every aspect of his upbringing. The prince's apartments could only be reached by way of the king's, and whenever he wished to leave the palace to hunt or joust, he was escorted out of a side door into a private park and accompanied at all times by the tightly knit body of attendants appointed by his father.

'It is quite wonderful how much the king likes the prince of Wales,' observed the Spanish ambassador. 'Certainly, there could be no better school in the world than the society of such a father as Henry VII.'[17] The prince did not share the ambassador's enthusiasm. Although outwardly content to defer to his father in all things, he privately resented his suffocating influence and would not defer to it for long. Prince Henry was growing into a handsome and athletic young man, admired throughout the world. His flame-red hair, soft complexion and sensual Cupid's bow mouth provided the perfect foil to his powerful physique, honed to perfection in the jousting arena and tournament ground. Towering over his increasingly stooped, emaciated father, the prince was described as 'gigantic' by the Spanish ambassador, who avowed that there was 'no finer youth in the world.'[18] His physical power was already formidable. One of his opponents, Richard Earl of Kent, was left with a broken arm after 'fighting with the prince' during a training session.[19]

Prince Henry had gathered about him a body of like-minded young men, all of whom shared his passion for the tiltyard. They included William Hussey, Giles Capel, Thomas Kyvet and Charles Brandon. Brandon, who had rapidly become a great favourite with the king's son, was seven years older but closely resembled him – so much so that some people referred to him as Henry's 'bastard brother'.[20] He came from a family of proven loyalty to the crown, and Charles had grown up in the royal household. He was already a consummate courtier by the age of seventeen, when he jousted at the wedding of Arthur and Catherine.

But Brandon's private life was somewhat less impeccable than his courtier-like credentials. In around 1503, he had fallen in love with Anne Browne, one of the queen's gentlewomen. Before long, Anne was pregnant. When the scandal broke, Brandon's patron, the Earl of Essex, insisted he marry the girl. But having agreed, Brandon subsequently broke off the engagement and married Anne's aunt, Margaret Mortimer, who was some twenty years his senior. Anne was so shocked that she miscarried their child. But Brandon's real motives were soon made clear when he sold off his new wife's property and used the proceeds to fund his extravagant lifestyle at court. Shortly afterwards, he had his marriage annulled on the grounds of consanguinity (being too closely related) and rode to Essex, where Anne was living in miserable seclusion. He carried her off to a church in Stepney and married her, with a few close companions as witnesses.

Encouraged by Brandon and his other wayward companions, Prince Henry, now in his early teens, threw himself into a life of sports, music, drinking and women. Together with his entourage and a select group of ladies, the prince would stay up dancing late into the night. Just as he had cast off his gown to dance at his brother's wedding, so he now caused a stir by dancing 'in his shirt and without shoes'.[21]

Alarmed, the king and his advisers resolved that the heir's penchant for vigorous sports and immoral pastimes should be 'repressed'. Their reasoning may have been sound, but if they expected young Henry immediately to comply with their wishes, they had seriously misjudged his character. During the closing years of Henry VII's reign, his son became ever more resolved to assert his independence. The physical embodiment of his maternal grandfather, Edward IV, he presented an increasingly appealing alternative to the dour, grasping old king whose despised counsellors, Richard Empson and Edmund Dudley, were making his regime more unpopular by the day.

Meanwhile, with the negotiations over his son's marriage to Catherine of Aragon still dragging on, the king ordered that she was to be refused access to the prince, even though they lived in the same palace for much of the time. If this was intended as a means of making the Spanish princess even more desperate to marry the prince, it succeeded. In a letter to her father, she confessed that she would 'rather die in England' than give up the idea of marrying her late husband's brother.[22]

For his part, although he had been allowed to spend little time with Catherine, Prince Henry seemed greatly enamoured of her – or at least, of the chivalrous idea of 'rescuing' this abandoned Spanish princess. He may also have developed a youthful crush on her when, aged ten, he had escorted her to marry his elder brother

Arthur. He once confessed to his father that he thought her 'a beautiful creature'. On one of the rare occasions when the couple were allowed to meet, New Year's Day 1508, the prince presented Catherine with a gift that was both romantic and patriotic: a 'fair rose of rubies set in a rose of white and green'.[23]

In the delicate and complex game of international diplomacy, the king was running out of time. His health had been failing for several months. A chronic cough that had plagued him each spring was becoming more persistent and he was steadily losing weight. Henry's household accounts reveal that when he was on progress around his hunting lodges, his entourage was obliged to tarry in each place for weeks at a time. Although the reason was not stated, it was likely that he was too weak to continue without a prolonged rest.

In February 1507, Henry suffered the first serious recurrence of the quinsy that had struck him down after Elizabeth's death. By the following month his symptoms had become so severe that his life was feared for. It is likely that Henry was suffering from tuberculosis, complicated by asthma. Closeted away at Richmond under the charge of his resourceful mother, who had stayed ever closer to his side in recent years, Henry languished, unable to swallow food or water, and struggling to breathe. By the middle of March, the king seemed close to death. Directing the few staff who were permitted to attend her son in his privy chamber, Lady Margaret was so certain of his impending demise that she paid the Garter herald, Thomas Wriothesley, twenty shillings for 'making of a book of mourning clothes', and £57 6s 8d for a substantial quantity of 'black material'. The king's chaplains were ordered to sing masses for his soul, and Lady Margaret's confessor, John Fisher, was told to be on standby. But against all the odds, by the end of the month Henry had rallied. On 31 March, the Spanish ambassador de Puebla was admitted to the privy chamber and found the king convalescing. The crisis had passed – for now.

That summer, Henry went on progress to East Anglia and Oxfordshire. He seemed in better health than he had been for years, and one observer remarked that he had 'grown fat'. Far from requiring frequent and prolonged rests, the king was now full of energy, 'going from one hunting place to another'.[24] For all his apparent good humour, however, the king was still beset by private fears. Access to him was increasingly restricted, and in the closeted world of his privy chamber, rumour and suspicion were ever rife.

One of his close attendants was the poet Stephen Hawes, who entered royal service in around 1503. In his poem, 'The Comfort of Lovers', he wrote of the highly charged atmosphere in the royal household, in which courtiers 'full privily' were forever trying to outmanoeuvre each other 'by craft and subtleness'. His position as a chamber servant made him privy to a number of illicit conversations, one of which shocked him because the speakers evidently 'did little love' their king. Hawes was obliged to report such treasonous talk. But rather than quietly relaying the conversation to his royal master or advisers, he publicly denounced the perpetrators in verses that he circulated around the court. As a result, he was accused of being a troublemaker and was set upon by a gang of unnamed courtiers, who gave him such a severe beating that he was 'in fear of death'. He was subsequently thrown out of the royal household.

In February 1508, Henry fell prey to a fresh bout of tuberculosis. At the end of that month, he made his way to Richmond Palace once more and sought privacy from the court, shut away in his chambers. Despite the secrecy to which his body servants were bound, reports leaked out that the king's breathing was laboured and that, unable to stomach any food, he had grown weak and emaciated. The fact that he was obliged to send a deputy to attend the habitual pilgrimage to Westminster to commemorate his wife's death reveals just how sick he was.

Yet again, the king's mother moved into Richmond so that she could attend her son. She brought her household with her, and took up residence in the lodgings that had been specially built for the purpose. Anxious about her son's condition, and frustrated that she was unable to do anything to alleviate it, she focused instead upon ordering new beds for him and sent a servant to London to buy a barrel of sweet muscadel wine.

In March, Henry rallied enough to receive an ambassador from Ferdinand of Aragon. Don Gutierre Gómez de Fuensalida was accompanied by a representative of the Aragonese branch of the Grimaldi bank, who carried bills of exchange as part of Catherine's dowry. The Spanish king had rightly judged that the only way finally to secure Henry's assent to the marriage between his son and Catherine was – literally – to show him the money. Struggling into a waiting barge, Henry was rowed to Greenwich, sheltered from the chill March air by thick carpets and cushions. He made a brief appearance before the assembled throng, then retreated to hold private discussions with the ambassador.

The king re-emerged two days later to watch the jousts that were held in honour of an embassy from Emperor Maximilian. His son was also present, looking on enviously as his companions entered the lists. Although Henry was keen to present his robust young heir as the public face of the Tudor monarchy, he kept him on an even tighter leash than before, closeting him away 'like a girl', according to Fuensalida. The ambassador noticed that the younger Henry was 'so subjected . . . that he doesn't say a word except in response to what the king asks him.'[25] But on this occasion, the king's illness obliged him to leave the prince in charge of the entertainments while he retired to his private apartments, greatly fatigued by maintaining the pretence that all was well. Prince Henry took full advantage of the opportunity. All those present admired the natural, easy grace and regal bearing that his father so painfully lacked. One onlooker observed that he sat 'in place of the king'.[26]

By April, the king's physicians reported that he had begun to show signs of recovery. But he remained shut away. Still weak, emaciated and exhausted from the long weeks of illness, he was described by his contemporary biographer, Bernard André, as 'depressed'. His mother's chaplain, Bishop Fisher, concurred that the king had suffered 'much displeasure and sorrow' from this 'wretched world'.[27] Increasingly, he took refuge in the minutiae of finance, personally checking and scrawling his initials next to each entry in his account books. These books include payment to minstrels who were sent to try and lift the king's spirits, as well as new chess sets and dice, and delicacies made by his French pastry chef to tempt his fading appetite.

In summer 1508, as the king and his court went on progress, the sweating sickness engulfed London. The symptoms of this most virulent disease, which had been introduced into England by Henry VII's army of prisoners and mercenaries in 1485, were terrifyingly swift and dramatic, with death often occurring within hours. Far from escaping the disease, Henry and his entourage were pursued by it everywhere they went. It even reached the household of the prince, killing three of his chamber servants. Great consternation ensued. With the king still in poor health and his only son perilously close to being infected by the disease known to be 'the easiest in the world to die of', the Tudor dynasty suddenly seemed desperately fragile.[28]

Henry and his entourage took what precautions they could. The eating of hot spices, leeks, garlic and wine was banned during each outbreak because they were believed to raise the body's temperature and thus the risk of infection. But it was in vain. Inevitably, given how closely bound were the two households of the prince and king, the sickness soon spread to the latter – penetrating to its very core. Hugh Denys, the king's closest body servant, was struck down, along with his chamberlain and Bishop of Winchester, Richard Fox, and another prominent attendant, Charles Somerset, Lord Herbert. But just as it looked set to wipe out the entire royal household, the disease suddenly abated. All three of the king's privy chamber servants recovered, and it soon became clear that both Henry and his son had escaped infection altogether.

If the king had avoided that most feared of diseases, however, it was obvious to those closest to him that he would not live much longer. In January 1509, he and his mother moved from Richmond to nearby Hanworth. Lady Margaret summoned a team of apothecaries and, tellingly, her three surviving grandchildren. Sensing that, this time, the tuberculosis and quinsy that had 'sore vexed' him in recent years would finally triumph, the king went to the Benedictine abbey of Chertsey in Surrey to offer up prayers for his soul.[29] He broke his return journey with a private visit to Richard Fox at Esher. The bishop was a trusted adviser of more than twenty-five years' service, and it is likely that the purpose of their meeting was to prepare the ground for a peaceful succession.

At the end of February, Henry returned to his favourite retreat of Richmond. In what had become a well-practised routine, his servants ensured that he was safely closeted away in his private apartments. The Aragonese ambassador, still hankering after an agreement for the prince's marriage to Catherine, noted with frustration that the king would 'not allow himself to be seen'.[30] Henry did, however, welcome the reassuringly familiar presence of his mother, who arrived at Richmond with her entourage in late March. She was clearly prepared for a long visit, having brought her favourite bed and quantities of 'kitchen stuff'. But by now, her son was unable to eat and each breath he took was an effort.

On the evening of the 20th, Bishop Fisher noticed a change in the king's breathing. Although it had been laboured for weeks, it now seemed to come out in short, rasping breaths as Henry fought 'the sharp assaults of death'. He clung on until the following evening when, at 11 o'clock, the final breath left his body. His confessor administered the last rites and placed a taper in Henry's lifeless hand, lighting his departed soul's path to heaven. One of his servants then stepped forward and closed the king's eyelids, masking the fixed stare of his penetrating blue eyes.

According to a German tourist who visited Richmond Palace in 1599, Henry had left instructions that upon his decease, his intestines were to be removed and 'slung full of blood against the walls of a chamber in the palace, as a symbol that he conquered the kingdom by force, slaying Richard III who had usurped the realm, in battle.' He claimed that 'many traces of blood were pointed out to us in one room'.[31] This gruesome report is unsubstantiated but chimes with Henry's relentless determination, born of insecurity, to assert his right to the throne.

England's first Tudor king had died in the private state from which he had always derived most comfort. The only people who knew of his death were his privy chamber servants, Bishop Fox and the handful of councillors who had been at his bedside. Anxious to set his affairs in order and ensure the security of the realm amid the uncertainty that always accompanied the death of a sovereign – even one with a living, and popular, successor – they ordered that the news be 'secretly kept'.[32] It was only announced two days later, when the court was filled with dignitaries for the Feast of the Order of the Garter.

Lady Margaret set aside her grief at the loss of her cherished only child and threw her energies into ensuring the smooth succession of her grandson. She also oversaw the plans for the late king's funeral, which took place on 11 May at Westminster Abbey. As her son had wished, his body was laid alongside 'our dearest late wife the queen'. Still also allowing herself no time for mourning, Lady Margaret turned her attention to her grandson's magnificent coronation, which was celebrated on 24 June. Having thus witnessed the triumphant accession of England's new Tudor king, this formidable old woman at last succumbed to her own physical frailty and died five days later.

4

'Their business is in many secrets'

THE ACCESSION OF Henry VIII in April 1509 seemed to herald a gloriously bright new future for the kingdom. Gone was his dour old miser of a father, whose final years had been beset by suspicion and paranoia. In his place was a young man of seventeen, bursting with energy and promise. Praise rang in Henry's ears as courtiers and diplomats clamoured to flatter the new king and draw favourable comparisons with his predecessor. 'The heavens laugh, the earth exults . . . Avarice is expelled from the country, extortion is put down, liberality scatters riches with a bountiful hand. Yet our King does not desire gold, gems or precious metals, but virtue, glory, immortality,' enthused Lord Mountjoy. 'If you could see how here all the world is rejoicing in the possession of so great a prince, how his life is all their desire, you could not contain your tears for sheer joy.'[1]

Henry VIII stood – literally – head and shoulders above most of his court. At six feet two inches tall, with a forty-two-inch chest and a thirty-one-inch waist, he was an imposing, athletic figure.[2] He had inherited the good looks of his Yorkist forebears and closely resembled his maternal grandfather, Edward IV. He was clean-shaven and wore his hair short and neatly trimmed. A Venetian diplomat who visited the English court in 1515 wrote a glowing report of the young king, whom he described as: 'the handsomest potentate I ever set eyes on; above the usual height, with an extremely fine calf to his leg, his complexion very fair and bright, with auburn hair combed straight and short, in the French fashion, and a round face so very beautiful, that it would become a pretty woman.' Thomas More, who would soon rise to prominence in Henry's court, was no less complimentary: 'Among a thousand noble companions, the King stands out the tallest, and his strength fits his majestic body. There is fiery power in his eyes, beauty in his face, and the colour of twin roses in his cheeks.'[3]

As well as being an accomplished sportsman who delighted in showing off his prowess in the jousting arena, Henry – a true Renaissance prince – also excelled at music, verse and languages. He pursued his private pleasures with the same remorseless energy and dedication that his father had applied to political matters. Henry had also inherited the famed charm and charisma of his mother's family. Affable, quick-witted and hugely generous, he was 'the man most full of heart' according to Erasmus. Thomas More concurred: 'The King has a way of making every man feel that he is enjoying his special favour.' The Venetian ambassador concluded that he was 'prudent, sage and free from every vice'.[4]

But the new king had an altogether darker side. Indulged in childhood, he had grown into a highly strung, impulsive and vain young man with a terrifying and unpredictable temper. Those who served him would soon learn how swiftly his favour could be lost. His father's deeply unpopular henchmen, Empson and Dudley, were thrown into the Tower on trumped-up charges of treason just days after Henry's accession and were executed the following year.

Forasmuch as he wanted to sweep away the remnants of his father's regime, Henry had not forgotten to whom he owed his kingship. Among his personal possessions were the Garter robes belonging to his late brother Arthur. Although Henry was not usually sentimental and gladly gave away clothes and possessions belonging to former favourites, he kept these robes safely locked away in his private wardrobe for the rest of his life – an acknowledgement, perhaps, that but for his sibling's death he would not have become king.

One of Henry's first acts as king was to put an end to the diplomatic wrangling surrounding his betrothal to Catherine of Aragon so that he could take her as his wife. They were married on 11 June, shortly before the groom's eighteenth birthday. Instantly, Catherine was transformed from an object of pity into one of envy. The years of eking out an existence on the meagre allowance allowed by her miserly father-in-law must have seemed a distant memory with her handsome and charismatic husband by her side, and her household filled with every conceivable luxury.

For all Henry's love of splendour and showmanship, his wedding was a quiet affair, held in one of the queen's private closets at Greenwich Palace. It was shrouded in such secrecy, indeed, that no details of it have been passed down to posterity. The only record is the form of words spoken by the bride and groom, which had been prepared in advance by William Warham, Archbishop of Canterbury.

Their wedding night would have been spent in the five-storey building that housed the royal apartments, overlooking the surrounding gardens, orchards and river. It was a very personal choice for Henry, Greenwich being his adored late mother's favourite palace. Elizabeth had commissioned improvements to the apartments shortly before her death, including new gardens, kitchen, tower and decorations.

Catherine was provided with a sizeable new household that included thirty-three women of good birth – countesses, baronesses, knights' wives and gentlewomen. Among their number was Elizabeth Boleyn, whose younger daughter would be Catherine's nemesis. These ladies prepared Catherine for her wedding night, although there is no record of the bedding ceremony or of the new queen's bloodstained sheets being paraded the following morning – a custom that had started to die out.

There seems to have been a strong attraction between the newly-weds. At twenty-three, Catherine was still in the bloom of youth and Henry, a true chivalric prince, loved the romantic notion that he had rescued the impoverished but beautiful Spanish princess. For her part, Catherine can hardly have failed to be impressed by the handsome and vigorous young husband who had delivered her from years of waiting and wondering.

This time, there was no doubt that the marriage had been consummated. It is likely that by the time of Catherine's coronation less than two weeks later, she was already pregnant. Her happy state was announced in November 1509. Henry wrote a triumphant letter to his father-in-law, Ferdinand of Aragon, telling him that his daughter 'has conceived in her womb a living child, and is right heavy therewith.'[5] The court rejoiced at the fertility of the newly married couple, confident that the royal nursery would soon be filled with their offspring. After all, they were both young, lusty and from very fertile stock.

Everything progressed well with the pregnancy, and preparations were duly made for the birth. A birthing or 'groaning' chair was ordered, together with a copper gilt bowl to catch the blood and placenta. Meanwhile, the same silver font in which Henry had been baptised was sent for from Canterbury Cathedral.

But at the end of January, disaster struck. At just seven months pregnant, Catherine went into labour, having experienced 'only a little pain in her knee'.[6] On the 31st, she was delivered of a stillborn daughter. Hope was not lost, however, for Catherine's belly remained swollen, which led her physicians to conclude that she had been expecting twins and there was still a live foetus in her womb. Preparations therefore continued for the queen's lying-in, and in mid-March 1510 she took her leave of her husband and the court and went into confinement at Greenwich.

As the weeks wore on and Catherine's bloated stomach began to deflate, it became obvious that no child would arrive. The king and queen were so embarrassed that they initially kept it a secret. But the inquisitive courtiers and diplomats could not long be held at bay, and the news was eventually announced. Catherine wrote to her father Ferdinand in May, admitting that she had miscarried. She remained in seclusion until the end of that month – some ten weeks since she had first entered her confinement.

The news sparked a rash of speculation across the kingdom and abroad. Luis Caroz, the Spanish ambassador, assigned the blame to Catherine's irregular menstrual cycle. This had been regularly reported by her physicians, who had made little attempt at secrecy: after all, a royal wife's fertility was a matter of justifiable public interest. Caroz therefore advised the new queen to change her diet. Others feared that her initial failure to bear a healthy child was an indication of a more serious problem.

In fact, by the time that she re-emerged into society, Catherine was already pregnant again. This meant that she had conceived during the period of her confinement – which, strictly speaking, meant that she had flouted the conventions laid down by her husband's grandmother, Lady Margaret Beaufort. These dictated that only after a royal wife has been 'churched' following her lying-in should she resume sexual relations with her husband. But Catherine and Henry may have judged that since she had not been pregnant during her confinement, the normal rules had been invalidated. They may in any case have been eager to lessen the embarrassment of the false pregnancy by making sure a real one would soon follow.

Catherine had another incentive to lure her husband back into her bed. To add insult to injury, during her ill-fated confinement, she had learned that Henry had started a dalliance with Anne Hastings, the married younger sister of the Duke of Buckingham. The king's groom of the stool, Sir William Compton, had been acting as an intermediary between his royal master and Lady Hastings. Elizabeth Amadas, wife of the master of the jewels, later alleged that Compton had arranged secret trysts for the king and his mistress in his own home on Thames Street, and that he had tried to persuade her to join his royal master there. However, rumours soon began to circulate that Compton had begun an affair with Lady Stafford himself, and these appeared to be corroborated when her brother found him in her room. Compton stanchly denied any wrongdoing but was forced to take the sacrament to prove it. Meanwhile, Anne's furious husband sent her to a convent sixty miles from court.[7]

Although Henry had been discreet, his wife soon heard of it – possibly as a result of Henry ordering her to dismiss Anne's sister, Elizabeth Fitzwalter, who was one of her favourite waiting women. Smelling a rat, Catherine confronted her errant husband and they had the first argument of their marriage. Henry thought it hardly worth the protest: he had been free to indulge his passion for women throughout his youth and he saw little reason why marriage should prevent his doing so now. Well versed though she was in the etiquette of royal marriage, the queen was smitten with her new husband and therefore wounded by his infidelity. Their frostiness towards each other was evident to the whole court.

The fact that Catherine was already pregnant again soon healed the rift, however. Eager to avoid the embarrassment of another false confinement, she and her husband kept the news a secret until it was beyond doubt. In the meantime, Catherine took great care of her health, resting at her husband's childhood home, Eltham Palace, for most of the summer and declining to accompany him on progress. Heeding the Spanish ambassador's advice, she also made sure to order the best available food. This may have included spinach mixed with butter, which was often recommended as a means of staving off constipation – one of the less pleasant side effects of pregnancy. If this failed, the expectant mother might be prescribed 'suppositors' made of honey and egg yolk, or of 'Venice soap' – a concoction that contained senna leaves.[8]

In December 1510, Catherine entered her second confinement that year, choosing the comforts of Richmond to wait out the days before the birth. She was appointed a suite of rooms on the first floor, overlooking the gardens and river. A single window was left uncovered, which afforded the queen a beautiful view south over a walled garden with the Thames flowing beyond.

Given Catherine's piety, she may have derived comfort from the popular ritual of laying a cross on her belly as her pains began. This time, they would result in a happy conclusion. In the early hours of the morning of New Year's Day 1511, the queen was delivered of a boy. She had succeeded in the only thing that mattered for a royal wife: to give the king a son and heir.

The infant prince was named Henry and the news of his arrival was proclaimed across London, prompting days of public rejoicing. Bonfires were lit, bells were rung and cannon were fired from the Tower of London. The king was overjoyed. Less than two years into his reign, his dynasty already looked secure. No doubt equally elated, particularly after the humiliation of her first attempt, Catherine remained in seclusion for at least three weeks after the birth, as tradition dictated. She did not attend her son's christening, which was conducted with great pomp and ceremony. She did, though, witness the magnificent jousts, pageants and feasts that were held on 12 and 13 February at Westminster to celebrate the birth. It was one of the most lavish and expensive series of entertainments conducted during Henry's reign. Shrouded in rich furs to keep out the cold, Catherine and her ladies watched from a gallery above as her husband assumed the role of Sir Loyal Heart, wearing a costume embroidered with his wife's initials.

Very soon afterwards, Prince Henry was established in a large household of his own, separate from his parents, and served by no fewer than forty-four male attendants, as well as an unknown number of nurses, cradle rockers and other women. Elizabeth Poyntz was appointed as chief nurse to the precious infant. His father, meanwhile, had undertaken a pilgrimage to Walsingham in Norfolk, the most popular of all the shrines scattered across the kingdom, to which pious subjects flocked to give thanks to the Virgin Mary.

But Henry's gratitude was premature. Just two months after his birth, the little prince died. The fireworks and banners that had heralded his arrival were replaced by black cloths and pallbearers as the tiny coffin was carried in solemn procession from Richmond to Westminster. Henry and Catherine were so grief-stricken that mourners were warned not to offer their condolences in case they sparked a fresh outpouring of tears. The chronicler Edward Hall described how the queen fell into 'much lamentation'. Appealing to her natural piety, her husband tried to comfort her with the notion that it was God's will. And the more one railed against that, the more likely it was that God would be angered. No blame was placed on the nursery staff. Elizabeth Poyntz was rewarded for her service with an annuity of £20 (£6,000 in today's money).[9]

Prince Henry's death brought his parents closer together, united in grief, and by September of that year rumours were circulating that the queen was pregnant again. In fact, they were groundless – sparked perhaps by gossip among Catherine's ladies that she was missing her monthly bleeds. If this was the case, then it was more likely due to her naturally irregular cycle, or the upset caused by her son's death. In any case, it would be another two years before hope sprang again.

Catherine fell pregnant in the spring of 1513. In contrast to her previous pregnancies, she was not afforded the luxury of rest. Her husband left to do battle in France soon after hearing the news, and in September that year Catherine was obliged to deal with a Scottish invasion. The Treaty of Perpetual Peace had not lived up to its name and, despite protests from his wife Margaret to adhere to the terms he had concluded with her brother, James had decided in favour of the 'Auld Alliance' between Scotland and France. In an act reminiscent of her warrior queen mother, meanwhile, Catherine rode north in full armour to address her troops, despite being by now heavily pregnant. They went on to secure a major victory at Flodden Field, crushing the Scottish forces. Relishing the triumph, Catherine sent news to her husband in France, enclosing a piece of the bloodied coat of James IV, who died in the battle, so that Henry might use it as a banner at the siege of Tournai.

As soon as the victory celebrations were over, Catherine travelled to Walsingham to pray for a safe delivery. But it may have been this journey, combined with the strain of leading the war effort against Scotland, that prompted another premature labour. On 17 September, she gave birth to a son who died shortly afterwards. Henry arrived home the following month and, yet again, grieved in private with his wife. They were observed to be so 'loving' that their courtiers 'rejoiced' at their obvious marital harmony.

Six months later, the queen was pregnant once more. By August 1514 her belly had grown so much that it was obvious to everyone who saw her. The Venetian ambassador reported that she was 'pregnant [and] clad in ash coloured satin with chains and jewels and on her head a cap of gold.' That this was her fourth pregnancy and she did not yet have a living child was not altogether unusual. In an age when knowledge of obstetrics was rudimentary, and diet and hygiene left much to be desired, rates of mortality among both infants and mothers remained consistently high and around one in five newborns failed to survive. The long and difficult labours suffered by their mothers were a key factor. Although the more experienced midwives were skilled and capable, others employed methods that had fatal consequences, such as attaching a hook to the baby's head in an attempt to yank it out. Post-partum infections were also extremely common in an age of poor hygiene and medical misunderstanding.

Even so, to have lost all three children was unfortunate, to say the least, and may have indicated an underlying problem with either Catherine or her husband. A popular theory is that Henry was suffering from syphilis. This is largely based on Henry's reputation as a womaniser who enjoyed the favours of a string of mistresses (and, later, wives). The fact that he displayed a number of symptoms – such as rashes, sores and mood swings – has been used to support this. But Henry's promiscuity has been overstated. There is only reliable documentary evidence that he had sexual relationships with a handful of women, other than his wives. Neither is there any evidence that his surviving children had congenital syphilis.

It is at least equally possible that the problem lay with Catherine. One theory is that she had a rhesus negative blood type, which causes the body to reject a foetus. But this expulsion usually occurs in the first trimester, and both of Catherine's miscarriages had occurred at around seven months. Another possibility is that in this age of poor hygiene, the food and water that she imbibed at court were infected with listeriosis, a bacteria that can trigger miscarriage, stillbirth and serious illnesses in newborn babies. Equally, her failed pregnancies might have been due to toxaemia (pre-eclampsia), and her strict observance of fasting days may also have been a contributory factor.

Catherine's latest pregnancy was not destined to end in success. In around November 1514, she was delivered of a stillborn son, who had arrived a month early. Now aged thirty and with no surviving child to show from her many pregnancies, the queen must have been close to despair. To make matters worse, she knew that her husband was courting various ladies at court, including her French maid of honour, Jane Popincourt. Jane had formerly served in the court of Louis XII, and had been appointed to Catherine's household on Henry VIII's accession. She had subsequently begun an affair with the Duc de Longueville, who was captured by Henry at the Battle of the Spurs in 1513 and brought back to England. Although there is no direct evidence of an affair with the English king, Henry did later make her a generous payment of £100. By then, Jane was so notorious that when it was proposed she might return to France and serve in the household of Louis' new wife, Henry's sister Mary, the French king indignantly rejected the idea because of her immoral character.

A more significant rival was already rising to prominence, however. In the New Year celebrations held at Greenwich in 1515, shortly after Catherine had lost her premature son, one of the queen's young maids of honour, Elizabeth Blount, was the centre of attention. Golden-haired and blue-eyed Elizabeth ('Bessie') was renowned for her skill in music and dancing, and partnered the king in the revels. Dressed in blue velvet with gold cap and mask, she was an alluring sight. The unsuspecting Catherine enjoyed the performance so much that she invited her husband and maid of honour to repeat it in her private apartments.

Henry can hardly have failed to be attracted to the comely Bessie, and she was no doubt flattered by his attentions. Although he was nine years her senior, at twenty-three years old he was at the height of his physical and sexual prowess. Diplomatic reports suggest that he was an affectionate and skilful lover – albeit a rather conservative one. His royal status made him all the more irresistible to the young women of his wife's household. And in the eyes of his contemporaries, Henry was justified in seeking other outlets for his sexual urges during Catherine's many pregnancies: indeed, he was simply playing the part of a caring and dutiful husband.

But the Tudor attitude to extramarital sex – indeed to sex in general – was rather more complex than that. Society was divided between those who believed that celibacy was the optimum state because it brought one closer to God, and those who believed in the holy state of matrimony. The former tallied with the teachings of ancient Greece and also had some basis in the Bible. St Paul taught that the celibate cared for the things of the Lord while the married cared for the things of the world. This was endorsed (in theory at least) by the 500-year-old legacy of communal celibacy within the hundreds of monasteries that dominated the English countryside.

At the same time, though, the Bible also promoted the values of family life. Christ is recorded as attending weddings, and his teachings on sex and marriage made it clear that he supported the spiritual and bodily union of men and women. From a practical point of view, many believed that sex was necessary for health. Even the Greeks, who propounded the benefits of celibacy, advised that regular (good) sex had a positive effect upon the appetite and digestion, made the body light and nimble, opened the pores and purged the phlegm. It also promoted good mental health, driving away melancholy and madness. 'Bad' sex, on the other hand, weakened both body and mind, and dragged a man down to the level of a common beast. Most authorities agreed that too much sex of any variety was detrimental to health. A commonly accepted theory was that every act of sex shortened a man's life by a day. It was therefore advisable to limit intercourse to once a week, with a temporary abstinence during the woman's menstruation.

Although Henry's affairs were justified on the basis of his needing a sexual outlet during his wife's pregnancies, they would have been frowned upon by the Catholic Church. In this pre-Reformation age, Henry considered himself to be a devout and traditional Catholic. Yet he was contravening the clearly articulated teaching that adultery was against the laws of God. Many believed that even within marriage, sexual intercourse should only be for the procreation of children. Pleasure was a secondary objective.

The 'wasteful spilling of seed', such as through masturbation or oral sex, had long been considered wicked and sinful by theologians. In the twelfth century, St Hildegard of Bingen opined that 'men who touch their own genital organ and emit their semen seriously imperil their souls.' This theme was taken up the following century by the lawyer and theologian William Pagula, who warned parish priests that 'if someone has knowingly and wilfully emitted the seed of coitus in any other way than naturally with his wife, he sins gravely.' Another authority cautioned that shedding sperm would harm a man 'more then if he should bleed forty times so much'.[10] In 1533 a new act was passed that made all 'unnatural' acts 'against the Will of man and God', including anal sex and bestiality, punishable by death. Children born outside of wedlock faced the social stigma of bastardy, and their parents could be subject to severe corporal punishment and fines.

This was all very well, but in an age when the vast majority of royal and noble marriages were made for dynastic, political and financial advancement, it was inevitable that men would often seek sexual gratification elsewhere. It was common practice for husbands to visit prostitutes or have affairs with lower-class women. The same blind eye was not turned to wives who might indulge in extramarital sex, however. Women were expected to do their duty and tolerate unsatisfactory marriages – and produce the necessary heirs into the bargain. Yet it was also widely believed that women were naturally more sexually voracious and uncontrolled than men. Comprised of cold, wet, phlegmatic humours, they had an uncontrollable urge for the hot essence of a man. And while men had the strength of mind to control their appetites, women were too weak to do so. This was also part of their essential wickedness, which dated back to the original sin of Eve. It was believed that a woman who indulged in excessive intercourse would render herself infertile because her womb would become too moist and slippery to hold on to a man's seed.

Medical theories about the sexual organs were confused and contradictory, to say the least. While some physicians maintained that a child was formed entirely from the male seed, with the woman's womb simply providing a place for it to grow, others argued that there was both a female and a male seed, and that the two needed to combine for conception to take place. Those who espoused the latter view believed that the female genitals were the same shape as the male, with two testicles nestling at the top of the vagina near the mouth of the womb. Writing in the 1570s, Thomas Vicary described a woman's reproductive organs as 'no other than those of a man reversed, or turned inward.'[11] It was believed, though, that a woman's seed was thinner, colder and weaker than that of a man.

In the confused and contradictory world of extramarital sex, it is perhaps not surprising that Henry VIII always employed the utmost discretion in his affairs. This makes it difficult (often impossible) to discern when they began and ended, and even who they were with. There is no reliable evidence that Henry did anything more than dance with Bessie Blount at Greenwich in January 1515. Even if their liaison had begun, Henry continued to visit his wife's bed, ever more painfully aware of the need for an heir. By May, Catherine was pregnant once more. It became public knowledge in October or November, and the court again held its breath as its queen entered her confinement at the Palace of Placentia, Greenwich, in January 1516. When, shortly afterwards, news arrived that Catherine's father Ferdinand had died, it was kept from the expectant mother for fear that it would cause another premature or stillbirth.

When the queen's labour began on 17 February, all of the usual rituals and precautions were observed. But this time, there was one important difference: Catherine called in the services of a male doctor. The records contain a payment to a Doctor Vittoria for services performed in the delivery of the child. It is not clear whether Catherine had flouted the strict conventions for the lying-in of a queen by having a man present in the birthing chamber, or whether Vittoria advised from a distance. That his assistance was sought at all was perhaps due to the fact that it was a particularly difficult birth and, having already endured four, Catherine was taking no chances.

At 4 a.m. on 18 February, the queen was delivered of a daughter, Mary. The child might not have been the son that Henry so craved, but she was at least healthy – and given Catherine's experience of childbirth, that was something to be thankful for. A lavish christening was held three days later at the Church of the Observant Friars, attended by the highest-ranking members of the court – including Thomas Wolsey, the king's chief adviser.

The queen, meanwhile, was given the traditional remedies to aid recovery from labour. These included powders of aloe and frankincense, which were applied to the abdomen. A difficult labour, such as Catherine had endured, could result in vaginal tearing. This was not treated but was left to heal naturally. In the absence of proper hygiene, however, the tear often became infected, with fatal results. Meanwhile, to help comfort and warm the parts that had been stretched, a woman might be wrapped in the fleece of a newly shorn sheep.

As Catherine recovered from the birth, her daughter was assigned to the care of a wet-nurse, Katherine Pole, the wife of one of the king's gentlemen ushers. Katherine nursed Mary for the first two years of her life. The princess also had a team of four rockers to keep her pacified in her cradle and, even more necessary, a laundress. Within days of Mary's birth, a treasurer was appointed to manage the finances of her household, and she was also given a chaplain and a gentlewoman. It was a court in miniature for the tiny princess, and its personnel would become her family – far closer to her than her parents. Unusually for a royal infant, however, there is no evidence that Mary was raised with the children of high-ranking noblemen to keep her company in her nursery and, later, her studies.

Mary's first Lady Mistress was Elizabeth Denton, an experienced matron who had superintended her father's nursery. But by the time of Mary's birth, Elizabeth was an old lady and in 1518 she was replaced by the bustling and capable Lady Margaret Bryan. The woman who would have the greatest influence upon the infant princess, however, was her Lady Governess, Margaret Pole, Countess of Salisbury. Her appointment was at the express wish of the queen, who was close friends with Margaret. The daughter of the disgraced Duke of Clarence, brother of Edward IV, Margaret had royal blood coursing through her veins and was regarded as one of the foremost women of the realm.

As a newborn baby, Mary would have been wrapped in the trad-itional swaddling bands. But as she started to become mobile at the age of about one, she was 'coated' – that is, put into ankle-length clothes. For little girls, these were usually a miniature version of adult female clothing, although they did not wear stays until the age of two or three (and even then they were less constrictive), and their bodices fastened at the back rather than with a stomacher at the front.[12]

Delighted with his new daughter though he was, the king still needed a male heir. He therefore continued to visit Catherine's bed regularly – conscious, no doubt, that her fertility was rapidly declining. Two years passed with no sign of another child, but in the spring of 1518 the queen had reason to hope that she was pregnant once more. Henry confided the news to Wolsey in April. Shortly afterwards, he hastened from London with his wife to escape the dreaded sweating sickness. Together with a skeletal court, they spent the summer travelling between country houses, hosted by various noble subjects. During that time, Catherine's pregnancy progressed from an uncertain 'likelihood' to a 'great hope', and preparations began for her lying-in at Greenwich.

The eyes of the world were once again upon England. Sebastian Guistinian, the Venetian ambassador in London, wrote to the Pope in late October that the queen's delivery was imminent and that he hoped the child would be a boy so 'that the King may be at liberty to embark in any great undertaking.' This was also Henry's dearest wish, but it seemed destined not to be fulfilled. The following month, Catherine was delivered of a girl, again born a month early. Guistinian reported the 'vexation' of Henry's subjects, who had 'looked for a prince'.[13] Seven days later, the little girl was dead. It was the fifth of Catherine's six pregnancies to end in either a stillbirth or a short-lived child.

Now on the cusp of her thirty-third birthday, Catherine's hopes for another child were rapidly diminishing. The age gap between her and Henry seemed increasingly wide. Her fertile years were almost over, whereas her husband was still in his vigorous prime. As if to prove the fact, during his wife's latest pregnancy, Henry had begun (or resumed) an affair with Bessie Blount. By the time that his short-lived daughter was born, his mistress was already carrying his child. If the queen could not give him a son, then perhaps another woman could.

During the early months of 1519, Henry VIII entrusted his chief minister, Thomas Wolsey, with a somewhat delicate matter. Bessie Blount, who was now very visibly pregnant, had been sent away from court in the interests of discretion and Wolsey was tasked with arranging her confinement. This was not to be the elaborate lying-in accorded to a queen, of course, but Henry was solicitous enough for the health of his bastard child to ensure that Bessie enjoyed as much comfort as possible.

Whether Catherine knew of the imminent birth of her husband's illegitimate child is not recorded. The lengths that Henry went to conceal Bessie's confinement at the Augustinian Priory of St Laurence in Blackmore, Essex, may have been to spare his wife's dignity rather than to keep her in ignorance. He succeeded to such an extent that the date on which Bessie gave birth can only be estimated as being in June 1519.

That Henry resisted the temptation to celebrate the birth at court must have required a great deal of restraint because he had every reason to be joyous. Bessie had given him what he had craved for the past decade: a healthy son. The timing could not have been better, for everyone except Catherine. Her recent miscarriage, after which there had been no signs of another pregnancy, served as proof that the problem lay not with the king, who now had a lusty son, but with his wife.

If there is no record of any overt celebrations at court, then Henry certainly made it clear to the world that Bessie's son was his. The christening was by no means as secret as the birth: the king's chief minister Wolsey stood as godfather and made Henry's paternity even more obvious by bestowing the name Henry FitzRoy upon the child. Her son's birth was the zenith of Bessie's affair with Henry, but it was also its end. A few weeks later, the king had her married off to Gilbert Tailboys, heir of George, Lord Tailboys of Kyme in Lincolnshire.[14]

Meanwhile, thanks to the ongoing failure of his wife to provide him with a son and heir, Henry was increasingly conscious of the need to project the stability of his dynasty in other ways. During the early years of his reign, resolved to make his court the envy of the world, he spent lavishly on creating a centre of culture, art, decadence and ceremony. Not content with the impressive array of royal palaces that he had inherited, he set about commissioning new ones. Henry was the most prolific builder of all the Tudor monarchs, and during the course of his reign, the stock of palaces rose from twelve to fifty-five. Most of these were heavily influenced by Burgundian architecture and also reflected the impact of the Italian Renaissance, with 'antique' ornamental motifs.

One of Henry's most spectacular palaces was Nonsuch in Surrey. Designed as a celebration of the power of the Tudor dynasty, its name was a boast that there was no other palace like it in the world. Built around a series of courtyards with tall octagonal towers at each end, it had stucco decoration on every available wall. Nearby, at Walton in Surrey, the grand mansion at Oatlands was acquired by Henry and transformed into a sumptuous courtyard palace. In the heart of London, meanwhile, Henry 'purchased all the meadows about St James's, and there made a fair mansion, and a park, and builded many costly and commodious houses for great pleasure.'[15]

Henry also renovated and embellished some of the palaces that he had inherited. At the most ancient of these, Windsor Castle, he made improvements to St George's Chapel. But Henry thought Windsor a gloomy place and stayed there only seldom. 'Methinks I am in prison,' he once complained, 'here be no galleries, nor no gardens to walk in.'[16] Far more to his taste was Hampton Court. Originally built by Wolsey, it later passed to Henry, who at once set about remodelling and extending it. He added a magnificent Great Hall, a new suite of royal apartments, an extensive tiltyard, a covered tennis court and other sporting facilities in order to create the perfect palace for pleasure and privacy. By the time that his works were completed, Hampton Court had no fewer than eight hundred rooms, all lavishly decorated with rich hangings and furniture, and was clearly designed to inspire awe.

Henry ensured that all of his palaces were gorgeously arrayed with luxurious furnishings and fabrics. The young king was particularly fond of tapestries, and by the end of his reign he had amassed a collection of more than two thousand.[17] At Hampton Court alone there were 430 hangings, and one set (the 'Story of Abraham') was valued at a colossal £8,000, second only to the crown jewels in value.[18] Woven with silken threads of the finest gold, silver, red, blue, green and a host of other bright colours, they would have presented a dazzling sight to visitors and courtiers alike, especially when illuminated by candlelight.

A separate team of craftsmen was employed to make and mend the hangings and tapestries that adorned the royal palaces. This comprised as many as twenty-six livery tailors and ten arras makers. In contrast to the men who worked on the king's clothes, however, they were only employed from June to September in order to save on heat and lighting. It was a rare example of thrift in Henry's otherwise lavish wardrobe expenditure.

An inventory of Henry's possessions taken at the end of his reign includes 800 carpets, 100 of which were 'great carpets' (measuring 4.5 to 10.5 metres long), used to cover tables as well as floors. Many were richly decorated with embroidered Tudor roses, classical figures and other symbolic motifs. One particularly lavish carpet was densely embroidered all over in gold and silver thread, with a central roundel and border of green velvet embroidered with gold and pearls, and roundels of crimson satin containing white and red roses. Most of the windows of the royal palaces would have had shutters, but those of the king's 'secret lodgings' were covered by curtains fashioned from rich fabrics.

Henry also spent extravagantly on furs, particularly his favourite – the beautiful and luxurious sables that came all the way from Russia. During the course of his reign, Henry amassed no fewer than 844 sable skins, most of which were stored in two iron chests in the old jewel house at Whitehall Palace. The king had many of these sables studded with priceless jewels and other embellishments. One of them was described in an inventory as having an animal's head mounted in gold, with pearls at the ears and rubies for the eyes, encircled with a collar of gold ornamented with four diamonds and four rubies, and with a clock at the head. The sable's feet were also of gold, with claws of sapphires.[19]

The luxury reached its height in Henry's private apartments. A bed that was commissioned for his 'dark bedchamber' at Whitehall Palace provides a glimpse into the magnificence with which he was surrounded during his private hours.[20] The canopy and tester were made from panels of cloth of silver and gold, edged with purple velvet ribbon and embroidered with Tudor roses, the French fleur-de-lys and the royal arms of England. The curtains that were drawn around it were fashioned from purple and white taffeta, with gold ribbon running along its seam. A staggering eight mattresses were then laid across the tightly threaded base.

A rare survivor from Henry's personal possessions is a beautiful writing desk, which may have been kept in his study. Crafted from stained walnut and gilded leather, it was decorated by Lucas Horenbout, a Flemish painter who specialised in miniatures. He painted the arms of the king and queen supported by putti, with trumpets, medallions, antique motifs and the figures of Venus and Mars. Elsewhere there is a painted figure of St George and the heads of Christ, Paris and Helen. The desk is lined with red velvet and has a number of drawers and hidden compartments.[21] Numerous other personal possessions are listed in the inventories of court. They include comb cases, shaving cloths, handkerchiefs and covers for prayer books. All were exquisitely crafted from the finest materials but, sadly, none has survived.

Henry might have been a natural showman and his court a magnificent theatre, but to uphold the pretence required a cast of thousands 'backstage'. These men and women would work long days (and often nights) to ensure that the king and his court were always displayed in as glittering a style as possible.

The number of Henry's privy chamber staff rose dramatically during the early part of his reign: from the handful of intimates that his father had retained to as many as fifty attendants. Whereas Henry VII's privy chamber had been the centre of his business and private life, his son filled it with his friends and confidantes, so that it became a forum for his social life.

Principal among the privy chamber staff was the groom of the stool, to whom Henry gave even greater prominence and honour than his father had done. Increasingly, Henry selected men of the highest rank for this role, and those who were his personal favourites. The first to be appointed was Sir William Compton, whom Henry had known since infancy. When Compton's father died in 1493, Henry VII had become his ward and appointed him page to his younger son. Although he was about nine years older than the prince, the two became close friends and one of Henry's first acts upon becoming king was to appoint Compton to the position. Within a year, Compton was referred to by the Spanish ambassador as the 'privado' or favourite of the king, and in 1511 the French ambassador asserted that Compton enjoyed more 'crédict' with Henry than any other servant.[22]

A consummate courtier, Compton was also an excellent soldier and would serve the king on a number of campaigns. As groom of the stool, he was required to attend his royal master wherever he went. Thus, for example, when Henry rode in disguise in a joust early in his reign, Compton was his sole companion. So that he might easily attend his master at all hours of the day and night, the groom of the stool's lodgings were directly beneath the privy chamber in each palace, linked by a private staircase.

Although his primary duty was still to attend the king on his close-stool, Compton had a growing portfolio of other duties. They included acting as Henry's most confidential messenger. As such, he was responsible for the highly sensitive and confidential task of conveying messages from his royal master to both the queen and his mistresses – as the affair with Anne Hastings had proved. Even more important was the groom's duty to help control access to the king, which greatly enhanced his own influence.

As part of his expansion of his private staff, in 1518 Henry created an additional set of higher-class officers, the gentlemen of the privy chamber. There were twelve gentlemen in total (including the groom of the stool), six of whom were on duty at any one time. They were marked out by their distinctive black damask gowns and doublets. The gentlemen were in an extremely privileged and influential position, able to advise and even manipulate the king, as well as to control access to his presence and exercise patronage. Thus, although many of the duties required of their post – fetching, carrying, dressing and undressing – could in theory be seen as demeaning for men of high birth and rank, the fact that they did them for the king, 'not . . . a man but . . . a more excellent and divine estate', transformed them into an honourable occupation.[23]

As well as performing their formal duties, the gentlemen of the privy chamber also served as the king's companions in his sports and other pastimes. They would go hunting and hawking with him, enter the jousts, take part in masks, play tennis, cards and board games. They were expected to be men of sufficient quality and education to share Henry's tastes and intellect so that he might converse with them on any subject. Henry chose men who were utterly trustworthy and could offer congenial companionship. They must have 'a vigilant and revered respect and eye to His Majesty, so that by his look and countenance they may know what lacketh or is his pleasure to be had or done.'[24] Many of the men whom Henry selected had served him as Prince of Wales and were personal, rather than political choices. The Duke of Buckingham grumbled, with some justification, that the king 'would give his fees, offices and rewards to boys rather than noblemen.'[25]

The gentlemen became known for their boisterous and intemperate behaviour, which was encouraged by their royal master. One of the greatest hell-raisers was Francis Bryan, son of the woman who was superintending Princess Mary's upbringing. He had come to court at a very young age and shared Henry's passion for jousting, gambling and tennis. Like the king, he took risks in pursuit of his sport and lost an eye during a tournament of 1526, which obliged him to wear a distinctive eye-patch thereafter. He was also an accomplished soldier, diplomat and man of letters, with a vicious wit and irresistible charm. Sexually promiscuous, on a trip to Calais he demanded 'a soft bed then a hard harlot'. Bryan's natural irreverence incited him to adopt what other courtiers viewed as an over-familiarity with his royal master. He was forever telling him jokes and speaking his mind, but Henry loved him for it and he remained in favour throughout the reign.

The other privy chamber staff included four esquires of the body. Trained knights, they would watch over the king at all times, helping him dress and informing the Lord Chamberlain 'if anything lack for his person or pleasaunce'. Like the gentlemen, they were also the king's confidantes: 'Their business is in many secrets,' remarked one contemporary.[26] Among the men appointed to this position were Edward Neville and Sir Thomas Boleyn. Neville was a distant cousin of the king and bore such a close resemblance to him that they were often mistaken for brothers. Boleyn, meanwhile, had begun his service at court under Henry's father in 1501. An unscrupulous social climber, he had married well above his station to Elizabeth Howard, daughter of the Earl of Surrey, and his principal estate was the fine castle of Hever in Kent. A man of learning as well as ambition, he spoke Latin and French better than anyone at court, and Henry employed him on a number of important embassies.

Two other esquires had served Henry since his youth. Henry Guildford was described as 'a lusty young man well beloved of the King'. He was always at the centre of court entertainments, such as a play of Robin Hood and his merry men that was performed in honour of the queen in January 1510. William Fitzwilliam, meanwhile, shared his master's love of the chase and was one of his closest companions. It was said that he understood the king's 'nature and temper better than any man in England'.[27] Unlike most other men at court, Fitzwilliam was genuinely committed to the king's service, rather than his own, and remained aloof from factional politics.

The four gentleman ushers were akin to masters of ceremonies and therefore had to be fully conversant with 'all the customs and ceremonies used about the King'. They guarded the door to his room, ushered visitors into his presence and watched over his valuables. Because they were among the more public-facing of the privy chamber staff, they must be 'courteous and glad to receive, teach and direct every man'.[28] They also had command of the more junior servants. The yeomen of the chamber, meanwhile, prepared the royal bed and lit the king's way with torches. They kept the passage leading to the privy chamber 'clear of rascals, boys and others', who tended to loiter there causing trouble.[29]

Like his father, Henry retained a number of grooms in his privy chamber. They were assisted by four pages of honour, or henchmen, who would wait upon their superiors in the privy chamber and walk close to the king's horse in public processions. These pages wore brightly coloured tunics with gold chains across the shoulder, and on ceremonial occasions they carried striped green and white staves. Together with the grooms, they would sleep in the presence chamber or the pages' chamber if there was one.

Six gentlemen waiters, three cupbearers, three carvers, two surveyors and three sewers were also among the privy chamber staff. The royal barber, physicians and surgeons were members of this department, too, as were the king's secretaries.

Every one of the king's considerable team of private attendants was crucial to creating the illusion of splendour and majesty in the public court beyond. But the private preparations that they super-intended were every bit as ceremonial as the formal state business and pageantry in which the rest of the court took part. The rigid structure and order to the process of preparing the king for his audience reinforced the hierarchies of the court: from the humble laundress who delivered his freshly washed clothes to the gentlemen of the bedchamber who supervised the ceremony of dressing. The art of majesty was as evident behind closed doors as it was in public.

5

'Lay hands upon his royal person'

IN THE EARLY years of his reign, when Henry was at the peak of his youthful vigour, he would rise at the crack of dawn and go hunting for several hours – sometimes until dusk. The courtier and diplomat Richard Pace reported to Cardinal Wolsey that during the summer, the 'King rises daily, except on holy days, at 4 or 5 o'clock [in the morning] and hunts till 9 or 10 at night.'[1] Henry would get up later in the colder months, typically around 8 o'clock. At first, he would always take a huge entourage of courtiers with him on the hunt. However, their boisterousness so 'hindered and impeached' his enjoyment that he eventually restricted the numbers to just a handful of intimates – including, often, his wife Catherine, who was a competent horsewoman.[2]

In order to get the king ready for his hunting expeditions and other courtly pastimes, his privy chamber staff had to rise even earlier than he did. The rules of court dictated that the grooms of the privy chamber should rise at 6 o'clock to clean and tidy the king's rooms before he emerged, although presumably they had to get up much earlier when their royal master was hunting. If they did not know of the existence of bacteria, the Tudors did at least appreciate the link between dirt and disease, so the royal apartments were kept free 'of all manner of filthiness'.[3] Henry also employed a team of permanent staff at each of his principal residences, whose job it was to give the palaces a thorough clean once the king and his court had moved on to the next place. No corner of these vast palaces was neglected as this team of men dusted and washed every inch of the floors, panelling and even ceilings.

Having cleaned the king's chambers, the grooms would then

wake the esquires of the body, who slept in the 'pallet chamber' next door to the royal bedchamber. They were not always successful: Henry complained more than once that his esquires were still snoring when he was up and dressed. When they had dragged themselves from their beds, the esquires would enter their royal master's bedchamber 'to array him and dress him in his [under]clothes'. These were kept in one of two chests in the bedchamber and would be strewn with fresh herbs to keep them sweet-smelling. The other chest held the dirty linen awaiting collection for washing by the king's laundress. If the esquires required any other clothes to complete the under layer of the king's apparel for that day, these would be handed to them at the bedchamber door by a groom, who in turn would have received them 'honestly and cleanly' from a yeoman of the Wardrobe of the Robes.[4] Although the yeomen were barred entry to the privy chamber itself, they wore the same livery as the servants within, to distinguish them from the other yeomen at court.

As well as delivering the king's clothes to the door of his privy chamber, the yeomen, along with the groom and page, were responsible for ensuring that they remained in mint condition. They brushed the clothes and kept them sweet-smelling, and also maintained detailed stocklists and inventories of everything in their charge. When their royal master and his court prepared to remove to a different palace, these attendants made sure that the right clothes were taken with them. Another duty that the yeoman of the robes might have undertaken was to make clothing and jewels available for portrait painters such as the celebrated Hans Holbein, so that they could capture the detail without taking up the sitter's time.[5] Tudor court portraits are unique in the level of detail that they provide of the sumptuous clothes worn by the king and his court, and this is as much due to the efforts of the yeomen in facilitating access to the royal wardrobe as to the skill of the painter.

When the Tudors found servants who proved their ability and trustworthiness, they not only rewarded them but appointed members of their family to succeed them. It was not unusual for several generations of the same family to fill the same office for successive monarchs. They were also sometimes promoted within the privy chamber. For example, a man named Richard Cecil was appointed as one of Henry VIII's yeomen. As well as dressing the king's person, he was also in charge of accessories, weapons and hunting equipment. Cecil had risen from the positions of page and then groom. His son was William Cecil, who later became chief adviser, Secretary of State, and Lord High Treasurer to Elizabeth I.

Having been 'loosely dressed' by his esquires, Henry would step into the privy chamber so that his six gentlemen could complete the ceremony of robing with whichever garments he had chosen for that day. Wolsey stipulated that the king's gentlemen should be ready by 7 o'clock

> to apparel and dress his Highness, putting on such garments, in reverent, discreet, and sober manner . . . and that none of the said grooms or ushers do approach or resume (unless they be otherwise by his Grace commanded or admitted) to lay hands upon his royal person, or intermeddle with preparing or dressing of the same, but only the said six gentlemen: except it be to warm clothes, or to bring the said gentlemen such things as shall appertain to the apparelling and dressing of the King's said person.[6]

A sartorially minded king such as Henry VIII no doubt had very specific ideas about how he wished to be dressed on any given day, while others might have been content to leave it to the discretion of their staff. Clothes were a major preoccupation for the young king – far more so than for his father, who had dressed magnificently out of political necessity rather than personal taste. When Henry came to the throne, his counterparts in Europe viewed English fashion with disdain. Baldassare Castiglione's influential *Book of the Courtier*, begun in 1508, provided an appraisal of most other nations' dress sense but completely omitted the English style. Just a decade later, Henry had changed all of that. Reporting to his master in 1519, the Venetian ambassador, Sebastian Guistinian, described Henry as 'the best dressed sovereign in the world'.[7]

Henry's very first Act of Parliament contained detailed sumptuary laws confining the use of certain fabrics and colours to the royal family. The 'Act against wearing of costly Apparel' was followed by three further Acts of Apparel. They stipulated that the royal family alone could wear purple; dukes and marquesses could fashion the sleeves of their cloaks from gold silks; earls could wear sables; barons were entitled to a mantle of fine cloth from the Netherlands trimmed with crimson or blue velvet; and knights were permitted a shirt of damask and a collar of golden tissue – a fabric woven with weft loops of metal thread.

Henry loved to show off his athletic physique (as well as his riches) in the quality and quantity of the cloth from which his garments were fashioned. His broad shoulders were emphasised by padded and embroidered sleeves, the curve of his calf muscles was shown off to best effect by white silk hose, and his improbably large codpiece symbolised his masculinity and power. Henry also had his doublets cut away at the neckline so that a good proportion of his shirts would be visible underneath. As well as signifying his wealth (clean white linen denoted that the wearer did not do any manual labour), this was blatantly exhibitionist on the young king's part because a shirt was an item of underwear. Like the rest of Henry's wardrobe, shoes were more exaggerated than those of his prede-cessor. A distinctive style, known as a high shoe, featured a square toe, which could measure as much as seventeen centimetres across. It was fashioned from leather, usually goatskin, and sometimes had textile uppers.

All of the layers that comprised Henry's outfits – shirt, doublet, jerkin, waistcoat, jacket and gown – created a rather bulky silhou-ette. This was intentional. Henry was well built, bordering on stocky, and the more slender of his courtiers sought to emulate his figure by adding extra layers to their outfits. Some even resorted to padded doublets. But most of Henry's courtiers had little need for such deception: even the basic layers of clothing provided most of the requisite bulk, and the hearty diet that they enjoyed at court provided the rest.

Not surprisingly, given his love of clothes and the frequency with which he hunted, Henry had an array of special riding and hunting coats fashioned by the royal tailors at great expense. He also had clothes for hawking, and employed a saddler and craftsmen to supply expensive silk textiles and metal thread to cover equipment for his hawks and hounds. The inventories kept by the officers of his wardrobe reveal an extensive collection of hunting equipment, including no fewer than 450 hawk hoods and 158 dog collars. These were of such value that they were kept within the closets and studies of the king's privy lodgings at the palaces of Greenwich and Whitehall, and in the privy jewel house at Hampton Court. Given the importance of horses for transporting the king and his possessions, as well as for jousting, hunting and ceremonial events, it is perhaps not surprising that the household accounts are also filled with references to saddles, harnesses, reins, buckles and other riding accoutrements. These were as lavish as every other aspect of Henry's personal wardrobe. They included a purple velvet saddle decorated with gold fleurs-de-lys, and an Italian-style harness bedecked with braids of black silk, together with buttons and tassels of black silk and gold for the reins.

The distinctive equipment that was made for the king's horses and hounds served a useful as well as decorative purpose. Henry was very fond of dogs and had a number of them, including a spaniel named Cutte and another dog called Ball, both of which had a tendency to get lost. The king was so distraught each time this happened that he would offer a substantial reward for their safe return, such as when Cutte disappeared in May 1530 and again in February 1531. The fact that the dog was wearing a high-quality collar would have helped track him down. The wardrobe inventories reveal that Henry's dogs wore elaborate collars of velvet and cloth of gold, studded with decorative scallop shells, roses and pomegranates, and emblazoned with the king's initials. Their chains were sometimes made of silver or silk – the latter dyed in the favourite Tudor colours of white and green. Anyone who found the prodigal hounds could have been in no doubt as to their owner.

The details of Henry's own clothing were even more carefully (and expensively) crafted. His doublets were fastened together with as many as forty gold-, silver- and diamond-encrusted buttons. His sleeves were punctuated with buttons down the forearm to the wrist, and more buttons could be displayed on the stiffened collars of his doublets. Buttons were a strictly male preserve during the first half of the Tudor period, when men's dress was arguably even more elaborate than that of the ladies at court.

The king's wardrobe was a riot of colour: cloth of gold, bright reds, deep blues, verdant greens and solid blacks were not only dazzling to the eye but damaging to the coffers. The more vivid a garment, the more expensive it was to produce. This meant that the king and his foremost courtiers literally stood out from the crowd, most of whom could only afford clothes dyed in more muted shades, such as pale blue, orangey-pink and mustard-yellow. The lowliest members of the court had to be content with undyed cloth.

A host of different men and women were employed in the business of making the king's clothes. A tailor, embroiderer, hosier and skinner (supplier of furs) made his garments, while a cordwainer, cutler, milliner and silkwoman were responsible for crafting his accessories. Henry initially retained his late father's tailor, Stephen Jasper, but just two years into his reign he had him replaced by William Hilton, eager perhaps to throw off his father's fashions and establish his own style. Hilton served in this post until his death in 1519, and was replaced by a Frenchman, John de Paris, which reveals the king's eagerness to keep up with the latest fashions from the country of his great rival, Francis I.[8]

The royal tailors did not design the king's clothes using contemporary style books or manuscripts. The first written manuscripts about clothing design only appeared later in the sixteenth century, but even then they were a rarity.[9] Instead, news of what was fashionable spread by word of mouth from the Continent, by descriptions in letters and by studying the construction of clothes that had been imported from overseas. Inspired by these, Henry's tailors would sketch out their own designs. One visitor to Whitehall noted that in the little study next to the king's bedchamber, there were 'diverse plates and patterns of gowns'.[10]

Among the few roles that a woman might take in the royal

wardrobe was that of silk worker. As such, she could trade in her own right and employ apprentices. Her job was to make ribbons, braids and trimmings, as well as to undertake the typically female tasks of laundering and starching, and mending sleeves, partlets and veils. Henry VIII's first recorded silkwoman was Lettice Worsop, and she was succeeded by a lady named Anne Cowper.

One item of clothing that did not fall under the authority of the wardrobe staff was the king's shirts. These were the responsibility of his most intimate body servant, the groom of the stool. The fact that shirts were worn closer to the body than most other items of clothing might account for their being cared for by the king's most personal servant. Little detail of Henry's shirts exists, except how they were decorated – for example with black and white silk, 'bands and ruffs of silver and gold', and 'ruffs of silk of sundry sorts'.[11]

Before long, Henry had accumulated an impressive and luxurious collection of clothing, textiles, embroidery, lace and jewels. Guistinian claimed that during the first decade of his reign, the English king spent 16,000 ducats on his wardrobe, which is the equivalent of around £1.6 million in today's money. In fact, this was probably an underestimation. An inventory of Henry's wardrobe in 1521 estimates its value at £10,380, which equates to almost £4 million today.[12] The high value of the contents covered by the Great Wardrobe made it one of the most important departments of the royal household. Spendthrift he may have been, but Henry was no hoarder. Eager to keep up with the latest fashions, he regularly purged the wardrobe and gave clothes away to favoured members of his court and household. His successors would do the same. The inventories show that the Tudor royals gave away hundreds of items of clothing as gifts each year.

It is thanks to the assiduity of Nicholas Bristowe, who served as clerk to the Wardrobe of Robes and Beds, that what may be a rare surviving item from Henry VIII's personal wardrobe has recently come to light. In 2014, Historic Royal Palaces was approached by a direct descendent of Bristowe, who had in their possession an exquisite hat that, family tradition has it, once belonged to the king. The story goes that upon witnessing the fall of Boulogne after a lengthy siege in 1544, a triumphant Henry threw his hat into the air and it was caught by Bristowe, who had accompanied his master on campaign. The hat is certainly rich enough to have belonged to the king. Fashioned from crimson silk, it is embellished with an ostrich feather and would have been studded with jewels. Scientific analysis has dated it to the late medieval or early Tudor period, so the legend that it was 'Henry's Hat' remains a tantalising prospect.[13]

When the king was dressed for the day, he would be seated on a chair with a footstool, and a kerchief was carefully laid around his shoulders. His barber, a man named Penny, would then step forward to begin shaving his royal master and dressing his hair. During the early years of his reign, Henry was clean-shaven, but he soon grew a beard, which the barber would ensure was neatly trimmed. This became the fashion for all gentlemen at court.

The royal barber had to be a man of impeccable character and infinite trustworthiness: after all, he would be holding sharp blades to the king's throat. A set of court ordinances made it clear 'that the said barber takes especial regard to the pure and clean keeping of his own person . . . without resorting to the company of vile persons . . . [and] avoiding such dangers and annoyance as by that means he might do unto the King's most royal person.' He should also have ready all of the instruments that he might need to perform his work efficiently, including 'water, cloths, knives, combs, scissors, and other stuff . . . for trimming and dressing the King's head and beard.'[14]

Luxury pervaded the business of hairdressing and shaving, as it did every other element of Henry's private routine. Inventories of his possessions include silver basins for shaving kept at the Tower and Hampton Court, where shaving cloths trimmed with black silk were also kept. The king had a comb of 'gold garnished with . . . stones and pearl', a toothpick case of gold, and an 'ear pick of silver'.[15]

When the barber had completed his work, the king would be examined by one of his four physicians, who would carry out their morning visits on a rotational basis. These men were easily distinguishable from the rest of the courtiers by their long, fur-sleeved gowns and black velvet caps. They frequently carried bladder-shaped flasks for inspecting the king's urine, and would also examine his stools. Henry was also regularly attended by the royal apothecaries and, when the need arose, by his personal surgeons.

In submitting himself to the frequent attentions of his medics, the king was merely following royal protocol. After all, a sovereign's health was of the utmost importance to the state, so any sign of illness must be detected and dealt with immediately. But Henry had always been prone to hypochondria and would be thrown into a panic at any sign of illness at court. The fact that his brother had died at the age of fifteen, before he had had the chance to bear any heirs, may have sparked Henry's paranoia. The French ambassador described him as 'the most timid person in such matters you could meet'.[16]

Henry's fear of sickness was not without justification, however. The court was such a crowded and contagious space that any disease would spread rapidly within its confines – particularly in summer, when the weather was stagnant and the river flowed with effluent. Henry himself fell prey to a number of serious illnesses, including a bout of smallpox in 1514, and in 1521 the first of what seems to have been repeated episodes of malaria. His love of vigorous sports, meanwhile, made him vulnerable to injury. The most serious of these were from jousting, but the king also once injured his foot while playing tennis. The pain was so acute and prolonged that he was obliged to wear a black velvet slipper for a month afterwards.

Ever master of his own destiny, Henry was determined to bolster his immunity against sickness and disease. For this reason, he took a keener interest than most in the medical practices of the day. In 1518, he chartered the Royal College of Physicians in London, and later in the reign he established the Company of Barbers and Surgeons.[17] During the course of his reign, no fewer than seven Acts of Parliament were passed aimed at regulating and licensing medical practitioners – legislation that remained unchanged for 300 years. Henry also created Regius Professorships in Medicine at Oxford and Cambridge.

Not content to meekly accept the diagnoses of the various medical professionals who surrounded him, Henry kept his own cabinet of medicines and regularly self-dosed. He was also fond of sharing recipes with family members and close friends, and once sent a remedy against plague to the Lord Mayor of London so that he might disseminate it among the people. This concoction was made up of herbs, elder and briar leaves and ginger, mixed with white wine. The king advised that it should be drunk for nine days. Whether the Mayor distributed this carefully thought-out but largely ineffective cure is not recorded.

Henry and his physicians believed firmly in the influence of the planets over a person's health, well-being and character. Born under the sign of Cancer, the king was thought to be governed by the watery and maternal cycles of the moon, which explained his obsessive interest in such feminine concerns as childbirth, lovemaking and romance. According to the chart that had been cast at the time of his birth, he would be a cheerful, frivolous and flirty child who would grow into a man of action. But he would also be short-tempered, restless and overly sensitive to criticism. The physical manifestations of his horoscope included poor sleeping patterns, a high sex drive, excessive wet dreams and a proneness to headaches and constipation. It would prove a remarkably accurate prediction.

The king was so obsessed with the movement of the planets that he later had an astronomical clock installed at Hampton Court. This sophisticated piece of Tudor technology showed not only the time, but the month, date and number of days since the beginning of the year. It also charted the phases of the moon, the movement of the constellations in the zodiac and, of more immediately practical use to Henry and his courtiers, the time of high water at London Bridge.

As part of their ministrations, the royal physicians used a range of tried and tested herbal remedies and had access to the many varieties of herbs and plants grown in the kitchen gardens of the palaces. Their potions varied in effectiveness. Sea holly or eryngium was used as an aphrodisiac, while comfrey was thought to ease backache caused by the 'over use of women'. Willow bark was distilled to provide a cure for headaches, which probably was effective because it contains aspirin. Daisy could reduce swelling and bruising, and alchemilla, henbane, selfheal and St John's wort were used to treat wounds and ulcers. The latter complaint would be particularly troublesome for the king, so his physicians also concocted a special paste of rose oil, myrtle seeds and 'half an ounce of long worms which have been slit and washed in white wine for two hours'. The alcohol in the white wine would have been effective at cleansing the wound and live maggots performed the same function, but the dead worms in this paste were unlikely to have had any beneficial effect. The royal physicians also devised a remedy for a more personal complaint. Known as 'The King's Grace's Ointment', this primarily comprised yellow sweet clover and was used to treat his 'inflamed member'.[18]

Later in the reign, the medics who attended the king included the barber-surgeons. This profession evolved during Henry's reign and, as the name suggests, fulfilled both a medical and a grooming function. There was a sound basis for doing so: the barber-surgeon was in an excellent position to gain knowledge of the state of his client's health from their skin, hair, breath and general odour. The barber-surgeons performed a range of duties, from blood-letting and tooth-drawing to cleaning and scraping teeth, cutting nails, syringing ears and extracting any worms or 'small beasts' therein, and removing any marks or blemishes from the skin.

Tudor medicine has an undeserved reputation for being entirely barbarous and ineffective. Although bleeding, purging and even chopping off limbs played their part, contemporary medical practice recommended a holistic approach to a patient's well-being. Physicians were therefore advised to pay attention to their mental state, daily habits and diet, and to observe the body as a whole, not just the part of it that was causing pain or difficulty. They also believed that a patient's character was dictated by whichever of the four humours was most dominant in his or her body. For example, anyone with an excess of bile would be peevish and bad-tempered, whereas too much phlegm sparked dull, apathetic behaviour.

In order to rebalance the humours, and thus achieve optimum health, physicians provided their patients with a *regimen sanitatis*, or guide to healthy living. This would encompass eating habits, relaxation, the avoidance of stress and keeping on good terms with colleagues and companions. Andrew Borde's *Fyrst Boke of the Introduction of Knowledge*, published in 1542, summed up this approach. He urged his readers that 'to comfort and to rejoice the spirits', they should 'live out of sin and follow Christ's doctrine'. He asserted: 'There is nothing that doth comfort the heart so much, beside God, as honest mirth and good company.' In short, laughter was the best medicine. For this reason he became known as 'Merry Andrew'. His dietary advice was sound, too, and he recommended a range of what might today be called 'superfoods', namely ginger, poached eggs and citrus fruits.[19]

This was all very well when a patient was in relatively good health, but during periods of illness physicians would resort to more interventionist methods. Blood-letting was particularly popular, and surviving medical texts provide detailed guidance on which veins should be opened depending upon the ailment. For example, the vein between the finger and thumb would relieve a migraine, diseases of the bladder were treated by opening the vein under the ankle, and a cure for melancholy was to cut a vein in the back. Laxatives, vomitaries and emmenagogues (herbs that stimulate menstruation) were also used. Henry took a genuine interest in the ministrations of his physicians and would spend long hours consulting them about the best means to ensure his well-being.

Having been washed, groomed, dressed and examined, the king was at last ready to appear before his court. In common with the rest of the court, the king would not take his first meal of the day until around 10.30 or 11 o'clock, although sometimes it was as late as midday.[20] This was known as dinner and was the most substantial of the day. Given that he often hunted from dawn, Henry must have taken this meal with him on occasion. Breakfast was not usually eaten at court during the first half of the Tudor period, except by labourers, small children, pregnant or breastfeeding women and the sick. Everyone else would earn their first meal by undertaking labour (for the lower classes) or dealing with matters of business, going hunting or enjoying some other leisure pursuit (for the richer classes).

An elaborate ceremonial was always observed when serving the king's meals, but to differing degrees, depending upon the particular meal and the degree of privacy. A handful of higher-ranking officials would superintend a team of waiters in preparing the dining room and laying the tables. Even though the king was absent while the table was being prepared, each of the gentlemen involved would bow to his empty place setting and kiss the towels and tablecloths in a reverential fashion. It was the responsibility of the groom of the stool to take delivery of the table linen, and after use it was returned to the ewery and then taken to the laundry before being stored ready for reuse.

One of the most luxurious pieces of table linen was the cover-pane, a beautifully embellished piece of material some three or four feet long. It was laid over the king's place setting of trencher, knife, spoon and fork (Henry owned 'suckett' forks, with a spoon on one end and a two-pronged fork at the other), salt and bread, and then removed once the meal had been set upon the table.[21] The inventory of Henry VIII's goods taken at the end of his reign includes a set of coverpanes 'wrought with gold and silk' dating from the reign of Edward IV or even earlier.[22] The rest of the court was obliged to bring their own knife and spoon to the table, and a separate linen napkin or long cloth was used as a napkin by all of those seated at each table.

In contrast to the popular image of Henry VIII devouring endless chicken legs and throwing the bones over his shoulder afterwards, he and his courtiers were the most fastidious of diners. First, the king would take part in an elaborate ceremony of handwashing. Once he was seated at table, the edge of the tablecloth would be lifted and placed on his lap. If he needed a napkin during the meal, this would be brought to him by a gentleman usher, who then folded it over his arm afterwards. In his manual on civility, Erasmus had opined: 'To lick greasy fingers or to wipe them on your coat is impolite. It is better to use the tablecloth or the serviette.'[23]

The image of most Tudor meals at court as huge and raucous feasts, presided over by the king on the top table, has little basis in reality. Only when entertaining ambassadors or other important guests would the king dine in great state, usually in his presence chamber. At other times, this was where the most senior members of court would take their meals. Linked to the presence chamber, usually by a gallery and closet, was the privy chamber. This was where the king most often took his meals, served by his personal staff.

A privy kitchen was installed beneath the king's privy lodgings so that his food could be prepared in close proximity and arrive piping hot on the royal table. It also enabled Henry's personal cooks to create the finest of dishes, unencumbered by the mass catering requirements of the Great Kitchen. Among his favourites were white broth with almonds, beef olives, leg of mutton with lemons, game pie stuffed with oranges, stewed capons, peacock royal, roasted deer, hog's liver and salmon roasted in sauce.

One of the king's most celebrated cooks was a Frenchman called Piero le Doux. His culinary skills were so appreciated by Henry that he was rewarded with numerous gifts of clothing, including a gown of tawny cloth furred with 123 skins of black budge (lamb-skin), a black velvet doublet and a black camlet jacket furred with white budge.[24] Only one woman is listed as being a member of Henry VIII's kitchens: Mrs Cornwallis. She worked in the confectionary and is listed in the household accounts as 'the wife who makes the King's puddings'.[25] The king so loved her sweet treats (particularly custards, fritters, tarts, jelly, cream of almonds and a quince marmalade so thick that it could be sliced) that he rewarded her with a fine house in Aldgate.[26]

Having his own privy kitchen also protected the king from the risk of poisoning because it contained only a fraction of the staff who were employed in the Great Kitchen. It also meant that Henry was not bound by the rigid timetable that the latter imposed on the rest of the court. This proved useful if, as often happened, he had 'gone further in walking, hunting, hawking, or other disports'.[27] Henry would regularly send for snacks late at night, and one of his favourites was a bowl of aleberry – a kind of bread pudding flavoured with ale.

At the more formal dinners, the king and those seated with him would be presented with an array of different dishes to choose from: as many as thirty-five at each course. The rest of the diners would be served with a strict number of dishes according to their status. The sumptuary laws of May 1517 that dictated the colour and style of dress at court also made provision for dining. Thus, for example, a cardinal was entitled to nine dishes at one meal, a duke, archbishop, marquis, earl or bishop to seven, lords, knights of the garter, mayors of the city of London and abbots to six, and those of the lowest rank were limited to three dishes per meal. But even they were hardly deprived, since a 'dish' could comprise an entire swan, peacock or 'fowls of like greatness'; four plovers, partridge or woodcock; eight quail; and twelve very small birds such as larks.[28] What was more, these laws only applied to certain foods. Others, such as pottages and dishes made of offal or oysters (which were cheap and widely available), could be served to everyone in abundance.[29]

Dinner was substantial enough to maintain the king and his court for the rest of the morning and afternoon. Supper was then served between 3 and 4 o'clock, and sometimes an evening snack, called 'rear night' or 'all night', was served between 8 and 9 o'clock.[30] For those who were lucky enough to dine at court, supper could be a full repeat of dinner. The royal family would be presented with a similarly bewildering array of different dishes, including soups, pottage, roasted meats, tarts, custards, fruits, nuts and cheeses. The Tudors set as much store by spectacle as by taste in creating their feasts. Contemporary cookery books include detailed instructions for making dishes into elaborate shapes in order to achieve dramatic impact. For example, a pig's stomach should be filled with ground pork and spices and covered all over with blanched almonds so that it resembles a hedgehog. A mythical beast known as a cockatrice could be created by sewing the front half of a capon to the rear part of a pig. To ensure maximum impact, such dishes would be paraded around the assembled court before being served.

The Tudors believed that the stomach was like a cauldron, heated by the rest of the body, and that proper digestion was vital for good health – as well as for fertility, which was a major preoccupation for the king. If a man had eaten a good meal, in the correct order, then his digestive process would produce a seed. Women, on the other hand, would be able to generate enough blood to line the womb and nourish the seed that was planted there. Wind-inducing food, such as beans, could inflate a man's penis at the desired moment. Meanwhile, the richest foodstuffs, namely red meat, sugar and wine, were thought to be the most effective in boosting sexual appetite.

The theory of digestion had a direct influence upon the order in which different dishes were eaten at court. This order is still followed today. Henry's physicians recommended beginning a meal with those foods that needed the most 'concocting' or breaking down, such as beef, peas and oatmeal – all of which were staple ingredients in soup. Soups were also ideal in forming 'juice' in the bottom of the cauldron for the rest of the food to be 'cooked' in. Bread was a good second course because it was also a strong food and would therefore help to line the stomach in preparation for the dishes to follow.

The meat course would come next, and boiled meats would be eaten before roasted ones because they were thought to be harder to digest. The Tudors ate far more meat than we do today, and the king ate more than most. On one occasion, he and his travelling household ate their way through 720 larks, 240 pigeons, 192 each of partridges, plovers and teals,132 capons, 84 pullets, 56 herons, 40 sheep, 34 pheasants, 24 peacocks, 20 storks, 12 pigs, 8 calves, 7 swans and 6 oxen in a single day. In order to ensure that meat was always in plentiful supply at court, Henry personally ordered a 'flesh day' every week 'from Easter until Michaelmas [29 September]', when the eating of meat was compulsory for his courtiers.[31] The predominance of meat in Henry's diet, and that of many of his courtiers, accounts for the fact that they regularly consumed between 4,500 and 5,000 calories a day – more than twice the intake recommended today for a healthy diet.

After the meat course, diners were advised to pause and take a long drink of ale or wine. This would help to top up the cauldron after all the solid food that had gone before. Tudor ale was much sweeter and thicker than modern brews, and was not very alcoholic. The king and his guests tended to drink wine, which was sometimes watered down. Fresh water was rarely drunk on its own because it was often unclean and carried the risk of sickness. Being teetotal at the Tudor court was therefore not an option.

Salad, fruit or other cold food usually followed. The Tudors did not eat as much fresh fruit as we do today because they were mostly limited to seasonal fruit. Thus, for example, strawberries and cherries were enjoyed by all levels of society, but only for a few weeks of the year. Only the king and his richest nobles could afford to import fruit, and in an age of slow transportation, the range of fruit that would survive the journey was restricted to such varieties as oranges and lemons. Most of the home-grown fruit was preserved for eating out of season. Nevertheless, Henry VIII did encourage the growth of more exotic varieties on home soil. The royal fruiterer, Richard Harris, was sent to the Low Countries and France to take samples of different varieties that he could then cultivate at a special fruit nursery in Kent. Thanks to this 'great cost and rare industry', Henry and his courtiers were able to enjoy the sweetest cherries, the crunchiest Pippins and the most succulent peaches and apricots.[32]

Vegetables were eaten in the form of 'sallats'. These contained cooked, preserved and fresh produce such as onions, chives, radishes, boiled carrots, parsnips, turnips, cabbage, lettuce and cucumber. Herbs and flowers such as violets and cowslips would be added to enhance the flavour and colour. They might be dressed with vinegar, oil and sugar. Like so many other dishes, sallats would often be highly decorative, with vegetables carved into elaborate shapes and other ingredients used 'for show only', according to an early seventeenth-century cookery manual.[33]

To round off the meal, cheese was served. This was believed to close the stomach, sealing in all the other foods. Given the staggering array of different dishes that were served to the king and his family, it is perhaps not surprising that many of them left the table untouched. These 'unbroken meats' would be given to their personal servants, and any other leftovers passed gradually down the chain of command so that the food that nobody else wanted was given to the poor people who always hung about the palace gates. In addition to these perks, those who worked in the royal household received a number of 'perquisites' to enhance their salary. For example, the men who worked in the boiling house could claim the dripping from roasts, the 'strippings' from briskets and the grease left in the bottom of the pot after the beef had been boiled.[34]

The king and his highest-ranking courtiers spent vast amounts on food. At the Field of the Cloth of Gold, an eighteen-day extrava-ganza of feasting and entertainments attended by Henry VIII and his French rival, Francis I, in 1520, a staggering £7,409 (£2.8 million) was spent on feeding the English king, queen and their nobles. Of this, £440 (£167,000) was laid out for spices alone. Henry's sea fisher was paid for 9,100 plaice, 7,836 whiting, 5,554 soles, 2,800 crayfish, 1,890 mackerel, 700 conger eels, 488 cod, 300 bream, 48 mullets, 30 turbots, 21 basses, 11 haddock, 5 dories, 4 trout, 3 crabs, 3 salmon, 1 sturgeon, 1 lobster and 1 dolphin. The quantities would be far higher on a normal day when the kitchen staff were catering for the full court. On average, it cost the equivalent of more than £6 million a year to feed the court.[35]

Even on an average day, catering for the king and his court was a task of truly gargantuan scale. The kitchen staff had to produce no fewer than six hundred covers twice a day. Little wonder that the kitchens at Hampton Court occupied one-third of the entire palace complex. They still survive today and are the best example of a Tudor kitchen in the world. Henry VIII employed around two hundred people in his kitchens, every one of whom worked excep-tionally long days peeling, chopping, plucking, boiling, roasting and decorating the vast array of different dishes that were served to their royal master and his courtiers every day.

The most senior member of the royal kitchen staff was the Clerk. A highly educated and trusted official, he held the key to the stores and was responsible for allocating provisions to the kitchen staff. He kept a close eye on every ingredient – from the precious spices to the humble shallot – and would list them all with great care in the accounts. He then presented these to the Board of the Green Cloth – the group of men responsible for the day-to-day running of the royal household.

Next in the strict hierarchy of the kitchen staff came the Master Cook. Like a modern chef, he was in overall charge of cooking but only carried out the most complex and difficult tasks himself. The more mundane tasks such as peeling and chopping vegetables and preparing the meat was left to more junior staff. There were three Master Cooks in the Tudor court: one for the main household kitchen and the other two for the king and queen's privy kitchens.

One of the worst jobs in the royal kitchens was that of turnspit. As the name suggests, their task was to spend many hours on end turning a spit full of huge joints of meat in front of the enormous fire. The heat of the fire and the draughts from the air that roared up the chimney ensured that the unfortunate occupier of this position was both boiling hot and freezing cold at the same time. The task was so arduous that it was one of the first to be mechanised. As early as 1536, there is a reference to a turnspit dog in the kitchens. The dogs were trained to run inside a small treadmill that powered the spit via a pulley attached to one end of it.

Keeping provisions and prepared food fresh was a considerable challenge in an age before modern conveniences such as fridges and freezers. Barrels were used to store not just wine and beer, but foods such as salt fish, olives and dried fruit. More expensive items like sweetmeats would be kept in wooden boxes, and there is also a reference to these being used to store marmalade. Fruit and vegetables would be kept in the wicker baskets used to transport them to the kitchens. Foods that were more prone to decay, such as jams and preserves, were kept in airtight earthenware jars known as gallipots, and large earthenware pots were used to store clarified butter. One of the most effective methods of keeping meat fresh was to wrap it in a thick crust of pastry and bake it. This would keep meats such as venison, wild boar, bacon, swan and porpoise fresh and moist for several days. Other meats were smoked and then hung from beams, out of reach of dogs, cats and vermin. Saltwater fish was wrapped in seaweed to keep it fresh, but other fish would be kept alive until the last possible moment. Most of the royal palaces had fishponds for this purpose.

At Hampton Court, there was a sophisticated network of larders for wet, dry and flesh goods, all of which led off from a single courtyard and were accessible by only one door. This would be kept locked in order to minimise the risk of pilfering. There were also three cellars at the palace, two beneath the Great Hall and one under the Great Watching Chamber. The wine cellar had a 'drinking house' attached, which was probably where the wine was tasted prior to serving. Henry and his court would drink their way through 300 casks of wine each year, and much of this was stored at Hampton Court. The great cellar was filled with hundreds of casks of ale – the most popular drink at court, with around 600,000 gallons being consumed each year. The finest wine and ale was reserved for the king and queen, and stored in the privy cellar.

Although fresh water was a rarity for many households, the royal court benefited from a sophisticated plumbing system. At Hampton Court, for example, fresh water was pumped from various conduit-houses at Coombe Hill, which lay four miles away, and reached the palace via conduits embedded in the Thames. Impressive though this was, it also constituted a security risk because the water could easily be poisoned at source. To safeguard against this, the conduit heads were built very solidly, with thick walls and double locking doors, and thistles and thorns were planted around them.[36] The king also took over the ownership of the land where the conduits lay.

The water did not just supply the kitchens, but also provided running water to the royal bathrooms, courtier lodgings and many household offices. The overflow from the cisterns was used to supply fountains, moats and fishponds, as well as to carry sewage away from the Great House of Easement. In order to keep this remarkable system working effectively, Henry employed a man to clean out all the sinks and drains in the royal palaces periodically and others to clean out the moats.

Henry's officials tried to attain high standards of hygiene in the royal kitchens. After each meal, every pot, pan, dish, glass and spit would be cleaned and scoured ready for reuse. Large kettles would be filled with water and set over the fire to boil. Alkaline lye made from wood ashes would be added to the water, or for more stubborn stains fine sand imported from Calais would be rubbed on with cloths.

One of the leading culinary experts of the day, Andrew Borde, advised: 'Of all things, let the buttery, the cellar, the kitchen, the larder-house, with all other houses of offices be kept clean.'[37] When Cardinal Wolsey discovered that some scullions were going about their duties 'naked, or in garments of vileness as they now do' (presumably because of the intense heat of the kitchens), he was horrified. An allowance was promptly given to the Clerk of the Kitchen to buy 'honest and whole garments' for his staff 'for the better avoiding of corruption and all uncleanness out of the King's house, which doth engender danger of infection and is very noisome and displeasant.' It was also expressly forbidden to 'piss' in the cooking hearths.[38]

But despite the best efforts of Wolsey and his fellow officials, the royal kitchens were hardly models of cleanliness. The overpowering heat from the ovens and fires and the constant press of bodies made for uncomfortable, sweaty conditions. A contemporary audit noted that the spitboys could not avoid 'interlarding their own grease to help the drippings'.[39] The kitchens were also overrun by dogs, cats and rats, which were undeterred by the many attempts to shoo them away with whips and bells.

Alexander Barclay, a monk who visited court early in the reign, was shocked by the laxity that existed below stairs. Having spent time among the royal servants, he thought them lazy and ill-behaved, and when he was obliged to share sleeping quarters with them, he was appalled:

It is great sorrow for to abide their shout,
Some fart, some flingeth, and other snort and rout;
Some buck and some babble, some cometh drunk to bed,
Some brawl and some jangle, when they be beastly fed;
Some spew and some piss, not one of them is still.
Never be they still till middle of the night,
And then some brawleth, and for their beds fight.[40]

Although he had a love of fine food, Henry did not like to linger over his meals, particularly during the first half of his reign, when he was impatient to be hunting, jousting, playing tennis or pursuing some other physical pastime. When the king was able to dine in his private apartments, this took up considerably less time than the formal court feasts, which could be of several hours' duration. Describing his first (brief) audience with the king at a dinner in September 1529, the Imperial ambassador Eustace Chapuys noted that Henry had been in a rush to finish his meal before resuming hunting and hawking for the afternoon.

For all his youthful exuberance, Henry did engage in a number of more sedate pastimes during his private hours. Renowned for his piety, he spent a significant part of every day in worship. The Venetian ambassador, Sebastian Giustinian, reported during his visit to the court in 1519 that the young English king was 'very religious' and noted: 'he hears three masses daily when he hunts and sometimes five on other days'.[41] His piety was something that Henry shared with his wife, Catherine, and he would attend two of the masses each day in her own private chapel.

Henry also had an oratory or 'privy closet' in his own apartments, in which he could perform his private devotions. Situated between his privy and presence chambers, this would contain a space for the king to kneel at a 'desk' or lectern, divided by a partition with a latticed opening from a slightly larger space to accommodate an altar and the chaplain. These private chapels were much smaller and more simply appointed than the 'holyday' or 'great' closets that divided the royal family from the main body of the public chapels in their palaces. In the latter, the king and queen would hear mass, sometimes in the company of important guests, such as visiting ambassadors. The holyday closets would therefore be lavishly decorated with ornate floors and ceilings, sumptuous furnishings and vestments, and glazed windows bearing the royal coats of arms and badges. The comparative privacy that they offered from the rest of the chapel also enabled the occupants to discuss confidential matters undisturbed while the service proceeded.

The king worshipped more in private than in public, but he would attend mass in the main chapel on Sundays and at certain key religious festivals, such as Christmas, Easter, Candlemas and numerous other feasts. On the more important of these dates, the king would wear purple, and the feast of Epiphany was considered so significant that it was also an occasion for 'crownwearing'. Although he would later institute a radical reform of religious practice in his kingdom, Henry was personally conservative and continued to observe the strict order of ceremony at all of the major services. For example, at Easter he would creep across the chapel on his knees to adore the cross. He also continued the tradition of touching for the 'king's evil' and blessing cramp rings, which were believed to cure epilepsy and muscle pains. Both ceremonies were designed to provide tangible proof of the divine nature of royal power.

Inspired with a love of learning in his youth, by the time that he came to the throne Henry was extremely well read and his private library was filled with classical and theological texts from across the world. He always took a selection of these with him on his regular removes between palaces. On one occasion, his coffers included four books in French, three in English, a religious treatise, 'a book of the Bible set forth with pictures' and 'one image of the crucifix in a case'. Henry also had a private interest in topography, and an inventory of his personal possessions includes a 'Mappa Mundi in parchment'. In addition, there was 'a purse of needlework containing table men of bone', which may have been a miniature chess set.[42]

Every so often, the king would take a bath in his private apartments. It is difficult to determine how frequent such occasions were, but the leading physicians of the age cautioned against regular bathing in hot water because it opened the pores and allowed deadly diseases such as the plague, sweating sickness and smallpox to enter the body. In his treatise, *This is the Myrrour or Glasse of Helth*, Thomas Moulton advised: 'Use no baths or stoves; nor sweat too much, for all openeth the pores of a man's body and maketh the venomous air to enter and for to infect the blood.'[43] Instead, cold water was to be used for washing the hands and face first thing in the morning and before and after every meal, in order to cleanse off any surface dirt.

Even if Henry's baths were infrequent, they were, predictably, luxurious. At Richmond and Whitehall, Henry had steam baths installed, and fragments of the latter are still preserved in the archaeological stores at Hampton Court Palace. These baths were rectangular in shape and sunk into the floor. The courtiers, meanwhile, had to make do with movable tubs that were brought into their rooms when required and set up in front of the fire.

The king was attended by his gentlemen throughout his bathing ritual. He did not enter the water naked but would wear a linen shirt or shift. A set of accounts for Henry's household reveals that he had a set of specially made bathing clothes, including 'slops' (loose-fitting smocks) and coifs.[44]

Sometimes hot stones were placed underneath the linen sheets lining the royal bathtub, along with cinnamon, cumin, mint or liquorice, to make a fragrant steam bath. The herbs were important because just as it was believed that evil airs could enter the body through open pores, so too could beneficial ones. Rosemary was thought to stimulate the brain and sharpen the memory, which is why Thomas More had a hedge of it planted underneath the window of his study. It was used in all of the most important church services: at marriages to remind the bride of her vows, at christenings to ensure that the godparents retained the promises they made on the child's behalf, and at funerals to help people remember the dead. Lavender, meanwhile, was understood to have calming and cooling properties. It would often be hung in bunches on bedsteads, or gathered in small bags and placed among the bedlinen. For the daytime, marjoram was a popular scent because it was believed to induce a 'merry' state of mind.

The royals and their nobles preferred to wash with flower-scented water rather than soap. The latter was made from tallow or whale oil and potash, which was too coarse and foul-smelling for them and was therefore used primarily by the labouring classes. This meant, however, that body odour needed to be tackled by other means, and perfume was popular. A contemporary treatise on health and hygiene advised: 'It is useful to press and rub the skin with a compound of roses.'[45] Perfumes made from essential oils were widely used to make oneself, and one's environment, as sweet-smelling as possible. In the early Tudor period, only members of the highest elite could afford such a luxury. Henry VIII and his household made regular use of rose oil, both for its appealing scent and for the fact that the rose was the symbol of the Tudor dynasty. Rose oil applied directly to the skin emitted such a heady aroma that it was believed to be an aphrodisiac. Another popular device for masking unpleasant aromas was the pomander, a small decorative perforated container that could be filled with fragrant herbs, scents and spices. It would be worn by male and female courtiers alike. After bathing, the king would be rubbed down with linen cloths and anointed with perfumed oil.

There are many myths surrounding the issue of personal hygiene in Tudor times. The generally accepted wisdom is that the vast majority of people – from the king down to his humblest subject – washed and bathed so infrequently that they stank to high heaven. This is only partially true. Personal hygiene and cleanliness were very important to the Tudor monarchs and their courtiers. In order to be considered respectable, one had to smell 'sweet', which meant that body odour was something to be dealt with, rather than ignored. Not only did this distinguish them from the poorer, working classes, but it made for a more pleasant existence at court, where hundreds of bodies were crammed up against each other. It was also essential for creating a good first impression for visitors, particularly those from rival courts overseas.

Because of the perils involved in bathing, people focused upon keeping their clothes clean, rather than their bodies. Underclothes would be changed and cleaned regularly because this was regarded as essential for good health. Wool, silk and leather were generally reserved for the outer layers of clothing because they were difficult to clean, and linen was recommended for garments that were in direct contact with the skin because it was so absorbent that it drew the sweat, grease and dirt from the body. Linen clothes included shirts, smocks, under-breeches, hose, ruffs, cuffs, coifs and caps. These items would be then changed or 'shifted' regularly by the king's servants and sent to be washed thoroughly. That the body odour was transferred from the skin to these undergarments is testified to by Shakespeare's *The Merry Wives of Windsor*. Falstaff hides in a laundry basket filled with 'foul shirts and smocks, socks, foul stockings, greasy napkins' and complains of the 'rankest compound of villainous smell that ever offended nostril.'[46] An early seventeenth-century verse, *In Praise of Cleane Linen*, neatly summarised the benefits of 'sweet and neat' linen, without which 'thou would'st stink above ground like a beast'.[47] The richer you were, the more often you would change your underwear during the course of a day, and – according to the accepted theory – the more healthy you would be.

Most ordinary people owned two or three sets of linen underwear, but members of the royal family had dozens of undershirts and would change several times a day. Their highest-ranking courtiers would have a similarly well-stocked linen cupboard and would change at least once a day. On average, each courtier would have about a week's worth of linen with them.

A courtier's outer garments were never washed because they were made from natural dyes and fabrics, and were covered with elaborate embellishments that were too delicate for being immersed in water and scrubbed. Odour, cleanliness and pests were therefore an issue, especially with heavy materials such as wool and furs. The latter were popular for practical as well as aesthetic reasons, given that they helped keep out the chill in the draughty royal palaces. A sumptuary law passed in 1532 dictated that the royal family alone could wear sable, but they and their nobles also favoured ermine and rabbit. Squirrel, lamb and even wolfskin could also be used. Henry VIII always wore a small piece of fur next to his skin in order to lure the parasites away from his body.

The Tudors tackled the challenge of keeping outer clothes clean and fresh in a number of ways. Sweet powders made from fragrant plants and herbs such as dried rose petals and lavender would be put into silk bags to lay between or within garments when they were stored. Perfume was also used to keep outer clothes smelling fragrant. The officials of the wardrobe were supplied with scent by the royal apothecary so 'that the Kings robes, doublets, sheets and shirts be fumed.'[48] While the clothes were in storage, it was the responsibility of the officers of the wardrobe to regularly check them for damp, mildew, dust, mice and moths. The yeoman of the robes was also required to light fires in the stores to air the clothes and to prevent damp.

The only way to clean an outer garment was to brush it, but this was not effective at removing every stain. Skilled royal laundresses would therefore carry out careful spot cleaning with special treatments. These included alkaline lye and lime-based buffering agents, acidic lemon juice, wetting agents such as ox gall, absorbents such as fuller's earth, and dispersants such as alcohol and egg-white.[49] When gowns, doublets and other outer garments became too malodorous with sweat and stains, the royal tailor would replace their linings. This was known as 'freshening'.

Accessories could be just as challenging to keep clean as outer garments. Leather gloves were an object of refinement that protected the wearer from dirt when riding or undertaking other outdoor pursuits, but if they became soiled (as inevitably happened) then they were extremely difficult to clean. The gloves worn by royalty and the richer members of their court were made from kid leather and were often heavily embellished with embroidery and spangles. Contemporary guidance recommended a painstaking procedure for keeping gloves in mint condition. They were to be treated with oil of jessamine and ambergris (wax) before being cleaned with a little malmsey wine and rubbed with grease such as cypress, pomade, or oil of cedar. Finally, they should be scented with grains of must, cinnamon, cloves, nutmeg, oil of lemon and civet or with water of orange flowers and musk rose.[50] Part of the status involved in wearing such high-value items was that only the very richest members of society could afford to have them looked after in this way.

The king and his court were always accompanied by a legion of laundresses and seamstresses to wash, sort and mend the linen that was worn and used by its occupants. When a king was in power, roles for women at court were limited, and royal laundresses tended to be the only permanent female members of the king's household. Given that they were directly responsible for the monarch's underwear and other linens, they were required to be women of proven discretion and trustworthiness.

Only very few of their names are recorded in the contemporary sources. Henry VIII's laundress, Anne Harris, is cited most frequently. A set of court ordinances specified her duties very precisely: 'The said Anne [Harris] shall weekly wash 7 long Breakfast clothes, 7 short ones, 8 Towels, 3 dozen of Napkins, and Pieces as need shall require; and by the same shall deliver as much . . . as shall be necessary to serve the King's Majesty.' Anne was also required to 'provide as much sweet Powder, sweet Herbs, and other sweet things, as shall be necessary to be occupied for the sweet keeping of the said stuff.'[51]

For the most part, though, the royal laundresses moved about court in as unobtrusive a way as possible, discreetly delivering their carefully wrapped bundles to the attendants of the king and his highest-ranking noblemen. The care that they took over their work was impressive. All whites were boiled to get them clean, and items such as linen 'smothers' and small irons were used to press and then pleat linens. The laundresses were also provided with a 'chafer', an ash bag and a pewter basin in which to starch some of the linens.

The majority of washing took place outdoors, where there were plentiful supplies of water and enough space to lay the linens out to dry and be naturally bleached by the sun during the summer, or hung next to braziers in winter. As a result, very little archaeological evidence remains, which means that it has often been an overlooked activity within the royal palaces. Although the laundering of the court linen would have taken place away from the immediate view of the palace, it would not have been so far as to make the task of carrying it back and forth too onerous. But the highest-status laundry, such as the underclothes worn by the king and his family, was washed, dried and ironed separately – probably inside the palaces, for the sake of discretion. The household accounts include receipts for wooden tubs 'occupied within the gallery [at Whitehall Palace] to wash the king's clothes in.'[52]

An indication of the sheer scale of the laundry operation at a royal palace is provided by looking at the allocation of table linen to one of the laundresses. She was issued with four table cloths, fifty-six breakfast cloths, twenty-eight hand towels and twelve dozen napkins, and was expected to clean a quarter of this linen every week. She would deliver it to 'the Serjeant or Yeoman of the King's Mouth' in order that the king be provided with a sufficient rotation of clean table linen. The same laundress would also be allocated a set number of his undergarments, although the details of these are not specified in the accounts.[53]

Unlikely though it seems, the practice of washing one's clothes rather than oneself actually worked. Linen was extraordinarily effective at cleansing the skin, so, provided the underclothes were washed regularly, people would have been free from body odour.[54] So effective was linen in keeping the skin clean and healthy that people often kept pieces of it to rub themselves down with each morning. The respected scholar and diplomat, Sir Thomas Elyot, advised his readers to 'rub the body with a coarse linen cloth, first softly and easily, and after to increase more and more, to a hard and swift rubbing, until the flesh do swell, and be somewhat ruddy.'[55] This ritual – a precursor to exfoliation, perhaps – was believed to transfer the toxins from the body to the linen cloth, which would then be thoroughly washed before the next rub-down.

While the rest of the court had to be content with using communal toilets, such as the 'Great House of Easement' at Hampton Court (which boasted an impressive twenty-eight seats), Henry had his own private close-stool in each palace. His 'stool chambers' at Greenwich and Hampton Court were kitted out with pictures and bookshelves to keep the king amused during the long hours that he spent there.

In order to ensure the king's comfort, as well as to display his magnificence even in this most private of rooms, a series of lavish close-stools was crafted for him. Made from pewter, they were covered in embroidered velvet, stuffed with swans' down and studded with gilt nails. When Henry went on progress, similarly luxurious close-stools would be constructed at each house that he stayed in and reserved for his sole use. This reinforced both the status of the king and the extreme privacy with which he expected to carry out his evacuations. It also reinforced the status of the groom of the stool as the only person privileged enough to attend his sovereign during these times.

Whenever the king left his privy chamber – after bathing, attending the close-stool, sleeping or enjoying some leisure – his attendants there would stay behind to guard it. He would often be gone for the whole day, particularly during the earlier years of the reign when hunting was his abiding passion. The privy chamber staff would while away the hours playing cards and dice, but even this 'leisure' time was directed by the rules of court. They must be 'loving together, and not to tattle about such things as may be done or said when the King goes forth.' Neither were they permitted to gossip or speculate about what their royal master was doing: 'They must leave enquiry where the King is or goeth, not grudging, mumbling or talking of the King's pastime, late or early going to bed, or anything done by His Grace.'[56]

With the onset of evening, the staff would busy themselves preparing for the ceremony of putting the king to bed, which was no less elaborate than his morning routine. His bed was stripped as soon as he got up each morning and would be left airing all day. It would then be prepared by no fewer than ten of his privy chamber staff. A groom would collect clean linen, pillows and blankets from the wardrobe of the beds. He would then stand at the end of the bed holding a torch while eight yeomen of the chamber and ward-robe lined up, four at each side of the bed. A gentleman usher would take charge of checking the bed for any hidden assassin, looking on as a yeoman thrust a dagger into the straw of the bottom mattress. The usher would make sure that the king's sword was hung within reach of the bed and that a poleaxe was also to hand, in case the king was attacked during the night.

A canvas cover would then be placed on the mattress, followed by a cover stuffed with down. A yeoman would 'roll up and down' it to ensure that no weapons were hidden inside. Only then could the bed be made up with the fine linen sheets, blankets, counter-point, bolster and pillows. With great reverence, each yeoman made the sign of the cross over the bed, kissed the places where he had touched it and sprinkled them with holy water.[57] The curtains were then drawn around the bed and a mantle of crimson velvet lined with ermine was laid out next to it, ready for the king to put on as soon as he got up the next morning. A 'nightstool and urinal' (a kind of chamber pot) would be placed within easy reach in case the king needed it during the night.

While the other attendants withdrew, the groom would remain kneeling by the bed so that he could guard it until the king arrived. This could be several hours later. Henry rarely retired before midnight, 'which is our accustomed hour to go to bed'.[58] An elaborate ceremony of disrobing began as soon as he stepped foot into the bedchamber. His gentlemen and esquires of the body would carefully untie, unbuckle and remove every item of clothing and then put on his nightgown, which was usually made of fine white linen or silk. Another attendant would bring a basin of water and a cloth so that he could wash his face and clean his teeth. The king's body servants would then comb his hair and cover it with a 'night-bonnet' of scarlet or black embroidered velvet before helping him into bed and lighting a candle next to it.

Their work complete, all but one of the privy chamber attendants bowed low and backed out of the room, leaving their royal master to his rest. The remaining gentleman would sleep on the pallet at the foot of the bed or sometimes even in the king's bed itself. Meanwhile, two yeomen of the chamber would sleep on pallet beds outside the door of the bedchamber, and two esquires of the body would sleep nearby in the pallet chamber. Beyond this private suite of rooms, the night watch of the yeoman of the guard would come on duty in the presence chamber and remain vigilant throughout the night for unwanted visitors, intruders or smells of burning – fire being an ever-present risk.

Every detail of this protracted routine would be observed each night without fail. It only differed when Henry chose to visit his wife. On such occasions, he would summon his grooms of the chamber, who would dress him in his nightrobe and escort him with lighted torches to the door of the queen's bedchamber. The king would rarely spend the night. Rather, his grooms would wait outside the door until their master was ready to return to bed. Such a lack of privacy for the king's conjugal visits, with all of the elaborate ceremony that surrounded them, was hardly conducive to spontaneous passion. But it was entirely acceptable to the royal couple and their court. After all, the begetting of heirs was a matter of intense public interest – as the queen knew only too well.

6

'She excelled them all'

I N 1523, THE thirty-seven-year-old queen was reported to be 'beyond the ways of women'. This was a euphemism for the menopause. That she had failed to give Henry the living son he craved was a source of intense sorrow to Catherine, made all the more acute by the fact that her husband was still busy siring children with his mistresses.

It could have been as early as 1520 that the elder of Thomas Boleyn's two daughters became the king's latest mistress. A combination of shrewd political acumen and advantageous marriages had transformed the Boleyn family from relatively obscure tenant farmers into titled gentry with a presence at court. Thomas's marriage to Elizabeth, daughter of the second Duke of Norfolk, had served him well, both politically and dynastically. She had given him the vital son, George, to carry on the family line, as well as two daughters, Mary and Anne, who might prove useful in the marriage market.

Born in 1499, Mary, like her sister Anne, had served in the household of the king's sister, Mary, during her short-lived marriage to King Louis XII of France, and had then transferred her service to Claude, wife of the new king, Francis I. Between that time and her return to England in around 1519, she acquired a dubious reputation and had almost certainly been the French king's mistress for a time. It may have been to salvage his eldest daughter's reputation that Thomas Boleyn recalled her to England and secured her a place in Catherine of Aragon's household. In February 1520, she was married to William Carey, a gentleman of the privy chamber. Henry VIII was the principal guest at the wedding and provided the newlyweds with rooms at court, close to his own.

Mary probably accompanied the court to France for the Field of Cloth of Gold – a lavish and ostentatious meeting between Henry VIII and his great rival, Francis I, held in June 1520. There is no evidence that she was yet Henry's mistress, however. The first hint that their liaison had begun was a series of royal grants made to her husband in the early months of 1522. There has been speculation that Mary was the lady for whom Henry jousted at the tournament held in honour of the Imperial ambassadors on 2 March 1522. The king rode a horse in silver caparisons embroidered with a wounded heart and the motto 'Elle mon coeur a navera' ('She has wounded my heart'). A few days later, Mary took part in a masque about the assault on the 'Château Vert'. The ladies wore white satin gowns and bonnets of gold, encrusted with gems and embroidered with their names. Mary featured as 'Kindness', and her sister Anne, who had recently returned from France, appeared (appropriately enough) as Perseverance.

Henry's affair with Mary was almost certainly under way by this time, and in around 1523, she gave birth to her first child, Catherine, who was generally acknowledged to be the king's rather than her husband's. The latter received a number of royal grants during the following two years, which may have been intended as some form of compensation. The paternity of Mary's second child, Henry, is more doubtful. He was born in March 1526, by which time his mother's affair with the king was almost certainly over. Inevitably, there were rumours that Henry had fathered another bastard son, but most of these were put about several years later.

Ignoring her husband's dalliances with queenly decorum, Catherine focused her attentions on their daughter, Mary, who was rapidly growing into an accomplished young princess. Although she had been raised within a predominantly female household, Mary was taught by men and benefited from a cutting-edge Renaissance education. This was dominated by the ideas of the Spanish humanist Juan Luis Vives, who was commissioned by Mary's mother to write *The Education of a Christian Woman*. 'Daughters', he opined, 'should be handled without any cherishing. For cherishing mars the sons but utterly destroys the daughters.'[1] He also taught that the purpose of a woman's education was to serve as her husband's companion, which was vital to the state. It was hardly an outlook to encourage independence and confidence in the young princess, but it was one that her mother entirely espoused.

As well as languages, religious instruction and classics, Mary was taught the courtly refinements of music and dancing, and it was in these that she particularly excelled. At the age of two, she made a visit to court and heard the Venetian organist, Dionysius Memo, playing for her father's guests. She was so delighted with his performance that when it had ended she ran after him calling for him to play some more. By the age of four, she could play the virginals, and she later learned the lute and regal (a kind of organ).

The Tudors set great store by physical exercise as part of a child's upbringing, appreciating that it was beneficial to health and helped ward off sickness. It was agreed that 'at seasons convenient, [Mary is] to use moderate exercise for taking open air in gardens, sweet and wholesome places and walks which may confer unto her health, solace and comfort.'² She was taught to ride from infancy, kept a pack of hounds and also enjoyed hawking.

At the age of nine, Mary was sent to Wales to continue her education. She was accompanied by her schoolmaster, Dr Richard Fetherstone, and her chaplain, Henry Rowle, and was established at Ludlow Castle with an impressive 300-strong household. By this time, she could already write in Latin and may well have been guided in this by the distinguished Oxford scholar and humanist, Thomas Linacre. But as well as her studies, Mary was given responsibility by her father for presiding over the Council of Wales and the Marches. This was largely symbolic – a nine-year-old girl could hardly be expected to take on the full scope of this role – but the fact that she was also accorded many of the other royal prerogatives normally reserved for a prince of Wales suggests that her father was beginning to resign himself to the fact that she might be his sole legitimate heir.

At the same time, the king was showing his bastard son great honour – so much so that it was rumoured he intended to make him his heir. In June 1525, Henry raised the six-year-old-boy to the peerage as 'right high and noble prince Henry, Duke of Richmond and Somerset'. He subsequently fêted his son at court, laying on lavish entertainments and feasts. The records of the royal kitchens reveal the extraordinarily rich diet to which the new duke was treated. One meal comprised a first course of pottage, boiled meat, beef and mutton, four green geese, three roast capons, a quarter of roast veal, and custard; and a second course of half a lamb, six rabbits, fourteen pigeons, one wildfowl, a tart, trenchers, four gallons of ale, two pitchers of wine and a selection of fruits. For all his indulgence, however, the king knew that his subjects would never accept FitzRoy as a legitimate heir. Even the prospect of his daughter Mary becoming queen regnant was better than a royal bastard on the throne.

Frustrated by his seemingly irresolvable dynastic problems, Henry increasingly sought diversions at court to help him forget them. Now in his early thirties, he still retained the physical vigour of his youth and would spend several hours a day hunting, shooting and pursuing other sporting activities. Sir William Kingston, who was a regular at Henry's court, observed that even after more than twenty years on the throne: 'The king hawks every day with goshawks and others . . . both before noon and after.'[3] Henry's regular companion in the joust was Charles Brandon, Duke of Suffolk. Despite being friends, the two men were fiercely competitive. In 1524, for example, Henry rode out with his visor raised and, rather than warning him, the duke rode at full pace and struck his opponent above the right brow. A couple of inches lower and Henry would have lost an eye. The king, who thrived on the danger of the sport, bore him no malice.

As well as being Henry's most intimate friend, Brandon was also his brother-in-law, having married the king's beautiful younger sister Mary without his permission. It is a testament to his favour with Henry that Brandon had emerged unscathed from this scandal and had been quickly forgiven. With his increasingly stout physique and full beard, Brandon resembled the king more than ever. On one occasion, at the Christmas celebrations of 1524, the two men even appeared at court wearing identical clothes – a singular honour for Brandon.

Bowling was another popular pastime. Like archery, it was practised by all classes across the kingdom, from village alehouses to the specially commissioned bowling alleys that became a fashionable feature of palaces and stately homes. When Henry VIII acquired Cardinal Wolsey's lavish palace of Hampton Court, he immediately set about enhancing its sporting facilities, including the addition of a bowling alley.

Henry had inherited his father's love of tennis and would play it most afternoons. Having been tutored in his early youth by specially appointed coaches, it was a sport at which he excelled. The Venetian ambassador was impressed by his prowess and observed: 'It is the prettiest thing in the world to see him play, his fair skin glowing through a shirt of the finest texture.'[4] The king took great pride in being dressed for the occasion, whether that was a tennis match or an ambassadorial reception. His wardrobe accounts from 1517 include a close-fitting black and blue velvet coat that was intended as an outfit for the game. During the 1520s, he abandoned his tennis coats in favour of crimson satin doublets, which presumably enabled him to move around the court with greater ease. Henry also had special tennis shoes made.

Formal tennis courts were the preserve of the wealthy, which made the sport itself rather elitist. More popular among the lower classes was football – or 'camping', as it was sometimes known. In stark contrast to tennis, the early forms of this game were lacking in rules, which led to brawls and other bad behaviour during matches. Thomas Elyot denounced it as entirely unsuitable for gentlemen, 'wherein is nothing but beastly fury and extreme violence, whereof proceedeth hurt.'[5] Nevertheless, the king himself was not averse to the occasional game and had a pair of football shoes made, even though he hardly played often enough to justify the expense.

Sport dominated Henry's possessions. His jewel house at Hampton Court included a set of pewter weights 'to exercise a man's arms'. At the same palace, his private closet, next to the privy chamber, was decorated with numerous hunting trophies (including heads and tusks) and elaborate falcon hoods. His closet at Greenwich, meanwhile, contained the king's tennis rackets.[6]

Together with his coterie of irrepressible young favourites, Henry threw himself into the pursuit of pleasure in all its forms, and on one occasion even entered a snowball fight. Another pastime favoured by the king and his companions was cock-fighting. He had a purpose-built cock-fighting ring installed at Whitehall Palace so that he could enjoy this bloody spectator sport whenever he pleased. The audience would watch a host of fights in quick succession and would gamble large sums on the outcome. Bull- and bear-baiting were also popular blood sports in Tudor times, and Henry enjoyed both.

Huge sums could be won and lost on the outcome of these grisly spectacles. The Tudors loved to gamble, and Henry was no exception. As well as betting on spectator sports, he was very fond of playing cards and board games such as dominoes. The privy purse records from January 1530 include a staggering £450 (equivalent to £145,000 today) lost by the king in a single game of dominoes. Although it must have taken a brave man to beat Henry, a further £100 was spent on honouring his losses at cards to various gentlemen of the privy chamber. Henry's luck had improved little two years later, when he lost £45 at 'shovelboard', a game that involved sliding small coins across a table towards marked targets and knocking the coins of one's opponents out of the way in the process. Ironically, this same game had been deemed unlawful by Henry's government because it had become such an obsession that it was tempting men away from their archery practice.

Interestingly, it was not just gentlemen of status who enjoyed the privilege of playing cards with the king. Richard Hill, the sergeant of the cellar, was a frequent gambling partner of Henry between the years 1527 and 1539. Indeed, the Tudor monarchs had a very different relationship with their lowlier servants than the traditional 'upstairs downstairs' approach of the Victorian era. Far from being invisible and ignored, the below-stairs staff could expect to be regularly noticed by the king and his family, who might engage them in conversation, involve them in games or other pastimes, and reward them with gifts and other honours.

Working as a servant in the royal household also offered excellent long-term security. Even though the Tudor monarchs ran short of money from time to time, it was vital to uphold the magnificence of their court to the outside world, so the size of their household was never reduced. If a servant performed well, they could expect to work in the royal household for life, and to secure jobs for their children and other family members. If they fell sick, they were paid board wages, and they would be supported during long-term illness or old age. The prospects for promotion were also excellent for those who proved their competence. Sir John Gage, for example, held the posts of esquire of the body, controller, vice chamberlain and Lord Chamberlain under Henry VII and Henry VIII, and although his son entered the royal household as a lowly groom during the latter's reign, by the time that his successor was crowned he had risen to master of the household.

Henry VIII loved to dance and, as with most other physical activities, he excelled at it. A waspish ambassador from Spain described his efforts as 'prancing', but everyone else who saw the king in action eulogised about his ability. The Venetian ambassador remarked that Henry had 'acquitted himself divinely', and the Milanese envoy was astonished by the fact that 'he does wonders and leaps like a stag'.[7] On the latter occasion, Henry may have been performing the tourdion – a dance that comprised four high leaps and a cadence where the dancer landed on both feet. There was no pause in between leaps, so it required a high level of fitness. To enable one to catch one's breath, it was often interspersed with the more sedate *basse danse*, in which partners move quietly and gracefully in a slow gliding or walking motion without leaving the floor.

During the early years of his reign, Henry was partnered by his favourite sister, Mary, whose 'deportment in dancing is as pleasing as you would desire.'[8] His wife Catherine was more reserved and preferred to practise her steps in the privacy of her rooms, with just a few ladies for company. Her frequent pregnancies also excused her apparent reticence to take part. But this left the way open for the graceful and self-confident beauties of court to show off their prowess on the public stage – and in so doing catch her husband's eye.

Like his father, Henry enjoyed the spectacle of theatre. Mystery plays were still popular during the earlier part of his reign, but as the Reformist ideas began to spread from the Continent, these moralising religious tales were gradually eclipsed by secular themes. So fond was Henry of the performances that took place regularly at his court that he employed four professional actors and their boy apprentice as part of his household.

Another member of Henry's entourage who was employed for the business of entertaining the king was his fool. Henry had had a fool as part of his household from the age of ten, when 'John Goose my lord of York's fool' is listed in the accounts.[9] Now that he was king, it was natural that he should wish to retain such a person for his entertainment. Moreover, 'mirth' and laughter were considered essential for well-being, which was an important consideration for this health-conscious king.

By far the most famous of Henry's fools is William (Will) Somer.[10] Far from being skilled performers who acted the fool in order to earn a laugh, most court fools in the early Tudor period were 'natural fools', or people with learning disabilities. This was the case with Will, who had a keeper appointed to care for him. Natural fools were defined as being 'abortive of wit, where Nature had more power than reason', and were either incapable or insensible of their actions.[11] The Tudors had an ambiguous attitude towards people with mental disabilities. They had traditionally been objects of fear and derision, and their disabilities were interpreted as a sign of sinfulness. This made them susceptible to ill treatment and stigmatisation. But Erasmus's The Praise of Folly (1511) presented an alternative view. Drawing on the writings of St Paul, that 'all men were fools before God, and the foolishness of God was wiser than men's wisdom', he argued that fools possessed an essential goodness and simplicity that meant they were incapable of sin and closer to God. Erasmus's work was very influential at the Tudor court, which is perhaps why the 'fools' there were shown great favour, given rich clothing and allowed to spend many private hours with the king.

The date of Somer's birth is not known because he was of obscure origins, but he was probably younger than his sovereign. The first reference to him in Henry's service is dated 28 June 1535. The image of Somer as a witty adviser who regularly challenged the excesses of his royal master owes more to plays penned after his death, such as Thomas Nashe's *Summer's Last Will and Testament* (1592). If he was not a traditional fool, then he appealed to Henry in other ways because he rapidly become one of the most trusted and favoured members of the court, spending more time with the king than even some of his highest-ranking courtiers. He certainly played a prominent role in the entertainments at Henry's court and is most often mentioned in connection with a group of royal musicians. There are numerous records of gifts of clothing presented to Somer, especially for ceremonial and masquing events. He was provided with a royal livery to wear at court, and with lavish costumes for disguisings.

Court jesters were allowed to show greater familiarity towards the king and his ministers than most other members of the court. 'They can speak truth and even open insults and be heard with positive pleasure,' observed Erasmus. 'Indeed, the words that would cost a wise man his life are surprisingly enjoyable when uttered by a clown.'[12] As Henry's reign progressed and he became increasingly weighed down by affairs of state, Will Somer provided much-needed light relief.

A painting of the royal family that was completed ten years after Somer first appeared at court reflects his position as favoured royal retainer. He is one of two figures that flank Henry VIII and his family, and is shown in an archway at the extreme right of the painting. A pet monkey is perched on his shoulder – one of the animated props favoured by court fools. An even more vivid depiction of Somer is contained in a psalter presented to Henry in 1540. The illustration refers to a verse from Psalm 52: '*Dixit insipiens in corde suo non est Deus*' ('The fool has said in his heart there is no God'). Henry is depicted as the psalmist David, while Somer is shown as a stocky man, dressed in a green knee-length coat and wearing a purse at his belt. His hair is short-cropped or shaved, as most fools wore it, his hands are clasped in front of him, and his eyes stare out rather anxiously. His shoulders are raised and perhaps slightly deformed.

Many of the leading households of the realm also retained a fool for their entertainment. One of the most renowned was a man named Sexton, also known as Patch, who became famous for his witty and nonsensical jests. He was in the service of the king's chief minister, Wolsey, and probably entertained Henry himself during his visits to the cardinal's various palaces. When Wolsey later fell from grace, he gave Patch to the king in an attempt to win back his favour.

For all of the entertainments that occupied the king's private hours during the 1520s, by the middle of that decade he had found a new diversion. The birth of the woman who would become the scandal of Christendom was of so little concern that its date was not even recorded. It is now generally accepted as having been around 1500 or 1501.[13] The second daughter of Thomas Boleyn, Anne soon emerged as the more intelligent of the two girls. Her father noted that she was exceptionally 'toward' and resolved to take 'all possible care for her good education'. This education included a good deal more than the cursory studies usually afforded to a young woman of gentry stock. When she was probably no more than eleven years old, Anne left England to take up a position in the most sophisticated court in Europe: that of Margaret of Austria, Regent of the Netherlands, to which country Thomas Boleyn had just been appointed ambassador. By all accounts, Margaret was delighted with Anne, and wrote how 'bright and pleasant' she was for her young age.

But it was in France that Anne's education in court life reached its zenith, and her experiences there would have a profound effect upon her character and demeanour. Like her sister Mary, she was appointed to the household of Henry VIII's sister upon her marriage to the King of France and stayed on to serve the new queen, Claude. In stark contrast to her sister, Anne preferred the cultural and intellectual diversions of this dazzling court and earned a reputation as one of the most graceful and accomplished ladies of the queen's household.

So entirely did Anne embrace the French manners, language and customs that the court poet, Lancelot de Carles, observed: 'She became so graceful that you would never have taken her for an Englishwoman, but for a French woman born.'[14] Anne was particularly admired for her exquisite taste and the elegance of her dress, earning her the praise of Pierre de Brantôme, a seasoned courtier, who noted that all the fashionable ladies at court tried to emulate her style, but that she possessed a 'gracefulness that rivalled Venus'. She was, he concluded, 'the fairest and most bewitching of all the lovely dames of the French court.'[15]

By the time that Anne returned to England in 1522, she had blossomed into an attractive young woman. Her slim, petite stature gave her an appealing fragility, and she had luscious dark brown hair, which she grew very long. Her most striking features, though, were her eyes, which were exceptionally dark and seductive, 'inviting conversation'.

But Anne was by no means a conventional beauty. 'Madam Anne is not one of the handsomest women in the world,' observed the Venetian ambassador, who was clearly at a loss as to why men found her so attractive. 'She is of middling stature, swarthy complexion, long neck, wide mouth, bosom not much raised, and in fact has nothing but the English King's great appetite, and her eyes, which are black and beautiful, and take great effect on those who served the Queen when she was on the throne.'[16] Although Anne was known to be rather flat-chested, the reference to her bosom being 'not much raised' may have been more to do with the fashions of the day. The ideal Tudor woman would have a soft décolletage, as depicted in Holbein's portraits of prominent court ladies. The boning in a bodice ended below the line of the bust in order to suppress, rather than enhance the cleavage. The fastenings would be at the back or sides, which would have the effect of drawing the bust down and not pushing it up.[17] Anne also had a large Adam's apple 'like a man's' and, most famously, the appearance of a sixth finger on one of her hands.[18]

Anne's greatest assets were her personal charisma, style and grace, rather than her physical appearance. Among her many admirers was the (married) poet Thomas Wyatt, who observed that Anne's looks 'appeared much more excellent by her favour passing sweet and cheerful; and . . . also increased by her noble presence of shape and fashion, representing both mildness and majesty more than can be expressed.'[19] Her allure, honed to perfection at one of the most sophisticated courts in the world, set her apart when she made her entrée into Henry VIII's court in 1522 as a lady-in-waiting to the queen. 'For behaviour, manners, attire and tongue she excelled them all,' her sixteenth-century biographer George Wyatt later claimed.[20] If Thomas Boleyn's intention in bringing Anne to court had been to find a good match for her, then it looked set to be realised soon after her arrival when she attracted the attention of Henry Percy, later sixth Earl of Northumberland. Percy rapidly grew so besotted with Anne that he tried to break a prior engagement in order to marry her. Anne seemed to return his affection, and they were secretly betrothed, probably during the spring of 1523 – while Anne's sister Mary was pregnant with the king's child.

Percy was a page in Wolsey's household, and when the cardinal heard of it he upbraided him, since permission to marry had not been sought from his father or the king. It is possible that the latter already had an interest in Anne by this time and had discreetly instructed Wolsey to dissolve the betrothal. There is no reliable evidence to support this, however, and it was not until 1526 that Henry VIII began to pay Anne serious attention. Whether he had been instructed or not, Wolsey's actions had made an implacable enemy of the king's new sweetheart.

In the year that Anne Boleyn rose to prominence at court, Wolsey drew up a set of detailed ordinances for the government of the royal household. The Eltham Ordinances, as they became known, may have been partly inspired by the cardinal's desire to safeguard his influence over the king and counter the rising power of the Boleyns.

The primary target of Wolsey's reforms was the privy chamber, which had become increasingly crowded with men hostile to the cardinal's influence. They included the chief of them, Sir William Compton, groom of the stool. Three years earlier, Wolsey had attempted to loosen Compton's hold over the king, upon whom he was in constant attendance, by sending him to serve on the Scottish borders in 1523. This was the longest that Compton had been away from his royal master, but when he returned, he found his favour undiminished – much to Wolsey's frustration. As part of his reforms in 1526, Wolsey succeeded in having Compton removed from post and replaced by Sir Henry Norris, who was much more favourable to his cause.[21]

Now that he had an ally in this most influential of privy chamber posts, Wolsey enhanced its prestige still further. The Eltham Ordinances described the groom of the stool as the sole servant of the king's 'bedchamber and other privy places as shall stand with his pleasure.' For the avoidance of doubt, they further stated that none of the other privy chamber servants were 'to presume to enter or follow his Grace' to these rooms, save by the king's specific command.[22] The ordinances also confirmed the importance of the gentlemen of the privy chamber as the only men who were permitted to touch the king. By contrast, the grooms and ushers must not 'approach or presume . . . to lay hands upon his royal person.'[23]

The most dramatic change brought about by the Eltham Ordinances, though, was to reduce the number of privy chamber staff from around fifty to just fifteen officers. Wolsey claimed that this was to safeguard the privacy of the king and prevent his being constantly besieged by ambitious place-seekers, but it was clear to everyone that it was as much an attempt to tighten his own control over Henry. The ordinances also stipulated named individuals (mostly associates of the cardinal) who 'shall diligently attend upon his person in his said privy chamber; doing humble, reverent, secret, and lowly service.' The cardinal also ordered that those appointed must not resort to 'pressing his grace, nor advancing themselves, either in further service than his grace will or shall assign them unto; or also in suits, or intermeddle of any causes or matters whatsoever they be.' He added that those lucky enough to serve in this inner sanctum must always remember that 'the more higher his Grace hath called them unto his person, the more to be humbly reverent, sober, discreet, and serviceable, in all their doings, behaviours, and conversations.'[24]

Wolsey's reforms reinforced the importance of the king's privy chamber as a place where he could retreat from the noise of the court and restore his spirits with relaxation: 'Inasmuch as in the pure and clean keeping of the King's privy chamber, with the good order thereof, consisteth a great part of the King's quiet, rest, comfort and preservation of his health.' He argued that if commoners could enjoy privacy, then so should a king:

> Considering that right mean persons, as well for their more commodity do retire and withdraw themselves sometimes apart, as for the wholesomeness and sweetness of their chambers, do forbear to have any great or frequent resort into the same; much more it is convenient, that the King's Highness have his privy chamber and inward lodgings reserved secret, at the pleasure of his grace, without repair of any great multitude thereunto; it is therefore ordained, that no person, of whatever estate . . . from henceforth presume, attempt, or be in any wise suffered or admitted to come or repair into the King's privy chamber; other than such only as his grace shall from time to time command.[25]

This was a noble sentiment, but Wolsey knew better than most that a king's private life was subject to a whole suite of restrictions and interventions, and could hardly be compared to that of his subjects.

The Eltham Ordinances succeeded in bringing greater order to the king's household and more closely defining the roles of those within it. But as a means of safeguarding Wolsey's position, they were a failure. By the time that they had been implemented, the woman who was rapidly becoming his arch-enemy had already secured such a hold over the king that it seemed nobody would ever break it.

The relationship between Henry and Anne Boleyn seems to have developed gradually out of a charade of courtly love. By late 1526, all the court knew that she was the king's latest inamorata. But this was very different to his previous infidelities, for Anne proved to be the most unyielding of mistresses. Having learned from the example of her sister, she sensed that Henry would lose interest as soon as she had succumbed to his desires, so she kept her eyes focused on a much greater prize. In her favour was the fact that after almost twenty years of marriage, the king was still without a male heir and his wife looked unlikely to bear him any more children. Anne, on the other hand, was in her mid-twenties and came from very fertile stock. Her mother had been pregnant at least seven times, and her paternal grandmother had borne ten children, eight of whom had survived infancy.

Henry wrote a series of increasingly passionate letters to Anne, complaining that he had 'been more than a year wounded by the dart of love, and not yet sure whether I shall fail or find a place in your affection.' He begged Anne to 'give yourself up, body and heart, to me' and promised that if she assented, he would make her his 'sole mistress', a privilege that he had afforded to no other woman before.[26] But Anne was determined to hold out for more and told him: 'I would rather lose my life than my honesty . . . Your mistress I will not be.' She proceeded to play the king with all the skill and guile that she had learned during her years at the French court, giving him just enough encouragement to keep him interested, but rebuffing him if he tried to overstep the mark. She evidently allowed Henry some sexual favours, without consenting to the full act, because one moment Henry was writing with gleeful anticipation at the prospect of kissing Anne's 'pretty duggs [breasts]', and the next he was lamenting how far he was from the 'sun', adding mischievously, 'yet the heat is all the greater'.[27]

Henry's privy purse accounts reveal that among the gifts that he sent to Anne in his attempt to seduce her was a black satin nightgown.[28] This was a deliberately intimate choice. Nightgowns were only worn in the presence of family or very close friends and attendants. They formed a welcome contrast to the constrictive layers of outer dress, but were often luxury items in their own right and became particularly elaborate during Henry's reign. The richer nightgowns were made of velvet and lined with fur for warmth, which was the case with the one Henry chose for Anne. If he was not permitted to share Anne's bed, then Henry was determined to at least enjoy the sight of her in this new night-time attire as often as he wished. He therefore commissioned Holbein to sketch Anne wearing it. In the portrait, Anne is shown wearing a typical high-collared embroidered linen smock underneath the nightgown. On her head is a linen coif, wrapped around with a frontlet – a band of linen worn around the forehead. Intimate it may be, but it is not the most flattering portrait of Henry's great love. Her gaze cast downwards, she has a pronounced double chin and looks decidedly plain.[29] Such is the contrast with the more famous portrait of Henry's dark-haired beauty that some doubt has been cast that it really is Anne, despite the contemporary inscription.

Knowing that Anne shared his love of fine clothes, Henry lavished many other such gifts upon her, including lengths of priceless crimson satin, cloth of gold and jewels. One eyewitness at court noted that not long after becoming the king's favourite, Lady Anne 'began to look very hault [haughty] and stout [proud], having all manner of jewels, or rich apparel that might be gotten with money.'[30]

Personal attire was one of the foremost weapons in the increasingly public battle between Anne Boleyn and Catherine of Aragon. When, in June 1527, Henry told his wife that he had begun to doubt the validity of their marriage, one of Catherine's first responses was to dress more richly than before. Determined to assert her superiority over Anne, she doubled her expenditure on dress that year, as her wardrobe accounts prove.[31] She had always favoured rich dark colours such as black and purple, which were regal but pious. Her religious devotion had been shown in other ways too, such as by wearing the habit of Saint Francis under her clothing and dressing modestly in private. But now she appeared in rich colours and fabrics – a highly visual assertion of her status as queen. She might also have been hoping to make herself more attractive to her husband and to draw his attention back to her.

But this was a battle that Anne, with her natural sense of style – not to mention the many gifts of clothing and rich fabrics she received from the king – was always destined to win. She showed off her slender physique to best effect in an array of striking and increasingly regal gowns, which made her rival appear dumpy and old-fashioned by comparison. To push home her advantage, Anne had '*Ainsi sera, groigne qui groigne*' ('This is how it is going to be, however much people grumble') embroidered onto her household livery.[32]

Henry's affection for his wife declined in directly inverse proportion to his increasing desire for Anne, and he instructed Wolsey to find a way to have his marriage annulled. This was a shocking and, as far as his subjects were concerned, deeply unpopular move. Although the king's real motivation was obvious, he claimed to be acting out of conscience because he had come to realise that God was displeased with him for marrying his brother's wife. Much was made of the passage in Leviticus that warned: 'If a man shall take his brother's wife, it is an unclean thing . . . they shall be childless.'[33] Little matter that Henry and Catherine had a daughter, or that the Pope had sanctioned their marriage because Catherine had always attested that her marriage to Arthur had not been consummated.

In 1528, Henry confided to the papal legate, Cardinal Campeggio, that he had not had sex with Catherine for two years, even though they continued to share a bed regularly for appearances' sake. If Henry was sleeping with neither his wife nor his mistress, did he remain celibate? It is possible that, as he claimed, he was so stricken with love for Anne that he could not so much as look at another woman. But given his healthy sexual appetite, which had been demonstrated by Catherine's frequent pregnancies and the various illicit liaisons that he had conducted throughout their marriage, it seems unlikely that he would have abstained altogether. More probable is that Henry eased his frustrated lust by bedding other women – possibly those of a lower class rather than court ladies, so that Anne would not hear of it.

All the while, the tortuous negotiations for an annulment of his marriage to Catherine dragged on, with apparently little prospect of success. The fact that the queen's nephew, Charles V, was the most powerful man in Europe and even held the Pope in sway proved a significant obstacle to Henry's ambitions. Even his able minister Wolsey failed to resolve the matter and was ousted from power because of it, leaving the way open for the cardinal's shrewd and talented protégé, Thomas Cromwell, who rapidly rose in favour.

The longer that Anne held Henry in thrall (and at bay), the greater her influence at court became. She was his constant companion in his private apartments, and hunted, danced and prayed with him. The only thing she did not do was to sleep with him. Increasingly, Henry chose to dine with Anne in the privacy of his 'secret lodgings'. In 1528, for example, he was recorded as having dined at Hunsdon in 'a chamber within a tower where his highness sometimes used to sup apart.'[34]

As Anne's status grew, so did her pride and haughtiness. She became insolent towards her mistress the queen, and was once heard loudly to proclaim that she wished all Spaniards at the bottom of the sea. A foreign visitor to the court was dismayed to encounter Anne, whom he described as a young woman of 'bad character, whose will is law to him [the king]'.[35]

For her part, Catherine maintained a quietly dignified stance and insisted that she was the king's lawful wife. As if to prove that nothing was amiss, she continued to perform the wifely duty of making her husband's shirts. The queen had always been fond of sewing and had spent many of her leisure hours in this pursuit. The household accounts include references to her handiwork, such as 'a table cloth of fine diaper with a towel and napkins thereunto wrought with red Spanish stitch'.[36] But the fact that Catherine was still making her husband's shirts was due to more than her love of sewing. Shirts were among the most intimate items of clothing that the king wore, so the gesture was hugely symbolic – and not lost upon Anne who, when she found out, put a stop to it immediately. Thereafter she herself supplied Henry with shirts – although she commissioned a shirt-maker, rather than make them herself. Henry should have taken note: his mistress was not made of the same dutiful and domestic stuff as his wife.

Catherine's stoicism was in vain. In 1531, she was banished from court and Anne was established as queen in all but name. Things now moved rapidly in Anne's favour. The combined efforts of Thomas Cromwell and another man sympathetic to her cause, Thomas Cranmer (who was made Archbishop of Canterbury in October 1532), brought the annulment within reach. If the Pope would not grant the divorce, then they would simply remove the need for his permission by making their royal master head of the

English church. It was a shockingly radical concept, but by now Henry was desperate enough to embrace it.

During the long years of negotiating for an annulment, preoccupied by such weighty matters and no longer enjoying the physical energy of his youth, Henry increasingly withdrew from court life and spent the majority of his leisure hours in private. As a result, there were far fewer court entertainments than there had been in the earlier years of the reign, and courtiers were obliged to ward off the boredom of waiting for the king to appear by making use of the recreational facilities at the palaces. Perhaps at least partly in recognition of this fact, Henry commissioned new sports complexes at Greenwich, Hampton Court and Whitehall after 1530. These included tennis courts, bowling alleys and tiltyards. The latter was particularly impressive at Hampton Court and included a series of viewing towers, which doubled up as banqueting houses.[37]

Although Henry still enjoyed taking part in these sports himself, his personality was undergoing a profound shift as he became ever more paranoid and suspicious of those around him, calling to mind memories of the father to whom he had always presented such a stark contrast. 'He does not trust anyone alive,' remarked one observer.[38] Only those who attended him in his inner sanctum were trusted and beloved. Increasingly, they included men who were also close to Anne Boleyn.

Francis Weston, who was made a gentleman of the privy chamber in 1532, often partnered the king at tennis and Anne at cards. An up-and-coming favourite was William Brereton, who had served as page since 1524 and accompanied both Henry and Anne to the hunt. But the most highly favoured was Henry Norris, who had been appointed groom of the stool in the same year that Anne had first attracted the king's notice. Like Compton, Norris had been known to Henry for many years by the time he was promoted to the most sought-after position at court. He had previously served as a gentleman of the bedchamber and had received many honours at the hands of his royal master. The French ambassador described him as 'du roy le mieulx aimé' ('the king's most loved').[39]

Norris was quick to realise the potential of his position, particularly in controlling access to the king. In 1530, for example, the Vice Chancellor of the University of Oxford arrived at court with a delegation to sue for the continuance of Cardinal College, which was under threat following Thomas Wolsey's fall. But, lacking 'friends' to recommend them, they were kept waiting for eleven days on the basis that the king was preoccupied with 'great business'. Eventually, Norris took pity on them and they found themselves in the king's presence within a matter of hours.[40] Norris also proved adept at the groom of the stool's traditional role in facilitating the king's illicit liaisons. As part of the evidence that Elizabeth Amadas provided upon her arrest for treason in 1532, she alleged that Norris had intrigued with Anne Boleyn on his royal master's behalf.[41] Norris was assisted by Thomas Heneage, an associate of Cromwell. Heneage took pride in every aspect of his private attendance upon the king and once reported: 'There is none here but Master Norris and I to give attendance upon the King's Highness when he goeth to make water in his bed chamber.'[42]

In November 1532, Henry took Anne with him as his official consort to Calais, where he met his great rival Francis I in another show of accord. Fully aware of what it signified, Anne was determined to dress the part. Eustace Chapuys, the Imperial ambassador, disapprovingly noted that 'the Lady has been busy in buying costly dresses; and the King, not content with having given her his jewels, sent the duke of Norfolk to obtain the Queen's as well.' That her husband should demand her jewels for his 'concubine' was too much for Catherine to bear. She angrily retorted that it was against her conscience to give her jewels 'to adorn a person who is the scandal of Christendom'.[43] But when the king gave his express command, there was little she could do to resist and, painfully conscious of the symbolism, she surrendered all the jewels she possessed.

Meanwhile, for Anne the visit to Calais was a triumph in every respect. Not only was she there as the king's consort, bedecked in his estranged wife's jewels, but during their stay Francis I also promised his support for their marriage. It may have been this that convinced Anne finally to sleep with Henry, although it has also been conjectured that she and Henry had undergone a private ceremony of betrothal before embarking for Calais. The need for secrecy in their sexual encounters was still paramount, given the delicate stage that the proceedings for an annulment had reached. But that something had changed between the couple was almost immediately apparent to the courtiers in attendance. Henry was, at least initially, even more besotted with Anne now than he had been before. 'The king cannot leave her for an hour,' remarked Chapuys, with barely concealed disgust.

The Tudors believed that it was possible to influence the sex of a child by undertaking various rituals. These included tying a ribbon around the man's left testicle during intercourse, this being where all the female seed was supposedly stored. Certain sexual positions were also recommended for the conception of a boy. Just as a man's right testicle contained all the male seed, so the right side of a woman's womb was considered to be more receptive to this seed. Many couples would therefore opt for a position that allowed the seed to fall down into the right side of the womb. It is interesting to speculate whether this is why Anne was not content with the traditional missionary position favoured by Henry, who later confessed to having been shocked by her sexual knowledge.

By December, Anne was pregnant. Once she was certain of her condition, her royal lover had to act fast if the baby was to be born legitimate. He therefore set aside the ongoing wranglings with the church and married Anne in secret, probably on 25 January 1533 in his private chapel at Westminster. Their discretion was so successful that, even to this day, the date and location of their wedding is not certain. But Henry's courtiers quickly noticed a difference in Anne's status because of her clothing. Chapuys reported to his master Charles V: 'On Saturday . . . dame Anne went to mass in Royal state, loaded with jewels, clothed in a robe of cloth of gold frieze . . . and was brought to church, and brought back with the solemnities or even more, which were used to the queen.'[44]

It was another four months before the king's marriage to Catherine was annulled, by which time Anne's condition was obvious to everyone at court. Given the Boleyn family's fecundity, there was no reason to doubt that the pregnancy would progress smoothly

– and that it would be the first of many. Anne's health was generally good, and as one observer remarked, she seemed 'likely enough to bear children'. What was more, she had fallen pregnant almost immediately after becoming Henry's lover, which surely augured well – both for this and all future conceptions.

Nevertheless, Anne had conceived her first child considerably later than most women in her family, thanks to the seven years during which her new husband had tried to rid himself of his first wife. When Henry had first started courting Anne, she had been in her mid-twenties and at the peak of her fertility; now aged about thirty-two, she was nearing the end of it. Her husband, meanwhile, was forty-one. As such, they would have been considered old by Tudor standards to be starting a family.

Anne's pregnancy proceeded without incident, however, and she took delight in boasting of her condition, on one occasion loudly declaring a craving for apples. This was rapidly reported back to courts across the Continent, where the English king's marriage to the 'Concubine' was the source of much gossip. For all her boasting, the new queen was secretly worried about the toll that pregnancy was taking on her famously slender figure. She no doubt feared that as her attractiveness waned, the king would seek diversion elsewhere, particularly as they were expected to abstain from sex until after the baby was born. Although her ladies were obliged to loosen Anne's gowns, she took care to dress as stylishly as before.

Anne was also quick to make her mark on the apartments in her husband's palaces that his former wife had vacated. The household accounts reveal the luxury of the furnishings and fabrics, many of which were decorated with Anne's personal emblem and the intertwined initials 'HA'.[45] These included a series of priceless carpets that covered the floors of her private apartments. One was crafted from cloth of gold, silver and silk needlework and decorated with the new queen's monograms, red and white roses, a border of honeysuckle, acorns and the letters H and A. Honeysuckle symbolised love and devotion, while an acorn was an emblem of fertility, growth and new life. Another was wrought with the royal arms and the white falcon of Anne's emblem. Throughout the public rooms, too, Anne made sure that the change of queen was made obvious. In the Great Hall at Hampton Court, for example, the royal carpenters were obliged to replace Catherine's initials with the now familiar intertwined 'HA'.[46]

In August 1533, as Anne was preparing to enter her confinement, rumours of a secret liaison between the king and a 'very beautiful' woman began to spread throughout the court. The new queen's enemies at court were quick to encourage the king in his courtship, as the eagle-eyed Chapuys noted: 'The King's affection for her [Anne] is less than it was. He now shows himself in love with another lady, and many nobles are assisting him in the affair.' By the time that Anne heard of it, the tale had been embellished: Henry had slept with at least one other woman, possibly more. His new wife was by no means as willing as her predecessor to turn a blind eye to her husband's indiscretions. Chapuys noted with satisfaction that she was 'very jealous of the King, and not without legitimate cause.'[47] Furious at such humiliation, Anne confronted Henry. To her dismay, rather than offering placatory assurances, he spat back that she must 'shut her eyes and endure' as more 'worthy' persons had done. As a wife, Anne no longer held the same appeal to a man who thrived on the thrill of the chase. 'She ought to know that it was in his power to humble her again in a moment, more than he had exalted her before,' Chapuys shrewdly observed.[48]

The quarrel dragged on for several days, but by the time Anne entered her confinement at Greenwich, she and Henry seemed to have resolved their differences. Confidently expecting the birth of a male heir, it was hardly in the king's interests to send his wife into her enforced seclusion full of anger and suspicion. Anne shared her husband's confidence about the sex of their child. At her orders, letters announcing the birth had been written in advance, thanking God for sending her 'good speed, in the deliverance and bringing forth of a prince.'[49] The king, meanwhile, had already decided that the boy would be christened Henry or Edward. He had also been busy planning a splendid joust to mark the safe delivery of his son. One courtier remarked that he had never seen His Majesty so 'merry'. All except one of the kingdom's leading astrologers and soothsayers were in agreement that the child Anne carried was a boy. Only the renowned 'seer', William Glover, disagreed. He had dared to tell Queen Anne that he had had a vision of her bearing 'a woman child'. His prediction had not been well received.

On 26 August, Anne heard Mass in the palace chapel before hosting a feast for all the lords and ladies of the court in her Great Chamber, which had been richly decorated for the occasion. There, 'spices and wine' were served to the queen and her guests, and soon afterwards she was escorted to the door of her bedchamber with great ceremony by two high-ranking ladies. Having taken formal leave not just of the king, but of all the male courtiers, officials and servants, she stepped forward into the exclusively female world of her confinement chambers.

Although Anne was keen to adhere to the strict ordinances set down for a royal birth, she judged that these alone were not enough to convince the world that she was the rightful queen and that her child would be the legitimate heir. She therefore ordered a number of embellishments, all loaded with symbolism. For example, the tapestries that hung in her chamber showed the story of Saint Ursula and her eleven thousand virgins – a theme that would prove remarkably fitting.

The centrepiece of the birthing chamber was 'one of the richest and most triumphant beds' in the king's possession.[50] Worth around £500,000 in today's money, it was said to have formed part of the ransom of a French duke who had been captured at Verneuil in 1424. If this was true, then perhaps it was intended as a reminder that the queen had served in the French royal court during her youth. The bed was bedecked with an elaborate counterpane, 'richly embossed upon crimson velvet', lined with ermine and edged with gold. A crimson satin tester and curtains embroidered with gold crowns completed the effect, with the queen's arms being added as another reminder of her lineage – and therefore her right to the throne.

But Anne had one final, very cruel demand before she would be content that everything was ready for the birth of her child. She asked the king to procure from his former wife the 'rich triumphal cloth' that Catherine had brought with her from Spain for the baptism of her future children. This was more than mere spite. The cloth was a symbol of legitimate, royal blood, and Anne was desperate to secure it for her unborn child. But for Catherine, it was one of the few possessions she had left and was a poignant reminder of all her children who had been stillborn or died within days of birth. The former queen was outraged when she heard of the request and refused to hand over the cloth. Eager though he was to placate his expectant wife, even Henry cringed at her insensitivity and refused to press the matter. Anne was therefore forced to relent with as much good grace as she could muster.

On 7 September, the eve of the Feast of the Virgin, Anne went into labour. This was just twelve days after she had entered her confinement, so it was assumed that either the baby was premature or the midwives had miscalculated. It is also possible that Anne had told them that the date of conception had been a little later that it actually was, given that the child had almost certainly been conceived outside of wedlock. Anne knew that its legitimacy was already being called into question, so she would have wished to keep this fact to herself.

Anne's labour progressed smoothly, although was 'particularly painful', and at 3 o'clock in the afternoon she was delivered of a healthy child.[51] But Anne had done no better than her predecessor: she had given birth to a girl. Although she must have been panic-stricken that she had failed to give Henry a son after all the turbulence he had created in order to marry her, Anne brazened it out. 'Henceforth they may with reason call this room the Chamber of Virgins,' she told the assembled ladies, 'for a virgin is now born in it on the vigil of that auspicious day when the church commem-orates the nativity of our blessed lady the Virgin Mary.'[52] Upon visiting his new daughter for the first time, Henry managed to suppress what must have been bitter disappointment. 'You and I are both young,' he told Anne, 'and by God's grace, boys will follow.'[53] It was less a consolation than a demand.

'A thin, old, and vicious hack'

ALTHOUGH SHE HAD every reason to resent her new daughter, Anne appeared to dote upon her. To the great surprise of the court, she had a velvet cushion placed next to her throne so that the baby, who had been christened Elizabeth, could remain next to her as she conducted the duties required of her position. It was highly unusual for a queen to keep her child with her, rather than entrusting it to the royal nursery, but Anne went further still by declaring her intention to breastfeed Elizabeth herself. This was such a shocking concept that it called into question Anne's suitability as queen. When he heard of it, the king was outraged and insisted that Anne employ a wet-nurse as her predecessors had done. A woman called Mrs Pendred was duly assigned to the task. Three months later, Elizabeth was sent with a sizeable retinue to Hatfield House, where she would be raised away from her parents at court, as royal tradition dictated.

Anne had little time to grieve over the departure of her daughter. She knew that she had to conceive again as quickly as possible in order to secure her position as Henry's queen. It seems that she succeeded. At Christmas 1533, she gave her husband a fertility symbol: a gold fountain flanked by three naked women whose nipples spurted water. This prompted rumours that she was pregnant again, and they were apparently confirmed the following April when the court goldsmith was commissioned to make a silver cradle decorated with Tudor roses and precious stones. At the same time, the royal seamstresses began work on a set of baby clothes fashioned from cloth of gold.

On 27 April, a courtier reported from Greenwich that the queen 'hath a goodly belly, praying our Lord to send us a prince', and a planned trip to Calais was postponed until after the birth because Anne was 'so far gone with child'.[1] She joined in a series of entertainments at Hampton Court on 26 June, by which time she must surely have been heavily pregnant if the rumours were true. But no plans were made for her confinement, and no baby appeared. By September, some of the court gossips were speculating that she had delivered a premature son at the end of June, while others claimed that she had never been pregnant at all. It is possible that Anne, desperate to give Henry a son, had experienced a phantom pregnancy – when a woman's mind convinces her body that she is with child, leading to some if not all of the usual symptoms of that condition. This would explain the swollen belly that courtiers had remarked upon, as well as a number of other physical symptoms commensurate with a real pregnancy. That Anne had been mistaken, rather than having miscarried, is supported by Chapuys' report in September that the 'Concubine' was 'not to have a child after all'.[2]

Preoccupied though she was with the need to give the king a son, Anne had by no means neglected her infant daughter. When court affairs would allow, she visited Elizabeth at Hatfield, and the princess was occasionally brought to see her at court, such as in the spring of 1535. But such visits were all too rare, so Anne consoled herself by maintaining a regular correspondence with her daughter's governess, Lady Margaret Bryan, and ensuring that Elizabeth had everything necessary for her proper upbringing. This included a plentiful supply of linen with which to swaddle the infant princess. Her nappies and bibs were made from the same material.

In the autumn of 1535, after the princess had celebrated her second birthday, Anne and Lady Bryan conferred over her weaning. The governess affirmed that her charge was now old enough to drink from a cup and therefore no longer needed a wet-nurse. Even this most intimate of matters had to be referred to the king and council, who duly agreed that 'my lady princess' should be weaned 'with all diligence'.[3] Lady Bryan was put in charge of the task, but Anne sent her a private letter, possibly with her own maternal instructions about how it should be accomplished. All of this was exactly in accordance with the accepted wisdom of the time, which stated that children should be fully weaned after two years. They would then continue to be fed largely on milk, and only gradually would poultry and other white meats be introduced. Rich food was considered unsuitable, even for royal offspring, so Elizabeth's first solid foods would have been rather plain.

At around the same time that her daughter was weaned, Anne fell pregnant again. During the previous eighteen months she had suffered at least one, possibly two miscarriages. This had not helped her relationship with Henry, which had rapidly deteriorated since Elizabeth's birth. Increasingly, the king sought diversion among the other ladies of court. In February 1535, the ever vigilant Chapuys reported that the queen's cousin and lady-in-waiting, Mary Shelton, had been enjoying the king's favour. She was almost certainly his mistress by this time and their affair lasted for about six months.

In the summer of 1535, the king and his court went on progress to Wiltshire and Somerset. The choice of location was deliberate for it enabled Henry to pay a visit to Wolf Hall, the home of the Seymour family, which lay in the heart of the Savernake Forest. The Seymours boasted an ancient lineage but were of gentry, rather than noble status. Nevertheless, Sir John Seymour's sons, Edward and Thomas, were rising to prominence at Henry's court, so the visit was entirely appropriate. But it was their sister Jane whom the king was most eager to see.

Jane Seymour was one of Anne's ladies-in-waiting, but had formerly served her predecessor, Catherine of Aragon, whom she greatly admired. She had attracted little notice at court, being of a quiet demeanour and rather plain. Fair-haired and pale-skinned, she had a large, plump face with a double chin. Her eyes were small and beady, and her lips were thin. One onlooker at court dismissed her as being 'of middle stature and no great beauty'.⁴ Neither did Jane have the sparkling wit and intelligence of her royal mistress: in fact, she was barely literate.

It was therefore the source of much surprise – not to mention bemusement – when in late 1534 the king started paying Jane particular attention. She was then in her mid-twenties – some seven or eight years younger than Anne. Henry employed his customary discretion in courting her. The first hint of their attachment came in a letter from Chapuys, who reported in October that Henry had become 'attached' to 'a young lady' of the court.[5] Although delighted that the 'Concubine' appeared to be losing her hold over the king, the ambassador was at a loss to explain what he saw in her lady-in-waiting. He could only conclude that she must have a fine 'enigme', meaning 'riddle' or 'secret', which in Tudor times referred to the female genitals.[6]

Jane's true appeal to Henry, though, lay not in her looks but in her demeanour. Anne's tempestuous, passionate nature might have stoked the king's desire during the long years of their courtship, but they were hardly fitting qualities in a royal wife. By contrast, Jane appeared meek, docile and placid. While Anne sparked dissent and faction at court, Jane was praised as a peacemaker. Henry himself singled out this quality above all others, commending her as 'gentle and inclined to peace'.[7] And while Anne was derided as the 'Concubine' and loved to flirt with her coterie of male admirers, Jane was unquestionably chaste. Thomas Cromwell described her as 'the most virtuous lady and veriest gentlewoman that liveth.'[8] Chapuys concluded that the prospect of replacing Anne with Jane was 'by many a one compared to the joy and pleasure a man feels in getting rid of a thin, old, and vicious hack in the hope of getting soon a fine horse to ride.'[9]

By the time that Anne and her husband visited Wolf Hall in late summer 1535, Anne was fully aware of her husband's growing infatuation with her sallow-faced lady-in-waiting. Rather than complain of it, as she had with his other indiscretions, she resolved to take decisive action. She knew that no matter how besotted Henry might be with his latest favourite, if she gave him a son, her position as his queen would be assured. She therefore employed what was left of her once famously seductive charms and enticed Henry back to her bed.

It seemed the gamble had paid off: Anne fell pregnant once more. Although delighted at his wife's condition and outwardly solicitous of her every need, Henry could not put aside the distaste that he had come to feel for her, and courtiers noticed that in private he 'shrank from her'.[10] While in the past, Anne would have shrugged this off, confident of regaining his affection, the uncertainties and betrayals of the past two years had left her plagued with insecurity and fear.

But at the beginning of 1536, events turned more decisively in Anne's favour. On 8 January, Catherine of Aragon, the woman whom most of England still regarded as the rightful queen, died at Kimbolton Castle. Anne and Henry were so overjoyed that they celebrated at court 'clad all over in yellow from top to toe'.[11] Their joy was premature. Just three weeks later, on the same day that the old queen was laid to rest at Peterborough Cathedral, Anne miscarried. At around fifteen weeks, her pregnancy was far enough advanced to tell that the foetus was a boy. Chapuys was quick to convey the news to Charles V. With barely suppressed satisfaction, he told his master: 'The Concubine had an abortion which seemed to be a male child which she had not borne three and a half months, and on which the King has shown great distress.' His conclusion was brutal but accurate: 'She has miscarried of her saviour.'[12]

Desperate to prove that the fault did not lie with her, Anne blamed her latest miscarriage upon the shock that she had received when her uncle Norfolk had told her about the king's jousting accident. This was the most serious that Henry had suffered in all his years in the tournament field. He had fallen from his horse while jousting at Greenwich, and although reports that he lay unconscious for two hours are unsubstantiated, he certainly suffered a nasty injury to his leg. This subsequently turned ulcerous and caused Henry considerable pain. Three months after the accident, a member of court reported: 'The King goes seldom abroad because his leg is something sore.'[13] It would prove a defining moment in the formerly athletic king's reign. No longer able to take regular and vigorous exercise, he rapidly gained weight and became increasingly irascible.

Forasmuch as his wife tried to deflect the blame, however, the king needed no further proof that his marriage to Anne was cursed, and he set his chief minister Thomas Cromwell to work in getting him out of it. In the meantime, avoiding Anne, he switched his attentions firmly to his new mistress, showering her with 'great presents'. Jane now employed some of the same tactics that she had seen Anne use to such powerful effect. After all, there was now a precedent for a mistress becoming a queen. Like Anne, Jane refused to sleep with Henry, and gently rebuffed his advances with a show of maidenly modesty. When in April 1536, he sent her a purse of money with an accompanying declaration of love, Jane reverently kissed the letter before sending it back unopened, begging the king to consider that there was 'no treasure in the world that she valued as much as her honour, and on no account would she lose it, even if she were to die a thousand deaths.' She cunningly added that if the king wished to send her such a present in future, then he should wait 'for such a time as God would be pleased to send her some advantageous marriage.'[14]

While Henry and Jane played out the now predictable game of courtship, Cromwell quietly gathered evidence that would rid his master of his second wife. An annulment would not suffice this time: it would make a mockery of all the turbulence and trouble involved in dissolving the king's first marriage. Besides, Cromwell had his own reasons for getting rid of Anne on a more permanent basis because, by 1536, they were sworn enemies: the queen had made no secret of wishing to see the chief minister's head off his shoulders. Cromwell therefore devised a plot inspired by Anne's naturally flirtatious behaviour with the group of male courtiers who were often in her presence – men such as Henry Norris, William Brereton, Mark Smeaton, a court musician, and even the queen's own brother, George Boleyn. All had positions in the king's privy chamber, which – Cromwell rightly judged – would make the case all the more scandalous.

That Anne's relationships with these men had gone no further than flirtation has been convincingly proved.[15] But Cromwell had spied the means to bring her down and wasted no time in collecting gossip from her ladies that could be twisted into damning evidence. When he secretly presented this to Henry, the latter did not hesitate. It is an indication of how much the king wished to be rid of his second wife that he was willing to play the cuckold. Society took a dim view of men who had been cheated on by their wives. Far

from being an object of pity, they were derided as weak and inef-
fectual, unable to satisfy their wives in the marriage bed. For a king
who had prided himself on his sexual potency, this was humiliating
indeed. But Cromwell helped ensure that the case against Anne
would be so damning, her actions so wicked and perverted, that
nobody would point the finger of blame at her husband.

The May Day tournament was held as usual at Greenwich, but
a contemporary chronicler noted that 'suddenly from the jousts the
king departed having not above six persons with him . . . Of this
sudden departing many men mused, but most chiefly the queen.'[16]
She had good reason. On 2 May, Anne was arrested without warning
and taken to the Tower. Her trial took place a little over two weeks
later and she faced a string of lurid and scandalous charges. Her
crime was not just adultery, but incest and perversion. The testimonies provided by her ladies, as well as some of the men with
whom she was alleged to have conducted illicit affairs, were scandalous and explicit. Driven by her 'frail and carnal lust', she had
kissed her brother by 'inserting her tongue in his mouth, and he in
hers', and had incited others in her entourage to yield to her 'vile
provocations'.[17] So insatiable had been her sexual appetite that she
had taken Henry Norris to her bed just six weeks after giving birth
to Elizabeth.

One of the lesser-known charges against Anne might seem trivial
to modern observers, but it was damning in the eyes of her contemporaries. It was said that she and her brother had laughed at the
king's clothes.[18] That this was included when other, greater charges
were sufficient to condemn them shows the importance accorded
to clothing by Henry and his court. Clothes were an extension of
the man, so to laugh at his apparel was to laugh at the king himself
– a shocking and unforgivable transgression.

Anne gave an eloquent defence, calmly insisting upon her innocence. Although she had not lacked the opportunity to conduct
adulterous liaisons, thanks to the separation of the king and queen's
private apartments, she insisted that none of the accused men had
been allowed close access. Only on one occasion, at Winchester,
had she admitted Mark Smeaton to her chambers so that she could

listen to him playing the virginals. But, as she was at pains to point out, 'there my lodging was above the king's'.[19]

No matter how flimsy the evidence against her, however, there could only be one verdict. Indeed, her estranged husband had already sent for the expert executioner from Calais before the trial had even begun. The fallen queen was duly convicted of adultery, which was treason in a royal wife, and sentenced to be executed. Her marriage to the king was also annulled, rendering their daughter Elizabeth a bastard.

On 19 May 1536, Anne was led the short distance from her apartments in the Tower to the scaffold site. Elegant to the last, she wore a mantle of ermine over a loose gown of dark grey damask trimmed with fur and a crimson petticoat. The latter may have been for warmth (wearing red was believed to generate heat), but it was also the colour of martyrs. When she had mounted the scaffold, her ladies removed her headdress to reveal a white linen coif covering her hair. After she had delivered her final speech, Anne's attendants blindfolded her so that she did not see the executioner's sword, which killed her with one clean strike. The crowd looked on aghast as Anne's eyes and lips continued to move, as if in silent prayer, when her head was held aloft. Her weeping ladies sought in vain for a coffin in which to lay their mistress's body. In one final indignity, they were compelled to use an old arrow chest, and it was in this that Henry's second queen was laid to rest in the Tower chapel of St Peter ad Vincula.

The following morning, Jane Seymour travelled in secret by barge to the king's apartments at Hampton Court, where she and Henry were betrothed. In the preceding days, she had received large amounts of clothing and material from the king. These were more than mere tokens of his affection: Henry was providing his new consort with the items she would need to raise her status from lady-in-waiting to queen. It is likely that some of the gowns had come straight from Anne Boleyn's wardrobe. Henry had no scruple about recycling clothing and jewels from his fallen wives and courtiers. Sometimes, they still bore the monograms and symbols of their former owners when they were transferred to the next person.

Henry and Jane were married on 30 May 1536 in the queen's closet at Whitehall. The king was said to have worn white for the ceremony – a symbol of purity and rebirth that suggests with this marriage he was wiping the slate clean: Jane was his first legitimate and true wife. Although his primary motive in marrying her was to beget a son, at forty-five he was past his sexual prime and there are some hints in the sources that he lacked the prowess of his younger days. Anne Boleyn was rumoured to have said that he had 'neither vigour nor virtue' as a lover, and Chapuys speculated that 'he may make a condition in the marriage [to Jane Seymour] that she be a virgin, and when he has a mind to divorce her he will find enough of witnesses.'

Henry himself confided to Chapuys that he feared he would not have any children by Jane . The accident that he had suffered while jousting at the beginning of the year had rendered him incapable of vigorous exercise, and his descent into obesity can be traced from that time. He was still complaining of the acute pain from his ulcerated leg the following summer. But he was desperate to keep his incapacity private, conscious of the imperative for a sovereign to appear invincible to his people. In a letter to the Duke of Norfolk written in June 1537, Henry instructed him to announce the official reason why he had cancelled a planned excursion from court, but confided: 'To be frank with you, which you must keep to yourself, a humor has fallen into our legs, and our physicians advise us not to go so far in the heat of the year, even for this reason only.'[20] Far from improving, the injury would plague Henry for the rest of his life.

Jane may have lacked the beauty and charisma expected of a royal wife, but Henry ensured that she would at least dress like one. For her first appearance as queen at court on 4 June, he ordered no fewer than 560 pearls to adorn her clothes. An inventory of Jane's clothes at Whitehall reveals an extensive wardrobe containing twenty-seven gowns, thirty placards, sixty-four pairs of sleeves, fifteen kirtles and thirteen stomachers. There were also numerous coifs, hats, furs and mufflers. The inventory also refers to several 'babies', or fashion dolls. These would have been shown to the queen dressed in miniature versions of gowns designed for her by the royal tailors so that she could choose which ones she wished to have made up.

Although she enjoyed the trappings of royalty, Jane was determined to differentiate herself from her predecessor by adopting a modest, very English style of dress. Many of her garments were embroidered with naturalistic designs such as strawberry leaves – a typically English motif. The new queen forbade her ladies from wearing the elegant French hood, which was closely associated with Anne Boleyn, or any other items inspired by the court of France. Jane also made her ladies wear extra fabric at the neckline so that their bosoms were well hidden.

Just three months after the wedding, with his new bride showing no sign of pregnancy, her husband was already hinting in private that he regretted his hasty choice. Jane's simple plainness and modesty had appealed to Henry when Anne Boleyn had been alive. But now that she no longer formed an appealing contrast to a wife whom he wished to be rid of, she seemed to lack the attributes to keep him interested. In August, the king confessed to Chapuys that he wished he had noticed the two beautiful women who had made their appearance at court shortly after the wedding.

Nevertheless, Henry felt the need for a male heir more keenly than ever, as his illegitimate son, Henry FitzRoy, had died in July that year. This evidently inspired him to perform his marital duty. Shortly afterwards, one eyewitness reported that the king had placed his hand on his new wife's belly saying 'Edward, Edward'.[21] In fact, it would be another four months before Jane conceived, at the end of 1536. Her happy condition was formally announced in February, ending weeks of speculation among a court that had been watching the new queen intently for any signs of pregnancy. Now that the secret was out, Jane was able to indulge the whims of her condition, which included a craving for cucumbers – dutifully provided by her stepdaughter, Mary.

Jane's other stepdaughter, by contrast, seems to have been entirely forgotten. Her mother's shameful demise had immediately reduced Elizabeth from the rank of princess to merely 'Lady'. As heir to the throne, the infant princess had been served with all the reverence expected of her status, and her household at Hatfield had been run with great order and ceremony. But within days of Anne Boleyn's execution, Elizabeth's governess was writing in alarm to Thomas Cromwell about the disarray into which her household had fallen.

Whereas before, the child had been served meals in her own private apartments, now she was allowed 'to dine and sup' with the adults of the household. When her mother was alive, Elizabeth's diet had been restricted to the plain foods that were prescribed for newly weaned infants, but now the precocious young girl took full advantage of the rich fare that was – literally – within her grasp. Lady Bryan was scandalised. 'It is not meet for a child of her age to keep such rule,' she told Cromwell. 'If she do, I dare not take it upon me to keep her Grace in health; for she will see divers meats, fruits, and wine, that it will be hard for me to refrain her from.' She therefore urged the minister to order Sir John Shelton, who presided over the household, to arrange for Elizabeth to dine in private once more, away from the temptations of grown-up food.

It was a trying time for Henry VIII's youngest daughter. As well as being denied the flavoursome dishes that she had enjoyed only fleetingly, Elizabeth was also teething. 'God knoweth my lady hath great pain with her great teeth [molars], and they come very slowly forth,' Lady Bryan told Cromwell. For all her strictness, she felt so sorry for the discomfort that this had caused her charge that she admitted it 'causeth me to suffer her grace to have her will more than I would.' She had clearly grown very fond of the motherless child, and assured Cromwell: 'She is as toward a child and as gentle of conditions, as ever I knew any in my life.'[22]

Back at court, it may have been to celebrate Jane's pregnancy, as much as to honour her status as queen, that the greatest portrait painter of the age, Hans Holbein, was commissioned to take her likeness. For this, Jane wore a rich gown of deep red velvet. It was a colour that defied her image as a quiet, unassuming wife, and it now became her favourite. An inventory of her clothes at Whitehall Palace included several gowns of 'crimson velvet', complemented by sleeves and embellishments of cloth of gold.

Splendid though the overall effect was, Holbein's mastery of detail reveals the private side of this very public statement. At the front of the dress is a 'placard': a piece of fabric worn under the front lacing of a gown or pinned in place over the bodice. It was often stiffened with paste, reeds or whalebone to provide a foundation for embellishments and to shape and compress the stomach and breasts, giving a distinctive rigid bodice shape.[23] A series of tiny pinheads, visible around Jane's placard, shows how it was kept in place. The fact that it was worn over her bodice suggests that she was pregnant at the time that the portrait was painted. Placards were commonly worn in this way by expectant ladies because they allowed for the expanding belly.

That Holbein chose to show the pinheads on Jane's placard may have been deliberate. The more observant of Henry's courtiers would have understood that they symbolised the queen's happy condition. Pregnancy was not a state often depicted in portraiture, but such was Henry's joy at his new wife's condition that he would have approved of the artist's choice.

Before long, the whole court knew that 'the Queen's Grace is great with child, and shall be open-laced with stomacher.'[24] As well as making her more comfortable, this also signalled that the baby had quickened. This change in Jane's attire took place at the beginning of May 1537, when she travelled to Hampton Court to enjoy its comfort and relative seclusion for the summer. Henry had inherited the palace from Cardinal Wolsey in the late 1520s and had immediately set about remodelling it in lavish style. His improvements also signalled a significant shift in the relationship between the royal family's public and private life. Wolsey's palace had included a series of royal apartments, spread over several floors. The king now abandoned these in favour of a pair of matching apartments for himself and his queen – who, at the time when the works had begun, was Anne Boleyn. These were on the same floor and were reached by a grand staircase that led from the privy gardens.

At the same time, Henry enhanced the prestige of those men who were permitted to attend him in his private apartments. The groom of the stool was given the additional office of gentleman of the privy chamber. Then, in 1537, the barons of the exchequer declared that the officers of the privy chamber gave service 'not merely to the body natural' of the prince '[but] to the Majesty of the body politic . . . which includes the body natural'.[25] This set the privy chamber staff apart from the king's other personal servants, such as his physicians and surgeons. Thanks to these developments, the privy chamber was now acknowledged as second only to the Privy Council in the order of power at court.

The importance of the privy chamber staff was quickly demonstrated when, that same year, one of its gentlemen, Ralph Sadler, a protégé of Thomas Cromwell, was sent as ambassador to Scotland. His instructions directed that he:

> shall, as of himself, affirm to the King of Scots, that being he of his uncle's [i.e. Henry VIII's] privy chamber, and of long season acquainted with his proceedings, he knoweth the King his master's true meaning, upright dealing, and proceedings to be of such reason, truth and innocency, as he wisheth all the world might know the ground and very secrecies thereof.[26]

In short, Ralph was the personification of the king and thus fully empowered to act on his behalf.

Meanwhile, plans were well under way for the queen's confinement. Just prior to Jane's arrival at Hampton Court, a new private gallery had been built overlooking her privy gardens and the River Thames. This connected her chambers with those of the royal nursery. She passed the entire summer at the palace in order to avoid the plague that was raging across London. Her husband stayed close by at Esher, anxious not to put Jane at any risk of infection. She was attended regularly by the royal physicians, who noted in mid-July that her belly was 'large'.

On 16 September, Jane formally took to her chambers to begin her confinement. The room in which she was to give birth was decked out with luxurious furnishings, including tapestries depicting 'the history of Pompey'. Nearby was a chamber in which 'the history of Tobias [was] worked and embossed in gold relief on the tapestry.'[27]

Three weeks later, Jane's labour pains began. It is a testament to how much Henry believed that she was about to deliver a son that he ordered his most trusted doctor, Sir William Butts, to attend the queen. To have a man present in the royal birthing chamber was highly unusual, but Jane would have much need of Butts' wisdom and experience. Although her pregnancy had been very straightforward, her labour was not. It dragged on for two long days and three nights until at last, at around 2 a.m. on 12 October, she was delivered of a healthy son – 'the most beautiful boy that ever was seen'.[28] He was christened Edward in honour of its being the eve of the feast of the translation of Edward the Confessor.

It was later rumoured that the precious prince had been born by Caesarean, and that Henry had been forced to choose between mother and child (opting for the latter). This is unfounded, however, and such procedures were not performed in England until considerably later. Only in cases when the mother was dead or dying would a living foetus be cut out of her. Sixteenth-century obstetrics would have made the chances of survival virtually non-existent if such an operation had been performed on a living woman, and Jane showed every sign of making a normal recovery from the birth.

Transported with joy, the king rode to Hampton Court to meet his new son, the saviour of his dynasty. Meanwhile, the happy tidings were conveyed to all corners of the kingdom, as well as to the potentates of Europe. Two thousand rounds of ammunition were shot off from the Tower of London, and wild celebrations broke out in cities and villages across the country.

A lavish christening was held three days later in the chapel at Hampton Court, beneath the dazzling blue hammer-beam ceiling, which was decorated with angels and gold stars. A fire pan of perfumed coals was lit, and a special basin was prepared to wash the precious infant. A huge octagonal platform was built in the centre of the chapel, upon which the font was raised so that the many guests could get a good view of the moment when the baby prince was anointed by Archbishop Cranmer. The christening was held at night, and the long procession was guided by a series of torch bearers. Both of Edward's half-sisters – the four-year-old Elizabeth and the twenty-one-year-old Mary – were in attendance, and six gentlemen of the privy chamber held a rich canopy over him as he was carried to the chapel, clad in a white gown. After the ceremony, the guests were served wine and specially made wafers.

Edward was then carried back to his parents to be blessed. His triumphant mother sat upright in bed, wearing a gown of red velvet edged with ermine. She seemed well and plans were already under way for her churching. But then disaster struck. The queen suddenly began to sicken, complaining of a fever and nausea. Her attendants swathed her in furs and gave her the rich foods she asked for, but her condition rapidly deteriorated. A number of doctors – including Butts – were hastily summoned to her bedside, and reported that 'All this night she hath been very sick.'[29] On 24 October, the Earl of Rutland told Cromwell that Jane had been bleeding heavily. Her almoner, Robert Aldrich, administered extreme unction to her later that day and informed the king of his wife's perilous condition. She died just before midnight.

Jane's death has commonly been attributed to puerperal fever, a bacterial infection caused by lack of hygiene in the delivery room. The necessity of cleanliness was not appreciated at the time, and midwives and other attendants would not have washed their hands regularly. The potential for transmitting germs was therefore high. More recent theories suggest that Jane had not delivered all of the placenta. The symptoms associated with this problem are commensurate with those exhibited by the dying queen, notably heavy bleeding and fever. Such conditions were not known of at the time, however, and in the wake of Jane's demise, members of Henry's court were quick to ascribe the blame elsewhere. Cromwell, for example, opined that it was 'the fault of them that were about her which suffered her to take great cold and to eat things that her fantasy in sickness called for.'[30]

'Divine Providence has mingled my joy with the bitterness of the death of her who brought me to this happiness,' Henry lamented in a letter to his French rival, Francis I.[31] It is not certain whether he had been with his third wife when she died. He was at Esher when Aldrich's message had arrived, but he had not left for Hampton

Court immediately. Ever paranoid about sickness, he had claimed the continuing prevalence of the plague as an excuse.

Jane Seymour has gone down in history as the only wife whom Henry really loved. Certainly he revered her memory – as well he might, given that she alone had succeeded in bearing him a son. The mourning period was pronounced, and courtiers and servants were issued with black gowns and black cloth. The king and his immediate family wore the traditional royal mourning colour of deep blue. Even five months later, Princess Mary was obliged to write to Thomas Cromwell, anxious to know whether she should still wear mourning at the Easter court.[32] Jane's clothes are the only ones, of all his wives, that Henry kept, carefully preserved at the palace of Whitehall. Hers was the only portrait that hung in the royal collection by the time of Henry's death. But this does not necessarily mean that it had been a true love match. Rather, Jane's memory would be forever sacred because she had been the only wife to succeed in the one thing that mattered to Henry.

Just days after Jane's death, the diplomat Sir John Wallop reported that the 'king was in good health and merry as a widower may be'.[33] But Henry observed the necessary decorum in the run-up to her funeral on 13 November and retired to a 'solitary place to pass his sorrows'.[34] The preparation of a king or queen's body for burial required an elaborate ritual. This involved purging the corpse, which was then eviscerated and embalmed with spices before being wrapped in a cerecloth. Encased in lead and sealed in a wooden coffin, Jane's body was displayed in the presence chamber at Hampton Court until 31 October. Throughout this period, the ladies and gentlemen of her household maintained a sombre vigil.

Any lingering regret that the king felt about his wife's passing was assuaged by the knowledge that their young son was thriving. Far from being the sickly child that history has often portrayed him as, Edward was a robust little boy and, as Cromwell put it, 'sucketh like a child of his puissance'.[35] But Henry was taking no chances. He ordered that the son whom he referred to as 'this whole realm's most precious jewel' should remain at Hampton Court, well away from the perpetual sickness that plagued the capital.[36] More conscious of hygiene than most of his contemporaries, the king provided a new washhouse at the palace and ordered that the walls, floors and ceilings of Edward's apartments should be washed down several times a day. Everything that might be handled by the prince had first to be washed. Only those of the rank of knight or above were permitted to attend the prince, and they must all be scrupulously clean before touching him, as well as free from sickness. They were not permitted to speak with persons suspected of having been in contact with the plague, and they were strictly forbidden from visiting London during the summer, when outbreaks of the disease most commonly occurred. Any servant who fell ill was ordered to leave the household at once. Serving boys and dogs were specifically barred because they were clumsy and prone to infection.'

Situated in the north range of Chapel Court, Edward's suite of rooms was laid out in a similar manner to the king's. A magnificent cradle of state took pride of place in the presence chamber, where privileged visitors could catch a glimpse of the precious infant. This was accessed via a processional stair and a heavily guarded watching chamber. Edward's privy chamber served as a day nursery, and he slept in the bedchamber or 'rocking chamber' in a cradle protected from the sun by a canopy. Next door was a bathroom and garderobe, which still survives.

Henry also commissioned a privy kitchen for his son at Hampton Court in order to ensure that there was no contamination from the main kitchens that served the rest of the household. Once he had been weaned, all of the prince's food would be tested by a servant before being given to him, his clothes were washed, brushed and tried on before being worn, and any new garments were to be washed, dried by the fire and anointed with perfume before they were deemed fit for Edward to wear. No detail was overlooked. A rare glimpse of the prince's bedchamber at Hampton Court is provided by a reference to the making of 'a frame of scaffold polls over the prince's bed to keep away the heat of the sun.'[37] The same strict standards were applied to the other residences that Edward and his sizeable household stayed in, notably Richmond Palace, Havering-atte-Bower and Hunsdon.

But all of the king's assiduous care was administered at a distance: Henry adhered to royal tradition by being as absent a father to Edward as he was to Mary and Elizabeth. A rare glimpse of him paying a visit to his infant son was recorded in May 1538, when he spent the day with Edward 'dallying with him in his arms a long space and so holding him in a window to the sight and great comfort of all the people.'[38]

By contrast, Edward's elder half-sister Mary was a regular visitor to the nursery. Aged twenty-one at the time of his birth, she had a strong maternal instinct and lavished affection on her motherless baby brother. She also gave him various gifts – all of which were more personal (and no doubt welcome) than those he received from his father. At New Year 1539, for example, she gave him a made-to-measure coat of crimson satin embroidered with gold and pearls and with sleeves of tinsel. The king, meanwhile, presented him with a lavish gilt standing cup – the same gift that he might have given one of his adult courtiers. Throughout his childhood, and before their relationship was soured by differing religious views, Edward was very fond of his elder sister. He 'took special content' in her company and once assured her that despite his infrequent letters: 'I love you most.'[39] He was also fond of his other half-sister Elizabeth, to whom he was much closer in age. Elizabeth had learned to sew by the age of six and she made a shirt of cambric or fine white linen for her brother. Upon trying out a new quill, she wrote 'Edwardus' across the page in her careful, childlike scrawl.

For the first years of his life, Edward was raised 'among the women', as he recalled in his journal some time later.[40] They were responsible for teaching the young prince these fundamentals of etiquette, as well as for catering to his every need. They included his nurse, 'Mother Jack', and Sybil Penn, who took over from her in October 1538 and remained in that post until 1544.[41] Edward adored Sybil and on one occasion, when she carried him in to be presented to some visiting dignitaries at court, the young boy was overcome with shyness and refused to look at them, but clung to his nurse and buried his face in her neck. Sybil's brother-in-law, William Sidney, a member of the king's privy chamber, was appointed Chamberlain to the prince. Numerous other officials were appointed for Edward's care, and in its first year alone his household cost £6,500 (the equivalent of almost £2 million) to administer.

Principal among Edward's household was the experienced Lady Margaret Bryan, who had proved her ability and trustworthiness as the 'Lady Governess' to both of the king's daughters, Mary and Elizabeth. Capable and efficient, she had been a stern mistress to the princesses, but she had something of a soft spot for their baby brother. In March 1539, she reported the seventeen-month-old prince's progress to Thomas Cromwell: 'My lord Prince is in good health and merry. Would to God the King and your Lordship had seen him last night. The minstrels played, and his Grace danced and played so wantonly that he could not stand still.'[42]

The troupe of minstrels described by Lady Bryan had been appointed to the prince by his indulgent father, who was determined that he should have everything that his young heart might desire. Little wonder that the few visitors who were permitted access to his apartments described him as a contented child. He was also a strong one. In August 1539, Lord Chancellor Audley paid a visit to the prince's nursery and reported back to Cromwell that Edward 'waxeth firm and stiff'. He could stand unaided and would probably have been able to walk if his nursemaids had let him.[43]

Although Henry undoubtedly devoted the greatest attention to his precious son and heir, he was a doting (if distant) father to all of his children. Among his personal possessions at Whitehall was a collection of mementos from their infancy. An inventory of the palace includes a 'little box of crimson satin embroidered, containing shirts and other things for young children.'[44] Whether these were keepsakes from Edward, Mary and Elizabeth, or were made for the short-lived babies and pregnancies of Catherine of Aragon and Anne Boleyn, is impossible to say.

8

'True carnal copulation'

HENRY REMAINED A bachelor for two years after the death of
Jane Seymour. This was the longest period that England had
been without a queen since the beginning of the reign and it had
profound consequences for the structure of the court. With no
queen, there was no need for the scores of women who made up
her household. This altered the sexual dynamics of the court considerably, depriving not only the king but his male attendants of the
more pleasurable diversions that court life had to offer. Given that
Henry had traditionally chosen his wives from among these ladies,
action needed to be taken. He might have had a son at last, but his
own childhood had proved the necessity of having a spare heir.

The turmoil of his marital history thus far had perhaps made the
king more inclined to allow politics, not passion, to dictate the
choice of his next bride. There was another reason why Henry was
prepared to settle for a less than ideal wife. Aged forty-six at the
time of Jane's death, he was considered an old man by the standards
of the time. The jousting accident of 1536 had set in train increasingly frequent (and painful) bouts of ill health, the most serious of
which occurred in 1538 when the skin on his ulcerated leg closed
over. This caused the infected matter to seep into his body, as the
French ambassador Castillon reported: 'The King has had stopped
one of the fistulas of his legs, and for 10 or 12 days the humors
which had no outlet were like to have stifled him, so that he was
sometime without speaking, black in the face and in great danger.'[1]
The king was so ill on this occasion that his life was despaired of
and frantic preparations were made for the succession. The condition that Henry was suffering from may have been osteomyelitis, a

septic infection of the bone resulting from the jousting injury. This causes splinters of bone to break away, and when they periodically work their way through the skin, there is sudden swelling and intense pain, relieved only by a discharge of pus and the removal of the bone shard.[2] Another theory is that Henry was suffering from deep vein thrombosis, as a result either of his injury or of his penchant for wearing a tightly bound garter below his knee. Immobility and obesity can render this condition severe enough to cause ulceration.[3] Whatever the cause of his painful (and pungent) ulcer, from thenceforth the royal physicians resolved to keep the wound constantly open.

Henry recovered from this scare, but his immune system had evidently been weakened because he soon afterwards fell ill with a bad cold and a chill. For the latter, his physicians administered a laxative and an enema. The humiliation that such treatments involved must have served as an uncomfortable reminder to Henry that he was no longer the virile and athletic man of his early years as king, when he had been the envy of the world. A telling remark that he made in 1537 reveals that he was painfully aware of this fact. A Parisian jeweller named Jehan Langues had presented a range of fashionable items to the English king that year, including an embroidered gown and hose. He subsequently confided to a fellow countryman: 'The King was very glad to see such riches. I told him they were made for him. He said he was too old to wear such things, but he offered 4,000 crowns for both.'[4]

Another reminder of his advancing years was the fact that the King of England was no longer considered such a prize in the international marriage market. Among the various ladies who were proposed as his fourth wife was Christina, the beautiful Duchess of Milan, who at nineteen was thirty years his junior. She made no secret of her distaste for the idea and tartly replied that if she had two heads, then one would be at Henry's disposal.

The English king soon found consolation for this scornful rejection in the form of Anne, sister of Duke Wilhelm of Cleves, whom the English ambassador claimed outshone Christina of Milan as the sun did the moon. Anne had first been mooted as a potential bride in the closing weeks of 1537, very soon after the death of Jane Seymour. She was then twenty-two years of age, and had already been betrothed to François, heir to the duchy of Lorraine, in 1527. This had come to nothing, leaving her free to marry elsewhere. Henry's chief minister Cromwell championed the match enthusiastically because Cleves, like England, had rejected papal authority. If the marriage went forward, it would therefore give a much-needed boost to his religious reforms.

Henry had initially proved reluctant, having heard no reliable accounts of Anne's beauty, but by 1539 he was in need of new allies overseas and was therefore willing to reconsider. In March, he finally agreed that negotiations could begin, but insisted that Master Holbein be dispatched to Cleves to take the lady's likeness. Cromwell may have secretly briefed Holbein before he departed because the artist so famed for his accuracy seems to have rather flattered the lady – or at least, painted her from the most favourable angle. The king was delighted when he saw the finished piece, which displayed Anne's pretty, doll-like face, her fair hair, dark eyes, delicate mouth and chin, and demure, maidenly expression to perfection. With considerably more enthusiasm than he had shown before, Henry told Cromwell to bring the negotiations to a speedy conclusion. His minister needed little prompting: the marriage treaty was swiftly drawn up and was signed by both parties on 4 October.

Anne duly set out from Cleves and made her way with great ceremony to meet her new husband. Henry, meanwhile, busied himself with preparing the court for his bride. Gleefully anticipating the wedding night, he commissioned a beautiful headboard, fashioned from oak and decorated with painted carvings, all on the theme of conjugal pleasure and fertility. At one end was a man with a bulging codpiece and at the other a woman with meek, downcast eyes, holding a sword and serpent, which were well-known phallic symbols. That the king hoped their union would result in the birth of new heirs is made plain by the carved cherubs flying over the heads of the couple.

The object of Henry's lustful imaginings reached England in the closing days of 1539 and saw in the New Year with lavish celebrations at Rochester Castle. The next day, eager to meet his exquisite new bride, Henry rode south with his attendants. Following the custom favoured by Renaissance monarchs who were betrothed to foreign brides whom they had not met, Henry hastened to greet her in disguise. The theory was that the lady would instantly recognise her true love, despite his disguise. Unfortunately, things turned out rather differently. When Henry and his entourage crept into the castle, Anne was watching a bullfight. She was not expecting to meet her new husband for another two days, so had not donned her finest clothes or prepared herself in any other way. Then, suddenly, a group of masked men burst into the room. Still reeling from the shock, she was assailed by one of them, who strode up to her and tried to kiss her. She angrily repelled him, cursing in German.

Anne had not only failed to recognise her 'true love' but had shown a complete ignorance of the courtly games that he so enjoyed. For Henry at least, the die was cast. Anne did not possess the courtly refinements that he expected in a wife. She was dressed in 'monstrous habit and apparel' and wore a headdress of 'her own country fashion'. The French ambassador reported that her clothing looked 'strange to many', and her ladies 'were dressed so heavily and unbecomingly they would almost be thought ugly even if they were beautiful.'[5]

Neither was Anne endowed with any of the physical charms that Henry looked for in a consort. In contrast to the petite stature of his first three wives, she was tall and big-boned. She had a large nose that had been cleverly disguised by the angle of Holbein's portrait, and her skin was pitted with the marks of smallpox. Her body odour was so strong that it was remarked upon by several members of the court.

As soon as the meeting was over, the king rounded on Cromwell, shouting: 'I like her not! I like her not!' He ordered his minister to get him out of the match immediately. Miserably, Cromwell admitted that the contract was watertight and his royal master had no choice but to go ahead with the marriage. Henry and Anne met again on 3 January. This had been intended as their first meeting, and if it had been then things might have worked out differently, for Anne was fully prepared this time. Dressed in a magnificent cloth of gold and wearing a headdress studded with oriental pearls, a coronet of black velvet and a necklace of sparkling stones, she displayed an 'amiable aspect and womanly behaviour'. Henry, meanwhile, gave every appearance of the doting husband-to-be, beaming 'with most lovely countenance and princely behaviour'.[6] But he did not fool everyone. 'It was much noticed that the King came along with her, but showed in his face he was disappointed,' observed the author of the *Spanish Chronicle*. 'It was noticed that from that day forward the King was not so gay as usual.'[7]

In truth, Anne had more reason to be disappointed in her betrothed than he was in her. Up to his mid-thirties, Henry had been exceptionally athletic and had taken part in regular, rigorous sporting activities. But the jousting injury that he had suffered almost four years earlier had forced him to spend more time indoors. Thereafter, he had rapidly gained weight and frequently complained of ill health. The French ambassador Marillac was astonished by the king's 'marvellous excess' in eating.[8] His expanding waistline is demonstrated by the measurements of his suits of armour. Between 1514 and 1536, Henry had gained only two inches around his waist, but by 1541 his measurements had expanded by a staggering seventeen inches so that his waist was now fifty inches. His chest, meanwhile, had expanded to fifty-seven inches – an increase of twelve inches. Little wonder that in the latter year, the royal armourer described his sovereign as 'very stout'.[9]

A sketch by the Antwerp artist Cornelius Matsys taken four years later shows the king as a grotesque figure. His beady eyes and tiny, pursed mouth are submerged in the layers of flesh that surround them. He appears to have no neck, and his enormous frame extends beyond the reaches of the sketch. 'The King was so stout that such a man has never been seen,' observed one contemporary. 'Three of the biggest men that could be found could get inside his doublet.'[10]

This is corroborated by a portrait painted in around 1542, which shows the king in an enormous loose-fitting coat that he wore over several layers of clothing in an attempt to disguise his bulk. In his left hand he grasps a gold-topped staff, upon which he would lean

heavily even for short walks around his palaces. As Henry's immobility increased, so his staffs became more elaborate. Some were
equipped with a variety of accessories, such as a pomander, inkpot
and pen, and gold counters. Eager to flatter their king by imitation,
his courtiers added ever more layers and padding to their own outfits.
They also wore bonnets, which had become fashionable since Henry
had been obliged to wear them to hide his thinning hair.

The king's diet, and in particular his love of red meat, had
caused other problems for his health. As he grew into middle age
and his metabolism slowed down, he suffered from painful constipation, which necessitated prolonged and often painful visits to
his close-stool. Henry also drank lots of red wine, which meant
that he needed to urinate frequently. It also made him dehydrated
– his thirst was said to be 'unquenchable' – which exacerbated his
constipation.

In 1539, Thomas Heneage, groom of the stool, reported on a
particularly bad bout of constipation to his patron, Thomas
Cromwell, who took a keen interest in every detail of the king's
business. To alleviate their royal master's symptoms, the physicians
had prescribed a pill and an enema – a pig's bladder with a greased
metal tube fixed in it, which was inserted into the king's anus. The
bladder would contain more than a pint of a weak solution of salt
and infused herbs, which would remain in the anus for one or two
hours. Having thus administered this uncomfortable treatment, the
physicians advised their royal master to go to bed early – although
it is hard to imagine that he would have been able to do much
else. Heneage noted that the king 'slept until two of the clock in
the morning and then his Grace rose to go to the stool, which, by
working of the pills and the glyster [enema] that his Highness had
taken before, had a very fair siege, as the said physicians have made
report; not doubting but the worst is past by their perseverance,
to no danger of any further grief to remain in him.' He added,
though, that the king had 'a little soreness in his body.'[11] Having
suffered recurrent bouts of constipation such as this, Henry developed piles. These were treated with rhubarb, which offered some
relief but did not eradicate the problem altogether. Despite his

discomfort, Henry showed no inclination to moderate his diet. Instead, his consumption of rich foods increased as his reign progressed.

If it was not exactly a match made in heaven for either Henry or Anne, they had little choice but to make the best of it. The king grumbled that he had to 'put my neck in the yoke', and snarled at Cromwell: 'My lord if it were not to satisfy the world and my realm I would not do that I must do this day for no earthly thing.'[12] He and Anne duly made their way to Greenwich, where several days of wedding celebrations had been planned. The contemporary chronicler Edward Hall described the sumptuous decorations on nearby Blackheath, which included 'a rich cloth of gold and divers other tents and pavilions in the which were made fires and perfumes for her [Anne] and such ladies as should receive her grace.'[13] It is tempting to speculate that the heavily fragranced tents were devised to mask the bride's pungent aroma. Her ladies also interlaced Anne's coronet with sprigs of rosemary.

Henry himself gave no hint that he was anything less than delighted at the prospect of marrying Anne. He certainly dressed for the occasion, being resplendent in 'rich cloth of gold traversed lattice wise square, all over embroidered with flat gold of damask, pearled on every side of the embroidery, the buckles and pendants were all of fine gold.' To keep out the chill winter air, the king wore a coat of purple velvet, the sleeves and breast of which were tied together with 'great buttons of diamonds, rubies and orient pearl'. To complete the splendid outfit, he wore a hat 'so rich of jewels that few men could value them'.[14]

Meanwhile, Anne's ladies were busy putting the finishing touches to her wedding clothes. The end result was no less impressive than the outfit of her betrothed. When she heard that the king was approaching, she emerged from her tent in a rich gown of cloth of gold. Like Henry, she wore a cap decorated with pearls, and around her neck was a chain studded with such large stones that they 'glistened all the field'.[15] All of the attendants were similarly apparelled so that the whole wedding party made such a dazzling sight that the watching crowds – who were well used to the spectacle of Tudor pageantry – had never seen the like. It was as if Henry was trying to blind them to the true farce that was being played out before their eyes.

Ironically, there are more detailed and laudatory descriptions of this, Henry's least favourite wedding, than any other. It took place early in the morning of 6 January, three days after the couple's arrival in Greenwich, and was celebrated with enough pomp and ceremony to fool even the most eagle-eyed guest that it was an occasion of heartfelt joy for both parties.

By nine o'clock they were man and wife and, after hearing Mass, each departed to their own chambers to prepare for the wedding feast. Henry immediately changed out of his wedding clothes (a telling detail that was innocently reported by Hall), whereas Anne remained in hers for the feast. Only then did she change into an unflattering outfit that was described as being 'like a man's gown, of tissue with long sleeves girt to her, furred with rich sables.' At length, after all the elaborate ceremonials were over, she and her new husband retired 'to take their rest'.[16]

If the king was prepared to do his duty in public, in private it was a very different matter. Among the records of Henry's reign is a detailed account of what happened on the wedding night. The bride and groom were put to bed with the usual ceremony, each giving every appearance of joyful anticipation of what lay ahead. As soon as the servants had departed, Henry ran his hands all over Anne's body in a half-hearted attempt to 'stir up lust', but was so repelled that he was incapable of doing more. They spent the rest of the night sleeping chastely next to each other. The following morning, Henry graciously took his leave of Anne and hastened to his own bedchamber, where he found Cromwell anxiously waiting for news. Tentatively, his minister asked how he liked his new queen, to which Henry retorted: 'As you know, I liked her before not well but now I like her much worse.' He went on to complain: 'She is nothing fair, and has very evil smells about her.'

More damningly, Henry claimed that there had been certain 'tokens' to suggest that Anne was no virgin: 'I have felt her belly

and her breasts and thereby as I can judge she should be no maid.'
His conviction rendered the king incapable of consummating the
union. 'I had neither will nor courage to proceed any further in
other matters', he told Cromwell, insisting: 'I have left her as good
a maid as I found her.'[17] There is nothing to substantiate his claim
that Anne was not a virgin, and it is likely that Henry had already
seized upon the idea of having the marriage annulled on the basis
of her previous betrothal. Hinting that she had previous sexual
experience was a good way of setting the ball rolling.

But there may have been another explanation for Henry's failure
to consummate the marriage. He was more than twice his young
bride's age and had become increasingly incapacitated in recent
years. Although he still liked to play the game of courtly love, there
had been no talk of a mistress for some time. It is therefore possible
that he was impotent. Kings, even more than ordinary men, prided
themselves on their sexual potency. This was more than mere vanity:
it was vital for the continuation of their dynasty. Even though Henry
was so desperate to secure an annulment that he was willing to
suffer the humiliation of admitting in public that he had been unable
to consummate the marriage, he was at pains to stress that this had
been entirely due to Anne,. rather than any physical shortcomings
of his own. He told his physician, Dr Butts, that he had had 'two
wet dreams', and made sure that this became public knowledge.[18]
But the more he protested, the less credible his explanation seemed.

Anne's own account of the wedding night suggests that she was
entirely innocent in the ways of the world. She believed that Henry's
chaste caresses amounted to a consummation and that she might
already be pregnant. 'How can I be a maid . . . and sleep every night
with the King?' she demanded of her ladies. 'When he comes to
bed he kisses me, and taketh me by the hand, and biddeth me,
Goodnight, sweetheart: and in the morning kisses me, and biddeth
me, Farewell, darling. Is this not enough?' The Countess of Rutland
retorted: 'Madam, there must be more than this, or it will be long
ere we have a Duke of York, which all this realm most desireth.'[19]

Taking the cue from her ladies, Anne soon realised something
was seriously wrong and sought to remedy the situation. She started

by asking the advice of Thomas Cromwell, rightly judging that he had a vested interest in making sure her marriage was consummated. This was hardly a subject for a man more used to dealing with legal and financial matters, however, and Cromwell shrank from the task. Instead, he instructed Anne's Lord Chamberlain, the Earl of Rutland, to advise her how to 'stir up lust' in her new husband.[20] Cromwell probably also instructed Rutland's wife, who served in Anne's privy chamber, to report on the royal couple's sexual activity.

At the same time, Cromwell quietly urged the king's deputy groom of the stool, Anthony Denny, to whisper words of encouragement in his royal master's ear, taking 'evermore occasion to praise [Anne] to the King's highness'. This was an unenviable task, and the hapless Denny soon admitted defeat. Henry upbraided his groom: 'He would utter plainly to him, as to a servant whom he used secretly about him . . . that he could never . . . be provoked and stirred to know her carnally.'[21]

A few months later, when Henry's lawyers were striving to secure an annulment, the king called upon Denny to bear witness to his 'lack of will and power to consummate the same'. The king was confident his servant would 'testify according to truth; which is, that I never for love to the woman consented to marry; nor yet, if she brought maidenhead with her, took any from her by true carnal copulation.'[22] That Denny would have known for certain whether his royal master had consummated his new marriage reveals the intimate nature of the groom's relationship with the king.

For now, though, Anne was doing her best to please her new husband. Contemporary descriptions attest that she was assiduous in her dress, choosing the richest fabrics and finest jewels. In order to mask her 'evil airs', her ladies may have scented her clothes with herbs and spices, such as lavender, mint and nutmeg, or prepared sweet-smelling pomanders to carry about her person. But it was all in vain. Although Henry continued to visit Anne's bedchamber, nothing more passed between them than affectionate sentiments and goodnight kisses.

With the king spending as little time as possible with his new wife, Anne had many hours to while away in her privy chamber.

Her attendants soon understood why the king thought she lacked the refinements expected of a consort. The education of noble ladies in Cleves was very different to that in England. The English ambassador there noted that although Anne could read and write in her own language, she was unable to speak any other. Neither could she sing or play an instrument. But she still enjoyed music and during her time at the English court she employed a troupe of musicians to entertain her. Among them were several members of the Jewish Bassano family from Italy, who were skilled recorder players and had been discovered by Cromwell's agents in Venice. Anne also enjoyed gambling with her ladies at cards or dice, and took delight in the beautiful gardens of her husband's palaces.

The king, meanwhile, was seeking diversion with another lady at court. He had probably met Katherine Howard, the attractive young niece of the Duke of Norfolk, on the very same night that he first laid eyes upon Anne of Cleves, because she was among the latter's maids of honour. Her age is not certain, but she could have been as young as fifteen at the time of her entrée to court. Although young, Katherine was no innocent. She had been raised by her father's stepmother, the Dowager Duchess of Norfolk, whose household was notorious for its immorality. Katherine was probably only about twelve years old when she had her first sexual liaison, with her music teacher. This was soon followed by an affair with her kinsman, Francis Dereham. That they had had full sex is well attested: one eyewitness recorded that there was much 'panting and puffing' in the communal bedchamber and that they were forever 'hanging together by the belly like sparrows'.[23] Katherine herself later admitted that she knew how to 'meddle' with a man without conceiving a child, so she was clearly very experienced for her years.[24]

Methods of contraception were rudimentary in Tudor times, to say the least. Among the more obvious (and reliable) was the withdrawal method. More outlandish ones included placing a hemlock plaster on the man's testicles, or hiding a cockerel's testicles under the bed. A primitive form of barrier was made from a sponge soaked in herbs or vinegar, while other women went to the more extreme measure of using wax to seal up the uterus. The first condoms, made from linen, lambskin or animal gut, were introduced in the sixteenth century and were popularly known as the 'Venus Glove'.

Although the Dowager Duchess had allowed Katherine a great deal of freedom in her household, when she discovered that she had been having sex with Francis Dereham, she decided to act. With her stepson's help, she had secured Katherine a position in the new queen's household as a means of safeguarding her reputation.

Pretty and vivacious, Katherine provided a perfect antidote to the king's new wife. Her ambitious uncle, Norfolk, was quick to spy an opportunity and therefore began to arrange meetings between her and Henry. In April 1540, the king gave Katherine a gift of land, together with '23 lengths of quilted sarsenet [fine soft silk]'. This did not escape the notice of one sharp-eyed courtier, who noted that Henry 'crept too near another lady'.[25] Anne herself was aware of it, and on 20 June complained to the Duke of Cleves' ambassador in London. Meanwhile, tutored by her uncle, Katherine was careful to play the maid with her royal suitor, who was all too willing to believe that she was innocent in the ways of men.

Events now moved apace. On 24 June, Anne received orders from the council to remove herself from court and go to Richmond Palace. From there, she learned that her marriage to the English king had been called into question because Henry was concerned about her prior betrothal to the Duke of Lorraine, and had therefore refrained from consummating the union. An ecclesiastical inquiry was duly commissioned, and a delegation of councillors arrived at Richmond in early July to seek Anne's cooperation. Shocked by this sudden turn of events, she fainted. Having recovered her composure, she steadfastly refused to give her consent to the inquiry.

But Anne had learned from the example of her predecessors and was too great a pragmatist to stand out on principle for long. The marriage was duly declared illegal on 9 July, and the annulment was confirmed by parliament three days later. With great dignity, Anne told her estranged husband: 'Though this case must needs be most hard and sorrowful unto me, for the great love which I bear your most noble person, yet, having more regard to God and his truth than to any worldly affection . . . I knowledge myself hereby to accept and approve the same.' She also admitted to the king's 'clean and pure living with me', and offered herself up as his 'most humble servant'.[26]

Anne was richly rewarded for her compliance. She was given possession of Richmond Palace and Bletchingley Manor for life, together with a considerable annual income. This was further boosted by her right to keep all of her royal jewels, plate and goods in order to furnish her new properties. Any sense of disgrace was avoided by according her the exalted status of the king's 'sister', which meant that she took precedence over all of his subjects, with the exception of his children and any future wife that he might take. Henry later granted her some additional manors, including Hever Castle, the former home of Anne Boleyn. This was to become her principal residence, and she lived a very comfortable life there on the fringes of public life. She was also permitted to visit court from time to time, and her former husband favoured her with several visits, which, by all accounts, were very convivial. It says much for Anne's strength of character that she managed to accept and adapt to her new life with dignity – and, perhaps, a certain feeling of relief.

Once the annulment had been confirmed, the king wasted no time in marrying Katherine Howard. Their wedding took place on 28 July 1540, the very same day that his disgraced minister Cromwell was executed. It was conducted in some secrecy and only made public two weeks later, on 8 August. Henry commissioned a French craftsman to create an ornate 'pearl bed' for the wedding night, at great expense. The contrast to his previous marriage could not have been greater. While Anne's unattractiveness had apparently rendered Henry impotent, he could not keep his hands off his nubile young wife. 'The King is so amorous of her that he cannot treat her well enough and caresses her more than he did the others,' reported the scandalised French ambassador.[27]

It is easy to understand what Henry saw in Katherine. She had a playful exuberance and vitality that must have appealed to the ageing king, who was desperate to recapture his own youthful vigour. Small in stature with a curvaceous figure, auburn hair and sparkling eyes that resembled those of her late cousin, Anne Boleyn, she dressed stylishly in the rich clothes and jewels to which she now had ready access. Knowing his young wife's passion for adornments, as part of his wedding gift Henry gave her an upper billiment (the decorative trim at the top of her French hood) of 'goldsmith work enamelled and garnished with 7 fair diamonds, 7 fair rubies and 7 fair pearls', together with a gold pendant set with 'a very fair table diamond and a very fair ruby with a long pearl hanging at the same', and a necklace 'containing 28 rubies and 29 clusters of pearls being 4 pearls in every cluster'.[28] Courtiers looked on with a mixture of dismay and amusement as their sovereign lavished such gifts upon his new bride, who was content to treat him like a sugar daddy. 'The King had no wife who made him spend so much money in dresses and jewels as she did, who every day had some fresh caprice,' observed one visitor to court. 'She was the handsomest of his wives, and also the most giddy.'[29]

As a further demonstration of favour towards his new wife, Henry appointed Katherine's brother Charles as a gentleman of his privy chamber. Other members of her family soon found preferment. Her brother-in-law, Robert Radcliffe, Earl of Sussex, was appointed Lord Great Chamberlain, and her cousin, the Earl of Surrey, became a Knight of the Garter.

Thrilled though she was at becoming queen, with all of the attendant luxuries and privileges of the position, Katherine can hardly have been attracted to her ageing, corpulent husband. If she found him repellent, though, she was wise enough not to show it. Besides, she may have escaped the distasteful business of having sex with him. For all Henry's pawing desire for his new bride, there is no evidence that he was any more able to consummate this marriage than he had been his previous one. If the king had once more found himself to be impotent, his doctors may have administered a number of remedies. One of the most popular was a concoction made from the testicles of quail mixed with large winged ants, bark oil and amber. This was then applied liberally to the affected member. Alternatively, the left testicle could be trussed up in a tourniquet, or the phallically shaped mandrake root was prescribed – whether to eat or imbibe in some other way is not clear.

It was probably in an attempt to regain his lost vigour that, towards the end of 1540, Henry embarked upon a new health and fitness regime. Ambassador Marillac observed that the king would now 'rise between five and six a.m., hear mass at 7 a.m., and then ride until dinner time, which is 10 a.m.'[30] For a man of Henry's size and debilitating ailments, such excursions must have been extremely uncomfortable (for horse as well as rider), but Henry was not giving up. He began to experiment more and more with his own remedies, as well as consulting the leading physicians of the day.

Although the king declared himself 'rejuvenated' after embarking upon his new lifestyle, he was struck down with another serious illness in March 1541. This left him depressed, as well as incapacitated. 'Besides the bodily malady, he had a *mal d'esprit*,' reported the French ambassador, Marillac. He went on to describe how paranoid and suspicious the king had become, so that he eschewed the company of formerly trusted favourites and advisers. In place of the famously pleasure-loving prince was an insular, watchful and menacing king who seemed to become more like his father every day. 'He spent Shrovetide without recreation, even of music, in which he used to take as much pleasure as any prince in Christendom,' the ambassador continued, 'and stayed at Hampton Court with so little company that his Court resembled more a private family than a king's train.'[31] This tendency to retreat into his private domain became ever more pronounced during the years that followed.

If the rumours at court were to be believed, despite his physical shortcomings, the king and his young wife were able to have full sexual intercourse. On 10 April, Marillac reported: 'The Queen is thought to be with child, which would be a very great joy to this king, who, it seems, believes it and intends, if it be found true, to have her crowned at Whitsuntide.' Before long, rumour had turned to firm conviction and certain 'young lords and gentlemen of this court' were seen practising for the jousts and tournaments that would accompany the queen's coronation – which, presumably, would only take place when she had borne the king a child.[32] But it had either been a false alarm or Katherine had miscarried, because there was no talk of her pregnancy thereafter, and by the end of June the king and his court prepared to go on a progress to the north.

At the same time, a scandal was beginning to unfold in the queen's private affairs. Shortly before her husband's fiftieth birthday on 28 June, Katherine began an adulterous affair with Thomas Culpeper, a gentleman of the king's privy chamber. Described as a 'beautiful youth', Culpeper was something of a sexual predator and had been accused of raping a park keeper's wife in 1539. Only his favour with the king had enabled him to escape punishment. As well as being among Henry's closest body servants, Culpeper had also attended important occasions of state, such as the reception of Anne of Cleves upon her arrival in England. He and Katherine had struck up a secret flirtation that April, just as rumours of the queen's pregnancy had started to circulate. Henry had been incapacitated with illness that month, which had allowed his young wife more hours of private leisure.

Katherine would have come into regular contact with the men of her husband's privy chamber because they were by now in more or less constant attendance upon the king. Thus, for example, when the couple went on a short winter progress in 1540, they took with them only four Privy Councillors and 'the Ladies, Gentlemen, and Gentlewomen of their Privy Chambers.'[33] Not surprisingly, therefore, when the new queen accompanied the king on his progress to York that summer, Culpeper went with them.

The logistics for this progress would have been even more complex than usual, given the king's deteriorating health and mobility. Although his personal servants had devised increasingly sophisticated means of transporting their royal master up and down the stairs of his palaces, the same devices were not available at the homes of private individuals. Thus, when Henry and Katherine visited Sir John Russell's Buckinghamshire home of Chenies that year, their host was obliged to arrange for a special state bed, with cloth of gold and silver hangings embellished with Henry's arms, to be placed in the 'lower chamber'.[34]

Meanwhile, the queen was also taking a more than usual interest in the accommodation that would be provided for her on progress – albeit for very different reasons. In order to prepare the ground for her secret trysts with Culpeper, Katherine secretly took steps to discover the layout of her privy lodgings at each of the houses that she and the king were due to visit. According to her later testimony, Lady Rochford, the widow of Anne Boleyn's brother and a lady-in-waiting to the new queen, 'would at every lodging search the back doors and tell her of them if there were any.'[35] Bolstered by this information, every evening Culpeper would creep up the back stairs to Katherine's apartments and spend the night cavorting with her. Another of the queen's ladies, Margaret Morton, acted as lookout when the progress reached Lincoln and Katherine 'went two nights out of her chamber, when it was late, to Lady Rochford's chamber.' Katherine did not return to her own rooms until 2 a.m., and when Margaret duly went to bed herself, her colleague and room-mate, Katherine Tilney, awoke and exclaimed: 'Jesus! Is the Queen not abed yet?' Miss Tilney had not been made privy to her royal mistress's indiscretions, but 'was barred from entering the Queen's room, being stopped at the previous closet room.'[36]

To make matters worse, it was at around the same time that Francis Dereham returned from exile in Ireland. Rather than distancing herself from her former lover, the queen (perhaps submitting to blackmail) took a staggering risk by appointing him as her private secretary and usher of her chamber. Dereham soon proved a liability, boasting to anyone who would listen that if the king died then Katherine was sure to marry him. He also hinted that she had already granted him a number of sexual favours, which aroused Culpeper's jealousy when he heard of it. The new queen had also been obliged to take another former acquaintance into her service. Joan Bulmer had attended her in the Duchess of Norfolk's household and had acted as a messenger between Katherine and Dereham. Now she, too, crawled out of the woodwork demanding employment. 'I know the Queen of England will not forget her secretary.' she wrote to Katherine, in a thinly veiled attempt at blackmail. It worked, and Katherine reluctantly appointed Joan as her chamberer.

The young queen might have got away with her adulterous

activities inside the royal palaces, with their rambling suites of apartments that provided for much greater privacy for those within. But life was very different on progress, when courtiers – and even the royal family – were obliged to adapt to far more restricted living conditions, and privacy was a luxury that few, if any, could enjoy. One of her ladies later testified that Katherine had to resort to meeting Culpeper in the queen's stool chamber.

Katherine had experienced similarly cramped conditions in the Dowager Duchess's household, but had still indulged in sexual dalliances, confident that her fellow residents would turn a blind eye to her indiscretions. But the same was not true of the royal courtiers, who were ever watchful for any signs of scandal. By the time that Henry and his court returned to London, gossip about the queen's indiscretions was rife. One of her household confessed that such significant 'looks pass between the Queen and Culpeper' that she thought 'there was love between them'.[37]

When he heard the rumours, Archbishop Cranmer, who was no friend of the new queen's uncle, decided to investigate. Before long, he had secured the testimony of Mary Lascelles, a member of the Duchess of Norfolk's household who knew of Katherine's scandalous past. Cranmer wasted no time in breaking the news to Henry, who was at prayer in his privy closet, that his wife was not as pure as he had believed. The king's first reaction was disbelief. Even if, behind closed doors, he had been unable to have sex with his beautiful young wife, he still worshipped her. Desperate to prove the allegations against her were false, he ordered an immediate inquiry. This soon found ample evidence to corroborate the rumours that Katherine was no maid when she had married Henry.

Confronted with the shocking and sordid burden of truth, the king called for a sword so that he could slay the queen. He then broke down in tears, complaining to his council of his bad fortune to have met 'such ill-conditioned wives'.[38] Thereafter, Henry fell into a deep depression. His infatuation for Katherine had blinded him to her true character. When he realised she was not his 'rose without a thorn', it broke his heart. To assuage his sorrow, he commissioned a new set of tapestries. Henry had always loved to surround himself by richly woven tapestries and had had hundreds made during his reign. The subjects revealed much about his state of mind, ranging from the 'Story of David', which asserted his arguments in favour of the divorce from Catherine of Aragon, to the lavish religious scenes during the height of the Reformation in the 1530s. The latest set was rather less stridently self-confident. It represented the 'Story of Vulcan and Venus' and depicted the cuckolding of Neptune by Vulcan. In case anyone should miss the message, the scenes were bordered with moralising inscriptions bewailing the painful and deceptive nature of love.

While the king licked his wounds in private, his errant wife and her ladies were confined to her privy lodgings. Even before she was aware of the full extent of the catastrophe, the young queen knew that something was badly wrong because her husband's groom of the stool, Thomas Heneage, had not called by her apartments, as he had at six o'clock every evening, to ask on the king's behalf 'how she did'.[39] The reason for his absence soon became clear when Katherine and her ladies were subjected to intense questioning by Henry's ministers. So far, the evidence only pointed to sexual misconduct before her marriage to the king. But Dereham, who was interrogated in the Tower, asserted that Culpeper 'had succeeded him in the Queen's affections'. The news was relayed at once to the king, who was so distraught upon hearing that his wife had betrayed him – and, worse still, with a beloved private servant – that he left Hampton Court 'suddenly after dinner' and rode to Whitehall.

Although the queen admitted to having flirted with her 'little, sweet fool' Culpeper, she stoutly denied having committed adultery with him. But one by one, her ladies began to confess what they had seen during the summer progress and before long the case against Katherine was compelling. When the full sordid truth began to emerge, as a deliberate act of revenge, Henry confiscated all of his new wife's fine clothes and jewels, ordering that 'Mr Seymour shall remain there [at Hampton Court] with all the jewels and other things of the queen's till she be gone and then to bring them hither.'[40] In vain, Katherine begged her estranged husband to 'bestow some of her clothes on those maid-servants . . . since she had nothing else left to recompense them.'[41] The request fell upon deaf ears. Katherine was now reduced to wearing plain, unadorned dresses – a tangible symbol of her fall from grace. The wardrobe accounts specified that the disgraced queen was allowed 'six French hoods . . . [with] no stone or pearl . . . likewise, as many pair of sleeves, six gowns and six kirtles . . . except always stone and pearl.'[42]

That the queen had been stripped of her fine clothes was typical of the fate of other fallen favourites. The day before his execution on 28 July the previous year, the clothes belonging to her husband's chief minister, Thomas Cromwell, had arrived at Hampton Court. These, along with other of his more valuable personal effects, had been distributed among important courtiers, with the exception of his Garter robes, which had remained 'at Hampton Court by the King's command'. The items had been carefully recorded by the ruthlessly efficient Nicholas Bristowe at Cromwell's home of Austin Friars. It was not the first time that he had been charged with surveying the possessions of attainted or deceased courtiers on the king's behalf.[43] Clothes might be among the most personal of a courtier's goods, but they were also the most valuable and were therefore naturally forfeit to the crown.

In the midst of the scandalous unravelling of the king's fifth marriage, he received alarming news from the household of his son Edward. In October 1541, the prince, who had been thriving in the cosseted world of his nursery, had suddenly fallen prey to a quartan fever – a form of malaria. In great distress, the king summoned the best doctors from across the country to attend his son. One of them was shocked by how fat the four-year-old boy was and bluntly described him as 'so gross and unhealthy that he could not believe, judging from what he could see now, that he would live long.'[44] Edward recovered, however, and for a time the king's doctor, William Butts, kept a close eye on the boy, ensuring that he ate nothing but broths and soups. The prince soon tired of this, however, and ordered Butts to go away. His father and attendants, relieved that he had recovered, allowed him to return to his indulgent lifestyle.

On 23 November 1541, Katherine was deprived of her title as queen and imprisoned at Syon Abbey in Middlesex, where she remained for the rest of the winter. Culpeper and Dereham were executed in December, but Katherine remained in limbo until parliament passed a bill of attainder against her on 7 February 1542. The groundwork had been prepared by the Royal Assent by Commission Act, which made it treason – and punishable by death – for a queen consort to fail to disclose her sexual history to the king within twenty days of their marriage, or to incite someone to commit adultery with her. This made Katherine unequivocally guilty.

On 10 February, Katherine was taken to the Tower. Her barge passed under London Bridge, where the decaying heads of her former lovers were still impaled. As she mounted the steps at St Thomas's Tower (better known as Traitors' Gate), observers noticed that she was dressed in simple black velvet, in stark contrast to the colourful gowns in which she had been bedecked as queen.

In the privacy of the apartments that had been assigned to her, Katherine spent the night before her execution practising how to lay her head upon the block, which had been brought at her request. Having enjoyed the status of queen for so little time, and being so young (perhaps only eighteen), she was nevertheless determined to conduct herself with regal dignity. As she was led to the scaffold on 13 February, she struggled to maintain her composure, and appeared pale and terrified. She needed help to climb the scaffold but was able to deliver a brief speech, describing her punishment as 'worthy and just'. According to tradition, her last words were: 'I die a Queen, but I would rather have died the wife of Culpeper.'

Katherine's remains were buried in the chapel of St Peter ad Vincula, along with those of her disgraced cousin, Anne Boleyn. She had paid the ultimate price for believing that even a queen could enjoy a private life.

'Kings and Emperors all be but mortal'

IN THE WAKE of Katherine Howard's execution, Henry kept to his private chambers more than usual. Even before her demise, his desire for greater privacy was becoming ever more pronounced. This had resulted in significant changes to the operation of his household. Many of the functions of the presence chamber and council chamber were transferred to the privy chamber so that the king could conduct more matters of business without leaving his inner sanctum. In blurring the lines between the king's private and political life, this meant that before long the privy chamber was as rife with faction as his Privy Council. It also caused the ranks of the privy chamber staff to swell so much that it no longer offered a peaceful refuge in which Henry could relax with a few favoured companions.[1]

Access to the privy chamber was therefore not the prize that it had once been. Increasingly, the bedchamber was where the king's private life was centred. In contrast to the earlier part of the reign, when the king's privy chamber gentlemen slept in the same room as their master, now they required permission to enter his bedchamber. To signal this increasing gulf between the king and his court, a new lock was made for the royal bedchamber and was carried from palace to palace.

This important development was reflected in the architecture of Henry's palaces. At Hampton Court, a new suite of secret lodgings known as the 'Bayne Tower' was built, away from the presence and privy chambers. On the ground floor was an office and a strongroom for the king's treasurer and privy chamber officers. The first floor contained his bedroom, bathroom and a private study. Henry took a keen interest in the decoration of the latter and commissioned the

Italian artist Toto del Nunziata to paint murals on the upper walls, as well as four large panel paintings of biblical scenes, one of which was Christ washing the apostles' feet. He also ordered the installation of wall cupboards and new furniture. The bathroom, meanwhile, was one of the most sophisticated in the world. Water was pumped through a lead pipe from a spring four miles away in Coombe Hill and spurted out either hot or cold from two large bronze taps. Cold water cisterns were installed on the roof of the Bayne Tower from which water could be piped into the fixed stone hand basins. There was also a round wooden bath lined with linen to prevent splinters. On the top floor of the Bayne Tower were the king's jewel house and library, which contained cases with glazed, lockable doors and curtains to protect the precious books from sunlight. The ceiling was beautifully decorated with gilded battens and balls.[2]

Henry expanded the 'secret lodgings' in his other great palaces too, transforming them from a modest suite of lodgings to a sizeable complex of private rooms. These were roughly divided into an outer and inner sanctum for the king. The outer part was known as the privy lodging and comprised the privy chamber, bedchamber and a council chamber where, after Thomas Cromwell's ordinances of 1540, full meetings of the Privy Council were often held. The king's most intimate body servants might also have lodgings nearby or, in the case of the groom of the stool, directly adjacent to the king's bedchamber.

Beyond these, the inward lodgings comprised a handful of 'secret' rooms. At Whitehall, these were constructed just off the privy gallery, which was henceforth out of bounds to courtiers. Meanwhile, at Henry's other favourite palace at Greenwich, a network of small rooms was built beyond the king's bedchamber. As well as being where the king slept and spent his most private hours, these rooms were also filled with his most personal and valuable possessions. As at Hampton Court, the king's secret lodgings at Whitehall included his private jewel house. These not only housed his priceless jewellery and plate, but also large amounts of cash. The privy coffers at Whitehall and Greenwich contained as much as £50,000. The value of the contents of these rooms was one of the reasons why access to them was more restricted than to any other part of the palace.

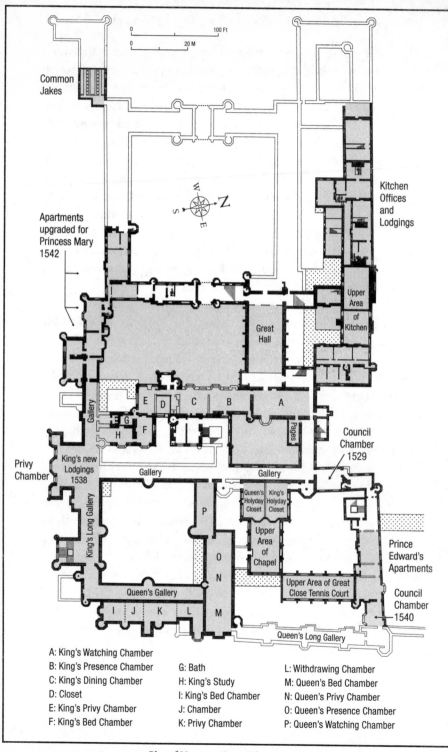

Common
Jakes

Apartments
upgraded for
Princess Mary
1542

Privy
Chamber

King's new
Lodgings
1538

Great
Hall

Upper
Area
of
Kitchen

Kitchen
Offices
and
Lodgings

Pages

Council
Chamber
1529

Gallery

Gallery

Gallery

Gallery

King's Long Gallery

Queen's Gallery

Queen's Long Gallery

P

O
N
M

I J K L

Queen's
Holyday
Closet

King's
Holyday
Closet

Upper
Area
of
Chapel

Upper Area of Great
Close Tennis Court

Prince
Edward's
Apartments

Council
Chamber
1540

100 Ft
20 M

A: King's Watching Chamber

B: King's Presence Chamber

C: King's Dining Chamber

D: Closet

E: King's Privy Chamber

F: King's Bed Chamber

G: Bath

H: King's Study

I: King's Bed Chamber

J: Chamber

K: Privy Chamber

L: Withdrawing Chamber

M: Queen's Bed Chamber

N: Queen's Privy Chamber

O: Queen's Presence Chamber

P: Queen's Watching Chamber

Plan of Hampton Court Palace c. 1547

All of these new lodgings were so secret that very little information about them survives. The king could remain there for days on end, hiding sickness or melancholy, conducting secret business, or simply enjoying some repose away from the glare of the court. The ambitious place-seekers who crowded the public rooms beyond were quick to notice that the king now appeared so seldom that they could 'no longer molest his person with any suit.'[3]

Henry had much to reflect upon during his hours of solitude. In less than a decade, he had married no fewer than four times, his wives changing places with a speed that reflected the endless power play at court – not to mention the king's fickle affections. But he could console himself with the knowledge that at least one marriage had been worth it, for he now had a precious son to continue the Tudor dynasty.

That son was, by all accounts, thriving. Closeted away from the rest of the world in a succession of luxurious nurseries, Prince Edward had been allowed to indulge in a diet of rich foods. One tactful visitor noted in October 1541 that Edward was 'well fed', hastily adding that he was also 'handsome' and 'remarkably tall for his age'.[4] Still under the supervision of Lady Bryan and the other women of his household, Edward was already being groomed for his future role.

All Tudor children, regardless of their status, had to learn a complex set of social rules and behaviours almost from birth. From the time that Edward took his first, tottering steps he would have been taught a range of postures for walking, standing or sitting that communicated his superior social position. He was forbidden from crossing his arms because the great scholar Erasmus had deemed it foolish. A miniature of Will Somer, the favourite fool of Edward's father, shows him in just such a pose. By contrast, for a man to stand with his legs apart, hips pushed forward and gaze fixed straight ahead was indicative of strength, virility and martial prowess. Henry VIII had famously adopted this pose for Holbein's full-length portrait of him at the height of his powers.

In order to distinguish themselves from the labouring classes, most of whom worked the fields in a slow, plodding gait, young noblemen would walk with a swagger, thrusting their hips forward so that their swords, bucklers (shields) or purses swung about noisily, announcing their presence. It is from this showy practice that the word 'swashbuckler' originates.

Perfect posture was only achieved if one was taught it from the earliest days of childhood. It was not a skill that could be learned in adulthood, so the origins of those who managed to rise through the ranks as a result of trade or good fortune would be forever betrayed by the way that they stood or walked. Edward had received formal instruction in the arts of movement from his tutors and dancing masters. As these arts were subject to the whims of fashion, his masters ensured that he adhered to the very latest styles of posture.

People living in the sixteenth century had to negotiate a minefield of different codes of conduct that were devised to create a strict pecking order between the sexes and social classes. Boys were encouraged to be bold and assertive, as described by Thomas Elyot in his treatise of 1531: 'A man in his natural perfection is fierce, hardy, strong in opinion, covetous of glory, desirous of knowledge.' Women, on the other hand, were expected to be 'mild, timorous, tractable, benign, of sure remembrance, and shamefaced.'[5] It is interesting to note that Edward's half-sister Elizabeth, who was four years his senior and shared his education, hardly conformed to this ideal.

Age commanded a great deal of respect in Tudor times, so children were expected to show deference to almost all adults, even those who were significantly below them on the social scale. Erasmus wrote a code of conduct for children entitled *Civilitie of Childhood*. First published in 1532, this gained widespread circulation, running into several editions, and would almost certainly have influenced the upbringing of Henry VIII's two younger children. One of the fundamentals of polite behaviour among children was the art of bowing and curtseying. Edward and Elizabeth would have been taught this from the age of four. A simple doff of the cap for a boy and a little bobbing movement for a girl would suffice at this young age. A more formal bow, such as Edward might have made to his father the king, would have involved dropping to one knee. Elizabeth, meanwhile, would have been taught to keep her head perfectly erect and her back very straight as her eyes were lowered. Her hands would be open and slightly to the side, thus making the whole effect very like a *plié* in ballet.

There was no shortage of manners books published in the Tudor period, each of which set down strict rules for every childhood activity: from dressing and eating to talking and playing. No circumstance was overlooked. If a child had a runny nose but no handkerchief, they were instructed to pinch the phlegm away with finger and thumb and allow it to drop to the ground, where it should be trodden in so that it should not sully the shoes of a passer-by. Wiping your nose on your sleeve was strictly forbidden, as was nose picking, squinting, pulling a sad face, resting your elbow on the table and talking with your mouth full.

While Henry's two younger children were being shaped into exemplary royals, their father was turning his attention to other, more personal matters. Although he had been devastated by his fifth wife's betrayal, rumours soon began to circulate about which lady he would marry next. There were a number of candidates, but one of the favourites was Anne of Cleves. Upon hearing of Katherine Howard's fall, she had moved immediately to Richmond so that she was close at hand in case the king should wish to take her back. She and Henry exchanged New Year's gifts in 1542, and Anne seemed keen to revive their association. But the king made no indication of wishing to remarry the wife who had so revolted him, and when Anne heard that he was looking elsewhere for a new wife, she was rumoured to be bitterly disappointed.

The gossips at court did not have to wait long for the question of the king's marriage to be resolved. Within a year of Katherine's execution, he was courting another lady of the same name, but an altogether different disposition. The thirty-year-old Katherine Parr was a twice-widowed lady of gentle birth and strong court connections. Her mother Maud had served Henry's first wife, Catherine of Aragon, and had given her daughter an exceptionally enlightened education by the standards of the time. Maud herself was strong-minded and articulate, and the programme of studies that she devised for Katherine had at its heart the premise that women were the intellectual equals of men.

Katherine had thrived in her mother's intellectually stimulating household, and by the time that she reached adulthood, she had grown into an able, assertive and fiercely independent woman. For all that, she knew she was expected to take a husband as soon as a suitable one was offered. Her first marriage, to the son of a Lincolnshire baron, took place in 1529, when Katherine was aged seventeen. The match was not a happy one, but her husband died unexpectedly just four years later. The following year, she married John Neville, third Baron Latimer of Snape Castle in Yorkshire. After nine years of apparently happy marriage, Lord Latimer died. This does not seem to have come as a shock to Katherine, who some months before had already secured herself a place in the household of the king's eldest daughter, Mary, towards the end of 1542.

Katherine was just four years older than Mary, and the two women soon established a close rapport. Among Katherine's duties was the very personal task of ordering the princess's clothes. Her service was to be of an unexpectedly short duration, however, for it brought her to the attention of Mary's father, who, undeterred by his disastrous marital history, began to pay court to her.

Katherine was a comely, pleasant-looking woman. A portrait of her painted in 1545 shows her to be well-dressed and with a pleasing, dignified appearance. She was tall and slender, with rich auburn hair and soft grey eyes, as well as the pale, flawless skin that was favoured at the time because it was thought to signal purity. For all that, she was not acknowledged as a great beauty. Anne of Cleves was said to have bitterly reflected that she was even less attractive than herself. But it may have been Katherine's character, more than her physical charms, that first drew her to the attention of the king. Witty and engaging, she enjoyed lively conversation and could speak knowledgeably on a wide range of subjects. Described by the king's principal secretary, Thomas Wriothesley, as a woman of 'virtue, wisdom and gentleness', she had a naturally queenly demeanour, being calm and dignified with great presence.[6] She was also well versed in the more courtly accomplishments of music and dancing, and loved fine clothes and jewels.

For all her suitability as a consort, there was one significant drawback. By the time that Henry started to pay her attention, Katherine was already in love with another gentleman at court. Her choice betrayed a lack of judgement: Thomas Seymour was the handsome but volatile brother of the late queen and a notorious troublemaker at court. But Katherine seemed blind to his imperfections and, having experienced two arranged marriages, she was eager to marry for love.

It was therefore only with considerable reticence that Lady Parr acknowledged the king's affections. This was a very different courtship to the ones that had gone before, however. Katherine Howard's betrayal had dealt Henry's confidence a severe blow. He was also painfully aware that, far from being the 'adonis' of his youth, he was dogged by poor health and excessive weight. Perhaps in the hope that it might inspire him to adopt a healthier diet, Henry invited the renowned physician Andrew Borde to attend him in 1542. Having examined his royal patient, Borde focused on the positives. Henry's hair was still plentiful and red, even though it was thinning a little on top, his pulse was strong and regular, and his digestive system appeared to be functioning well. But the physician admitted that the king's diet needed urgent attention because years of overeating had caused him to become obese. Henry's own physicians went further still and opined that their master was 'not of constitution to live long'.[7]

'Few, if any, ladies at court would henceforth aspire to such an honour,' remarked the acerbic Chapuys upon hearing that parliament had passed an Act in January 1542 declaring it treason for an unchaste woman to marry the king.[8] Henry was equally gloomy about his marriage prospects. Rather than showering the new object of his affections with love tokens and grand gestures, he assumed a melancholy attitude whenever Lady Parr was around, appearing 'sad, pensive and sighing'.[9] He was plagued with jealousy when he learned of Katherine's love for Thomas Seymour, and found an excuse to send the latter away from court. This did little to allay Katherine's reluctance, but she was well enough versed in the politics of court to know that the king could not be gainsaid. With not a little regret, she therefore put aside her own desires and consented to be the sixth wife of this much-married monarch.

The wedding took place on 12 July 1543 in the queen's private apartments at Hampton Court Palace and was attended by just eighteen guests. Although all five of Henry's previous marriages had been played out on a very public stage, the weddings themselves had all been very private affairs – with the notable exception of the ill-fated Anne of Cleves union, which had been a deliberately public and formal occasion.

Although the marriage prompted renewed hopes of a new heir, there was even less chance of this than there had been with Henry's previous two wives. Despite being married twice, for a total of thirteen years, Katherine had had no children and there is no evidence that she had ever fallen pregnant. Anne of Cleves could not resist opining that the new queen had 'no hope of issue, seeing that she had none by her two former husbands,' and added a rather insincere expression of 'great grief and despair'.[10] Perhaps by now resigned to his impotency, Henry may have been content to take a wife more for intellectual than physical stimulation.

But even if he was gradually submitting to the physical infirmities caused by his ulcerated leg and rapidly expanding waistline, the king still took pride in his appearance. His marriage to Katherine seemed to inspire a burst of activity in the royal wardrobe – for himself and his new wife. Among the luxurious new adornments that Henry ordered his wardrobe staff to make for Katherine were some new nightgowns, one of which was described in the inventory as being of black damask with two borders and an edge of black velvet furred with budge.[11]

Katherine welcomed these gifts and was quick to commission other items for her wardrobe. Although she had a natural sense of style, she was anxious to dress appropriately to her status. She therefore appointed John Scut, who had been tailor to all of Henry's previous queens. Only Catherine of Aragon had been born royal, so the others (Katherine Parr included) must have found it reassuring to be guided by an experienced royal tailor in the early days of their queenship. While she was content to adhere to the expected style of queenly dress, Katherine added some touches of her own – notably a selection of masculine-style velvet caps.[12] She also loved ostentatious accessories, such as a fan made 'of black ostrich feathers set in gold garnished with vi counterfeit stones and some pearls', and a black velvet scarf 'garnished with twenty rubies . . . and fully furnished with pearls'.[13]

For the first years of her reign, Katherine favoured crimson and cloth of gold, but an indication of her increased confidence in her role is that she began to wear royal purple for important occasions. Her outfit was particularly impressive for the court reception of the Duke of Najera on 18 February 1544, when she wore 'an open robe of cloth of gold, the sleeves lined with crimson satin, and trimmed with three piled crimson velvet, the train more than two yards long.' Around her neck she wore 'two crosses, and a jewel of very rich diamonds, and in her headdress were many rich and beautiful stones. Her girdle was of gold, with very large pendants.'[14]

Katherine had a particular weakness for shoes and in a single year ordered no fewer than forty-seven pairs in various colours, many trimmed with gold.[15] She also owned a pair of mounted and jewelled sable skins, which she kept locked away in a little square coffer covered with needlework. That she valued her material possessions is suggested by the fact that she kept notes on her clothes and jewels, together with a looking glass, inside another square coffer, which was locked inside a 'great standard' or chest.[16]

Katherine's suitability as a royal wife was obvious to everyone at court, not least the king himself, who derived a great deal of comfort from his 'dearly and most entirely beloved wife'.[17] 'His majesty never had a wife more agreeable to his heart than she is,' observed Wriothesley. Katherine was 'quieter than any of the young wives the king had, and as she knew more of the world, she always got on pleasantly with the King and had no caprices.'[18]

The new queen soon set about ordering her household, which she filled with members of her family and those who shared her ideological affiliations. Her sister Anne became chief lady-in-waiting, and she also found positions for her cousin Lady Lane, and two stepdaughters from a previous marriage. Above all, though, she favoured those of the Reformist faith. Careful to remain outwardly orthodox, Katherine was a religious radical and gathered around her a like-minded group of women. They included Jane, Lady Lisle, Lady Elizabeth Hoby and Katherine Willoughby, Duchess of Suffolk. Most of the queen's private hours were spent not in the usual pastimes of gossip and embroidery (although she excelled at the latter), but in debating and writing about the radical opinions that she and her ladies espoused.

Less controversial among the members of Katherine's household was an Italian consort of viols. The new queen shared her husband's passion for music and also loved to dance. Keen to curry favour with her stepdaughter Mary, she sent a message with one of her personal musicians, 'who will be, I judge, most acceptable, from his skill in music, in which you, I am well aware, take as much delight as myself.'[19]

In 1543, Henry commissioned a new suite of lodgings for his sixth wife at Hampton Court. Katherine filled her apartments at each palace with flowers, which she adored. Her accounts reveal that she ordered fresh floral arrangements every day, as well as 'perfume for her chamber'. Her favourite scents were juniper and civet. Katherine also paid a great deal of attention to her personal hygiene and fragrance. She took regular milk baths and adorned her body with expensive oils and perfumes such as rose water. She also used lozenges made from sage, liquorice and angelica to sweeten her breath.

She may not have married for love, but Katherine grew fond of her ailing husband and was assiduous for his welfare. During his last quest for military glory in France in the summer of 1544, she sent him an affectionate letter together with a gift of venison.

To her stepchildren, too, Katherine was a loving and caring figure. Keen to present a united Tudor family to the eyes of the court, she employed a number of personal touches. For example, for the New Year celebrations of 1544/5, she had matching clothes made for herself, Princesses Mary and Elizabeth, and Prince Edward, all in cloth of silver.[20] Henry must have been delighted to see his wife and children presented in such sartorial harmony. He subsequently approved the purchase of various other sumptuous gowns for his children, and there was a notable improvement in Mary and Elizabeth's attire during their father's latest marriage. No longer consigned to the background, they were now proudly displayed at court bedecked in bold-patterned cloths of tissue, gold and silver.

Katherine's relationship with her stepchildren was based upon something far less superficial than her clever use of image, for she invested a great deal of time in cultivating the good graces of each of them. Recognising Elizabeth and Edward's intellectual abilities, she took a keen interest in their schooling and may have influenced the appointment of their tutors. The young prince, who shared his half-sister's love of learning, gratefully enthused to his 'most dear mother': 'I received so many benefits from you that my mind can hardly grasp them.'[21]

Edward had turned six years old shortly after Katherine had married his father. This age (also known as 'breeching' because it was accompanied by a change to adult-style attire) was viewed as a milestone by the Tudors, who believed that it marked the beginning of adulthood. An order of clothing from March 1544 provided the young prince with two doublets and matching slops (loose breeches) of crimson velvet and black satin, with buttons and loops of Venice gold.[22] The following year, the king's skinner, Thomas Addington, provided the prince with a range of furs, including thirty sable skins. At the same time, Edward's private apartments were restyled so that they more closely resembled those of his father, and were stuffed with every conceivable luxury. The walls were hung with Flemish tapestries depicting classical and biblical scenes and his books were embellished with covers of enamelled gold set with rubies, sapphires and diamonds. Even his cutlery was studded with precious stones and his napkins sparkled with gold and silver thread.

The transformation of Edward's household was more than simply decorative. Any female attendants were replaced so that his became a predominantly male establishment. Edward was also assigned a tutor, Richard Cox (described as 'the best schoolmaster of our time'), with John Cheke acting as deputy, 'for the better instruction of a Prince, and the diligent teaching of such children as be appointed to attend him.'[23] The serious business of moulding him into a future king had begun.

The prince was not alone in his new schoolroom. He was joined by fourteen boys of a similar age, sons of high-ranking noblemen and favourites at his father's court. They included Henry, Lord Hastings; Robert Dudley, a favourite of Edward's sister Elizabeth; and Henry Brandon, son of the king's oldest friend, the Duke of Suffolk. Henry Brandon's childish doodles can still be seen on Edward's schoolwork. The prince's favourite companion was Barnaby Fitzpatrick, who was from an Irish noble family. Barnaby was appointed to the unenviable position of royal whipping boy, which meant that he had to suffer the punishments that Edward should have received. The prince's half-sister Elizabeth also continued to share his studies, but now she was far outnumbered in this male-dominated household.

The inventory of Henry VIII includes a number of items for kitting out his son's schoolroom. No detail was overlooked. Edward had his own personal writing desk, which was covered in black velvet and embroidered with the letter 'E'. Another desk, in green velvet, contained writing tools and instruments. There was a cabinet filled with paper, knives, a wooden compass, scales and weights, and – for one of the more recreational aspects of his studies – a little black coffer containing a chess set. Elsewhere in the room were two tables of slate for writing upon, five astronomical instruments and two spectacle cases. A visitor to court later observed that the prince seemed to suffer from poor eyesight.

Edward's education was heavily influenced by the curriculum known as *bonae litterae* ('good letters') espoused by the Northern European Humanists – notably Erasmus. This emphasised the importance of Latin and Greek grammar and rhetoric, classical authors and scripture above the more traditional elements of a prince's education, such as hunting, hawking and dancing. 'What could be more foolish,' opined Erasmus, 'than to judge the prince by accomplishments like these: dancing gracefully, playing dice expertly, drinking liberally, giving himself airs [and] plundering the people on a regal scale?'[24] Henry, though, could not countenance a complete absence of tradition, and ordered that his son (but not his younger daughter) should be given lessons in fencing, horseback riding, music, etiquette and other gentlemanly pursuits.

The basic skills of reading and writing were taught separately, usually by different tutors. Reading came first and was practised by printing letters on a piece of paper stuck to a wooden board with a sheet of transparent horn over the top. Children were taught to chant the alphabet while their tutor pointed to each letter. The first set of words that a child would read was usually the Lord's Prayer.

Edward and his companions learned to write with a quill fashioned from goose, swan or raven feathers, dipped in ink and scratched across a piece of paper. Poorer children had to make do with slate or even tracing letter shapes in sand. Most Tudor letters were the same as those we use today, but with a few notable exceptions. The modern-day lower case 'r', for example, was the letter 'c' to the Tudors. The letter 's' had three different forms, depending on where it appeared in a word. While most people wrote in 'secretary hand', a new style of handwriting, known as italic, was developing in Italy. By the time of Edward's education, it had been introduced among the elite in England, who were keen to embrace Renaissance culture in all its forms. Being able to write in any form was an indication of social status. At the beginning of the Tudor period, only 5 per cent of men and 1 per cent of women were able to write. By the end of the sixteenth century, this had risen to 25 per cent of men and 10 per cent of women.[25]

Although Edward proved to be a serious and conscientious student, at times he displayed flashes of his father's notoriously savage temper. Reginald Pole, later Archbishop of Canterbury, claimed that in a fit of rage, the young prince once tore a living falcon into four pieces in front of his tutors.

Edward had never known his mother but from his earliest days he had been taught to revere her memory. As the only one of Henry's wives to give him the son he craved, the late queen was spoken about in the most reverential terms by the king and his court, and her brother Edward, who played a prominent role in his nephew's upbringing, would have helped craft her saintly image in the young boy's mind. A remark made by the prince in later years suggests that he harboured more than a little guilt about her death. 'How unfortunate have I been to those of my blood,' he lamented, 'my mother I slew at my birth.'[26] Among his possessions in the private study next to his bedchamber were some documents concerning his mother.

Edward's other possessions were as playful as one might expect for a young boy. They included a comb in the shape of a horse with a rider on its back, a puppet, a spear and javelin, and a staff of 'unicorns' horns garnished with silver gilt'. The prince also evidently shared his sister Elizabeth's fascination with magic and astrology. Among his toys was a red box filled with 'small tools of sorcery' and two 'instruments of sorcery of silver white called spattelles'.[27] He would almost certainly have owned some of the most popular toys of the day: miniature figures, vessels and other shapes fashioned out of base-metal such as pewter. As a baby, he might have been given a rattle decorated with little bells, which served as both entertainment and a teething aid. Often, these were fashioned from coral and wolf's tooth, both of which were thought to have supernatural powers.

Although Edward was the most cherished of the king's children, thanks to Katherine's influence both Mary and Elizabeth were restored to the succession shortly after she married their father. To mark this important event, Henry commissioned a new portrait of himself and his heirs. *The Family of Henry VIII* was idealised because it included Jane Seymour, even though she had been dead for eight years. The other sitters were the king himself, along with his three children. Although the purpose of the painting was to reinforce the strength of the Tudor dynasty and confirm the succession, the king's youngest daughter used it as a means of conveying her secret loyalty to her mother. Anne Boleyn's name had been banned from court ever since her execution, for the king hated to be reminded of her. Elizabeth knew this all too well, and was also painfully aware that her return to favour at court was entirely dependent upon the king's notoriously fickle goodwill. But such was her private devotion to her late mother that when she sat for the artist, she wore Anne's 'A' pendant around her neck. This would have been clearly visible in the preliminary sketches, but is barely perceptible in the finished painting. Certainly it was discreet enough to escape the king's eye, but Elizabeth must have secretly triumphed every time she saw it.

Even though the two women were ideologically opposed, the new queen's gentle and tactful disposition helped her to win over the staunchly Catholic Mary. The elder princess appreciated her stepmother's efforts in persuading the king to look more favourably upon her, and she felt sure enough in his renewed affection to send him a gift at New Year 1544. The gift she chose was both very personal and also hinted at her father's increasing infirmity. She commissioned a beautifully embroidered chair from the master embroiderer, Guillaume Brellont, and went to some considerable expense in having the panels mounted onto a wooden frame before being transported to Hampton Court.

The stepchild that Katherine was closest to, though, was her husband's youngest daughter, Elizabeth. The earliest surviving letter of the princess was to her beloved stepmother and reveals the genuine affection that existed between them. Writing in July 1544, the ten-year-old princess laments the 'inimical fortune' that has deprived her of Katherine's 'illustrious presence' for a whole year. 'I am not only bound to serve you, but also to revere you with filial love,' she assured her.[28] Although Elizabeth had good reason to court the woman who had been the means of reconciling her to her father, this was more than mere statecraft. Katherine was the first of Elizabeth's stepmothers to recognise, and seek to nurture, her love of learning and of the reformist faith. Increasingly, the young princess was invited to take part in the religious debates that took place in the queen's privy apartments.

Shortly after writing to her stepmother, Elizabeth joined Katherine at Hampton Court Palace, where she was holding court as regent for her husband, who had gone to France. Henry had decreed that his wife was to have full royal authority in his absence. Elizabeth was observed to be in constant attendance upon her stepmother, both in public and private. It would prove a hugely formative experience for the young Elizabeth. She looked on as courtiers and ambassadors paid court to the queen with as much state as they had to her father. Until now, Elizabeth had witnessed only kingly rule, with her father's wives relegated to the domestic sphere. Now it was her stepmother sitting in state in the presence chamber, being served on bended knee and deciding upon all matters of state. The sight of some of the most powerful men in the country bowing low before a woman made a profound and lasting impression on the princess, who was just shy of her eleventh birthday. It may have been from that moment that she cherished private ambitions to be a queen regnant herself one day.

As soon as Henry had returned from his largely futile attempt to assert England's military might, Katherine relinquished her duties as regent. But the stereotypical portrayal of her as little more than a nursemaid to the king in his last years has little basis in truth. She may have alleviated his condition by diverting him with witty and lively conversation, but as far as Henry's medical needs were concerned, he had plenty of doctors on hand. The treatments recommended for his ulcerated leg were as varied as they were ineffective. Andrew Borde's *Fyrst Boke of the Introduction of Knowledge* was one of the more sensible medical texts. He advised against excessive sleep as this led to sluggishness as well as sinfulness, and directed that if a patient must sleep during the day then he should do so in a chair or leaning against a cupboard. He recommended that certain foods should be avoided, such as eggs, salmon, shellfish, beef and duck, along with ale, beer and red wine. Patients were also prohibited from committing 'acts of venery' on a full stomach.

The extent to which Henry followed this advice is questionable. The *Propre boke of new Cokerye*, published in 1545, included an array of rich and exotic recipes favoured by the king. They included boiled peacocks stitched back into their original skin and feathers, which were made to breathe fire using camphor; hens presented in six different colours; meatballs dressed as oranges; and almond cream eggs served in real shells.

Recent analysis has suggested that Henry may have been suffering from Type 2 diabetes. This would explain his enormous appetite and his seemingly unquenchable thirst. The fact that his ulcerated leg never healed but got progressively worse is another possible indication of the disease. Another theory is that the king was Kell positive and suffered from McLeod syndrome, which meant that he belonged to a rare blood group that can prevent a healthy partner bearing an infant after a first pregnancy. If a Kell positive male impregnates a Kell negative female, she may develop antibodies against a second or subsequent foetus's red cells, which can result in miscarriage, stillbirth or early neonatal death. Henry may have inherited this condition from his maternal great-grandmother, Jacquetta Woodville. It certainly closely reflects the reproductive history of his first two marriages. McLeod syndrome is related to the condition and can cause marked physical and behavioural changes, including restricted movement and psychoses. It usually manifests itself in late middle age.[29]

Whatever the cause, it was obvious to everyone at court that by the summer of 1546, Henry was dangerously ill. By now morbidly obese, his mobility was so restricted that he had to rely on specially designed devices to manoeuvre him around the palaces.[30] The chronicler Edward Hall claimed that 'the King was now overgrown with corpulence and fatness, so that he became more and more unwieldy. He could not go up or down stairs unless he was raised up or let down by an engine.'[31] An inventory taken at the time of his death includes two chairs 'for the king's majesty to sit in to be carried to and fro in his galleries and chambers' in Whitehall Palace. These were richly made to ensure both comfort and splendour, being 'covered with tawny velvet all over [and] quilted with a cordaunte of tawny silk.'[32] Even bathing now tired the king, and a special bed was installed in an adjoining chamber to his bathroom in the Bayne Tower at Hampton Court. Although it was just intended for short rests, rather than sleep, the bed was typically sumptuous, being painted and gilded, and bedecked with hangings embroidered with the king's badges. Henry would be escorted to it by his attendants, dressed in linen robes, so that he might rest after the exertions of being washed and then helped out of the bath.

Neither was the king able to worship as frequently as he had in his youth. By the 1540s, he was attending significantly fewer masses each day, as the French ambassador, Charles de Marillac, reported. Although he was still an avid reader, he was growing increasingly short-sighted and ordered spectacles ten pairs at a time.

Henry's ability to carry out the routine business of government was also diminishing. In 1545, he had entrusted the deputy groom of the stool, Anthony Denny, with the authority to affix the royal stamp on all documents emanating from the monarch. Sparked by Henry's growing infirmity, this enabled Denny to wield ever greater influence. The antiquary John Leland claimed that the entire court was aware of the deputy groom's 'gratia flagrans'.[33] Sir Thomas Cheyney, one of Henry VIII's Privy Councillors, was warned during marriage negotiations with Sir Anthony Denny that he was 'the man to be near about the king and so unmeet to be trifled or mocked with in any cause.'[34] Denny's pre-eminence was confirmed in 1546, when he was promoted to groom of the stool. He was also appointed keeper of the Palace of Whitehall, which may explain why a selection of Henry's shirts (which were the responsibility of the groom of the stool) were recorded as being in the care of Denny's deputy at Whitehall, James Rufforth.

The king's wardrobe accounts also hint at his growing infirmity. During the last four years of his reign, there were orders for items of clothing that were intended for warmth and comfort rather than glamour and public display. They included a number of 'petticoats' or waistcoats that could be worn over a shirt for added warmth, but concealed under a doublet. Meanwhile, the court skinners, Catherine and Thomas Addington, were tasked with adding a fur lining to twenty-eight pairs of buskins, eight coats, six gowns and nightgowns and a pair of quilted hose. The king favoured sable, budge, coney, lamb, squirrel and even leopard fur. Now that he was a good deal less mobile than in former years, he would have felt the cold while sitting in his draughty palaces and going for short walks outside, so it was imperative that his clothing should be adapted for his comfort.[35] The engraving by Cornelius Matsys shows the ageing Henry with his furs drawn closely around his neck. He owned several sable mufflers, one of which was made from black velvet ornamented with gold chains, pearls, rubies and diamonds, with a chain of gold enamelled in green with pearls hanging from it. This was considered to be of such value that a special case of black leather was made to store it in. The accounts also list twelve knee bands, six lined with taffeta and six with scarlet, which were designed to ease the pain caused by Henry's ulcerated leg.

The accounts reveal a sense of insecurity on the king's part as he felt his grip on the throne weakening. Throughout his reign, his wardrobe had been dominated by clothes of black and crimson, with white also predominant, but in these final years, an unusually high number of purple garments were recorded. This was the colour of kingship, so it represented a deliberate attempt by Henry to reassert his authority.

Only his closest body servants knew the full extent of the king's illness. They saw the suppurating ulcer on his leg, the stench from which was enough to turn the strongest of stomachs. When they undressed their royal master each evening, they also had to take care not to aggravate the pus-filled boils that covered other parts of his body.

Tormented as much with the constant pain as the knowledge that he was dying, Henry frequently lashed out at those around him – including the queen herself. In 1546, a conspiracy led by Stephen Gardiner and the other conservatives at court almost succeeded in turning this paranoid and irascible king against his wife, who was growing less discreet in her adherence to radical religious views. A warrant was drawn up for her arrest, but by chance Katherine heard of this before it could be carried out and wisely threw herself upon her husband's mercy, begging him to forgive her womanly weaknesses. Despite his paranoia, Henry cherished enough affection for his sixth wife to forgive her at once, and he angrily upbraided Gardiner and Wriothesley for daring to accuse her. He proceeded to lavish favours upon the queen whom he had almost condemned. Between July 1546 and early December, he ordered French, Flemish and Italian jewellers to bring to court 'all manner of jewels, pearls, and precious stone . . . of skins and sable furs . . . clothes and new gentlenesses of fashion . . . as he or they shall think best for the pleasure of . . . our dearest wife, the Queen.'[36]

At the beginning of December 1546, Henry moved to Oatlands Palace and was seen on the 7th taking exercise in the grounds. But three days later he was laid low with a fever so severe that for thirty hours his doctors tried every remedy they knew to keep him alive. Although he rallied, when the Imperial ambassador François van der Delft saw him shortly afterwards, he noted that his face was ashen and his body 'greatly fallen away'. In private, Norfolk confided to the ambassador that the king 'could not long endure'.[37]

Determined to keep up appearances, Henry travelled to London in slow and painful stages. His close advisers and body servants succeeded in keeping the gravity of his illness a secret. The king was no less eager to conceal his decline and made his way to Greenwich in order to uphold the tradition of celebrating Christmas there. But he soon had to admit defeat, and left that palace on 22 December, never to return. He travelled on to Whitehall Palace and retired to his private apartments. In stark contrast to the many raucous Christmas celebrations that Henry had enjoyed in the past, he now ordered that the palace should be closed to all 'but his councillors and three or four Gentlemen of his [Privy] Chamber.'[38] Although the queen and his daughters had accompanied him to Whitehall, on Christmas Eve he told them to return to Greenwich so that they might represent him at the festive celebrations.

Only the king's closest body servants and physicians stayed with him to the end, doing what they could to alleviate his suffering and make him more comfortable. He fell ill with another fever on 1 January 1547. A week later, rumours were circulating that he was dead because 'whatever amendment is announced, few persons have access to his chamber.' The queen and her eldest stepdaughter Mary hastened back to Whitehall on 10 January, but even they were denied access to the king. They remained there, however, and on 26 January Katherine's patience was rewarded by a summons to the king's bedside. She found her husband in a state of physical and emotional distress. 'It is God's will that we should part,' he told her, before breaking down in tears. Unable to go on, he sent her from him.[39]

The following day, Henry saw his confessor and received Holy Communion. By evening, he was fading fast. But as yet, nobody had been brave enough to tell the king, who had always hated to show physical weakness, that he was dying. 'His servants scarcely dared speak to him to put him in mind of his approaching end,' observed Edward Hall, 'lest he, in his angry and imperious humour, should have ordered them to be indicted.' At length, his groom of the stool, Sir Anthony Denny, warned his master that 'in man's judgement, he was not like to live' and urged him to confess his sins 'as becometh every good Christian man to do.' To Denny's relief, Henry reacted with calm acceptance. When his groom asked if he would like to speak to any 'learned man', the king replied: 'If he had any, it should be Dr Cranmer, but I will first take a little sleep, and then, as I feel myself, I will advise upon the matter.'[40] These were his last recorded words.

Cranmer was hastily summoned from Croydon and arrived in the early hours of 28 January. By then, his royal master was beyond speech. When the archbishop asked him to give some sign that he died in the faith of Christ, the king 'did wring his hand in his as hard as he could.' Shortly afterwards, at around 2 a.m., on what would have been his father's ninetieth birthday, Henry breathed his last.

Bedecked in sumptuous nightclothes and surrounded by the opulence of his private bedchamber, he might have reflected upon the words that his former bishop, John Fisher, had spoken some twenty-six years before at the Field of the Cloth of Gold. Then, they would have seemed curiously out of place, but now they were entirely apposite:

Kings and Emperors, all be but men, all be but mortal . . . All the rich apparel that can be devised, can not take from them the condition of mortality. They be in them self but earth and ashes, and to earth they must return, and all their glory well considered, and beholded with right eyes, is but very miserable.[41]

'Being yet but a child'

THE PRIVY COUNCIL brought the late king's son and youngest daughter together to tell them of their father's death. Edward rushed into his sister's arms and they wept together for several hours, astonishing the councillors with their public show of grief. For five days, their father's body lay in state in his privy chamber at Whitehall, the coffin draped with gold. On 3 February, the body was moved to the palace chapel, where a select group of mourners heard a requiem mass. There followed a series of continual services for the next ten days and nights, after which the coffin was taken with great solemnity to Windsor to be buried in St George's Chapel, as Henry had decreed, next to the remains of his third wife, Jane Seymour.

Just four days later, on 20 February 1547, the nine-year-old king, Edward VI, was crowned. Henry VIII's will had not provided for the appointment of a protector to rule during his son's minority. Instead, it entrusted the government of the realm to a regency council that would rule collectively with 'like and equal charge'. Nevertheless, within a week of Henry's death, the executors had chosen to invest almost regal power in the new king's uncle, Edward Seymour, Duke of Somerset.

Somerset had proved his worth both at court and on the battlefield, having achieved notable military successes in Scotland and France. However, it was perhaps an indication of his insecurity as much as his ambition that he was quick to embrace all of the trappings of power. This included plundering the late king's wardrobe. Within days of assuming the protectorship, Somerset arranged for the transfer of furs from some of Henry's gowns to his own robes so that he could wear them during the coronation celebrations. The inventory of Henry's possessions notes that the king's skinner removed some lynx furs from a gown of russet damask embroidered with Venice gold and transferred them to a gown of black cloth of gold. If Somerset had been the same size as the late king, he might have taken the garments piecemeal, rather than going to the trouble of having the furs removed.

Somerset had been able to seize the late king's private treasure thanks to the closet assistance of Henry's former groom of the stool, Sir Anthony Denny. In the division of the spoils that followed Henry's death, Denny himself was quick to claim ownership of a rather less savoury collection of items. The officer who drew up the inventory of the late king's goods made a marginal note that 'all which parcels [i.e. close-stools] the said accountant [Denny] claimeth to have by virtue of his said office of the Groomship of the Stool at the death of the late king. Which parcels we the said commissioners do allow to the said Sir Anthony as pertaining to his said office.'[1] Quite what Denny chose to do with his late master's close-stools is not recorded.

Denny retained his post as groom of the stool to the new king and forged a powerful alliance with Protector Somerset, who was keen to control every aspect of his nephew's existence. The rest of Edward's privy chamber was staffed by several grooms who had been his companions since early childhood. They included Edward Rogers, who had served the new king's father as an esquire of the body. There was continuity, too, in other private offices at court. Even the royal barbers remained on the payroll for six months, despite the fact that they served a beardless boy.

In August 1547, Somerset initiated a change in the personnel of the privy chamber, prompted by preparations for the war with Scotland. His alliance with Denny had proved short-lived, the latter being replaced by Somerset's brother-in-law, Sir Michael Stanhope, who set about excluding all of the Protector's rivals from this inner sanctum. Stanhope wasted no time in restricting direct access to the young king and fostering a deliberate distance between him and his subjects. This soon created an unwelcoming and austere atmosphere throughout Edward's private apartments. Even if he had wished to, Edward was prevented from spending lavishly on furnishings or entertainment. Stanhope managed his privy purse expenditure and kept him so short of funds that the boy was obliged to accept illicit gifts.

As well as undertaking the usual duties of the groom of the stool, Stanhope took control of the Revels, organising such court ceremonial as he deemed suitable for the king to take part in. Before long, a staid, almost puritanical atmosphere pervaded Edward's court, mirroring that of his private apartments. This presented a dramatic and unwelcome contrast to the glory of his father's court in its heyday. At the same time, the contemporary records suggest that standards of behaviour among Edward's courtiers had started to slip. Just seven months after Henry's death, a proclamation was issued forbidding any person to 'make water [urinate] or cast any nuisance within the precinct of the court . . . wherein corruption may breed and tend to the prejudice of his royal person.'[2]

Stanhope's controlling influence over the boy king was obvious to everyone at court. One observer referred to his 'governance' of his royal master. But Edward had a mind of his own and was determined to exert his authority – particularly in the sphere of religion. Influenced by reformist ideas in his schooling, he was growing into an exceptionally devout young man. He began each day, upon waking, with a prayer. This was hardly unusual. In fact, every man, woman and child at all levels of society was taught that their first waking thought should be of God, and their first words in his praise.

Morning prayer remained an essential part of everyone's daily routine throughout the Tudor period, but the wording changed after the break with Rome. In 1545 a new 'primer' or prayer book was introduced, with all references to the Pope and purgatory removed, and with much less focus on the Virgin Mary. During Edward's reign, his subjects were obliged to say the Lord's Prayer in English when they woke, either reciting it by heart or reading it from their primer. Children were also taught to recite the catechism by rote.

Edward would repair to his privy closet several times a day to perform his private devotions, and, like his subjects, would say another set of prayers before going to sleep. The most commonly employed themes were pleas for forgiveness of the day's sins; an opportunity to wipe the slate clean before beginning afresh the next morning. Surrendering oneself up to sleep was like putting oneself in God's care, hence the popular prayer: 'I commit my body and soul, this night and evermore, unto his most holy hands.' The oblivion of sleep was seen as a shorter version of the eternal one of death.

For all his piety, Edward was by no means unconcerned for the trappings of kingly wealth and power. He had certainly inherited his father's love of ostentatious clothes. Every item of his attire was crafted from the finest materials, and his wardrobe was filled with cloths of gold embroidered with silver and decorated with priceless gems. Even the buttons of his clothes were made from solid gold, and his caps and other accessories were studded with diamonds and sapphires. His most prized possession was a gold dagger with a large green stone embedded in the hilt. The dagger was attached to a rope of pearls and its sheath was encrusted with diamonds, rubies and emeralds. Little wonder that one visitor to court claimed that the prince made entire rooms sparkle when he moved about his palaces.

For his coronation in February 1547, Edward had been dressed in a gown of cloth of gold and a cape furred with sable to keep out the chill winter air. Like his father, he would favour sable above other skins throughout his reign. Underneath, he had worn a jerkin and cape of white velvet with silver embroidery, embellished with rubies, diamonds and pearls.[3] Some of his father's jewels had been recycled to make his crown, and a number of gemstones and pearls had been removed from Henry's caps and bonnets and sewn onto 'certain caps made for the king's majesty that now is'.[4]

Edward's personal preference for highly decorated clothes had a political motive too. Given his minority, they were an important means of projecting his kingly authority. For this reason, Edward's style deliberately emulated his father's. A portrait of him as king, painted in around 1547, shows him in opulent fabrics with the wide and bulky Henrician silhouette created by the fashionable doublet and fur-lined gown. Keen to project his majesty, he adopts the same strident pose that his father had famously struck for Holbein's iconic portrait. Slender as he was, however, the new king could not hope to emulate his father's enormous frame, and his doublet appears padded. The intended effect was to reinforce the continuity of the Tudor dynasty and to project masculine strength, even though he was just a nine-year-old boy.[5] In fact, he appears more as a child dressing up in adult clothes.

Nevertheless, Edward continued to take clothing seriously, and he personally drafted the 1552 bill for restraint of apparel. This was far less detailed than Henry's legislation, however, and made only a few amendments – such as restricting the wearing of ostrich feathers (which were now the fashion) to the rank of gentleman and above. The young king was particularly fond of caps and had a new set made for a visit by the French ambassador in 1550. He chose white, black and crimson, which echoed the colours favoured by his late father. He also shared the Tudor love of fine jewellery. An inventory of his possessions includes the purchase, in 1551, from a jeweller in Antwerp of: 'A fair flower of gold having set in the same three table balases set without foil and between every balas a pearl and in between the three balases a large pointed diamond and a pearl pendant at one of the balases.' The young king also acquired 'a fair great table diamond ring set in fair work enamelled black red white and blue.'[6]

Although Edward always tried to emulate the majestic image of his predecessor, he and his courtiers also took care to adhere to the latest fashions. These included the use of 'Moresque' or Islamic designs in embroidery patterns for clothes and furnishings. Naturalistic patterns for birds and flowers were also popular, thanks to publications such as Conrad Gesner's *Historia Animalum* (1551). As usual, the royal court dictated the fashion for the rest of the kingdom, and the homes of Edward's richest subjects were soon filled with embroidered clothes, cushions and tapestries all containing Moorish and naturalistic designs. The young king liked his apartments to smell as appealing as they looked. A blend of rose water and sugar boiled together was said to have given Edward's bedchamber such a heady scent that it was 'as though it were full of roses'.[7]

Although he is often depicted as a serious, sober-minded young man, Edward did not lack a sense of humour. He retained his father's favourite fool, Will Somer, and was solicitous enough of his welfare to pay for his keeper. A warrant dated 1551 authorised the payment of forty shillings to one William Seyton, 'whom his Majesty hath appointed to keep William Somer'.[8]

No doubt thanks to the minstrels who had entertained him as a child, Edward was as fond of music as the rest of his family and the number of musicians at court increased during his reign. The household accounts include payments to eighteen trumpeters, seven vial players, four sackbuts, a bagpiper, drummer, harpist, rebeck player and eight minstrels. The king himself was a talented musician and had been taught to play the lute by his father's favourite musician, Philip van Wilder. He also delighted in theatrical performances and even acted in plays at court. He shared his father's love of gambling, too, and once ran up the substantial sum of £143 17d as 'money lost in play', along with ten yards of black velvet, to Sir Thomas Wroth, a gentleman of his privy chamber.

Edward enjoyed the vigorous sports at which his father had so excelled, such as hunting and fencing, and was also keen on archery and tennis. An inventory of his possessions reveals that he also went fishing and hawking, and that he kept greyhounds, fighting bears and a pet monkey. The latter may have belonged to his fool. Even though he was now king, however, Edward was still subjected to the same suffocating protectiveness that had restricted his activities as a child. An Italian visitor to court shrewdly observed that the king went hunting regularly 'so as to have an excuse to ride, because his men, out of fear for his life, often seem to keep a rather tight rein on him in this area.'[9]

The young king's closeted existence was reinforced by the fact that he was largely deprived of the company of his half-sisters, both of whom chose to live away from court. Neither did he see his former stepmother, Katherine Parr. There was good reason. While the kingdom and court mourned the passing of their charismatic, domineering and – towards the end – tyrannical king, his widow had soon turned her attention elsewhere. Painfully aware that she had no real place at court now that she had been altogether excluded from the regency council, Katherine Parr had left for her manor at Chelsea straight after Edward's coronation.

As soon as she was certain that she was not pregnant by her late husband, this famously discreet and dignified woman threw caution to the wind and married her old love, the king's uncle, Thomas Seymour, Lord High Admiral. Quite when the wedding took place is not known because the ceremony was conducted with the utmost secrecy, but it was likely to have been in May 1547. Katherine knew that the council would have refused permission for her to marry again so soon.

Such an impetuous action was at odds with the calm good sense for which Katherine was so well known. There is a hint of defiance in her actions, prompted by her being excluded from the government of the country. Perhaps, too, after three duty marriages, she felt that she should be allowed to follow her heart. At thirty-four – an advanced age for marriage in Tudor times – becoming Seymour's wife must have seemed like her last chance of happiness, and of bearing children. Although, for Katherine, it was undoubtedly a love match, her new husband was not quite so besotted. Before Henry VIII's death, he had contemplated marrying various other well-born ladies at court – including the king's own daughters.

When news of the Queen Dowager's marriage to the Lord Admiral broke, the scandal reverberated throughout the court. The official period of mourning was far from over, and the man of her choice could hardly have been less suitable. The ministers who controlled the court and its young king were outraged: Seymour was foolish and arrogant, but also dangerously volatile. Nobody was more disapproving than his own brother. The young king noted in his journal: 'The Lord Seymour of Sudeley married the Queen whose name was Katherine, with which marriage the Lord Protector was much offended.' Katherine bitterly resented his disapproval, telling her husband: 'It was fortunate we were so much distant for I suppose else I should have bitten him.'[10]

Katherine's stepdaughter, Princess Mary, was also highly affronted.

She and her half-sister Elizabeth had joined Katherine's household shortly after returning to court to pay their respects to their late father. Because the new king had no queen, it was not considered fitting for unmarried ladies to be present without a female household in which to serve, and their stepmother had been delighted to oblige. Seriously misjudging the situation, Seymour had sought Mary's help in persuading Katherine to marry him. This had been met with a sharp rebuke. Close though she had been to her last stepmother, Mary left her household immediately and never fully forgave Katherine for what she saw as a shocking insult to her late father.

Elizabeth, though, in typically pragmatic fashion, chose to stay with her stepmother at Chelsea. When her half-sister Mary heard of this, she was horrified. She wrote at once, urging Elizabeth not to associate with Katherine, considering the 'scarcely cold body of the King our father [has been] so shamefully dishonoured by the Queen our stepmother.' With unusual prescience, she claimed that Elizabeth's reputation would suffer if she remained at Chelsea and therefore offered her a place in her own household at New Hall in Essex. Elizabeth wrote a respectful but philosophical reply, telling Mary that they must 'submit with patience to that which could not be cured'. She cleverly added that although Katherine's behaviour had not been entirely proper, 'the Queen having shown me so great affection, and done me so many kind offices, I must use much tact in manoeuvring with her, for fear of appearing ungrateful for her benefits.'[11]

The younger princess, now aged thirteen, may have had other, less honourable reasons for staying at Chelsea. Although the rumours that Seymour had courted her for a time were unsubstantiated, she seems to have developed something of a crush on her stepmother's new husband and was seen to blush whenever he was spoken of. She was evidently glad of the opportunity to spend more time with him, even though (as she thought) there was no prospect of a renewed courtship.

The manor of Chelsea, part of Katherine's inheritance from the late king, was situated on a beautiful stretch of land close to the River Thames, surrounded by gardens and woodland. It was a handsome building of red brick, two storeys high and furnished with well-appointed rooms. It also had many amenities that would have been considered a luxury at the time, including piped water from a nearby spring.

As well as having the guardianship of Elizabeth, Katherine and her new husband had also purchased the wardship and marriage rights of Lady Jane Grey, the great-granddaughter of Henry VII and a cousin of the princess.[12] Jane's ambitious father, the Duke of Suffolk, later claimed that he had agreed to this because Seymour had promised to secure King Edward as her husband. Jane was installed at Seymour Place, although she did occasionally visit Chelsea and she may have joined Elizabeth's lessons under the tutelage of the renowned scholar, William Grindal.

Both girls shared a love of learning and an exceptionally sharp intellect. Elizabeth was far more worldly than her cousin, however. During these harmonious months in Katherine's household, the young princess developed sexually as well as intellectually. At four-teen years old, she was blossoming into a young woman, with fine features and an abundance of the trademark red hair of the Tudors. She was an alluring prospect to any suitor, and a fatally irresistible one to her stepmother's husband.

Early one morning before the household had risen, Elizabeth and her faithful governess Kat Astley were shocked by the sudden appearance of the Lord Admiral in her bedchamber. Noting their expressions, he smilingly told them that he had simply come to bid the princess good morrow.[13] Before long, Seymour's morning visits to Elizabeth's bedchamber had become a regular habit. And the more often he came, the more outrageous his behaviour grew. 'He would come many mornings into the said Lady Elizabeth's Chamber, before she was ready, and sometimes before she did rise,' Kat Astley later recounted. 'And if she were up, he would bid her good morrow, and ask how she did, and strike her upon the back or on the buttocks familiarly.'

Far from safeguarding Elizabeth from Seymour's scandalous attentions, Kat, who was utterly devoted to her royal mistress but dangerously indiscreet, actively encouraged them. She engineered clandestine meetings between the couple, flouting the restraints to which a young lady should have been subject – particularly one of royal blood. On one occasion, she even allowed her charge to go on a romantic boat ride on the Thames at night with only the Lord Admiral for company.

It was not long before things got out of hand. Kat described how her young charge would hide under the covers, tempting Seymour to 'come at her'. By now, even Mistress Astley was alarmed, and when the Lord Admiral 'strived to have kissed her [Elizabeth] in her bed', she admonished him, telling him to 'go away for shame'.[14]

What may have begun as harmless flirtation had deepened into something altogether more serious. Although the timing of the scandal is uncertain, it is likely to have coincided with Katherine falling pregnant, late in 1547. Overjoyed that she was at last to have a child, Katherine may have been too preoccupied to notice her husband's growing obsession with her young stepdaughter. Perhaps the sickness of early pregnancy obliged her to spend more time than was usual in her own chambers. She and Seymour would in any case have refrained from sexual intercourse in order to preserve the health of the child.

In vain, Kat Astley tried to restrain Seymour as he came again and again into Elizabeth's bedchamber, dressed only in his night-gown. She cried that it was 'an unseemly sight to come so bare legged to a maiden's chamber', which prompted an angry retort from the sexually frustrated Seymour. 'What do I do?' he shouted. 'I would they all saw it!' Then he stormed out in anger.[15] Elizabeth's governess decided she must tell Katherine all about her husband's antics. But Katherine refused to take her seriously and insisted that Seymour was simply expressing his affection for his new stepdaughter. As a concession, however, she offered to accompany her husband on his morning visits to Elizabeth in future.

Katherine soon realised that there was more than enough to corroborate Kat's suspicions. Bizarrely, though, far from restraining her husband, she became an apparently willing accomplice to his 'jests'. On one notorious occasion, she pinned back Elizabeth's arms while her husband cut the girl's dress 'into a hundred pieces'.[16] This has been interpreted as naïve compliance on Katherine's part. More likely is that she understood that if she insisted Seymour leave Elizabeth well alone, it would only increase the girl's appeal in his eyes. She may therefore have judged that the best way to cure him of his temporary infatuation was to allow him at least a taste of the prize that he sought.

But if this was Katherine's strategy, it backfired spectacularly. Far from being satisfied by the fleeting touches and caresses that his romps with Elizabeth allowed him, these merely served to intensify her husband's desire. By the time that the household moved to Hanworth, a manor house to the west of London, in spring 1548, Seymour's behaviour had got so out of hand that his wife felt obliged to take action. She instructed Kat Astley to 'take more heed, and be as it were in watch betwixt the Lady Elizabeth and the Admiral.'[17]

As it happened, it was a discovery made by Katherine herself that brought things to a head. Going in search of her husband and stepdaughter one day, she 'came suddenly upon them, where they were all alone, (he having her in his arms)'. Furious at being so deceived, she ordered Elizabeth to leave her house at once.[18] When Elizabeth protested her innocence, it served only to infuriate her stepmother even more. The two women were barely on speaking terms by the time that Elizabeth left the household that June. But despite the hurt and anger at discovering her stepdaughter's apparent disloyalty, Katherine still cherished some affection for her. As Elizabeth took her formal leave, she told her that she would send warning if she heard that any rumours about the affair had begun. This would prepare her stepdaughter to defend her reputation, which Katherine knew was one of the most precious things she possessed.

Elizabeth and her governess made their way to Cheshunt, the Hertfordshire home of Kat's brother-in-law, Sir Anthony Denny. The house provided much-needed privacy for the princess, who hoped that the inevitable gossip that her sudden departure had prompted among the servants at Chelsea would not spread to the court.

But there is some speculation that Elizabeth's retreat to Cheshunt was for more than just decorum's sake. Jane Dormer, a lady-in-waiting to Princess Mary, reported the rumour that Elizabeth had given birth to Seymour's child while staying at the house. 'There was a bruit of a child born and miserably destroyed,' she recounted. 'Only the report of the midwife, who was brought from her house blindfolded thither . . . said it was the child of a very fair young lady.'[19] There is some evidence (albeit circumstantial) to corroborate this. Elizabeth was kept in strict seclusion at Cheshunt, and Kat Astley reported that her charge was sick with an unspecified illness of several weeks' duration. But Jane Dormer was notoriously hostile towards Elizabeth, and there is little else to support her story. It would be one of many rumours to circulate about Elizabeth, and the question of her virginity would dominate court gossip both in England and across Europe for more than half a century.

For now, though, it looked like the whole sorry affair would blow over. As soon as she arrived at Cheshunt, Elizabeth wrote a letter of humble supplication to her stepmother, thanking her for her kindness and expressing her heartfelt sorrow about what had happened.[20] Katherine was quick to forgive her stepdaughter's behaviour, which she put down to youthful indiscretion.

Although the affair quickly died down, it had taken its toll on Katherine's health. This, her first pregnancy at the comparatively advanced age of thirty-six, had not been an easy one. Her stepdaughter had noted that she had seemed very ill when they had said goodbye at Hanworth, and she sent anxious enquiries after her health now that she was 'great with child'.[21] Even though Katherine assured her that she was much better, she was clearly still unwell. In addition to the increasing exhaustion and discomfort of her pregnancy, she had injured her wrist so badly that she was barely able to reply to her stepdaughter's letters.

Shortly after Elizabeth's departure in June, Katherine had decided to move to her husband's beautiful castle of Sudeley in Gloucestershire to prepare for the birth of her child. Marital harmony restored, she wrote to Seymour at court, assuring him that his 'little knave' was in good health and kicking her boisterously to prove it. Seymour mischievously replied that she should keep the child lean by feeding it a good diet and taking regular exercise, so that 'he may be small enough to creep out of a mousehole'.[22]

A few weeks later, the Lord Admiral joined his wife at Sudeley. Her pains began shortly afterwards, and on 30 August she was delivered of a girl. The baby was christened Mary in honour of the eldest princess, whose attitude towards Katherine had softened upon hearing that she was with child. Although everything appeared well, a few days later Katherine became suddenly feverish with what may have been puerperal fever. In the delirium of her 'unquieted' state, all of the suppressed pain and humiliation caused by her husband's betrayal came spilling out and she ranted against him as he looked on aghast by her bedside. 'I am not well handled,' she cried to one of her ladies, 'for those that be about me careth not for me, but stand laughing at my grief.' In vain, Seymour tried to calm her with gentle assurances that he had meant her no harm. But Katherine spat back: 'No my Lord, I think so; you have given me many shrewd taunts.' The more her husband tried to pacify her, the more Katherine dealt with him 'roundly and shortly'.[23]

In the early hours of 5 September, racked by pain and sorrow, Katherine breathed her last. She was buried the same day at Sudeley Castle. Lady Jane Grey, who had replaced Elizabeth as Katherine's protégée, was the chief mourner. Despite his indiscretions, Lord Seymour was reported to be 'the heaviest man in the world' upon the sudden loss of his wife, for whom he had apparently cherished a genuine affection.[24] His daughter was given to the care of Katherine's friend, Baroness Willoughby, but did not survive infancy.

Many of Katherine's personal effects were sent to Edward VI a few months after her death, by which time they were the property of the crown, thanks to her widower's actions. They included a set of cramp rings, which were commonly used by pregnant women because of their alleged healing properties.

Elizabeth was grief-stricken at the loss of her beloved stepmother. She bitterly regretted the pain that her foolish flirtation with Seymour had caused, and had learned a great deal from it. The same was not true of Kat Astley. With an astonishing lack of both sensitivity and judgement, she told Elizabeth that her 'old husband, appointed at the king's death, was free again, and she might have him if she wished'. Elizabeth immediately dismissed Kat's foolish proposition, pointing out that her marriage was a matter for the king and council to decide.

If she had left the matter there, Kat would have avoided a great deal of future trouble. But she seemed infatuated by Lord Seymour and determined to have the vicarious pleasure of seeing him married to Elizabeth. She therefore wheedled and pleaded, constantly praising Seymour's qualities and insisting that it was Elizabeth whom he had loved all along. For all her sage judgement, the princess was still just a girl of fifteen and she was gradually seduced by her governess's appealing theory. While she refrained from writing to the Lord Admiral herself, she agreed that Kat could do so.

Triumphant, Kat told her husband all about it. Recognising his wife's attraction for Seymour, John Astley furiously upbraided her and warned with some considerable foresight that 'the admiral's suitors would come to an evil end'. Annoyed by her husband's obstinacy, Kat left for London, no doubt intending to seek out Lord Seymour, despite Elizabeth's instructions to the contrary. Seymour evidently knew of Kat's weakness for him and played on it, sending her a flirtatious message to enquire 'whether her great buttocks were grown any less or no?'[25]

Kat failed to gain an audience with Lord Seymour, but sent a message to him via Thomas Parry, Elizabeth's cofferer, that 'she would her Grace were your wife of any man living'. Seymour sensibly retorted that his brother, the Lord Protector, would never agree to it. He could not resist suggesting, though, that he pay a visit to Elizabeth on his way to Sudeley Castle. Even Kat realised that this would be unwise and she rejected it out of hand. When she told Elizabeth, the latter was 'much offended with her', telling her that she should not have committed the matter to paper because then there would be proof that she knew of the proposal.[26]

But the princess failed to disguise her renewed infatuation with Seymour, and when Parry returned to Hatfield, she immediately besieged him with questions about everything that had passed between him and the Lord Admiral. She listened, enraptured, as he told her of Seymour's 'gentleness and kind offers', and urged him to go and tell Kat what he had just told her, knowing that her governess would share in her excitement.

Delighted, Kat could not resist gossiping about it all when she dined with Thomas Parry and his wife a short while later. She even told Parry that the Dowager Queen had once found Elizabeth in Lord Seymour's arms, and that this had been the cause of their peremptory departure from her household. Registering the shock on Parry's face, she knew that she had gone too far. Begging him not to repeat what she had said, she took her leave.[27]

But this scandalous knowledge proved too great a temptation for Parry. By Christmas 1548, the rumour that Lord Seymour was on the verge of taking Elizabeth as his wife was the talk of the court. It was said that Seymour had retained his late wife's ladies so that they could wait upon the princess once he had married her.

Things now began to unravel with alarming speed. Jealous of his brother's power, and of Stanhope's intimacy with the king, Seymour set about cultivating his young nephew, visiting him in secret and giving him generous gifts of money. But patience was not his strong point, and in January 1549 he executed a reckless plan to kidnap the king. Having obtained copies of the keys to the privy apartments, late one night he stole into the king's privy garden at Hampton Court, waking one of Edward's pet spaniels. To silence his barking, he shot and killed the dog, which raised the alarm. To be caught outside the king's bedroom with a loaded pistol was a serious offence, and his brother was quick to interpret it in the worst possible terms.

Seymour was arrested on suspicion of high treason and thrown into the Tower. A key part of the evidence against him was that he had conspired to marry the king's sister without the council's permission, an offence punishable by death. Shortly afterwards, Kat Astley and Thomas Parry were also committed to the Tower.

Determined to wrest a confession, the interrogators had Elizabeth's governess moved to one of the darkest, most uncomfortable cells in the fortress. 'Pity me . . . and let me change my prison, for it is so cold that I cannot sleep, and so dark that I cannot see by day, for I stop the window with straw as there is no glass,' she pleaded. Her loyalty to Elizabeth overcame her terror, though, and she remained tight-lipped.[28]

The same was not true of Thomas Parry. A month after his arrest, he gave way and told his interrogators every detail of Seymour's relationship with Elizabeth, from the half-naked romps in the princess's bedchamber to their being caught in an embrace. When she heard of this, Kat realised she had little choice but to reveal everything she knew. Her account of the increasingly indecent romps at Chelsea tallied exactly with Parry's, and she admitted that she and her royal mistress had talked of the prospect of marriage 'diverse times'.[29]

When the news was relayed to Elizabeth at Hatfield, she was 'much abashed, and half breathless', but soon mustered her formidable courage and insisted that although she had talked of the Lord Admiral with her governess 'many times', she had always made it clear that nothing could be done without the council's consent.[30] This latter fact, which was backed up by Kat Astley's and Thomas Parry's confessions, was what saved Elizabeth.

But nothing could save Seymour. His scandalous relationship with Elizabeth aside, he had already signed his own death warrant by plotting to kidnap the king. He was convicted of no fewer than thirty-three charges of treason and was executed on 20 March. Elizabeth was careful to show no regret when she heard of Seymour's death. She had learned a brutal but invaluable lesson: for a person of royal blood, private desires could have deadly outcomes.

Anxious to repair the damage that had been done to her reputation, Elizabeth transformed her image. A portrait painted of her in around 1546 clearly demonstrates her love of rich clothes and jewels. Her crimson satin gown is underlain with cloth of gold and silver. Her headdress, décolletage and waist are lined with exquisite pearls (the princess's favourite), and there is a string of larger pearls around her neck. The overall effect is as striking as Elizabeth intended.

But now, three years later, the sixteen-year-old princess made a conscious ploy to swap her vivid and ostentatious gowns for plain black dresses such as her cousin Lady Jane Grey favoured. Their tutor, Roger Ascham, approved of the transformation. 'With respect to personal decoration, she greatly prefers a simple elegance to show and splendour, so despising the outward adorning of plaiting the hair and wearing of gold, that in the whole manner of her life she rather resembles Hippolyta than Phaedra,' he observed.[31] Another of her tutors, Roger Aylmer, recounted that although her father had bequeathed his youngest daughter a set of 'rich cloths and jewels', even seven years after his death she 'never in all that time looked upon that rich attire and precious jewels but once, and that against her will.' So plainly and 'virtuously' did Elizabeth now attire herself that other young ladies of her rank were 'ashamed to be dressed and painted like peacocks'. On one splendid court occasion, 'when all the ladies . . . went with their hair frownsed, curled and double curled, she [Elizabeth] altered nothing, but kept her old maidenly shamefacedness.'[32] To further emphasise her virtue, Elizabeth always took care to carry prayer books wherever she went.

All of this would have won the approval of her half-brother Edward. Although he had been shocked by the scandalous revelations of Elizabeth's private life, at eleven years old the king had little interest in or understanding of matters of the heart. He was in any case growing into a serious, priggish young man for whom religion was all-consuming. 'In the court there is no bishop, and no man of learning so ready to argue in support of the new doctrine as the king,' reported the Imperial ambassador, 'according to what his masters tell him, and he learns from his preachers.'[33] Fiercely committed to furthering the Protestant cause, he spent much of his short reign implementing a series of radical reforms, notably the first Book of Common Prayer, published in 1549, which aimed at achieving uniformity of worship for all, and the Prayer Book of 1552, which provided a model for worship within the Church of England for the next four centuries. His council also banned a number of old Catholic rituals, such as the use of rosaries, the casting of holy water and the undertaking of pilgrimage.

This had a profound impact upon the private lives of Edward's subjects. The stripping away of Catholic rituals affected more than just religious worship. Women in labour were no longer allowed to take comfort from chants, relics 'or other such superstitious things'.[34] Midwives who continued to perform the same rituals that had provided solace to women racked with the pain of childbirth suddenly found themselves under suspicion of sorcery and witchcraft, and had to adapt their practices quickly to avoid arrest.

The religious reforms also affected those closest to the young king. An entry in Edward's journal for January 1552 records: 'The Emperor's ambassador moved me severally that my sister Mary might have mass, which, with no little reasoning with him, was denied him.'[35] By contrast, the younger of Edward's sisters, who had shared his reformist views since their education together as children, was openly conformist. As a result, Edward grew closer to her and expressed his favour with occasional gifts, such as when he sent Elizabeth 'a fair diamond' by one of his servants.

Elizabeth was careful to cultivate her young brother in return. Having spent so much time together in their youth, she would have recognised his rather spoilt, wilful nature and therefore knew that no matter how much they had in common, she could never completely trust his favour. Even though she lived away from court, she resolved to keep herself in his thoughts. In 1550, she sent him a private letter, together with her portrait. She hoped that her 'inward good mind toward your grace might as well be declared as the outward face and countenance shall be seen,' and could not resist adding: 'For the face I grant I might well blush to offer, but the mind I shall never be ashamed to present.' Elizabeth also assured her brother that although her appearance 'may fade by time', her loyalty towards him never would, as she hoped the years to come would prove. Elizabeth fully appreciated that the surest means of securing a sovereign's favour was to be regularly in their presence, and that Edward was surrounded by men who were potentially hostile to her. She therefore ended the letter: 'I humbly beseech your majesty, that when you shall look on my picture, you will vouchsafe to think, that as you have but the outward shadow of the body afore you, so my inward mind wisheth that the body itself were oftener in your presence.'[36]

In October 1549, the Duke of Somerset was ousted from power following a coup by his rival, John Dudley, Duke of Northumberland.

This sparked a dramatic change in the personnel of the privy chamber. No longer content to be dominated by ambitious courtiers, Edward put his own stamp on this most intimate of court departments. The men whom he chose as his closest body servants shared two characteristics: the king's religion and his personal favour. They included his former whipping boy, Barnaby Fitzpatrick, along with another childhood companion, Sir Robert Dudley, who by now had forged a close friendship with Elizabeth.

There were also men of Northumberland's choosing, including his 'intimate friend', Sir John Gates. According to one source, Gates became 'the principal instrument which he used in order to induce the King to something when he did not want it to be known that it had proceeded from himself.' The same observer claimed: 'All of the others who were in the [Privy] Chamber were creatures of the Duke.'[37]

Northumberland arranged for the structure of the privy chamber to be overhauled, as well as the personnel. The office of first gentleman was replaced by the four principal gentleman of the privy chamber. Two of these officers were given the weighty responsibility of being constantly in attendance upon the king. Another two officials were to be stationed outside the royal bedchamber each night, and it was decreed that only the principal gentlemen could have access. No other officer of the privy chamber was to be allowed entrance to the 'inner chamber'.[38]

The duke himself was exempt from these restrictions – in practice, if not in theory. In order to strengthen his hold over the young king, he paid regular secret visits to him at night, 'unseen by anyone, after all were asleep'. As a result, Edward would come into the council chamber the following day and voice opinions 'as if they were his own; consequently, everyone was amazed, thinking that they proceeded from his mind and by his invention.'[39]

Realising that Edward was eager to prove his kingly power, the Duke of Northumberland transformed his education. Six councillors were appointed to attend the king in his privy chamber to oversee his education in 'these his tender years'. This strengthened the links between the two traditional rival departments of court: the Privy Chamber and Privy Council. It also ensured that Edward was better informed and more able to participate in discussions of policy.

The more scholarly aspects of Edward's education were increasingly overshadowed by the traditional military training of a royal prince. The Venetian ambassador observed that the duke had Edward 'taught to ride and handle his weapons, and to go through other similar exercises, so that his Majesty soon commenced arming and tilting, managing horses, and delighting in every sort of exercise, drawing the bow, playing rackets, hunting . . . indefatigably.'[40] The formerly studious young man was now often arriving late for his lessons because he had been too absorbed in such physical pastimes. But Sir John Cheke ensured that he did not entirely neglect his studies, which continued until his fourteenth birthday. By then, Edward had amassed a considerable body of knowledge. His memory was almost photographic and he could recite the names of all the ports, havens and creeks in England, Scotland and France, along with 'the names of all his justices, magistrates, gentlemen that had any authority'.[41]

As well as feeding Edward's insatiable appetite for knowledge, Cheke also encouraged him to keep a diary. He was the only Tudor monarch to do so, and it is an invaluable – if rather dry – source for the remainder of his reign. The pages of Edward's journal reveal a boy who was precociously intelligent, as might be expected for Henry VIII's cherished only son, having been assigned the best tutors from his infancy. But he also appears as cold, unfeeling and uncompromising – a dangerous blend of traits that might have hardened into tyranny if he had lived to maturity. Although he had been close to his uncle, the ousted Lord Protector Seymour, Edward afforded his demise no more than the following cursory mention in his journal: 'The Duke of Somerset had his head cut off upon Tower Hill between eight and nine o'clock in the morning.'[42]

The young king was not completely devoid of feeling, however. When the sweating sickness claimed the lives of his old school companions, Henry and Charles Brandon, in July 1551, he was said to be devastated. Rather than reveal his grief at court, he penned an oration on the subject of mourning the death of friends. He also revered the German Protestant reformer Martin Bucer and treated him almost as a second father. When Bucer fell ill in late 1550, Edward made a payment of £20 out of his privy purse accounts for 'Mr Bucer his relief in sickness'. His accounts reveal a number of other charitable donations, such as to one Alexander Ginzam 'for the finding of his two sons', and to Margaret de la Rose for 'her loss by fire'.[43]

Edward's tender years protected him from the gossip that usually surrounded a monarch's love life. As a king, the question of his future marriage was still a matter for discussion, however. Although Elizabeth of Valois, Lady Jane Grey and Mary, Queen of Scots were mooted as potential brides, none of them came to fruition. Of them all, Edward was closest to Lady Jane, who shared his keen intellect and strong Reformist faith. She was also unusually modest for a young lady and eschewed the fine clothes and jewels that her status permitted her to wear. Upon receiving a gift from Princess Mary of 'tinsel, cloth of gold and velvet, laid on with parchment lace of gold', Jane was perplexed rather than delighted, and asked: 'What shall I do with it?' 'Marry,' replied one of her ladies, 'wear it.' 'Nay,' insisted Jane, 'that were a shame, to follow my lady Mary against God's word.'[44]

Such pious austerity was even too much for the puritanical king, who rejected the suggestion to marry Jane because he preferred the idea of 'a foreign princess, well stuffed and well jewelled'.[45] As it was, though, Edward showed little inclination to marry at all. He was too preoccupied with statecraft, and probably considered that he had plenty of years yet to deal with more domestic matters.

In April 1552, Edward recorded in his journal that he was 'sick of the measles and smallpox'.[46] The latter was a particularly virulent, often deadly disease. Although the young king recovered, declaring that 'we have shaken that quite away', his constitution may have been fatally weakened. Measles can suppress natural immunity to tuberculosis, and it is likely that Edward contracted this soon afterwards – with fatal results.

In late October, the Italian physician and astrologer Hieronymus Cardano was summoned to the privy chamber to attend the king, who had just turned fifteen. This was prompted by the council's concern at his obvious decline, but Edward himself would have approved of the choice as he had a keen interest in astronomy. 'What is more natural', he once wrote, 'than understanding of the principles, the sky, the constellations, the stars, the planets through the courses of which our bodies . . . and all grasses, flowers, trees, grains, wines and all others are governed and ruled?'[47]

Cardano provided a detailed account of their meeting. Although he included the predictable praise of this 'miracle of nature', with his 'excellent wit and forwardness, being yet but a child' and 'his cleverness and sweetness of manner', the astrologer admitted that Edward 'carried himself like an old man; and yet he was always affable and gentle, as became his age.' He described the young king as being 'of stature somewhat below the middle height, pale-faced with grey eyes, a grave aspect, decorous and handsome,' but added that 'he was rather of a bad habit of body, than a sufferer from fixed diseases.' Cardano noticed that Edward had 'a somewhat projecting shoulder-blade', but was quick to point out that 'such defects do not amount to deformity'. He also recorded that the king was a little deaf and suffered from poor sight. As well as wearing spectacles, Edward also had 'a glass to read with', and when his eyes grew sore they were treated with red fennel, sage, ground peppercorns, white wine, honey and 'the water of a man-child that is an innocent', all of which was mixed together and applied with a feather.[48]

Having thus examined the young king, Cardano set to work on casting his horoscope – a task that took him one hundred hours. He concluded that, although he would suffer from various illnesses, Edward would enjoy a long life. His prediction was soon to prove false.

By the following March, Edward's health had deteriorated to such an extent that, on the advice of his doctors, he kept to his privy chamber in case a change of environment should place his life at risk. He seemed to rally the following month, thanks to a carefully devised diet and exercise programme, and he was seen outside in Westminster Park. But by the end of April, his condition had worsened again and the traditional Garter celebrations had to be postponed. The royal doctors reported his symptoms with a mixture of alarm and confusion. 'The matter he ejects from his mouth is sometimes coloured a greenish yellow and black, sometimes pink, like the colour of blood,' they observed.[49]

The young king was moved to Greenwich in the hope that the cleaner air would speed his recovery. Although he improved again for a short time, on 12 May the Imperial ambassador confided to his master that Edward was so 'indisposed' that 'it is held for certain that he cannot escape'.[50] Exhausted by a hacking cough and high fever, he had also developed ulcers across his swollen body. As his councillors struggled to contain the rumours that the king was dying, Edward was attended only by his most trusted privy chamber servants.

Despite his rapidly deteriorating condition, the king's mind remained sharp. Knowing that Mary would undo all of the reforms for which he and his council had worked so hard, he was determined to prevent her from inheriting his throne. But he went further still by proposing to disinherit his other half-sister, Elizabeth, on account of her bastardy. To do so would be to overthrow the laws of inheritance, not to mention his late father's wishes. But Edward was driven by his desire to safeguard the new faith, and was also under pressure from the Duke of Northumberland, who had his family's interests at heart. In late May, he signed a 'Devise' for the succession, leaving his crown to Lady Jane Grey, granddaughter of Henry VIII's sister Mary and, as of 21 May, daughter-in-law of Northumberland.

Thereafter, the young king's condition seriously declined. John Banister, a twenty-year-old medical student, gleaned reports of Edward's illness from his father, who was a minor official in the royal household. Banister confided these to Jean Scheyfve, the Imperial ambassador, who no doubt rewarded him for his pains. 'He does not sleep except when he be stuffed with drugs, which doctors call opiates,' reported Scheyfve. 'First one thing then another are given him . . . The sputum which he brings up is livid, black, fetid and full of carbon; it smells beyond measure; if it is put in a basin full of water it sinks to the bottom. His feet are swollen all over. To the doctors these things portend death, and that within

This portrait of Henry VII was commissioned in 1505 for Margaret of Savoy, whom he hoped to marry. It failed to persuade her of the ageing king's charms.

Thought to have been made for Henry VII and Elizabeth of York in 1495, this may be the only Tudor royal bed in existence.

Some Tudor birthing methods were surprisingly modern, such as the positions that were recommended in the final stages of labour.

Bust of a laughing boy, thought to be the future Henry VIII aged about seven, by Guido Mazzoni, c.1498.

Extract from an illuminated manuscript showing Henry VII and his children after the death of Elizabeth of York. His young son Henry is shown in the top left hand corner, his face buried in his hands.

The deathbed of Henry VII, 21 April 1509. Hugh Denys, Groom of the Stool, is fourth on the King's right hand.

Henry VIII appears rather stout in this miniature, but he was at the height of his physical vigour and had probably just started courting Anne Boleyn.

Years of ill-fated pregnancies had taken their toll on Catherine of Aragon's figure, but her piety remains undiminished: she wears a jewelled cross and a brooch with the letters IHS – the first three letters of 'Jesus' in Greek.

This intimate sketch by Hans Holbein shows Anne Boleyn in a nightgown, a linen coif covering her hair. She has a pronounced double chin and looks rather plain.

Anne Boleyn and Henry VIII were so confident that their first child would be a son that they had letters prepared announcing the birth of a 'prince'. An extra 's' was subsequently added.

William Fitzwilliam, Earl of Southampton, esquire of the body to Henry VIII, was said to understand the king's 'nature and temper better than any man in England.'

Sir Henry Guildford was appointed to Henry VIII's household when they were both young boys. They struck up an instant rapport and Guildford served Henry for the rest of his life.

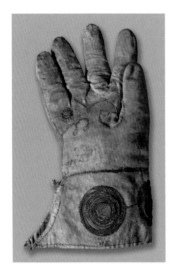

Henry VIII's leather hawking glove and hawk's hood. Sport was an abiding passion for Henry VIII, and his wardrobe was filled with specially made clothes and equipment.

Henry VIII dining in his privy chamber. Although relatively private, such meals still involved elaborate ceremony and an army of attendants.

This beautiful writing desk is thought to have belonged to Henry VIII. It is crafted from stained walnut and gilded leather, and decorated by Lucas Horenbout.

Ceremonial bed head made for Henry VIII's marriage to Anne of Cleves. The panel on the right bears the 'AH' monogram for Anne and Henry, and the carved male and female figures symbolise fertility.

Clock Court, Hampton Court Palace. This beautiful courtyard is named after the astronomical clock, a sophisticated piece of Tudor technology.

This exquisite hat is thought to have belonged to Nicholas Bristowe, clerk to the Wardrobe of Robes and Beds. Legend has it that it was once worn by Henry VIII.

A boy's shirt of fine linen. This material was commonly used for underclothes because it was highly effective at drawing toxins and odours from the body.

An illustration of c.1531-2 showing the various stages involved in the process of washing, drying and bleaching linen.

An 'eavesdropper' in the Great Hall ceiling at Hampton Court Palace, which served as a reminder that 'there is not a single bruit anywhere which he [Henry VIII] does not hear among the first, even to little private matters.'

This unnamed man is easily recognisable as a royal official by his bright red coat emblazoned with 'HR' (Henry Rex).

This luxurious suite of 'secret' lodgings, known as the Bayne Tower, was built for Henry VIII at Hampton Court towards the end of his reign and reflected his desire for greater privacy.

A mid-seventeenth century close stool from Hampton Court Palace. Henry VIII's close stools would have been very similar to this.

Henry VIII and the Barber Surgeons. The king had always taken a keen interest in the medical profession, and in 1540 he formally established the Company of Barbers and Surgeons.

Henry VIII in old age with his favourite fool, Will Somer, and his children: Edward, Mary and Elizabeth.

Edward VI as prince. He holds a pet monkey, which may have belonged to his father's fool, Will Somer.

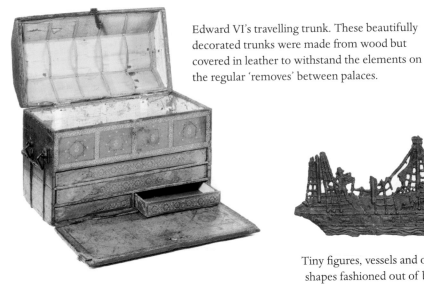

Henry Brandon, second earl of Surrey. The son of Henry VIII's favourite companion, Henry joined Edward's household when the prince turned six years' old.

Edward VI's travelling trunk. These beautifully decorated trunks were made from wood but covered in leather to withstand the elements on the regular 'removes' between palaces.

Tiny figures, vessels and other shapes fashioned out of base-metal such as lead alloy were popular toys in the Tudor period.

The ambitious and volatile Thomas Seymour, Lord High Admiral, caused a scandal when he tried to seduce Edward VI's young sister Elizabeth.

In this, her earliest surviving letter, the ten year old princess Elizabeth writes in Italian to her stepmother, Katherine Parr: 'I am bound not only to serve you but to revere you with a daughter's love.'

Mary I is at ease but her husband Philip appears awkward and uncomfortable. Theirs was not a happy marriage and it sparked rebellion amongst Mary's xenophobic subjects.

Elizabeth I at a stag hunt. The Queen shared her father's love of hunting and did not flinch from cutting the throat of a deer or stag, as shown here.

A locket ring, c.1575, owned by Elizabeth I, showing portraits of herself and her mother Anne Boleyn.

Queen Elizabeth receives a delegation of Dutch ambassadors in her presence chamber. Such sparsely furnished rooms are typical of the Tudor period.

Queen Elizabeth playing the lute, at which she excelled. She preferred to practice in the privacy of her chambers, 'to shun melancholy.'

Elizabeth I at prayer, 1569. Like all the Tudor monarchs, the queen was renowned for her piety and spent many hours in her private devotions.

Medal commemorating Elizabeth's recovery from smallpox, 1562. The young queen almost died from the disease whilst staying at Hampton Court.

An armillary sphere, which was a sign of heavenly wisdom and was used in later portraits of Elizabeth. On the facing page is a poem written in Elizabeth's own hand.

A pair of gloves presented to Elizabeth I on her visit to Oxford University in 1566. Elizabeth was very proud of her exceptionally long, slender fingers.

The 'Rainbow Portrait', by Marcus Gheeraerts the Younger, c.1602. The exquisitely embroidered altar cloth below may have been fashioned from the bodice that Elizabeth wears in the painting.

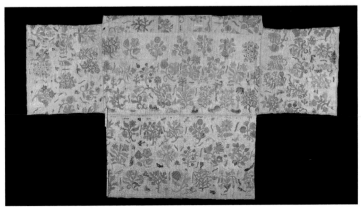

François, Duke of Alençon and Anjou, was the last serious contender for Elizabeth I's hand in marriage. The queen grew very fond of her 'frog', who was more than twenty years her junior.

Elizabeth enjoyed a close relationship with Robert Dudley, Earl of Leicester, for almost fifty years, prompting endless speculation that they were lovers.

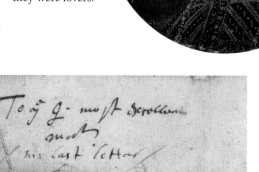

Robert Dudley wrote to Elizabeth just days before his death, on 4 September 1588. The grief-stricken queen inscribed it 'his last letter'.

Known as 'Fair Geraldine', Elizabeth Fitzgerald, Countess of Lincoln, had been a companion of Queen Elizabeth since childhood and was said to be the lady 'in whom she trusted more than all others'.

Lady Anne Dudley, Countess of Warwick. The sister-in-law of the queen's great favourite, Robert Dudley, Anne was the most influential member of Elizabeth's privy chamber.

Elizabeth Vernon was one of several young 'flouting wenches' who served the queen in her later years. When her royal mistress found out that she had fallen pregnant by the Earl of Southampton, she was 'grievously offended'.

Although the queen liked to appear ageless in her portraits, the so-called 'mask of youth' occasionally slipped – as this painting shows.

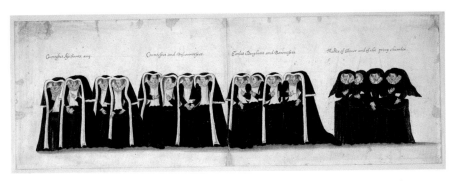

Elizabeth I was buried with great ceremony at Westminster Abbey on 28 April 1603. Following directly behind the coffin were her ladies in waiting.

three months.' Another report claimed that Edward had lost most of his hair and even his nails, and that his fingers and toes were becoming gangrenous. Unable to keep any food down and racked by constant pain, the king whispered to his tutor Cheke: 'I am glad to die.'[51]

In late June, the Imperial ambassador reported: 'It is firmly believed that he will die tomorrow, for he has not the strength to stir, and can hardly breathe. His body no longer performs its functions, his nails and hair are dropping off, and all his person is scabby.'[52] An atmosphere of barely restrained panic pervaded the city as Edward's subjects daily expected news of his death. Rumours of poisoning began to circulate. To reassure them, Edward dragged himself from his sickbed on 1 July and appeared at his window. But upon seeing his wasted body and ghastly pale complexion, the crowds that had gathered below were horrified. Although another appearance was promised, it never materialised.

Five days later, between eight and nine o'clock in the evening, Edward prepared for the end. Attended by his two chief gentlemen of the privy chamber, Sir Thomas Wroth and Sir Henry Sidney, his groom Christopher Salmon and his physicians, Dr Owen and Dr Wendy, he whispered: 'Lord God, deliver me out of this miserable and wretched life, and take me among thy chosen . . . O Lord God save thy chosen people of England! O my Lord God, defend this realm from papistry, and maintain thy true religion.' Only now aware of his attendants' presence, he turned his face towards them and said: 'Are you so nigh? I thought ye had been further off.' Sidney stepped forward and took his royal master in his arms. 'I am faint,' Edward whispered; 'Lord have mercy on me, and take my spirit.' They were the last words he ever spoke.[53]

On 10 July, Lady Jane Grey was proclaimed queen and entered the Tower of London with great ceremony – and reluctance. Aged just sixteen and of a diminutive stature, Jane lacked queenly presence and had no desire to take the throne. She was merely a puppet of her ambitious father-in-law. No doubt instructed by the duke, Jane's ladies attempted to make up for her shortcomings by a clever addition to her wardrobe. On the day that she was proclaimed queen, she was obliged to wear a pair of Italian-style 'chopines', or heeled shoes, to give her greater height – and therefore enhance her regal status. She was dressed in a gown of green velvet with long sleeves embroidered with gold. Her husband, Guildford Dudley, was dressed in white and gold. Together they presented a vision in Tudor colours, legitimising Jane's claim and reinforcing the dynastic continuity.

Powerful though clothes were as a political tool for the Tudors, they were not enough to convince the English people that Jane was their rightful queen, and her hold on the throne lasted for just nine days. For all her faults, Edward's elder half-sister Mary was a true Tudor princess and wasted no time in rallying thousands of subjects to her cause. Soon, the Privy Council turned its coat and declared for her. On 19 July, Mary was proclaimed queen amid great rejoicing.

I I

'*Thinking myself to be with child*'

MARY TUDOR WAS England's first queen for almost four hundred years. The last incumbent, the Empress Matilda, had been known simply as the 'Lady of the English' and had held on to power for only a few months. It was hardly an inspiring example of female sovereignty. In an age when women were generally regarded as inferior to men in every respect, Mary was not expected to fare any better. Setting aside their misgivings about the new queen's ability to rule, her subjects celebrated her accession with feasting and bonfires. At least she was a true Tudor princess and had ousted the usurper, Lady Jane Grey.

On 29 July 1553, Mary rode in triumph through the streets of London. Although she was determined to impress her new subjects with her queenly authority, she was naturally introspective and lacked her father's charisma. Responding awkwardly to the cheers, she progressed through the crowds appearing aloof and uncomfortable. When a group of poor children sang a verse in her honour, it was noted with disapproval that she 'said nothing to them in reply'.[1]

The queen appeared much older than her thirty-seven years. The turmoil of her youth, during which she had seen her beloved mother ousted by the 'Great Whore', Anne Boleyn, and had suffered from prolonged periods of ill health, had aged her prematurely, and the sombre, tight-lipped expression accentuated the lines on her face. Her appearance was not helped by the fact that she had lost nearly all of her teeth in her twenties. Diminutive in stature, she had none of her father's imposing presence. Among her most noticeable features were her eyes, which were so piercing that they 'inspire, not only respect, but fear, in those on whom she fixes them.' In fact, Mary's tendency to stare intently at people was due to severe short-sightedness. Her gruff voice, which was 'rough and loud, almost like a man's', did not make her any more appealing.[2]

Now that she was queen, Mary was determined to reinforce her status by dressing in as rich a style as possible. For her triumphant entry into London, she chose a 'gown of purple velvet [in the] French fashion, with sleeves of the same, her kirtle purple satin all thick set with goldsmith's work and great pearls, with her foresleeves of the same set with rich stones, with a rich baldrick of gold, pearl and stones about her neck, and a rich billiment of stones and a great pearl on her hood.'[3]

Like all of Henry VIII's children, Mary had been dressed in the finest clothes since her earliest days. For her first Christmas, she had received ten yards each of white gold tinsel and white silver tinsel, twelve yards of white satin and eleven yards of white damask to make four gowns, three of which had been furred with ermine.[4] She had continued to receive gifts of rich material and clothing from her father throughout his reign, even when exiled from court during Anne Boleyn's ascendancy. She had worn a gown of cloth of silver at the christening of her brother Edward in 1537, and had a sumptuous dress made for her role as chief mourner at the funeral of his mother shortly afterwards. The priceless garments that filled her wardrobe were under the care of its keeper, Sir Edward Waldegrave, who had been part of Mary's household since 1547 and had been imprisoned for a spell during her half-brother's reign for refusing to carry out the Privy Council's ban on Mary hearing mass. Like her grandfather Henry VII, the new queen chose a man of proven loyalty to serve in this most prestigious of household posts.

But for all the magnificence of her dress, Mary lacked a sense of style. She adorned herself in richly decorated gowns of bright colours that clashed with her red hair, rather than complementing it. Determined to put on a display of unity with her sister, she tried to make Elizabeth follow suit. The latter's tutor, Roger Aylmer, recalled: 'There never came gold or stone upon her head, till her sister [Mary] forced her to lay off her former soberness, and bear her company in her glittering gayness.'[5]

Although Elizabeth, anxious not to offend her sister, accepted such adornments, she made sure that the rest of her attire was as understated as possible. Her elegant simplicity and natural style provided a stark contrast to the garishness of her sister's gowns, and Mary suffered by the comparison. Even Mary's great ally the Spanish ambassador was forced to admit that if she dressed more stylishly, then 'she would not look so old and flabby'.[6] In fact, the new queen was far from overweight: dogged by stomach problems since puberty, she ate only sparingly. But she tended to hide her emaciated figure in heavy, high-necked gowns.

It is possible that Mary also avoided flaunting her sexuality because she feared it would hamper her authority as a female ruler in a male-dominated world. To most of her subjects (female as well as male), the idea of a woman ruling over them was not just abhorrent, it was unnatural. 'To promote a woman to bear rule, superiority, dominion or empire above any realm, nation or city, is repugnant to nature, contumely to God, a thing most contrarious to his revealed will and approved ordinance, and finally it is the subversion of good order, of all equity and justice,' railed the Protestant preacher John Knox in his tract against what he called 'The Monstrous Regiment of Women'. Citing Mary as an example, he argued that women were 'weak, frail, impatient, feeble and foolish: and experience hath declared them to be unconstant, variable, cruel and lacking the spirit of counsel and regiment.'[7]

Although Mary was descended from a long line of powerful women, notably her formidable grandmother, Isabella of Castile, and her bravely principled mother, Catherine of Aragon, she was every bit as conservative in her attitude towards women's place in society as her male courtiers. No matter how dedicated she was to her duties as queen, therefore, she lacked the vital ingredient of political confidence, convinced that her sex was a fatal impediment to ruling effectively. She was therefore resolved to marry as soon as possible so that she might at least have a male consort to guide her.

The accession of a queen regnant presented practical as well as political problems. The task of establishing her government and household was complicated by Mary's sex. Traditionally, officials in both the king's Privy Chamber and his council had been of equal importance, and in some cases interchangeable. But a queen must be attended by female servants, so this well-established arrangement could no longer continue. At a stroke, this effectively deprived the Privy Chamber of its political power because all of the key posts were now filled by women. Even though some of Mary's ladies exploited their position to gain influence, they did not have the same overt power that their male predecessors had enjoyed.

Moreover, Mary set the tone of court life by appointing ladies of irreproachable character, such as Cecily Barnes, Frideswide Strelley, Susan Clarencieux and Jane Dormer, who dedicated their lives to her service and had no ambition to interfere in matters of government. All of the queen's ladies were staunch Catholics, which, coupled with their high morals, transformed the privy chamber from a hotbed of intrigue and scandal into a sober and devout retreat. For all their admirable qualities, however, Mary's female attendants hardly provided the decorative backdrop that was expected of a queen's entourage. 'The Queen is well served with . . . many ladies, most of whom are so far from beautiful as to be downright ugly,' complained one male courtier, 'though I know not why this should be so, for outside the palace I have seen plenty of beautiful women with lovely faces.'[8]

If Mary's ladies presided over her privy chamber, then the responsibility for guarding access to it was the preserve of male officials. Almost all of these were drawn from the household that Mary had retained as princess. They included her Controller, Sir Robert Rochester, her vice chamberlain and captain of the guard, Sir Henry Jerningham, and her master of the horse, Sir Edward Hastings. As well as controlling access to the privy chamber, these men also guarded the queen's person and were therefore very prominent members of her court.

Despite her reputation (and that of her ladies) for sober-mindedness and piety, the new queen was not entirely devoid of fun. One of her favourite companions at court was her female jester, Jane Cooper, known as 'Jane Fool'. Jane had been the jester of Katherine Parr and may also have served under Henry VIII's second wife, Anne Boleyn. She is thought to feature in the painting of Henry VIII and his family that was completed in 1545. In this composition, a lady is shown through an arched doorway on the left-hand side, opposite Henry's fool, Will Somer, on the right.

Mary had enlisted Jane as her jester before she became queen. The first reference to her in Mary's privy purse accounts is as early as 1537, when a payment was made to a groom for stabling Jane's horse. This suggests that she was already in Mary's service, and it is possible that if Jane had been part of Anne Boleyn's household, Mary took pity on her after Anne's fall and offered her employment.

In common with other 'fools' of the period, Jane may have had learning difficulties. She conformed to the practice of male jesters and had her head shaved. Mary was extremely fond of her and gave her many valuable clothes, as well as an unusual number of shoes. Jane repaid her with loyalty and served the queen for the whole of her reign.

Although Jane was Mary's favourite fool, the queen also employed her father's old jester, Will Somer. It has been suggested that Jane and Somer were married, although this is based more upon the symmetry of the 1545 portrait than any firm evidence. Like Jane, Will was comfortably provided for by his royal mistress, who kept him supplied with both ordinary and ceremonial clothes. Mary seemed assiduous for his welfare, and her accounts include a payment for a supply of 'handkerchevers of Holland' to be given to Will, to deal with either an illness or a natural condition. Somer's first biographer claimed that he had a tendency to fall into sudden sleep in unexpected places, which may indicate that he was suffering from a progressive illness. Will was said to be the only man, apart from the playwright John Heywood, who could make the new queen laugh. Like Jane, he served her for the rest of the reign.

Another jester in the pay of the queen was a woman known as 'Lucretia the Tumbler'. She was part fool, part performer. Although the household accounts attest that she and Jane sometimes received identical clothes and performed together, Lucretia was a trained entertainer with impressive (and presumably acrobatic) skills.

As well as entertaining the queen, Jane Fool carried out some straightforward sewing for her royal mistress. The accounts include an order for 'green thread [and] needles for Jane'. Mary also employed a dedicated embroiderer named Bessie Cressy, who was regularly paid for 'working my lady grace's stuff'.[9] The queen herself shared her mother's love of needlework and had worked several fine pieces for members of her family during her youth. As was traditional for royal women, she spent a good part of her leisure hours in this gentle pursuit.

Mary was also an avid gambler and loved to play cards and board games. It was a preoccupation that had developed in childhood, and remained one of her chief sources of delight and recreation throughout her adult life. She also kept several pets, including a parrot and a spaniel, both of which had been given to her as gifts by members of the court. Like her father, she was fond of masques and plays, and her abiding love of music provided much-needed relief from the pressing concerns of state.

The new queen also loved to provide entertainments and feasts for her court. One Spanish visitor in 1554 claimed that she spent more than 300,000 ducats a year on her table, 'for all the thirteen councillors eat in the palace, as well as the household officers, the master of the horse, the master of the household . . . and the wives of all these gentlemen into the bargain. The Queen's ladies also eat by themselves in the palace, and their servants, as well as all the councillors, governors and household officials. And then there are the 200 men of the guard . . .' Feeding such a great number of courtiers and officials put an enormous strain on the royal kitchens, as the same observer noted: 'There are usually eighteen kitchens in full blast and they seem veritable hells, such is the stir and bustle in them.' Although she ate a good deal more sparingly than her father, like him Mary enjoyed a diet rich in meat, washed down with plenty of ale. 'The usual daily consumption is eighty to one hundred sheep – and the sheep here are very big and fat – a dozen fat beeves (cattle), a dozen and a half calves, without mentioning poultry, game, deer, boars and a great number of rabbits. There is plenty of beer here, and they drink more than would fill the Valladolid river. In the summer the ladies and gentlemen put sugar in their wine, with the result that there are great goings on in the palace.'[10]

For all her love of feasting and revelry, Mary found greatest solace in the many hours she spent away from the glare of the court in religious devotion. She heard no fewer than four masses a day and passed many more hours in private prayer. She began each day with the same prayer: 'Oh Lord my maker and redeemer, I thank thy goodness most humbly that thou hast preserved me all this night.'[11] Devout and pious from childhood, the religious reforms of her father and brother's reigns had pushed her towards an ever more ferocious determination to re-establish the traditional Roman Catholic faith. It was the faith of her late mother and her native Spain, the country to which Mary had always felt a passionate affiliation. Now that she was queen, her commitment to the 'old religion' deepened into a dangerous obsession.

As soon as her coronation was out of the way, Mary made it clear that her first priority was to find a husband. The Spanish ambassador, Simon Renard, shrewdly observed that the new queen was desperate to relieve herself of 'those duties which were not the province of ladies'.[12] Although her councillors assumed that she would consult them on such a weighty matter as marriage, Mary had already made up her mind. As with her faith, her choice was inspired by her mother's homeland. As a child, Mary had been betrothed to her cousin, Charles V, Holy Roman Emperor and King of Spain. In the event, he had married another cousin, Isabella of Portugal, but he now had a son of marriageable age.

At the time of Mary's accession, Philip of Spain was twenty-six years old, some eleven years her junior. Already inclined to favour him because of his Spanish blood, Mary fell madly in love with him upon first seeing his portrait. The likeness was painted by the renowned Italian artist Titian and was sent to the English queen in September 1553. The heir to Charles V's vast empire certainly appears quite handsome in the painting. His light-brown hair and neatly trimmed beard frame a pale, somewhat grave face. Fortunately, he had inherited the fine features of his mother, rather than the famously protruding Habsburg chin, but he had the same full lips as his father.

The Venetian ambassador Paolo Fagolo described Philip as 'slight of stature and round-faced, with pale blue eyes, somewhat prominent lip, and pink skin, but his overall appearance is very attractive.' He went on to say that Philip 'dresses very tastefully, and everything that he does is courteous and gracious.' The prince was rather cool and aloof, however, and one of his ministers observed: 'He had a smile that cut like a sword.'[13]

Even if she were aware of such reports, Mary would have paid little heed to them. There had been talk of marriage for her since she was a child, but nothing had ever come of it. As well as desiring a husband, she also had a strong maternal instinct, which she had displayed throughout her life, particularly in her relationship with her younger siblings. Even though she had every reason to hate her half-sister Elizabeth, she had soon taken pity on the motherless child and had lavished her with thoughtful little gifts. In 1538, for example, she had given the infant princess a box embroidered with silver thread. The following year, she had employed William Ibgrave, her father's embroiderer, to make her six-year-old sister 'a coat of crimson satin, embroidered with gold, with paunses of pearls, and sleeves of tinsel, and four aglets of gold.'[14]

Mary desperately wanted a child of her own but was painfully aware that time was running out. Philip already had a healthy son from a previous marriage, so his fertility was proven. This fuelled Mary's obsession. She refused to listen to the vociferous opposition from her council, who feared that England would become a mere satellite of the mighty Spanish empire. Neither did she appreciate the strength of feeling among her xenophobic people, who were reluctant enough to accept a female ruler, let alone one who was married to a Spaniard. 'The English . . . are most hostile by their nature to foreigners', remarked the Venetian ambassador.[15]

But Mary kept doggedly to her course and the marriage settlement was agreed in January 1554. As a compliment to her prospective husband, she and her courtiers began to adopt the fashions of his native Spain. These provided a marked – and sombre – contrast to the gaudy colours favoured at court since the beginning of her father's reign. Imports from the New World allowed the production of a truer black dye than had been achieved by English methods, and simpler lines, such as that imposed by the Spanish surcoat, now predominated.

News of the proposed Spanish marriage prompted uprisings in Kent, Hereford, Devon and Leicestershire led by Thomas Wyatt and a number of prominent noblemen, including Henry Grey, Duke of Suffolk, the father of Lady Jane Grey. The atmosphere at court was fraught with tension, and fresh plots against the new queen were feared on an almost daily basis. In February, under pressure from her council, Mary reluctantly ordered the execution of Lady Jane Grey and her husband Guilford Dudley. She also consigned her half-sister Elizabeth to the Tower.

Even though Wyatt had rebelled in Elizabeth's name, she was almost certainly innocent of involvement. But Mary was taking no chances with her younger sister, who was rapidly becoming a figure-head for any opponent to her regime. When she heard of her impending arrest, Elizabeth was residing at Ashridge with a small number of her most trusted ladies, including her childhood nurse Blanche Parry and her old governess, Kat Astley. Although to the outside world, the twenty-year-old princess appeared to be the very image of youthful vibrancy and health, in private Elizabeth would often suffer from attacks of sickness at times of extreme stress. Now faced with what was arguably the greatest crisis of her life so far, she collapsed with nervous exhaustion.

Frantic with worry, Kat Astley remained at Elizabeth's bedside throughout her illness, expecting with every passing minute to hear the queen's guards knocking on the door. Their arrival could not have come at a worse moment. Late into the night of 10 February, Elizabeth and her ladies were awoken by the delegation of officials from court who had been charged with bringing her to London for questioning. Legend has it that they disregarded the usual decorum and burst into her bedchamber, brushing aside Mistress Astley, who begged them to show mercy to the sick young girl. They paid no heed to her words, but without ceremony ushered a weak and protesting Elizabeth out of the safety of Ashridge and onto the road to London.

Upon arriving in the capital, Elizabeth was installed at Whitehall Palace. Despite her status, she was afforded neither comfort nor privacy, but was housed in cramped apartments below the principal floor of the palace. Sick with worry and weak from the journey, she endured long days holed up in her rooms waiting to be taken to the Tower. Her ordeal was made worse by the noise and smells that constantly emanated from the chamber above. This belonged to her cousin Margaret Douglas, Countess of Lennox, the woman whom it was rumoured Mary would name as her heir. Of a naturally haughty disposition, Margaret had no liking for Elizabeth and used the opportunity to emphasise her own superiority. Upon hearing that her cousin was to be housed in the rooms below, she gave orders that her own apartment be converted into a kitchen so that Elizabeth would be regularly disturbed by the preparation of her meals. It was a petty act of triumph, and one that the countess would live to regret.[16]

Frustrated by the long hours of waiting, Elizabeth resolved to act. Her only chance was to persuade her sister to relent and, having been denied access to her, she resorted to a long and impassioned letter. Lamenting that she was destined for 'a place more wanted for a false traitor than a true subject', Elizabeth confided her fear that 'evil persuasions [might] persuade one sister against the other'. She also expressed her sense of vulnerability at being denied access to the queen, telling Mary: 'I have heard in my time of many cast away for want of coming to the presence of their prince.' Insisting that she had had nothing to do with Wyatt's rebellion, she assured Mary of her utmost loyalty. Clearly not trusting that this private letter would be delivered intact, however, she scored lines across the blank space at the end of it so that nobody should add any incriminating postscript.[17]

This eloquent written plea went unanswered, and shortly afterwards the officials finally arrived to accompany Elizabeth to the dread fortress where her mother had met her death eighteen years before. She arrived by boat, as did the majority of prisoners, passing under St Thomas's Tower. As she mounted the steps beyond, Elizabeth's famously confident public face gave way to her private fears. Sinking down on the cold, wet steps she exclaimed: 'Oh Lord! I never thought to have come in here as a prisoner; and I pray you all, good friends and fellows, bear me witness, that I come in no traitor, but as true woman to the Queen's Majesty as any is now living.'[18]

Although she was comfortably housed inside the royal apartments, there was no doubt that Elizabeth was a prisoner. Denied any semblance of privacy, her every move and utterance was carefully recorded by those appointed to watch over her. Mustering her courage, Elizabeth defended herself stoically when subjected to intense questioning by the royal interrogators. But as soon as she was left to the company of her ladies (most of whom had been placed there by Mary), she gave herself over to her private fears. Painfully aware of the fate that had befallen her mother when she had been a prisoner in the Tower, Elizabeth was so convinced that she was going to die that she considered asking if she could be executed with a sword rather than an axe, because she had heard that it was the swifter death.

A few days after her arrival at the Tower, it seemed that Elizabeth's worst fears would be realised. The Lieutenant, Master Bridges, received a warrant for her execution. Thankfully, he had the presence of mind to seek confirmation of its validity from the queen. Horrified, Mary stoutly denied that she had issued it, and was furious to discover that it was the work of her Lord Chancellor, Stephen Gardiner, and his party. Shocked at how close her sister had come to being executed, her attitude towards Elizabeth immediately softened. She started to refer to her as 'my sister' again in public, and ordered that her portrait be reinstalled in its former position in the royal gallery. Elizabeth was released without charge on 19 May, the anniversary of her mother's execution.

Philip arrived in England in July. Having left the hot sun of Spain, he was dismayed to find his new kingdom in the throes of abysmal summer weather. Battling through torrential rain, he made his way to Winchester to meet his betrothed on 23 July. An English eyewitness recorded that the Spanish prince rode into that city at 6 o'clock in the evening, seated 'on a fair white horse, in a rich coat embroidered with gold . . . with a white feather in his hat very fair.' The prince was described as being 'well favoured' with a 'manly countenance . . . nature cannot work a more perfect pattern.'[19] After attending a service at the cathedral, he had a late supper at the Dean's House, where he was staying (and where Prince Arthur had been born in 1486).

Philip's first meeting with his intended bride was to be in relative privacy. He was escorted from the Dean's House 'by a privy way' to Wolvesey Castle, the former palace of the Bishop of Winchester, where Mary was waiting for him. By now, it must have been almost midnight, but the queen was anxious to meet her betrothed. Upon seeing him, 'her grace very lovingly, yea, and most joyfully received him'.[20] They talked, somewhat haltingly, for half an hour. Philip could not speak English, so they were obliged to converse in a mixture of Spanish, French and Latin. This was hardly conducive to meaningful conversation, but Mary cared little for that. Already deeply in love by the time they met, she was as delighted with her prospective husband in person as she had been with his portrait.

Philip himself was a good deal less enamoured. He confided to one of his attendants that Mary was rather older than he had been led to expect. Time had certainly not been kind to her. Afflicted by ill health for much of her life, she still suffered from a range of ailments. The Venetian ambassador, Giovanni Michiel, observed that the queen had a tendency 'to a very deep melancholy, much greater than that to which she is constitutionally liable, from menstruous retention and suffocation of the matrix to which, for many years, she has often been subject.'[21] In an attempt to alleviate her symptoms, her physicians regularly 'bloodied' her 'from the foot or elsewhere'. This only served to weaken her still further, and Michiel noted that she was 'always pale and emaciated'.[22] Mary had also had bouts of anorexia, suffered dental abnormalities and every winter would complain of aches and pains brought on by the cold, damp weather.

The queen's lack of style was noted with some disdain by a member of Philip's entourage, who described her as 'a perfect saint who dresses badly'.[23] Philip's most trusted attendant, Ruy Gómez de Silva, concluded: 'To speak frankly with you, it will take a great God to drink this cup [but] . . . the king realises that the marriage was concluded for no fleshly consideration, but in order to remedy the disorders of this kingdom and to preserve the Low Countries.'[24]

If Mary did not exactly inspire Philip with passion, then he was at least sufficiently well bred to hide his disappointment. Besides, the prospect of adding this powerful kingdom to his father's considerable dominions more than made up for his bride's physical shortcomings. Giving every appearance of the gallant prince, as he took his leave Philip asked Mary to teach him how to bid the assembled dignitaries farewell. She told him he should say 'Good night, my lords all', and the same eyewitness recorded that he 'said as the queen had taught him'.[25]

Mary and Philip met again the following day. This time, the Spanish prince was paraded through the streets so that his future subjects could see him in all his glory, clad in a cloak of black cloth embroidered with silver, set off with a pair of fine white hose. The very public nature of the meeting continued when Philip entered the bishop's great hall, where Mary was standing on a scaffold erected for the purpose. When she saw Philip, she walked down the steps and 'amiably receiving him, did kiss him in presence of all the people. And then taking him by the right hand, they went together in the chamber of presence, where after they had, in sight of all the lords and ladies, a quarter of an hour pleasantly talked and communed together, under the cloth of estate, and each of them merrily smiling on [the] other.'[26]

The next morning, 25 July, at ten o'clock, Philip and his entourage made their way to Winchester Cathedral for the wedding. Mary arrived half an hour later. Both she and her groom were richly dressed in ostentatious gowns fashioned from cloth of gold and 'so rich set with precious stones, as no man could esteem the value thereof.' But the queen had insisted that her ring be a 'plain hoop of gold without any stone in it . . . because maidens were so married in old times.'[27] It was a touching gesture of simplicity in an otherwise lavish and grandiose event.

Mary's ministers had made sure that her superiority over her husband was emphasised during the marriage ceremony. In the exact opposite of the traditional arrangements for royal weddings, she was always on Philip's right. Almost as soon as the ceremony was over, however, Mary made it clear that she intended to give her new husband a good deal more authority than the settlement had prescribed. She told the Lord Privy Seal 'to obey his [Philip's] commandment in all things.'[28] To confirm what she saw as their joint sovereignty, she then ordered a new coin to be struck in honour of their marriage. This showed the couple facing each other, and above their heads was a crown, equally placed between them. Nevertheless, whenever they appeared in public, Mary always stood on the right. She also occupied the king's apartments in her palaces and assigned the queen's to her husband.

The wedding breakfast took place at Wolvesey Castle. Even though there were 140 guests, it was an intimate occasion for the bride and groom because they chose to dine alone on one table, separated from the throng. There was dancing after dinner, then the royal couple took their leave. As they made their way towards the marriage bed, Mary must have been filled with nervous but joyful anticipation of what lay ahead. Philip was more likely to have felt resigned at the prospect of performing his duty. The bed was blessed by Stephen Gardiner who, as Bishop of Winchester, had officiated over the wedding ceremony.

'What happened that night only they knew,' remarked one of Philip's entourage. The groom was up at seven o'clock the following morning and heard mass as usual. The act of consummation had evidently lived down to his expectations. He confided to Gómez that his new wife 'is no good from the point of view of fleshly sensuality'. But he consoled himself with the knowledge that the match was made not 'for the flesh but for the restoration of this realm.'[29]

Mary, meanwhile, kept to the privacy of her chambers for the next two days. Although she had been used as a pawn in the international marriage market for almost thirty years, she had a fatal naivety when it came to the male sex. That her husband was not at all attracted to her was obvious to everyone except Mary. Even Cardinal Pole, son of the queen's beloved former governess, tactfully admitted: 'Philip is the spouse of Mary, but treats her so deferentially as to appear her son.'[30]

A month after the wedding, Mary wrote to Charles V, full of praise for his son. Proudly referring to Philip as 'The King, my lord and husband' (overlooking the fact that he had not been crowned), she enthused: 'This marriage and alliance, which renders me happier than I can say, as I daily discover in the King my husband and your son, so many virtues and perfections that I constantly pray God to grant me grace to please him and behave in all things as befits one who is so deeply embounden to him.'[31]

Meanwhile, the object of her affections was trying his best to act the part of a doting husband. De Silva remarked: 'The Queen is very happy with the King, and the King with her; and he strives to give her every possible proof of it in order to omit no part of his duty . . . He makes her so happy that the other day when they were alone she almost talked love-talk to him, and he replied in the same vein.' He shrewdly added in another letter: 'His Highness is so tactful and attentive to her that I am sure they will be very happy.'[32]

But there had to be more than just play-acting on Philip's part. The Habsburg dynasty must be firmly established in England, so the production of heirs was vital. The Spanish prince therefore had to perform his conjugal duty as often as possible, no matter how distasteful he might find the task. Within weeks of the wedding, it seemed that he had been rewarded for his pains. Mary's periods stopped, she felt queasy in the mornings and started to rapidly gain weight. In November 1554, Parliament gave thanks to God for 'the Queen's grace quickening', and a ballad was written joyfully anticipating 'our Prince that shall be'.[33]

Eager though Mary was to ascribe her symptoms to pregnancy, they were worryingly similar to those that she had regularly experienced since puberty. Her physicians had long since concluded that she suffered from 'strangulation of the womb', a condition that led to irregular or absent periods, abdominal swelling and frequent bouts of nausea and depression. In the past, Mary may have been subjected to one or more of the brutal treatments prescribed for the condition. They included the inhalation of noxious fumes in order to drive the blood downwards. Alternatively, a tube could be inserted into the vagina and steam sent up from a boiling liquid in order to 'fumigate' the uterus. Worse still, horse leeches could be inserted into the neck of the womb. From her teens, Mary had adapted her diet to try to alleviate the symptoms of her menstrual disorder. In March 1535 it was reported that 'the lady Mary . . . was much desirous to have her meat immediately after she was ready in the morning, or else she should be in danger eftsoons to return to her said infirmity.'[34] Upon the advice of her physicians, however, she subsequently refrained from eating until nine or ten in the morning.

A number of theories have been put forward by modern-day medical experts as to the cause of Mary's condition. One is that she had an ovarian tumour, which would have explained her lack of periods, swollen abdomen and frequent stomach pains. John Foxe dared to conjecture that 'she was deceived by a Tympanie [tumour] or some other like disease, to think herself with child.'[35] Her symptoms are also synonymous with prolactinoma, a benign tumour of the pituitary gland. This condition often causes infertility and changes in menstruation, with some women losing their periods altogether. Women who are not pregnant or nursing may begin producing breast milk.[36]

Yet Mary was so confident of her condition that in December 1554 she wrote joyfully to her father-in-law, Charles V, assuring him: 'As for that which I carry in my belly, I declare it to be alive, and with great humility thank God for His great goodness shown to me, praying Him so to guide the fruit of my womb that it may contribute to His glory and honour, and give happiness to the King, my Lord and your son.'[37] The fact that she felt it necessary to confirm that she was carrying a healthy child suggests that even at this early stage, there had been rumours that the pregnancy was false. Mary's menstrual problems were known throughout the court, and her advancing age was another cause to doubt that she had fallen pregnant so easily. It certainly suited the anti-Spanish party at court to doubt her condition, and they began to spread rumours that it was all a Spanish plot to pass off another infant as the queen's.

But Mary and her supporters continued to insist that her pregnancy was real. A Spanish envoy claimed that the queen's doctor had 'given me positive assurance' that there were other signs, apart from her nausea. Questions were evidently still being raised a few months later, but Renard affirmed: 'One cannot doubt that she is with child. A certain sign of this is the state of the breasts, and that the child moves. Then there is the increase of girth, the hardening of the breasts and the fact that they distill.'[38]

Although most of Mary's ladies assured her that they could feel the child move beneath her belly, Frideswide Strelley dared to express some doubt. 'Feel you not the child stir?' Mary had asked her eagerly. 'My fortune is not so great,' Strelley replied.[39] With an almost grim determination, Mary instructed her ladies to prepare for her confinement. Sumptuous cradles and baby clothes were ordered, and midwives and rockers were appointed. Hampton Court Palace was chosen as the place for the birth, and Mary duly made her way there in early April 1555, a little over a month before the baby was due. By now, her stomach was so swollen that even the more doubtful courtiers speculated that the baby might arrive at any day.

Among the ladies appointed to serve Mary in her confinement was her half-sister Elizabeth. Now aged twenty-one, the princess had grown into a striking young woman with long red hair, pale skin and the same bewitching dark eyes as her mother. Although the sisters had once been on good terms, their differences in religion were a growing source of friction and Elizabeth found herself subject to intense suspicion every time a fresh plot broke out against Mary's regime.

Late one evening, about three weeks after arriving at the palace, Elizabeth was led by torchlight to the queen's bedchamber. Knowing that her sister suspected her of plotting to take the throne, the princess humbly protested her innocence and devotion. Mary upbraided her for refusing to admit her guilt, but after a while she grudgingly uttered 'a few comfortable words' to her before abruptly sending her back to her apartments. According to John Foxe's account of the meeting, Mary's husband Philip had been hiding behind an arras the whole time, eager to spy upon this exchange between his ageing wife and her bewitching half-sister.[40] Although there are no other accounts to corroborate this, Philip certainly showed a keen interest in Elizabeth from that time forward.

As Mary's confinement progressed and the due date of 9 May drew closer, there was a fever pitch of anticipation, both at court and across the kingdom. Any scrap of information was seized upon and rumours swiftly became fact. At the end of April, the diarist Henry Machyn reported: 'The Queen's grace was delivered of a prince and so there was great ringing through London.' The next day, though, he admitted: 'It was turned other-ways to the pleasure of God!'[41] But the news had already spread, and great feasts were held across the capital in celebration. Scores of churchmen said prayers of thanks, and the parson of St Anne within Aldersgate 'after procession and Te Deum sung, took it upon him to describe the proportion of the child, how fair, how beautiful, and great a prince it was, as the like had not been seen.'[42]

News of Mary's happy delivery soon spread to the Continent. English merchants on the Channel set off cannons from their ships as a sign of joy, and bells were rung across the Spanish Netherlands in celebration.[43] The regent there, Mary of Hungary, rewarded the English sailors with 100 'pistolets' or Italian crowns. In this frenzy of celebration, one 'simple man' who lived close to Berwick, just south of the border between England and Scotland, dared to express doubts that the reports were true. 'Here is a joyful triumph', he remarked, 'but at length all will not prove worth a mess of pottage.'[44]

The date on which the baby should have been born came and went. 'Long persuasion had been in England, with great expectation, for the space of half a year or more, that the queen was conceived with child.' recounted John Foxe, who was writing just seven or eight years later and could therefore well recall the controversy.[45] The queen's physicians 'and others nigh about the Court' were obliged to reiterate their prognosis that Mary really was pregnant, 'divers were punished for saying the contrary and commands were given that in all churches supplication and prayer should be made for the queen's good delivery.'[46]

In late May, Mary was seen walking in her privy garden at Hampton Court. Gómez shrewdly observed: 'She steps so well that it seems to me that there is no hope at all for this month.'[47] But she remained confident: after all, first babies were often late. A little over three weeks later, on 1 June, she experienced some pains and her ladies hastily gathered around, assuming that the labour had begun. 'The time was thought to be nigh that this young master should come into the world,' observed John Foxe, who noted that an army of 'midwives, rockers and nurses with the cradle were all prepared in readiness.'[48] Letters were duly drafted announcing the birth of a prince to the Pope, Charles V, Henry II and all the potentates of Europe.[49] But the pains subsided and Mary and her attendants resumed their former waiting.

Philip was residing at Hampton Court throughout this time. As the weeks dragged on and there was still no news that his wife had been delivered of a child, he sought diversion with his sister-in-law. 'At the time of the queen's pregnancy, Lady Elizabeth, when made to come to the court, contrived so to ingratiate herself with all the Spaniards, and especially the King, that ever since no one has favoured her more than he does,' observed the Venetian ambassador.[50] Before long, it was rumoured that the queen's husband was so captivated by her half-sister's youthful beauty, which formed an attractive contrast to his wife's faded looks, that he resolved to have her for himself.

In fact, Elizabeth had been suggested as a bride for Philip at the age of just thirteen, when Henry VIII had been planning to forge an Imperial alliance. This had come to nothing, but now Philip, who was beginning to suspect that his wife's condition was due to something more sinister than pregnancy, may have considered resurrecting the scheme. His motives were almost certainly political. England played a critical part in the ongoing power struggle between his father's empire and France, and he would have been reluctant to relinquish it. What was more, the alternative claimant to the

English throne was Mary, Queen of Scots, who had been raised in France and was betrothed to the Dauphin. Elizabeth herself, though, later claimed that Philip's interest in her had been far more personal. She was fond of boasting that their relationship had begun with love, at least on Philip's part.

While Mary's husband amused himself with her half-sister, those with a vested interest in believing that her pregnancy was real surmised that the royal physicians had simply misjudged the due date. 'Her doctors and ladies have proved to be out in their calculations by about 2 months,' Renard reported to Charles V on 24 June, 'and it now appears that she will not be delivered before 8 or 10 days from now.' He could not help adding, with a note of anxiety: 'Everything in this kingdom depends on the Queen's safe deliverance.'[51] Those opposed to the regime, however, spread counter-rumours that the pregnancy and confinement had been nothing but an elaborate sham. To explain the queen's swollen girth, the French ambassador reported that she had been 'delivered of a mole or lump of flesh, and was in great peril of death.'[52]

As summer gave way to autumn and there was still no sign of a child, Mary was forced to admit defeat. Summoning her doubtful attendant, she cried: 'Ah, Strelley, Strelley, I see they be all but flatterers and none true to me but thou.' Humiliated and heartbroken, Mary left for Whitehall in August. 'There is no longer any hope of her being with child,' wrote Charles V to his ambassador in Portugal the following month.[53]

Once it became known that there would be no royal birth, the rumours started up again, growing ever more outlandish as the queen remained tight-lipped about what had really happened. While some speculated that the entire pregnancy had been fabricated 'for a policy', others affirmed that Mary 'did by some chance miscarry'. Some people even claimed that she had been 'bewitched'. Several years later, John Foxe related a tale that he had been told by a woman called Isabel Malt, who lived in Aldersgate Street in the City of London. She had been delivered of a boy on 11 June 1555, and had been astonished to receive a visit from Lord North and another member of the queen's council shortly afterwards. They had demanded that she hand over her son to them and had promised that he would be well provided for, making 'many fair offers if she would part with the child'. When Isabel refused, the men had gone away but had soon been followed by certain ladies from the queen's household, including one who had been appointed rocker to the non-existent child. Mrs Malt remained firm, however, and would 'in no wise let go her son'.[54] Foxe admitted that he had only been told this story thirteen years after the event and would not vouch for its credibility. No matter how unreliable such rumours may be, they reveal the extent of the public scandal caused by Mary's personal tragedy.

By now, Philip had tired of keeping up the pretence of affection towards this prematurely aged, sexually inadequate wife. The embarrassing farce of her phantom pregnancy had made him increasingly desirous to be rid of her – and her hostile country. To his relief, when it had become obvious that there would be no child, his father dispatched a summons to attend to Imperial business in the Netherlands. Whether this was as a result of a private plea on Philip's part is not known. When Mary heard of it, she was greatly distressed. In her grief and humiliation, her only comfort was to have her adored husband by her side. She wrote at once to Charles, begging him to withdraw his request: 'I assure you, Sire, that there is nothing in this world that I set so much store by as the King's presence.' Her appeals fell on deaf ears, and Philip prepared to embark for his father's dominions.

Much to the queen's resentment, her husband requested that Elizabeth should be among the party who travelled to Greenwich to bid him farewell as he sailed for the Netherlands. This was anathema to Mary, who already had her suspicions about his feelings for her half-sister. Philip's envoy later reported that one of the principal causes of Mary's resentment towards Elizabeth was 'her fear that if she died your Majesty would marry her.' Having just failed – very publicly – to produce a child, and painfully aware of her advancing years, Mary was taunted by the thought that her half-sister, who 'is more likely to have children on account of her age and temperament', would bear Philip many sons if they married.[55]

At length, she agreed to her husband's request, but only on condition that Elizabeth was conveyed to Greenwich discreetly by barge, rather than through the streets of London, where she could be cheered by the crowds. She herself was loath to be seen by her people, conscious that, some five months before, she had made her way in expectant triumph to her confinement at Hampton Court.

A far greater trial awaited Mary, though, when she was forced to bid farewell to her husband. To make matters worse, Philip's parting words included a commendation of the Lady Elizabeth, and he reiterated this in a letter to the queen written shortly after his arrival in Brussels. As she watched his ship embark from Greenwich, she sank into a deep melancholy that would last for many months. 'To say the truth the Queen's face has lost flesh greatly since I was last with her,' observed the Venetian ambassador, Michiel. 'The extreme need she has of her Consort's presence harassing her, as she told me, she having also within the last few days in great part lost her sleep.'[56] Her misery at being parted from her beloved husband was exacerbated by rumours that he was soon enjoying various liaisons with women at the Flemish court.

But Mary upheld the traditional festivities at court at Christmas 1556 and the New Year celebrations that followed. For all her shortcomings, she was unfailingly generous to those who served her, as is revealed by the three hundred or so gifts she gave to members of her court and household.[57] She did not forget anyone: from the great, such as Cardinal Pole, to the humble, such as her launderer, Beatrice ap Rice, who had been in her service since Mary was three years old. She also presented gifts to her late brother's nurse Sybil Penn, her fishmonger, fruiterer, hosier and the sergeant of the pastry. The latter reciprocated the Queen's kindness with a quince pie. Her sister, meanwhile, presented Mary with a kirtle and a pair of sleeves 'of cloth of silver, richly embroidered'.[58] It was a well-chosen gift. Elizabeth knew that Mary was in the process of updating her wardrobe in the hope that her husband would soon be returning to her side.

But as the months dragged on with no hint that Philip intended to return, Mary wrote to beg his father that he might restore her 'chief joy and comfort' to her, assuring him that without his son their kingdom was in a 'miserable plight'. Charles V was unlikely to agree to her request. In increasingly poor health, he was gradually ceding responsibility for significant parts of his vast empire, and in January 1556 he abdicated the Spanish crown in his son's favour. With such pressing new demands on his time, Philip had a genuine excuse not to return to his distasteful wife and it was not until March 1557 that he at last set sail for England. Overjoyed, Mary hastened to Greenwich to welcome him home.

Philip was a good deal less pleased to be back. A description of Mary at the time of her husband's return suggests that she had aged considerably. Although only forty-one years old, her face was lined with wrinkles 'caused more by sorrow than by years, which make her appear older than in fact she is,' remarked the Venetian ambassador, Giovanni Michiel. The traumas of the past few years had given her 'a grave and sedate cast', and Michele observed that she looked 'thin and delicate, and altogether unlike her father, who was tall and strongly made, or her mother, who, although not tall, was stout.' Mary's eyesight had also deteriorated, and she was now 'unable to read, or do anything else, without placing her eyes quite close to the object.' Michele insisted, though, that while the queen could no longer be described as 'more than moderately pretty', as in her younger days, neither 'should she ever be spoken ill of for want of sufficient beauty.'[59]

Mary barely had time to get accustomed to her husband's presence because in July 1557, after just four months back in England, Philip set sail once more. Utterly wretched at being abandoned for a second time, Mary retreated to her privy chamber, taking all of her meals there alone and refusing to appear in public. Desperate for consolation, she convinced herself that, this time, she was pregnant. Again, there were certain symptoms. Courtiers noted 'the swelling of the paps and their emission of milk', as well as her growing stomach.[60] She wrote at once to her husband, telling him the joyous news that their child would be born the following March. So confident was she, despite her earlier experience, that she also made a will, 'thinking myself to be with child in lawful marriage

... [and] foreseeing the great danger which by God's ordinance remain to all women in their travail of children.'[61] Privately, her husband was sceptical. But he dutifully wrote that the news had given him 'greater joy' than he could express, 'as it is the one thing in the world I have most desired and which is of the greatest importance for the cause of religion and the welfare of our realm.'

Few people believed that the queen was truly pregnant this time. No preparations were made for the birth, and even Mary herself delayed formally announcing the news. Aware of the widespread scepticism, she grew increasingly agitated. 'She the more distresses herself, perceiving daily that no one believes in the possibility of her having progeny,' observed one courtier, 'so that day by day she sees her authority and the respect induced by it diminish.'[62] The sixteenth-century antiquarian William Camden put it more bluntly: 'They [her subjects] had small hope of issue by the Queen, being now 40 years old, dry, and sickly.'[63]

Defying all of them, the queen doggedly went ahead with her plans for the birth. Loath to return to the site of her earlier humiliation, this time she chose Richmond Palace. In February 1558, her half-sister Elizabeth visited her there, ostensibly to offer her good wishes for a safe delivery, but in reality to judge for herself whether Mary was really pregnant. Although she soon realised that there was no more cause to believe this than there had been two years before, she went through the charade of presenting her elder sister with some baby clothes that she had made. She only stayed at Richmond for a week, which was long enough to satisfy herself that this pregnancy, like the first, was a figment of the queen's imagination.

Shortly after Elizabeth's departure, the queen entered her confinement. This time, there was little sense of anticipation. Only a handful of lords and ladies gathered at Richmond to await the birth, and those who attended Mary seemed resigned to the tedium of sitting it out until she admitted that there would be no child. As the weeks dragged on, she became increasingly despondent, weighed down not just by grief but probably also by a constant, nagging pain. It is likely that the swelling in her stomach was a cancerous growth – similar to the one that had killed her mother.

By the end of March 1558, Mary had accepted that there would be no child. Her doctors and attendants resumed their normal duties, and the matter was quietly dropped. In vain, the queen begged her husband to return, but he offered only weak excuses. In April, Mary had rallied sufficiently to visit her younger sister at Hatfield, where she was entertained with singing, bear-baiting and feasting. The true purpose of this apparently sisterly harmony was to signal to the world that, in the absence of any child from her own body, Elizabeth would be her heir.

In August, as she was travelling to St James's, the queen fell ill with a fever and was obliged to retire to the privacy of her rooms as soon as she reached the palace. Thomas Wriothesley had recorded that London had been afflicted by 'divers strange and new sicknesses' that summer, including a form of influenza. It may have been this that Mary, in her already weakened state, had fallen prey to.

As her condition worsened, the Spanish ambassador at court urged Philip to return to England so that he might be by his wife's side. But Philip clearly had no intention of doing so. While Mary had so mourned his absence during the previous few months that she had sent frequent letters and gifts to him, including some 'game pasties' that she knew were his favourites, Philip could not bring himself to pay his wife one final visit, even though he knew she was dying. Instead, he sent a message to the Privy Council, telling them: 'We are moved to send a person to England to attend certain business, visit her [the queen], and excuse our absence.' His neglect was said to have hastened Mary's decline, and some even blamed her illness entirely upon it. In her increasing delirium, she told the ladies who were gathered around her bedside that her dreams were filled with little children 'like angels playing before her, singing pleasing notes'.[64]

On 28 October, Mary was conscious enough to add a codicil to her will, finally acknowledging that there would be no 'fruit of her body', and confirming that the crown would go to Elizabeth. That it pained her to acknowledge her heretical half-sister as heir is suggested by the fact that she did not name her specifically, but merely referred to 'the next heir by law'. Shortly afterwards, Mary dispatched her most trusted servant and confidante, Jane Dormer, to relay her final wishes to Elizabeth. These were to uphold the Roman Catholic faith 'as the Queen has restored it', to be good to her servants, and to pay her debts.[65] Elizabeth's response was non-committal: she knew that the crown was now within her grasp.

Mary's adored husband was never far from the dying queen's thoughts, and her will included a touching bequest to her 'most dearest lord'. She begged him to 'keep for memory of me one jewel, being a table diamond', which had been given to her by Philip's father, Charles V, as well as another table diamond and 'the collar of gold set with nine diamonds, the which his majesty gave me the Epiphany after our marriage, also the ruby now set in a gold ring, which his highness sent me.' Mary had made this bequest before the codicil had been added, because she stipulated that her husband could dispose of these jewels 'at his pleasure' and, if he so wished, could pass them on 'to the issue between us'.[66] She must have known, at the time that this was written, that there was no longer any prospect of children, but she could not quite bear to relinquish this, her dearest wish.

On 14 November, the Duke of Feria, one of Philip's advisers in England, reported that there was now 'no hope of her [Majesty's] life; but on the contrary, each hour I think that they will come to inform me of her death, so rapidly does her condition deteriorate from one day to the next.'[67] Three days later, between four and five o'clock in the morning, having heard her final Mass, Mary slipped from a life that had been marked by tragedy and heartbreak. Her passing was so quiet that those around her did not immediately realise that she was gone. Upon hearing of his doting wife's death, Philip merely remarked that he felt 'reasonable regret'. It was a poor recompense for her unstinting devotion.

Among the personal effects that Mary left was a book of prayers, with a page devoted to intercessions for expectant mothers. It was stained with tears.

12

'We highly commend the single life'

ATTRACTIVE, CHARISMATIC AND vivacious, Elizabeth had already won the love of her people by the time she ascended the throne. After the brutality of her half-sister's reign, which had seen hundreds of Protestants perish in the flames, they welcomed a queen renowned for her moderation and tolerance. They were also glad to be rid of the overweening influence of Spain, which had always threatened to absorb little England into its vast empire.

But if there was ample justification for the feasting, bonfires, bell ringing and general revelry that swept across the kingdom in November 1558, there was also a feeling of profound unease that once again the people of England were subject to the rule of a woman. Mary had hardly been a shining example of queenship, and even though Elizabeth presented a more attractive and charismatic alternative, she was still hampered by her sex. Thomas Becon, a Norfolk clergyman, vehemently complained to God: 'Thou has set to rule over us a woman, whom nature hath formed to be in subjection unto man.' He could only conclude that 'this was an evident token of thine anger towards us Englishmen.'[1]

Far from railing against such blatant misogyny, Elizabeth appeared to collude with it. She constantly lamented that she had been born a 'weak and feeble woman', and whenever possible referred to herself as 'prince' and other masculine terms, as if to try to fit into a male-dominated world. But all of this was mere play-acting. Although the new queen was no champion of the female sex in general, she saw herself as a shining exception and, in stark contrast to her sister Mary, had no intention of being governed by a man.

As well as decrying her sex, Elizabeth also flaunted it. Having inherited her mother's natural flirtatiousness, she at turns delighted, frustrated, enticed and enslaved the male courtiers who flocked to pay her homage. A virgin queen, she was nevertheless as beguiling and sexually provocative as her sister Mary, the royal wife, had been naïve and frigid. At her coronation in January 1559, she wore the same robes of cloth of gold that Mary had worn. But whereas her late sister had worn the gown and kirtle loose, Elizabeth had the bodice remodelled to fit her body tightly.

From the very beginning of her reign, Elizabeth declared her intention never to marry. 'And, in the end, this shall be for me sufficient, that a marble stone shall declare that a queen, having reigned such a time, lived and died a virgin,' she told the first parliament of her reign in February 1559.[2] Her declaration was met with indulgent good humour. Few of her ministers believed that she truly meant it: this was surely a deliberate ploy to increase her value as a potential bride. She, like her mother, must have understood the need to allow men to experience the thrill of the chase.

It was inconceivable that the new queen would not wish to marry. She could not possibly hope to rule effectively without the firm guidance of a husband. Shortly after her accession, her sister's widower Philip II had told Elizabeth that she should marry him in order to 'relieve her of those labours which are only fit for men'.[3] Marriage was also, of course, essential for her to fulfil her primary function in life as the bearer of children. There was even more reason to suppose this in Elizabeth's case. For all her popularity, her position as queen was dangerously unstable. In the eyes of Catholic Europe, she was a heretic and a usurper, and the rightful heir to the throne was her cousin Mary, Queen of Scots. It was therefore vital to secure the new regime by marrying and producing an heir. Although a politically advantageous marriage was paramount, Elizabeth's contemporaries also acknowledged that in order for the queen to fall pregnant she must marry a man to whom she was sexually attracted. Contemporary medical theory still made a strong connection between female pleasure and conception. The Earl of Sussex confided to William Cecil that their royal mistress should marry according to her affections, 'which shall be the nearest ways with the help of God to bring us a blessed prince.'[4]

The social conventions of the day dictated that marriage was the desirable state for all women, not just queens. Those who remained single were derided as freaks of nature and a contemporary song claimed that women who died as virgins 'lead apes in hell'.[5] As well as needing a husband for practical and spiritual guidance, if a woman did not find an outlet for her sexual urges, it was thought to cause serious harm to her well-being. One authority claimed that women who did not have sexual intercourse would be tormented by 'unruly motions of tickling lust', and would also suffer from poor complexions and unstable minds caused by a 'naughty vapour' to the brain.

Elizabeth herself admitted: 'There is a strong idea in the world that a woman cannot live unless she is married, or at all events that if she refrains from marriage she does so for some bad reason.' Yet she herself had never shown any inclination to adhere to convention. During her sister's reign, when the question of her marriage was being discussed, she had told one of Mary's courtiers in no uncertain terms that she wished 'to remain in that state that I was, which best pleased me. I am at present of the same mind, and intend so to continue, with her majesty's favour. There is no life comparable to it.'[6]

In fact, Elizabeth had a number of very sound political reasons not to marry. The Tudors expected a wife to submit to her husband in all things, no matter if she was queen. Even though her half-sister's marriage treaty had strictly defined the powers of her new husband, the reality had been rather different and Mary had consciously ceded a good deal of authority to Philip. But Elizabeth had learned from that example and was also of a far more independent nature. When she told Sir James Melville that she was resolved never to marry, he shrewdly replied: 'Your Majesty thinks, if you were married, you would be but Queen of England; and now you are both King and Queen. I know your spirit cannot endure a commander.' In a similar vein, Heironimo Lippomano, the Venetian ambassador in France, disapprovingly noted 'the ambition which the Queen has by her nature to govern absolutely without any partner.' As if to corroborate this, when provoked by increasing pressure from her council to marry, Elizabeth angrily retorted: 'I will have but one mistress here, and no master!'[7]

Elizabeth therefore made no secret of her public reasons for wishing to remain single. But her decision may have had as much to do with powerful fears that she privately harboured about marriage. These occasionally found open expression, such as when she confided to the French ambassador that she would leave herself entirely vulnerable if she took a husband because he could 'carry out some evil wish, if he had one'. She later snapped at a German envoy that 'she would rather go into a nunnery, or for that matter suffer death' than marry.[8] A few years later, the queen abandoned her customary sang-froid and fiercely declared that she hated the idea of marriage 'every day more, for reasons which she could not divulge to a twin soul, if she had one, much less to a living creature.'[9]

The vehemence of Elizabeth's refusal to marry may have been rooted in the traumas of her childhood. She had been just shy of three years old when her mother had been executed at the orders of her father. Five years later, her stepmother, Katherine Howard, had followed Anne to the block. Old enough to understand the full horror of what had happened, the eight-year-old Elizabeth had confided to her close companion, Robert Dudley, that she would never marry. In the early years of her reign, she admitted to a Scottish envoy that certain events from her youth had made her afraid of marriage. Her opinion had changed little a few years later, when she declared: 'So many doubts of marriage was in all hands that I stand [in] awe myself to enter into marriage, fearing the controversy.'[10]

Tempting though it is to apply modern-day psychology to the traumas that Elizabeth suffered as a child (which would certainly be more than enough to foster a deep-seated fear of marriage), this is misleading. The Tudors occupied a far more brutal society than we do today. Violent death was commonplace, even – or especially – at court, where the stakes were highest and those seeking advancement often paid the ultimate price. Even minor misdemeanours were met with severe punishments: if you stole a loaf of bread, you could be tied to a post and publicly whipped, branded with a hot iron or have your hand struck off. The punishments for more serious crimes could be horrifyingly brutal. Attempted murder could result in the perpetrator being boiled alive, and if a woman was found guilty of petty treason (the betrayal of a superior by a subordinate) she could be burned alive. It was an age when people attended public executions for entertainment, and violent sports such as cock-fighting and bear-baiting were also popular. Elizabeth herself had a penchant for the latter.

Added to this is the fact that for almost all of Elizabeth's infancy, her mother had been a distant figure, making only occasional visits to her daughter. She had had even less contact with her third step-mother, Katherine Howard. It would likely have had more of an impact upon her outlook and development if one of her nursemaids or governesses had been suddenly wrenched from her. Nevertheless, the brutal world of the royal court had taught Elizabeth a valuable lesson, and one that she would put into practice when queen: love and politics could be a deadly combination. It had also given her a healthy cynicism about romance. 'Affection', as she would later remark, 'is false.'[11]

The disastrous marital history of the women in Elizabeth's early life had another impact upon her, too. It made her afraid of preg-nancy and childbirth – with good reason. Her mother Anne had lost her life because of her failure to bear Henry VIII a son, and had suffered three miscarriages in the attempt. Two of Elizabeth's stepmothers had died from complications in childbirth, and she had witnessed first-hand the pain and humiliation of her half-sister Mary's phantom pregnancies. Despite numerous marriages and mistresses, her father had only managed to sire two sons who had survived infancy, and there had been a string of stillbirths and miscarriages. The obstetric history of her Tudor forebears therefore hardly instilled Elizabeth with confidence about her own fertility. Little wonder that she was reluctant to gamble her throne on marriage, with all its attendant uncertainties and dangers.

But if Elizabeth was not inclined to marry, neither was she

prepared to restrain her sexual desires altogether. She made little attempt to conceal her fascination with sex and was clearly a woman of passion. One of the most notorious flirts in history, 'the Queen did fish for men's souls, and had so sweet a bait, that no one could escape her network,' as a favoured courtier, Sir Christopher Hatton, observed.[12] Elizabeth delighted in being at the centre of a game of courtly love that she herself had created, and loved to show herself off to her courtiers and foreign dignitaries as both a queen and a woman. She even personalised her relationships with her councillors by giving them pet names: Cecil was 'Sir Spirit', and Hatton was the 'Lids' to Dudley's 'Eyes' (which she wrote as ōō).

At times, her behaviour towards her male courtiers was so outrageously suggestive that many believed she must be conducting illicit affairs with them. Her relationship with her long-standing companion, Robert Dudley ('my bonnie sweet Robin'), prompted by far the most speculation. She had known the handsome courtier since childhood, and the two had become close during her years of uncertainty under Mary Tudor, when Dudley had taken great risks to remain loyal to her. They spent many hours together and shared a love of hunting, dancing and lively conversation.

When Elizabeth became queen, she made it clear that she had no intention of giving up her favourite. If anything, she found ways to spend even more time with him. Now that she was the focus of everyone's attention at court, this was only achieved with a great deal of subterfuge. A year after her accession, she had Dudley's bedchamber moved next to her private rooms in order to facilitate their clandestine meetings. Dudley showered his royal mistress with an array of very personal gifts, including a diamond necklace interspersed with lovers' knots, and a pair of gold bodkins, set with diamonds and rubies, for her hair.

Even though they were careful to stay within the bounds of decency in front of the watching court, their physical attraction was obvious to all. When conferring upon Dudley the Order of St George at the ceremony that admitted him to the ranks of the Garter Knights in April 1559, the queen could not resist tickling his neck, to the astonishment of the assembled dignitaries. On another occasion, after playing tennis with the Duke of Norfolk, Dudley snatched Elizabeth's handkerchief from her hand and mopped the sweat from his brow. His presumption shocked the onlookers, but the queen was far from offended. It was a telling indication of their natural, almost unthinking intimacy.

All of this was scandalous enough, but to make matters worse, the queen's favourite was already married. She was well aware of this, but evidently chose to put it out of her mind. The fact that Dudley kept his wife, Amy Robsart, safely tucked away at their Oxfordshire home made it all too easy. Before long, however, his relationship with the queen was causing a scandal not just in England, but in courts across Europe. Desperate to salvage her mistress's reputation, Elizabeth's old governess Kat Astley (who had apparently learned her lesson from the Seymour scandal) confronted her royal mistress in August 1559. Flinging herself at Elizabeth's feet, she passionately implored her to put an end to the 'evil speaking' that abounded about her relationship with Dudley.

Elizabeth's response was measured at first. She thanked her old governess for her care and assured her that she would give serious consideration to marrying in order to dispel the rumours and set her subjects' minds at ease. But she could not resist adding that marriage was a weighty matter and she had 'no wish to change her state' at present. Fully aware of her mistress's insincerity, Kat persisted until Elizabeth was provoked into throwing off the pretence. She cried that she had 'so much sorrow and tribulation and so little joy' in the world that she would not deny herself this one happiness. With characteristic stubbornness, she added that if she wished to lead an immoral life, 'she did not know of anyone who could forbid her'.[13]

Ironically, the sudden death of Dudley's wife in September 1560 removed any hope that Elizabeth might have privately cherished of marrying him. Amy Robsart was found dead at the bottom of a short flight of stairs at her home, Cumnor Place. The circumstances were suspicious. Her neck was broken and there were two small wounds to her head. On the day of her death, she had insisted that all of her servants attend the fair that was being held in Abingdon, 'and was so earnest to have them gone to the fair, that with any of her own sort that made reason of tarrying at home she was very angry.'[14] When they returned, they found their mistress dead. Whether it was an accident, suicide or murder has never been resolved beyond doubt. The finger of suspicion pointed at Dudley, whom his enemies claimed would not have flinched from having his wife put to death so that he could realise his ambitions of marrying the queen. Neither was Elizabeth free from blame: even her most faithful subjects feared that her passion for Dudley had driven her to get rid of his wife so that she could have him at last.

In fact, it is extremely unlikely that either Dudley or Elizabeth had any hand in Amy's death. They would hardly have taken such a risk, especially as they would have known that it would prove counterproductive to any plans they might have to marry one day. The scandal reverberated not just around the kingdom but across the courts of Europe, so that Elizabeth was obliged to distance herself from Dudley in order to avoid being implicated any further. This played directly into the hands of Dudley's chief rival, William Cecil, who may have had a hand in Amy's death. Another theory is that she had been suffering from breast cancer, which had spread to her spine and weakened the bones so much that even a minor fall could have broken her neck. There is also evidence that Amy had depression, so it has been posited that she took her own life.

Whatever the cause of Amy Robsart's death, it put paid – for now – to any hopes Elizabeth might have had of marrying Dudley. But in private, the queen refused to give up her favourite. Now that the scrutiny of the court was even more intense, she was obliged to go to ever greater lengths to conceal their meetings. In November 1561, for example, she disguised herself as the maid of Katherine Howard (later Countess of Nottingham) in order to enjoy the secret pleasure of watching Dudley shoot at Windsor.[15] Another attempt at discretion was less successful. When her close friend and attendant Lady Fiennes de Clinton helped Elizabeth escape court in disguise to meet Dudley at his house for dinner, Philip II's envoy heard of it and immediately reported it to his master.[16]

Elizabeth revelled in the even greater intimacy that she now shared with her favourite. They loved to talk of marriage, and although she would never commit, Elizabeth assured Dudley that if she had to marry an Englishman then he would be her choice. Dudley showered his royal mistress with personal gifts, such as a 'ring of gold with an agate made like two eyes with sparks about it of rubies'.[17] This was a reminder of the nickname of 'Eyes' that she had given him. The more affectionate they became, the more insistent the rumours that they were lovers and that Dudley 'hath got the Queen with child'.[18]

What exactly passed between the couple when they were closeted away in the queen's private apartments has been the source of endless speculation ever since. The question of whether Elizabeth was really the Virgin Queen is as hotly debated today as it was in the sixteenth century. The truth is, unless fresh evidence comes to light it will never be known. But while Elizabeth may have enjoyed some physical intimacy with her favourite, the likelihood of her having risked full sexual intercourse is remote. Elizabeth had fought too hard for her throne to throw it away on the discovery of an illicit affair or, worse, an unwanted pregnancy. Her authority would never have recovered from such a scandal, particularly as she was already battling against the slur of illegitimacy. If there had been certain proof that she was not chaste, it would have rendered her virtually worthless in the international marriage market. Even though Elizabeth had no intention of marrying, she fully appreciated the political necessity of keeping various foreign suitors in play.

In addition to the sound political and personal reasons why Elizabeth would have been unlikely to risk an affair are the practical ones. As she herself was at pains to point out: 'I do not live in a corner. A thousand eyes see all I do.' She reiterated the message to another diplomat: 'My life is in the open, and I have so many witnesses that I cannot understand how so bad a judgment can have been formed of me.'[19] As queen, she was constantly surrounded by her ladies and attendants, even when she slept. It would therefore have been virtually impossible to conduct an affair in secret. And even if only one or two of her most trusted ladies had been privy to any sexual transgressions, the truth would almost certainly have leaked out. There were few, if any, secrets at the Tudor court.

Perhaps most convincing, however, is Elizabeth's own testimony. In October 1562, she and her entourage were in residence at Hampton Court. On the night of the 10th, the queen complained of feeling unwell. She soon developed a high fever, and as her condition continued to deteriorate, her physicians confirmed everyone's worst fears: she had smallpox. This was one of the most deadly diseases in the sixteenth century and there was no known cure. Contemporary medicine was powerless against it and survival depended solely upon chance. Elizabeth's council was so convinced that she would die that they held an emergency meeting to decide upon her successor. The queen herself believed the end was near and felt the urge to confess her sins. But in so doing, she insisted that nothing improper had ever passed between her and Dudley. In this God-fearing age, when people spent their lives striving to secure their place in heaven, Elizabeth would have been unlikely to risk her eternal salvation by uttering a lie.

Even though Elizabeth was almost certainly a virgin queen, the fact that she chose to spend so much time with Dudley in private ensured that the rumours about their relationship never went away. Desperate to prevent her royal mistress from ruining her reputation and destroying any prospect of marriage, Kat Astley overstepped her authority by trying to advance negotiations with King Eric XIV of Sweden, one of Elizabeth's many foreign suitors. She sent a message to the king via an agent of William Cecil, solemnly assuring him 'that she thought that the Queen was free of any man living, and that she would not have the Lord Robert'.[20] When the negotiations began to flounder, Kat wrote to the Swedish chancellor in secret, urging him to persuade his master to come to England, where he would be assured of success. She claimed that she 'understood somewhat more than the common report is'.[21] The letter was intercepted by Cecil, who ordered an immediate inquiry and Kat was placed under house arrest. But Elizabeth privately knew that her old governess had been acting in her best interests and issued a swift pardon, restoring Kat to her former position.

The proposed marriage to Eric of Sweden came to nothing. Elizabeth's rejection of him was gracious but swift. On 25 February 1560, she wrote a letter filled with apparent regret that she could not share his feelings. Referring to a note that he had recently sent her, she apologised that: 'While we perceive therefrom that the zeal and love of your mind towards us is not diminished, yet in part we are grieved that we cannot gratify your serene highness with the same kind of affection.' Elizabeth also used her letter to help quell the rumours that were still circulating about her possible involvement in the death of Dudley's wife. 'We have never yet conceived a feeling of that kind of affection towards anyone,' she assured Eric, adding: 'We do not conceive in our heart to take a husband.'[22] The letter continued in the same polite but firm manner, and although it left little doubt as to Elizabeth's sincerity in rejecting the Swedish king, she added a postscript to make sure that he had got the message. Having heard that he planned to visit her, the queen urged him not to because 'nothing but expectation can happen to your serene highness in this business.'[23]

It was both the frankest and swiftest rejection by Elizabeth of any of her suitors. During the years that followed, she learned the value of keeping them in play by acting the flirt and sending romantic messages, even if they were full of 'answers answerless'. But the sentiment that she had expressed to Eric, that 'we do not conceive in our heart to take a husband but highly commend the single life,' still held as true by the end of her reign as it had at the beginning.

In the meantime, however, the queen's frank dismissal of King Eric only served to fuel the rumours about her relationship with Robert Dudley. Perhaps it was in an attempt to prove that she had no intention of marrying her favourite that, in 1564, she shocked everyone by proposing him as a suitor to her greatest rival, Mary, Queen of Scots.

Mary Stuart was Elizabeth's competitor in every way that mattered. The granddaughter of Margaret Tudor, sister of Henry VIII, she had a strong blood claim to the English throne.[24] She was also a Catholic, which further boosted her legitimacy in the eyes of her supporters – and Elizabeth's enemies. Nine years younger than the English queen, she was reputed to be far more beautiful. Impetuous, passionate and fatally naïve, she had always ruled by the heart, not the head. The contrast with Elizabeth could not have been greater.

Mary had spent most of her youth in the court of France, following her betrothal to the Dauphin, Francis. After his untimely death in 1560, she returned to Scotland to begin her queenship. Suddenly, Elizabeth had a rival to her position as the most eligible woman in Europe. Moreover, unlike her English cousin, Mary had no intention of remaining single and ruling her country alone.

The Scottish queen was well aware of the rumours that had been circulating about Elizabeth and Robert Dudley. When the news of Amy Robsart's death had reached Mary shortly before her return to Scotland, she had quipped that the Queen of England was about to marry her 'horsekeeper', who had killed his wife in order to make way for her.[25]

Perhaps it was at least partly in revenge for this remark that in March 1564, Elizabeth proposed that Mary should consider Robert Dudley, now Earl of Leicester, as a potential husband. She went further still by suggesting that the three of them live together at the English court, in what one historian has described as 'a virtual ménage à trois'.[26] Was this an attempt by Elizabeth to enjoy the pleasures of Dudley's bed vicariously through Mary? More likely is that it was a studied insult. Not only was Dudley one of her own cast-offs; despite his recent promotion to the earldom of Leicester, he still lacked the status to be the consort of the Scottish queen. To hammer home the point, in suggesting Dudley as a suitor to Mary, she referred to him as the man 'whom she would have herself married, had she ever minded to take a husband. But being determined to end her life in virginity, she wished that the Queen her sister might marry him.'[27]

At first, her ploy seemed to have worked. Mary sent a tart reply that Elizabeth should look to her own marriage first, given her advancing age. She claimed that 'for herself, the remembrance of her late husband [the Dauphin] is yet so fresh, she cannot think of any other,' and added: 'Her years are not so many but she may abide.'[28] She proceeded to play Elizabeth at her own game by pretending to warm to the idea of taking Dudley as a husband, professing to have 'so good liking of him' that she was prepared to accept him as a consort.

When Elizabeth heard of this, she was thrown into a panic. She had borne many sacrifices in her endeavour to become a great queen, but the prospect that Dudley might actually marry her cousin was too much to bear. But she could hardly admit that the whole scheme had been a sham so, when Mary's ambassador Sir James Melville arrived at court, she maintained the charade.

One night 'late after supper', the English queen invited Melville to her private bedchamber. Fully aware that only Elizabeth's most intimate courtiers and attendants were permitted into this inner sanctum, the astonished ambassador quickly accepted. Together they left the public rooms of court and Melville followed in the queen's wake as she led the way to her 'secret chambers'.

Once inside the dimly lit bedchamber, Elizabeth opened up a small desk, 'wherein were divers little pictures wrapped within paper, and their names written with her own hand upon the papers.' Among them was Dudley's portrait. When the Scottish ambassador spied this, feigning innocence he asked if he could borrow it to show his mistress, Mary, Queen of Scots. Abandoning all pretence at diplomacy, Elizabeth immediately refused, 'alleging that she had but that one picture of his'. Spying Dudley in a corner of the bedchamber, in whispered conversation with William Cecil, Melville slyly observed that she should not cling so to the portrait, since 'she had the original'.[29]

Regaining her composure, Elizabeth rifled through the other items and at length 'took out the queen's [Mary's] picture, and kissed it'. Next, the English queen showed Melville 'a fair ruby, as big as a tennis-ball'. To test her sincerity, the wily ambassador suggested 'that she would either send it or else my Lord of Leicester's picture, as a token unto the queen.' Quick as a flash, Elizabeth retorted: 'If the queen would follow her counsel, that she would in process of time get them both, and all she had.' In the meantime, though, she decided that Mary should be content with the smaller token of a diamond. She then drew the intimate audience to a close and commanded Melville to meet her at eight o'clock the next morning for her customary walk in the garden.[30]

That Elizabeth should allow – indeed, encourage – Sir James Melville to enter her private sanctum was a deliberate ploy. It was as if she hoped to so beguile him that he would fall under her spell and relinquish his own royal mistress. During his visit, she took even greater care than usual over her appearance, and her flirtatiousness grew ever more insistent. 'The Queen of England said she had clothes of every sort,' reported the ambassador, 'which every day, so long as I was there, she changed. One day she had the English weed [cloth], another the French, and another the Italian, and so forth. She asked me which of them became her best. I said, the Italian dress; which pleased her well.'[31]

Setting aside the political matters that Sir James had been sent to discuss, Elizabeth quizzed him upon every aspect of Mary's personal appearance and accomplishments. 'She desired to know of me, what colour of hair was reputed best; and which of the two was fairest,' he recalled. Melville diplomatically replied: 'She was the fairest Queen in England, and mine the fairest Queen in Scotland.' Not satisfied, Elizabeth asked who was the tallest, confident that she would be in the ascendancy. When the beleaguered ambassador admitted that the Scottish queen was the tallest, Elizabeth snapped: 'Then . . . she is too high; for I myself am neither too high nor too low.'

Determined to find something in which she excelled her cousin, the English queen turned to Mary's accomplishments, which she was sure would be inferior to her own. A keen hunter herself, she demanded to know what kind of exercise the Scottish queen took. Melville replied that when he had taken his leave of Mary, she had just returned from hunting in the Highlands. Irked, Elizabeth tried a different tack.

Upon hearing that Mary occasionally played the lute and virginals, she conspired to ensure that Sir James would 'accidentally' happen upon her as she was playing the virginals 'exceedingly well' in her privy chamber. Feigning surprise at his presence, she gave him a playful slap and chided him for so intruding upon her privacy, 'alleging she used not to play before men'. Then, as if the thought had only just occurred to her, she casually enquired whether she or Mary played best. 'In that I found myself obliged to give her the praise,' recalled Melville, who now entered fully into the charade, avowing: 'I heard such melody as ravished me and drew me within the chamber, I knew not how . . . and was now willing to endure what kind of punishment her majesty should be pleased to lay upon me for my offence.' Delighted, Elizabeth rewarded him as she would one of her lapdogs. 'She sat down low upon a cushion, and I upon my knees beside her; but she gave me a cushion with her own hand, to lay under my knee; which at first I refused, but she compelled me to take it.' Apparently only now realising that they were quite alone, which was unthinkable for a monarch, let alone for an unmarried queen, she then called for Lady Stafford (a lady of the bedchamber who was waiting – and listening – in the next chamber.'

Melville soon tired of the elaborate charade and begged leave to return to Scotland. Feigning offence, Elizabeth chided him that he was 'weary sooner of her company than she was [of his]' and compelled him to stay for another two days so that he might see her dance at a court gathering. As soon as the performance was over, she enquired of him 'whether she or my Queen danced best'. Sir James was forced to admit that Mary was her inferior in this respect, too. Satisfied, Elizabeth sent him on his way with a florid promise to meet her cousin Mary as soon as a convenient place could be found. Melville wryly retorted that he would be happy 'to convey her secretly to Scotland by post, clothed like a page, disguised.' Elizabeth appeared to like the idea but replied with a sigh: 'Alas, if I might do it.'[32]

The following year, Mary gave up the pretence that she was still considering Dudley as a suitor and married her cousin, Henry Stuart, Lord Darnley. She fell pregnant soon afterwards and wasted no time in flaunting her fertility to her English cousin. In April 1566, she sent her a letter, excusing her poor handwriting, which she claimed was due to her being 'in her seventh month'.[33] In fact, Mary's handwriting was always rather untidy so to use the rather dubious excuse of pregnancy was almost certainly intended to provoke her cousin's jealousy.

How much greater was Mary's pride when she gave birth to a male heir. She had fulfilled her duty as a woman and a queen. In the eyes of many of her contemporaries, Elizabeth had failed on both counts. 'The Queen of Scots was mother of a fair son, while she was but a barren stock,' Elizabeth was said to have lamented upon hearing the news. This account by Melville is not corroborated by any other source. Indeed, Philip II's envoy reported that 'the Queen seemed very glad of the birth of the infant.'[34]

But Elizabeth cannot have felt anything other than a deep resentment – personal as well as political – at the news that her chief rival had given birth to a son. By then aged thirty-three and with no apparent prospect of marrying or begetting an heir herself, Elizabeth was intensely jealous of her younger, more beautiful cousin, who was already on her second husband and had proven her fertility by falling pregnant almost immediately after the marriage. Mary had given in to her desires and had been rewarded for it. By contrast, Elizabeth had sacrificed her love for Robert Dudley to the interests of her crown and had been rewarded only by ongoing hostility both from within and outside her kingdom, together with the ever-present threat of invasion by a Catholic potentate.

Undeterred, Robert Dudley was stepping up his campaign to persuade his royal mistress to marry him. On Midsummer's Day 1565, he had thrown a party on the Thames for the queen and had made sure they shared a barge. Talk had soon turned to marriage and, spying a bishop on a nearby barge, Dudley had playfully suggested that he should marry them there and then.

At the same time, though, Dudley had started to flirt with one of Elizabeth's close attendants. Described as one of the best-looking women of the court, Lettice Knollys had auburn hair, smooth, pale skin and pouting lips. She shared kinship with Elizabeth (who was ten years her senior), being the great-niece of her mother, Anne Boleyn, and used this as an excuse not to show her royal mistress due deference. This was anathema to Elizabeth, who marked Lettice out as a rival from the earliest days of their acquaintance.

Despite the fact that she was already married, to Walter Devereux, Earl of Essex, Lettice was attracted to the queen's favourite and encouraged his attentions. She made little attempt to conceal this from her royal mistress: indeed, given her character, she was likely to have flaunted it. Elizabeth flew into a rage and upbraided Dudley for his disloyalty. He dutifully distanced himself from Lettice – for now at least. A few years later, however, he began an illicit affair with another of the queen's ladies, Douglas Sheffield, a beautiful young widow. She fell deeply in love with him and begged him to take her as his wife. Dudley refused, however, and told Douglas in no uncertain terms that: 'if I should marry I am sure never to have [the queen's] favour.'

Although Dudley refused to give up hope that he would one day persuade Elizabeth to marry him, her councillors and subjects were beginning to realise that for all her fair words, the queen had little intention of ever taking a husband. In an age when marriage was the primary – indeed, the only – ambition for a woman, this remained utterly perplexing to her contemporaries. It was not long before they began to speculate that Elizabeth's reticence had an underlying, physical cause.

Elizabeth's sexual health had been a matter of diplomatic interest from the earliest days of her infancy. As a baby, she had been displayed 'quite undressed' to the French ambassadors in order to prove that there were no impediments to her betrothal to Francis I's third son, Charles, Duc d'Angoulême. Now that she was queen, the issue of her fertility became a matter of even greater importance, for the security of her kingdom rested upon her ability to produce an heir to continue the Tudor dynasty. Her enemies therefore seized upon the rumours that there was some physical impediment to her bearing children. So prevalent did these become that all of Elizabeth's prospective suitors made careful and discreet enquiries into her gynaecological health. Before long, the queen's most private bodily functions had become a matter of intense public scrutiny.

One of the earliest diplomats to cast doubt upon the English queen's ability to bear children was Sir James Melville. Soon after Elizabeth's accession, he was asked to deliver a proposal to her from the Duke of Casimir, son of the Elector Palatine. But he declined the commission, claiming: 'I had ground to conjecture that she would never marry because of that story one of the gentlewomen of her chamber told me . . . knowing herself incapable of children, she would never render herself subject to a man.' [35]

Philip II's envoy, De Feria, was quick to propound this rumour. In April 1559, he claimed: 'If my spies do not lie, which I believe they do not, for a certain reason they have recently given me I understand she will not bear children.'[36] His successor, De Quadra, took up the theme two years later, alleging: 'It is the common opinion, confirmed by certain physicians, that this woman is unhealthy and it is believed that she will not bear children.'[37] This may have been based upon the opinion of Dr Huick, who was said to have counselled the queen that marriage and childbirth ought not to be attempted because of her 'womanish infirmity'. The exchange was reported by William Camden, Elizabeth's earliest biographer, who added that there were some 'hidden causes, which many times stuck in her mind, did very much terrify her from marrying.'[38] But his account was written almost half a century later, and Camden was only a young child when the matter of the queen's fertility was being discussed.

Any hint of a physical problem was seized upon by the gossips at court. In June 1559, a Venetian agent reported: 'Her Majesty was blooded from one foot and from one arm, but what her indisposition is, is not known,' adding cryptically: 'Many persons say things I should not dare to write, but they say that on arriving at Greenwich she was as cheerful as ever was.'[39] Speculation was rife that the queen had been blooded in order to correct the imbalance in her body caused by her lack of periods. Like her half-sister Mary, Elizabeth had suffered from irregular or absent periods for most of her life. Contemporaries were quick to ascribe this to her virgin state. Physicians opined that vigorous sexual intercourse was the most effective cure for all menstrual disorders.

The queen's menstrual cycle was soon a hotly debated topic among foreign envoys. 'She has hardly ever the purgation proper to all women,' observed the papal nuncio in France.[40] In the clamour for information, Elizabeth's closest body servants became the subject of intense pressure and even bribes. Philip II ordered one of his emissaries to pay Elizabeth's laundress for details of her menstrual cycle, judging that, having the task of washing the queen's intimate garments and bed sheets, she was best placed to know.

In fact, very little is known about how women coped with their periods in Tudor times. Perhaps not surprisingly, it was not considered a subject for polite conversation or open debate. However, some references hint that women wore linen rags held in place with a belt, and that they even used a form of tampon. Medical textbooks dating from the seventeenth century mention 'pessaries' of wool, linen, or silk. Women were instructed to ensure that a string was attached to whichever form of pessary they used so that it might be easily removed. Such devices would not have been used by a virgin, however, because of the risk of damage to the hymen, which could have cast doubt upon a woman's purity. Queen Elizabeth's household accounts list dozens of 'long and short vallopes [wallops or rags] . . . of fine hollande cloth'. She also had 'girdles of black jean silk . . . garnished with buckles, hooks and eyes whipped over with silk', which may have been the belt to hold the linen rags in place.[41]

The laundress was one of the most trusted servants at court, and once a woman had proved worthy, she would be retained for as long as possible. That is why Elizabeth had only two laundresses throughout the course of her long reign: Elizabeth Smith (or Smithson) from her coronation until 1576, and Anne Twiste thereafter. Both women were rewarded with gifts from the queen for their loyal service.[42] They were also given money to cover the cost of a horse and cart so that they could remain close to their royal mistress and accompany her wherever she went.

Given that Philip only seriously considered Elizabeth as a potential bride during the early years of her reign, the laundress whom he approached for information was almost certainly Elizabeth Smith. However, she did not divulge any details beyond affirming that her royal mistress was functioning normally as a woman – and that may well have been with the queen's sanction. The Spanish king was apparently satisfied because he continued to view Elizabeth as a potential bride for some time afterwards. Only when it became obvious that he was merely one of several pawns in her marriage game did he turn from suitor to enemy.

The other great powers of Europe also took a keen interest in the English queen's reproductive health. In 1566, the French ambassador, de la Forêt, quizzed one of Elizabeth's physicians in order to ascertain whether his royal mistress would be a suitable wife for the young French king, Charles IX. The physician's reply was unequivocal: 'Your King is seventeen, and the Queen is only thirty-two . . . If the King marries her, I will answer for her having ten children, and no one knows her temperament better than I do.'[43]

Writing after the queen's death, the poet and playwright Ben Jonson asserted that Elizabeth 'had a membrana on her, which made her incapable of man,' and claimed that 'At the coming over of Monsieur [the Duke of Anjou], there was a French surgeon who took in hand to cut it, yet fear stayed her.'[44] Even though there was no contemporary evidence to support this, the rumour is still perpetuated today, with some historians claiming that Elizabeth either had an abnormally thick hymen or suffered from vaginismus, a condition that makes sexual penetration extremely uncomfortable.

Motivated by the desire to find a foreign husband for their royal mistress, her ministers were at pains to point out that the queen was 'of the largest and goodliest stature of well-shaped women . . . and one whom in the sight of all men nature cannot amend her shape in any part to make her more likely to conceive and bear children without peril.' Loath though she was to marry, Elizabeth hated any suggestion that she was anything other than a perfect specimen of womanhood and proudly declared: 'I am unimpaired in body.'[45]

One of the most outlandish theories as to why Elizabeth never married is that she was really a man. In 1542, so the story goes, the future Elizabeth I (then aged nine) was sent to Overcourt House in the picturesque Cotswold village of Bisley, because the plague was rife in London. While there, she fell gravely ill with a fever and died. Knowing that Henry VIII was on his way to visit his daughter, her panic-stricken governess (presumably Kat Astley) was said to have searched the village in vain for a girl who resembled Elizabeth closely enough to fool the king. The only child of the right age and colouring was a boy, so in desperation Kat dressed him in the princess's clothes and the deception was complete.

This unlikely theory was first spouted by Thomas Keble, who was vicar of Bisley from 1827–1873. Keble recorded that during renovations at Overcourt, he had found an old stone coffin containing the skeleton of a girl aged about nine, dressed in Tudor clothing. It became part of local folklore, but gained more widespread renown in 1910 when it was written up by Bram Stoker, creator of Dracula, in his book, *Famous Impostors*. Conspiracy theorists seized upon it as an explanation for why the so-called Virgin Queen refused to marry and have children. A remark by William Cecil's son, Robert, that Elizabeth was 'more than a man, and, in truth, sometimes less than a woman', has been taken out of context to help prove the case.[46]

Yet for every account of Elizabeth's infertility or physical defects, there are others claiming that she regularly slept with her male courtiers and had several bastards by them. Among the rumours of the queen's sexual transgressions was one put about by a widow named Dionisia Deryck, who claimed that the queen 'hath already had as many children as I' – although she admitted that only two of them had survived into adulthood. Even Ben Jonson, who claimed that Elizabeth was 'incapable of man', added that she had 'tried many'. Sir James Melville, who knew Elizabeth well, was no less contradictory. Having sparked rumours of the English queen's infertility at the beginning of her reign, he went on to boast that he had tried to scare her off childbirth by relating how painful Mary, Queen of Scots' labour had been. If he had truly believed her to be barren, then he would have had no need to do so.

It is interesting to strip away the rumours and counter-rumours and examine the evidence that exists about Elizabeth's gynaecological state. The medical examinations that were carried out as part of the various marriage negotiations almost all confirmed that the queen was perfectly healthy and had no impediments to bearing children. Her laundress's testimony corroborates this. However, it is also certain that Elizabeth displayed a number of symptoms that might suggest she would have had difficulty conceiving or giving birth. The irregularity of her periods was something she had in common with her half-sister Mary, whose disastrous obstetric history she had witnessed first-hand. Elizabeth's amenorrhoea may have been due to the fact that she ate sparingly and was often described as being 'very thin'. She was also unusually pale – 'the colour of a corpse', according to one account – which suggests that she could have been anaemic. Although Elizabeth liked to boast of her physical vigour, she regularly experienced gastric attacks. 'Her Majesty [was] suddenly sick in her stomach,' reported William Cecil on one such occasion, 'and as suddenly relieved by a vomit.'[47]

Recent commentators have speculated that the queen might have suffered from Androgen Insensitivity Syndrome.[48] Victims of this condition are born with male XY chromosomes but develop outwardly as female, owing to the body's failure to produce male sex hormones. Depending on the severity of the symptoms, the female reproductive organs can either be impaired or entirely absent, making sexual intercourse difficult or impossible. Women with this condition, such as Edward VIII's mistress and later wife, Wallis Simpson, tend to be tall and lithe with 'strident personalities', thanks to the dominance of testosterone in their bodies.

Elizabeth certainly conformed to this outward description: she was unusually tall for a woman, and was very slim and small-breasted. She also had an extremely forthright manner and more energy and vigour than was usual in a woman. A tireless horsewoman, she could hunt and hawk for hours, long after her female attendants had retired, exhausted. Unlike many women who followed the chase, she shot as well as rode, and did not flinch from cutting the throat of a deer or stag when it had been cornered. In 1575, the French ambassador reported that the queen had killed 'six does' with her crossbow.

Even in old age, Elizabeth would still enjoy brisk, early morning walks in the gardens of her palaces, with most of her younger attendants struggling to keep up. It was said that she preferred the male steps of the galliard, a popular dance of the time, because these involved athletic leaps. She was often boisterous and, when amused, would laugh as uproariously as a man, and at other times would storm through her apartments, slapping and beating her ladies.[49]

Sixteenth-century medical opinion claimed that 'such [women] as are robust and of a manly constitution' were likely to be sterile.[50] And yet there is little evidence, apart from Ben Jonson's dubious testimony, that Elizabeth had any of the internal symptoms of Androgen Insensitivity Syndrome. Indeed, even the outward ones could have been the result of genetics, rather than the syndrome. Her father had been very tall, and her mother had had a slight frame and small breasts. Henry had also had the same restless energy, and both he and Anne Boleyn were notable for their extremely strident personalities. Interesting though the theory is, therefore, it can at best be described as speculative.

If, as the world's most famous unmarried sovereign, Elizabeth could not escape the rumours about her private life, she was always careful to define the parameters of her relationships with the men who surrounded her at court. Edward Dyer warned one of her greatest admirers, Sir Christopher Hatton: 'First of all you must consider with whom you have to deal, and what we be towards her, who though she does descend very much in her sex as a woman, yet we may not forget her place and nature of it as our sovereign.'[51] This was exactly what Elizabeth had intended: she could flirt with her courtiers as much as she pleased, but they must never take this as an excuse to disregard her supremacy as queen.

Elizabeth's flirtations may have been nothing more than play-acting, but she nevertheless demanded absolute fidelity, both emotional and political, from her male courtiers and would brook no rival for their affections. As one recent commentator has observed: 'There could only be one queen-bee in the hive.'[52] Her greatest favourite, Robert Dudley, would learn this to his cost.

13

'She seldom partakes before strangers'

ELIZABETH I's COURT presented a dramatic contrast to that of her late sister. 'She lives a life of magnificence and festivity such as can hardly be imagined,' observed the Venetian envoy with obvious disapproval, 'and occupies a great portion of her time with balls, feasting, hunting and similar amusements with the utmost possible display.'[1] Another foreign visitor concurred: 'They are intent on amusing themselves and on dancing till after midnight.'[2]

Elizabeth, like her father, Henry VIII, had a natural gift for public relations and fully appreciated the political importance of staging an obvious display of wealth and magnificence at her court. And while hostile commentators decried the 'levities' and 'licentiousness', the reality was that all of this seemingly decadent court display was carefully controlled by Elizabeth. She quickly established a strict etiquette and ceremony from which no courtier was allowed to stray. Ever watchful of her reputation as a young, unmarried queen, she was determined to ensure that merriment would never descend into drunkenness, or flirtatiousness into sexual transgression. 'The court of Queen Elizabeth was at once gay, decent, and superb,' remarked one shrewd observer.[3]

By the time that Elizabeth ascended the throne, the Tudors had a well-established structure for each of their palaces. The layout of the rooms was based around their public and private persona, and the new queen was careful to uphold this. Beyond the principal public rooms, namely the gallery, great hall and great chamber, lay the queen's private suite of rooms. The further a courtier was able to progress into them, the more important they were deemed to be.

First there was the presence chamber, which was filled with

ambitious subjects hoping to gain an audience with the queen. To get there, they would often have spent months writing letters, sending gifts or offering bribes, but even then they were not guaranteed an audience. Beyond this, there was the privy chamber, where the queen took her meals and enjoyed her hours of leisure and privacy. Only the highest-ranking members of court were admitted. These included privy councillors, ambassadors or those whom she 'favours extraordinarily'. Towards the end of Elizabeth's reign, her disgraced favourite, the Earl of Essex, lamented that although he had been given 'access' to the presence chamber, he had been denied 'near access' – in other words, admittance to the privy chamber.[4] Yet there was still a more exclusive sanctum, and this was the queen's bedchamber, which often had several other private rooms leading off it. It was exceptionally rare for any male courtier to gain admittance, for it was here that Elizabeth would seek refuge from the hustle and bustle of the court.

An account by André Hurault, Sieur de Maisse, ambassador of Henry IV of his visit to Elizabeth's court includes a tantalising description of his progression from the presence chamber through the privy gallery and finally into the privy chamber.

The Lord Chamberlain, who has the charge of the Queen's household . . . came to seek me where I was seated. He led me along a passage somewhat dark, into a chamber that they call the privy chamber, at the head of which was the Queen seated in a low chair, by herself, and withdrawn from all the Lords and Ladies that were present, they being in one place and she in another. After I had made my reverence at the entry to the chamber, she rose and came five or six paces towards me, almost into the middle of the chamber . . . She excused herself because I found her attired in her night-gown, and began to rebuke those of her council who were present, saying, 'What will these gentlemen say' – speaking of those who accompanied me – 'to see me so attired? I am much disturbed that they should see me in this state.'[5]

De Maisse's account neatly encapsulates the formal yet intimate nature of the audiences that Elizabeth held in her privy chamber. He was one of the privileged few who was allowed into this inner sanctum. Most visitors to court could only hope to behold the queen in the presence chamber. One such was a Swiss tourist named Thomas Platter, a German tourist who was granted an audience with the queen at Nonsuch later in her reign and was overawed by the experience.

> We were led into the presence chamber where we were placed well to the fore, so as better to behold the queen. This apartment like the others leading into this one was hung with fine tapestries, and the floor was strewn with straw or hay; only where the queen was to come out and up to her seat were carpets laid down worked in Turkish knot. After we had waited awhile here, somewhere between twelve and one, some men with white staffs entered from an inner chamber, and after them a number of lords of high standing followed by the queen, alone without escort, very straight and erect still, who sat down in the presence chamber upon a seat covered with red damask and cushions embroidered in gold thread, and so low was the chair that the cushions almost lay on the ground, and there was a canopy above, fixed very ornately to the ceiling.[6]

Although Elizabeth was like her father in many ways, she did not share his passion for building. Rather, she was an avid user and embellisher of the palaces she inherited. Her favourite palace was Richmond, where she spent most of her summers. Because of its sophisticated heating system, Elizabeth also liked to retreat there in winter and affectionately referred to it as her 'warm box'. The palace included a 'sweat bath' inherited from Elizabeth's father, as well as a prototype of the water closet. The latter was the invention of her godson, Sir John Harington. It carried waste away, rather than letting it fall into a pit beneath, so was more hygienic and less malodorous than the traditional close-stool. It would be many years before the same luxury was enjoyed by the rest of the court. At

Richmond, the queen let her taste for fanciful and sumptuous furnishings run wild. Among the many decorative features that she commissioned was a boat-shaped bed with 'curtains of sea water green' and quilts and valance of light-brown tinsel.[7]

Further upriver was Hampton Court, 'the most splendid and magnificent royal palace of any that may be found in England – or, indeed, in any other kingdom,' according to one foreign visitor.[8] The apartment in which Elizabeth liked to sit in state was hung with tapestries garnished with gold, pearls and precious stones, while her throne was studded with 'very large diamonds, rubies, sapphires, and the like, that glitter among other precious stones and pearls as the sun among the stars.'[9] Little wonder that it became known as the 'Paradise Chamber'.

At Hampton Court, Elizabeth preserved a great number of furnishings from her father's day, including his travelling bed, 'a very costly bed which the queen's mother and her ladies worked themselves' and 'a bed where the queen's brother was born'.[10] The queen's private library, meanwhile, was well stocked with books on a variety of different subjects, as well as a number of eclectic personal possessions. The latter included a walking stick made from a unicorn's horn, a receptacle for combs shaped like a man, and a horn cup that was reputed to break if it came into contact with poison.

The privy garden, which Elizabeth accessed via a staircase leading off the privy gallery, was decorated with columns surmounted by brightly painted and gilded heraldic beasts and no fewer than twenty sundials. The queen was particularly fond of the garden and appointed the Frenchman John Markye to carry out some improvements, replacing the myriad compartments with larger divisions in which her badges were set out in coloured gravel. She also ordered that the windows overlooking the ponds area to the south of the palace be blocked out so that she could 'walk secretly all hours and times without anyone looking upon her out of any place.'[11]

In most of her other palaces, the queen had a private garden for her personal use, which could be accessed from her privy apartments. The typical design was a garden enclosed by brick walls and rectangular in shape, divided into raised beds, around which were rails painted in the Tudor colours of green and white. Each of the beds was filled with sweet-smelling herbs and spices, and between them were 'fine walks grown in grass . . . surrounded by plants in the shape of seats'. Dispersed throughout the garden were high columns 'carved with various fine paintings; also different animals carved in wood, with their horns gilt . . . set on top of the columns, together with flags bearing the Queen's arms.'[12]

Despite the delights on offer at Hampton Court, and the fact that it had been her father's favourite palace, Elizabeth was not overly fond of it and hardly spent any time there during her long reign. Perhaps she never quite forgave it for being the place where she almost died early in her reign. Besides, she preferred the privacy that was more readily afforded at Richmond or, further west, at Windsor. The latter contained an exquisite royal bedchamber stuffed with treasures, such as a bird of paradise 'partially yellow' in colour and 'a beautifully embroidered cushion done by Queen Elizabeth herself in red and white silk'.[13] There was a large apartment filled with royal beds owned by her predecessors, which were still preserved in situ towards the end of her reign. Whether Elizabeth kept these beds for reasons of sentiment or thrift is not certain.

The queen's bathroom at Windsor had running water, and the walls and ceilings were covered with mirrors. Although mirrors had long been a priceless commodity, they were imported in much greater numbers during Elizabeth's reign. As well as elaborate looking-glass mirrors that adorned the queen's bedchamber and those of her higher-ranking ladies, the fashion for pocket mirrors or those attached to a belt or girdle ensured that even the most vain of court ladies could check her appearance as often as she desired.

Greenwich was another palace that Elizabeth had inherited from her predecessors, although she did not spend a great deal of time there. The few references to the palace during her reign hint at the same level of ostentation that prevailed at her other palaces, however. The inventory of the queen's private dining room at the palace includes a tablecloth made from peacock feathers sewn together.

At Whitehall, her chief residence in the heart of London, the queen had the Tudor equivalent of a sauna, heated by a ceramic tiled stove. There was also a splendidly arrayed bathroom that faced south onto the orchard and would have been warmed by the long hours of sunlight. As well as a large bath, it contained an elaborate water feature where 'the water pours from oyster shells and different kinds of rock'. The business of grooming was made as luxurious and entertaining as possible at Whitehall. Next to the bathroom was a room containing an organ 'on which two people can play duets, also a large chest completely covered in silk, and a clock which plays times by striking a bell.'[14]

Adjoining this room was the queen's personal library. The luxury continued in her bedroom, which overlooked the River Thames and was sumptuously decorated with a gold ceiling and rich hangings. Her bed was 'ingeniously composed of woods of different colours with quilts of silk, velvet, gold and silver embroidery'. Elizabeth's beds became even more sumptuous as the reign progressed. In 1581, a beautifully carved walnut bed frame was sent to her as a gift. Decorated with cloth of silver and velvet and lined with Venetian gold, silver and silk, the headpiece was crafted from crimson satin spun in Bruges and topped with six huge plumes of ostrich feathers sparkling with gold spangles.

Also in Elizabeth's bedchamber at Whitehall was 'a table covered with silver and a chair entirely fashioned out of cushions'.[15] Even courtiers of high status regularly sat on cushions on the floors of the royal palaces. De Maisse described a visit to court, when he was escorted to the presence chamber 'where there was a cushion made ready for me', and was obliged to sit on it for some time while he waited for the queen to appear.[16] A picture of Elizabeth receiving a delegation of Dutch emissaries shows her ladies reclining on cushions. The only furniture in the room is the royal throne, so the other people present are obliged to stand. Such sparsely furnished rooms are typical of the Tudor period, before the Industrial Revolution brought mass-produced and therefore cheap furniture.

The privy chamber at Whitehall was dominated by an enormous painting by Holbein of the Tudor dynasty, in which the figure of Elizabeth's father took centre stage. For all her love of decorative arts, she wanted those who entered her inner sanctum to be served a powerful reminder of her lineage. The privy gallery, which linked Elizabeth's private suite of rooms to the presence chamber, boasted a ceiling 'marvellously wrought in stone with gold' and panelled walls painted with 'a thousand beautiful figures'.[17] Had she so wished (and been able), she could have spent several days at a time in her private suite of rooms and gardens at Whitehall, amply entertained, without ever venturing out into the public court.

Later in the reign, Elizabeth acquired the palace of Nonsuch, built by her father during the last decade of his reign and subsequently sold to a private owner. This fairy-tale palace, with its octagonal turrets, gilded horoscopes and white marble fountains, was the perfect canvas for her increasingly extravagant tastes. She had her private suite of rooms luxuriously decked out with hangings of 'red damask embroidered with gold', carpets 'worked in Turkish knot' and tumbling piles of silk and velvet cushions. There was also a 'stonework' table into which were built four containers that dispensed red and white wine, beer and water when the queen was in residence. Her private gardens at Nonsuch were hailed as 'the finest in the whole of England'. They provided Elizabeth with a secret fantasyland of topiaried beasts, marble pelicans, snow-white nymphs and goddesses and an underground grotto. As a nod to the queen's advancing years, there was also a platform upon which 'either seated or standing, the Queen shoots at deer'.[18]

All of the royal palaces in London were built next to the Thames, travel by river being far more convenient than by road. The downside was the 'noisome smells' of the river, which could become very pungent, especially in summer. Elizabeth was particularly sensitive to unpleasant aromas and once greeted a gentleman who presented himself at court with: 'Tush man, your boots stink!'[19] She therefore ordered that perfumed oil be burnt in the royal barge so that her frequent trips along the river less malodorous. Thanks to the efforts of adventurers such as Sir Walter Ralegh, there was a regular supply of exotic spices to court, which meant that rose oil was no longer the primary scent. Heady blends of musk, civet and ambergris wafted through the queen's chambers and the public galleries beyond. She and her high-ranking courtiers would also have the floors of their chambers strewn with sweet-smelling herbs. Meadowsweet was a particular favourite with Elizabeth, and the contemporary herbalist John Gerard agreed that 'the leaves far excel all other strewing herbs to deck up houses, to strew in chambers, halls and banqueting houses in summertime, for the smell thereof makes the heart merry and joyful.'[20] Other herbs were known to repel insects, such as tansy, rue and wormwood. Knowing his royal mistress's fondness for scent, Elizabeth's favourite courtier, Robert Dudley, once spent the princely sum of £1 7s 9d upon herbs to scatter in his private chamber.[21]

So that they might be surrounded by pleasant smells wherever they went, Elizabeth and her ladies favoured the use of pomanders. Herbs, spices and sometimes essential oils were melted into a ball of wax or resin and placed in a perforated box that was tied to a cord and suspended from their girdles. As they walked around, the pomander would be knocked against their skirt, causing fresh waves of the aroma to emanate from it. If they encountered a noisome smell, they could lift the pomander to their nose to disguise it.

Despite their efforts, there was little that could disguise the unpleasant odours inside the palaces, which grew worse the longer that the court was in residence. Sanitation was poor, and the majority of courtiers had no access to bathrooms or flushing toilets. The latter mostly comprised a wooden bench with a hole cut out. The waste would fall into a pit below, and the 'gong scourer' (surely one of the worst jobs in history) was obliged to shovel out the waste on a regular basis, working by the light of a candle. In a court comprising hundreds of people, privacy was a luxury enjoyed by precious few. The problem of courtiers urinating against the walls of the palaces became so acute that stone or lead urinals were installed around the courtyards. To deter those who might still be tempted to relieve themselves there, red crosses were painted on the walls in the hope that no man would wish to desecrate the holy symbol.

Little wonder that after a few weeks' residence in any palace, the stench would become 'evil and contagious'.[22] Elizabeth and her court were therefore obliged to make regular 'removes' so that the palaces could be thoroughly cleaned and all the human waste disposed of. This also allowed the local farmers to replenish their stocks of animals and crops to supply the royal kitchens next time the court was in residence.

The same concern for the queen's privacy in her chambers at court extended to the regular removes from palace to palace. There was a flotilla of royal barges to carry the queen and her entourage to the next place of residence. Elizabeth's barge would be flanked by 'privy boats', presumably carrying her closest servants and some of her personal possessions.[23] Upon reaching the chosen residence, the queen could often alight from the barge and be conveyed straight to her privy apartments, without entering the public rooms of the palace. Special 'privy bridges' and landing stages were built at Richmond, Greenwich and Whitehall for this purpose. At Hampton Court, the landing stage was situated much further from the royal lodgings than at the other greater houses. To provide the royal party with the privacy they required, therefore, a long gallery had been built connecting the river gate with a privy stair that led directly to the privy lodgings.

Although Elizabeth maintained the routine established by her predecessors of holding regular meetings with her council, the real business of state was conducted in her privy chamber, which became the heart of her court. The queen would often keep her chief minister, Lord Burghley, 'till late at night, in discoursing alone, and then call out another at his departure'.[24] Walsingham was another trusted minister with whom the queen liked to confer in private, long after the rest of the court had retired. Elizabeth was always one to play her cards very close to her chest. Sir John Harington shrewdly observed: 'Her wisest and best counsellors were oft sore troubled to know her will in matters of state: so covertly did she pass her judgment,' and that 'by art and nature together so blended, it was difficult to find her right humour at any time.' Thus, while the queen would 'cause every one to open his most inward thought to her,' she would then 'ponder in private on what had passed' before reaching a decision.[25]

This same desire for privacy extended to other areas of the queen's life at court. Much as she loved the public feasts and entertainments regularly on offer, Elizabeth preferred to take her meals in her private apartments, where she would be served by a select group of her ladies 'with particular solemnity . . . and it is very seldom that any body, foreign or native, is admitted at that time and then only at the intercession of somebody in power.'²⁶ Increasingly, there was a gulf between the public world of the court and the private world of the queen. The magnificence of her sovereign state was reflected by the elaborate ceremonials that took place in the presence chamber and other public rooms, but the real centre of power lay where the queen herself resided: in the secret chambers beyond.

This is demonstrated by the experience of Thomas Platter. He described the ceremony attendant upon preparing and serving the queen's 'luncheon' at Nonsuch. Standing in the presence chamber, where Elizabeth had given an audience, he watched as she returned to her chamber. Her guardsmen 'wearing tabards, red, if I remember, with the royal arms on their backs embroidered in gold,' carried in two tables and set them down where the queen had been sitting. There followed a procession of other guards, gentlemen and 'a charming gentlewoman or lady-in-waiting, who bowed very grace-fully . . . thrice to the empty table.' Then no fewer than forty of the queen's guardsmen entered, 'tall, fine, strong men' with 'a weapon at their sides', each bearing a single covered dish of food. One by one, a gentleman removed the cover of each dish while the lady-in-waiting carved a large piece off and gave it to the guard to taste for poison. The wine and beer were also tasted. Finally, after the long table had been fully laid out with food 'and honours performed as if the queen herself had sat there, whatever dishes there were, were offered to the queen in her apartment for her to make her choice.' Platter noted: 'These were sent into her and she ate of what she fancied, privily however, for she seldom partakes before strangers.' The same performance was re-enacted for all three courses. The queen's musicians then gave a brief recital to signal an end to the spectacle, and everyone withdrew. Having watched this succession of mouth-watering dishes and smelt their delicious aroma, Platter hastened at once to find some luncheon of his own.²⁷

During Elizabeth's reign, breakfast became more popular and was eaten by most people at court soon after rising, although certain members still spurned it as being necessary only for workers and travellers. It was a modest repast compared to the other meals of the day and usually comprised manchet bread and either fish or meat. The main meal of the day was generally served at noon, followed by supper at around 5 o'clock.

Although she was content to put on as much of a show as her predecessors when it came to the ceremonies involved in preparing and serving the meals at court, Elizabeth herself was less interested in food and kept irregular dining habits. 'Precise hours of refection she observed not,' remarked one courtier, 'as never eating but when her appetite required it.'[28] Even if she ate little and mostly in private, however, she did not stint on the ceremony and luxury involved. During the course of her reign, drinking glasses began to replace pewter vessels. All glass was expensive, but Venetian glass was the most expensive of all and could cost five times as much. As such, it was a status symbol and took pride of place on the queen's table. Small forks were introduced for eating the candied fruits that were becoming popular among the fashionable elite. These were served at separate banqueting courses, rather than at the table. A banquet in Tudor times did not mean a feast, but an additional course of sweets, nuts, fruit and cheese that would be eaten in another part of the court, away from the main dining area, while wandering around.

An item of table linen made for the queen at the beginning of her reign is a rare display of her loyalty towards her late mother. The fact that Elizabeth seldom referred to Anne Boleyn has been taken as an indication that she shared her late father's distaste for the fallen queen. But Elizabeth's personal possessions suggest otherwise. These included a beautiful linen damask napkin that was made for her in the Flemish town of Kortrijk. It was embroidered with two busts of Elizabeth, above which were the falcons of Anne's emblem, together with her coat of arms. Her daughter was particularly fond of the falcon badge, which she used on the covers of her books. It would not have been politic to go further than such subtle means of expressing her loyalty by speaking out in defence of the woman who even in death was the scandal of Europe, or to have had Anne's remains reburied in great pomp and ceremony. Elizabeth was too painfully aware that this would have called her already fragile legitimacy as queen into question, given that the annulment of her parents' marriage had effectively rendered her a bastard. Throughout her reign, she therefore consoled herself with more covert means to demonstrate her abiding affection for the mother whom she had lost in infancy.

Many of the delicacies that Elizabeth enjoyed at mealtimes were prepared and cooked by her ladies. She would be offered an array of different dishes to choose from at each meal. Her first course might comprise beef, mutton, veal, swan, goose or capon, while the second provided a host of other meats, such as lamb, heron, pheasant, chicken, pigeon and lark. As her reign progressed, many exotic foods were imported from the New World, including rich spices such as cinnamon and ginger, as well as pineapples, chillies, potatoes, tomatoes and chocolate.

Elizabeth was known to observe humanist teachings on diet and health. She followed the advice of the fashionable humanist centres of medical learning such as Bologna, Padua and Paris that recommended the avoidance of excess in all things so as to prevent 'imbalances' of the 'humours'. An abstemious diet of well-cooked simple ingredients, watered-down wine, light exercise, keeping warm at night, and the avoidance of wantonness were all advised. Elizabeth therefore ate and drank 'sparingly'. The fact that she always had a very slender figure suggests that she must have only picked at the bewildering selection of dishes presented to her at each mealtime. She probably owned a copy of Sir Thomas Elyot's popular treatise, *Castel of Helth* (which had run into five editions by 1560), and almost certainly a copy of the *Salerno Regimen*, the most important medieval treatise on health and cleanliness, which had been translated by her godson, Sir John Harington.[29]

The queen's courtiers did not follow her example when it came to eating. Their diet was as rich in meat as it had been during Henry VIII's reign. A contemporary account of the quantity of meat cooked in the royal kitchens in a single year of Elizabeth's reign includes 8,200 sheep, 2,330 deer, 1,870 pigs, 1,240 oxen, 760 calves and 53 wild boar.[30]

For all her abstemiousness, Elizabeth had a weakness for dessert. In order to satisfy her famously sweet tooth, her privy cooks and ladies prepared increasingly elaborate and fantastical confectionery. For one feast, an entire menagerie was sculpted in 'sugar-work', including camels, lions, frogs, snakes and dolphins, along with mythical figures like mermaids and unicorns.[31] One recipe book even provided instructions for crafting sugar-work plates, cups, glasses 'and such like things, wherewith you may furnish a table [and] when you have done, eat them up.'[32] Jelly was another popular staple of Elizabethan cookery. Made from calves' feet or shavings of antler horn boiled for hours and clarified, or from a kind of gelatin found in fish, it was then flavoured with sugar, spices or wine and brightly coloured with plant dyes such as turnsole, which provided a violet or deep red hue.

The sugar used for such recipes was imported from Persia (modern-day Iran) via Antwerp, where it was refined and converted from sticky syrup into solid cones called sugar loaves. These would then be broken up by the cooks in Elizabeth's kitchens and ground with a pestle and mortar to make granules of varying fineness.

Knowing her weakness for sweet foods, Elizabeth's courtiers would regularly present her with comfits (seeds, spices or fruits covered with sugar), encased in beautiful gold and enamel boxes. Even the salads prepared for the queen were laden with sugar. A popular recipe comprised almonds, raisins, currants, olives, capers, spinach and red sage, all mixed together with a 'good store of sugar'.[33] The ingredients were then mixed with vinegar, oil and yet more sugar, and a layer of orange and lemon slices was laid on top. This would be surmounted by a layer of red cauliflower leaves, olives and pickled cucumber, then a layer of shredded cabbage lettuce, before a final topping of orange and lemon slices.

A healthier alternative (or addition) to such treats was the array of seasonal fruits that were served at each meal. The variety had increased as the sixteenth century progressed, so that the queen and her court enjoyed more fresh fruit than their predecessors. Apricots, peaches and plums were particularly popular, and there were more varieties of apples than ever before. The traditional summer treat, strawberries, were still eaten in great quantities and were thought to have several benefits to health, notably to 'cool the liver: quench thirst: provoke urine and appetite'.[34] However, they were not recommended for those suffering from palsy or weak stomachs. The Elizabethans liked to douse their strawberries in wine and, of course, sugar before eating them.

To drink, Elizabeth and her court took sweetened wine or ale with each meal, but the queen's own goblet comprised three parts water to one part alcohol. Even breakfast would be accompanied by ale, which was brewed with malt and water, sometimes with flavours added, such as mace, nutmeg or sage. As her reign progressed, beer (ale flavoured with hops) became more popular but tended to be 'strong and intoxicating'.[35] Wine was generally imported, although some fruit wines were produced in England. A form of cider referred to as 'apple-wine' was also prepared, along with mead, an alcoholic drink sweetened with honey. Hypocras, a spiced drink made by mixing wine with sugar and spices, such as cinnamon, ginger, cloves and nutmeg, was considered an excellent digestif and was often served at the end of a meal.

With typical self-control, Elizabeth was as sparing in her consumption of drink as she was of food, and never overindulged – in stark contrast to many of her courtiers. Even in the comparative privacy of her 'secret apartments', she preferred to keep a clear head – conscious, perhaps, that she was always on display.

Elizabeth enjoyed physical exercise as much for its health benefits as for its own sake. Like Henry VIII, she was a keen hunter and a very accomplished horsewoman. Her ladies were hard pressed to keep up with her as she rode at breakneck speed through the forests and parklands surrounding her palaces. Her more sedate hours of leisure were spent in a number of different pursuits. One of her greatest private pleasures was to read. Often, she would read to herself, but on other occasions she would command her ladies to read aloud (in several languages) for her amusement. She also enjoyed playing cards or gossiping with her ladies about the latest scandals and events at court.

Elizabeth and her ladies spent many hours in the traditional private pastime of female royals: embroidery. By the time that she became queen, Elizabeth was exceptionally skilled with a needle. At the age of just five years old, she had presented her infant brother Edward with 'a shirt . . . of her own working'.[36] She subsequently produced three exquisitely embroidered manuscript books, which she presented to her father and his sixth wife, Katherine Parr, as New Year gifts.

Another result of her refined upbringing was that Elizabeth was very fond of music and could play several instruments. A miniature by Nicholas Hilliard, one of her favourite artists, shows her playing the lute, at which she excelled. Although she sometimes displayed her talents to the whole court, the queen preferred to play the lute in her privy chamber with only a cluster of close attendants. She also liked to play 'when she was solitary to shun melancholy'.[37]

Elizabeth was an accomplished dancer and loved to show off her prowess by performing energetic routines such as the galliard or volta. The latter involved being thrown several feet into the air by a partner, so was not to be undertaken without a great deal of practice. Although Elizabeth moved with an easy, natural grace, this was the result of many hours spent rehearsing in her private apartments. There, with her ladies taking the part of the men, she would rehearse the complicated steps over and over again until they attained perfection. When the dances were performed, she would watch her ladies like a hawk, calling out sharp reproofs if they put a foot wrong. 'She takes such pleasure in it [music] that when her Maids dance she follows the cadence with her head, hand and foot. She rebukes them if they do not dance to her liking, and without doubt she is a mistress of the art,' remarked Monsieur de Maisse, who visited Elizabeth's court during the 1590s.[38]

The queen's love of dancing was shared by the vast majority of her subjects. Dancing had always been a popular pastime in Tudor England, but during Elizabeth's reign it became so prevalent that it started to attract criticism from some of the leading moralists of the day. They included Stephen Gosson, who in 1579 published a satirical tract in which he claimed: 'London is so full of unprofitable Pipers and Fidlers, that a man can no sooner enter a tavern, but two or three casts of them hang at his heels, to give him a dance before he departs.'[39]

As Elizabeth's reign progressed and new, puritanical beliefs started to take hold, dancing became the subject of increasing criticism as one of the causes of social ills. But dancing at court was exempt from such attacks and remained one of the most acceptable and enjoyable of pastimes. The same was true of gambling, which was slammed as 'evil' (albeit a 'necessary' one) 'on account of the very large number of people who play it'.[40] But nobody dared to criticise the queen who, like her father and sister before her, was fond of whiling away wet days or winter nights with games such as backgammon, chess or cards. Her palace at Greenwich contained a 'very costly' backgammon set that had been given to her by the Elector of Saxony. On the pieces were coloured portraits of great lords and queens shown in relief and covered with pure crystal. The edge of the board was inlaid with ebony and ivory and set with priceless jewels. Also at the palace was a 'pure silver game of chess and a wolf game, in which a wolf and a number of sheep are played.'[41] These games became infinitely more entertaining to Elizabeth and her courtiers when money was at stake.

Although her father's old fool, Will Somer, had been in attendance at Elizabeth's coronation in January 1559, he does not seem to have served her in an official capacity. Perhaps he was prevented from doing so by ill health because he died in June that year. Elizabeth subsequently employed a new fool, William Shenton, who is listed in the household accounts of 1574 and 1575, when he received a specially made (and rather garish) hat of taffeta decorated with brightly coloured lace and a feather trimmed with gold spangles.[42] Another of the queen's male fools was an eccentric Italian man called 'Monarcho'. A contemporary verse refers to his 'deep discoursing brain' and claimed that he was 'grave of looks' but 'of judgement quick'.[43] Shakespeare was so enthralled when he met him that he included him as a named character in *Love's Labour's Lost*. The queen also retained a young dwarf named Ippolyta the Tartaryan in June 1564, and another called Thomasine the Dwarf, who was dressed in clothing made from the queen's own gowns.[44]

Elizabeth was particularly fond of Thomasine and gave her many personal gifts during the twenty-five years that she served her. These included two gilt rings, six pairs of Spanish gloves, several ivory combs and a looking glass. Ippolyta, meanwhile, was given 'One Baby [doll] of pewter'; whether as a toy or a prop is not clear.[45]

Elizabeth's great favourite, Robert Dudley, also retained a fool. He accompanied his master to Windsor in 1565, when Dudley had been tasked with escorting two ambassadors around the park. Then, arriving at the queen's apartments, 'Leicester's fool made so much noise calling her that she came undressed to the window.'[46] It is tempting to speculate that he had been encouraged to do so by his master.

Another popular form of entertainment for the queen and her court was the theatre. Until now, this had been a mobile pastime, with troupes of players travelling around the country in the same way as musicians. But Elizabeth's reign saw the establishment of the first permanent theatre in London. Somewhat unimaginatively named, The Theatre was established in Shoreditch in 1576 by actor-manager James Burbage. It staged its first performance that autumn, led by Leicester's Men, a troupe of actors under the patronage of Robert Dudley. It proved so successful that the following year another playhouse, the Curtain, was built nearby. In 1597 this became the favourite venue of the celebrated playwright William Shakespeare and his company, the Lord Chamberlain's Men, before they built their own theatre, the Globe, on London's south bank, opposite St Paul's Cathedral.

There is no evidence that Elizabeth ever attended one of these public theatres, but she did invite Shakespeare and his players to perform for her at court. So delighted was she with the result that she insisted they return on numerous other occasions. One of the earliest recorded performances was at Christmas 1594, shortly after the Lord Chamberlain's Men had been established, when Shakespeare performed two comedies for the queen at Greenwich. He and his company were the star attraction of the Christmas celebrations again three years later, when they performed *Love's Labour's Lost* at Whitehall Palace.

The brightly painted sets provided a mere backdrop to the dazzling costumes, which grew ever more spectacular with the success of each performance. Elizabeth and her court demanded high standards of dress from the actors, as did the thousands of ordinary people who crowded into London's growing body of theatres. If audiences were prepared to use their imaginations to conjure up a street scene in Venice or an enchanted midsummer woodland, they expected an actor playing a king to be dressed like one, complete with cloth of gold and silver, vivid silks and velvets, and elaborate ruffs. Little wonder that the clothes worn by the actors at the Rose Theatre were valued as highly as the building itself. Such clothes were not easy to come by, but having a patron at court helped. Fashions there changed so rapidly that the leading members of court regularly handed on items of clothing after they had been worn a few times. Part of Robert Dudley's patronage of his troupe of actors was to supply them with items of his discarded clothing. Given that he was the best-dressed man at court, this was valuable indeed. Dudley had once paid more for a suit than Shakespeare had paid for a house in Stratford-upon-Avon.[47] Showcasing his wardrobe in this way also helped to promote his standing among those lower down the social scale, who rushed to see Leicester's Men perform in the public theatres and gawp at their lavish costumes.

For a queen who loved words as much as Elizabeth, Shakespeare's plays were a stimulating delight. The playwright made up thousands of new words, more than 1,700 of which are still in common usage. They include: 'bedroom', 'moonbeam', 'hobnob', 'lacklustre' and 'submerge'. His genius for inventing pithy phrases such as 'all of a sudden', 'a foregone conclusion' and 'dead as a doornail' also greatly enriched the language not just of the court, but of all levels of society. Repeating words and phrases heard in the latest Shakespeare comedy or tragedy began as an in-joke for those who had attended, but rapidly spread into common parlance.

A significant portion of the queen's leisure hours was spent in the less frivolous occupation of private devotion. Like her predecessors, she had a private closet for worship but also regularly attended services in the public chapels of her palaces. A committed

Reformist, she had nevertheless learned from the example of her half-sister and had no intention of creating further turmoil by forcing her private beliefs upon her subjects. She famously declared: 'I would not open windows into men's souls', and her moderate religious settlement of 1559 bore this out.

During her reign, the rote-learned prayers that had been prescribed by Edward and Mary were abandoned in favour of more personal devotions. The Protestant teachings promoted a more direct approach to God, stripping away the unnecessary interventions of priests and chants, and encouraged people to come up with their own words.

For all her Reformist beliefs, Elizabeth's private religion incorporated elements of the 'old faith'. Some of her closest companions were Catholic, and it was said that she was not averse to hearing mass in private when the mood took her. But when the Dean of St Paul's gave a nod to his royal mistress's religious ambivalence with a New Year's gift in 1561, she angrily rebuked him. A foreign visitor had given the Dean several woodcuts and pictures representing the stories of various saints and martyrs. Thinking they would make an ideal gift for the queen, he had them 'richly bound' with a Common Prayer Book, and placed the gift on Elizabeth's kneeling cushion ready for her use. But upon seeing the book, she 'frowned and blushed', and then slammed it shut '(of which several took notice); and, calling the verger, bad him bring her the old book, wherein she was formerly wont to read.'[48]

As soon as the service was over, the queen immediately called for her carriage and rode straight to the vestry, where she furiously upbraided the hapless Dean. He pleaded that he had intended the book as a New Year's gift, but Elizabeth retorted: 'You could never present me with a worse.' She continued: 'You know I have an aversion to idolatry, to images and pictures of this kind . . . Have you forgot our proclamation against . . . Romish relics in the churches?' Only when the Dean humbly admitted that the mistake was born of ignorance, not opinion, did the queen relent. But she could not resist adding: 'God grant you his spirit, and more wisdom for the future.'[49] The message was clear: Elizabeth might blur the lines between the Protestant and Catholic faith in her own private worship, but in public the purity of the former must be upheld.

Forasmuch as the queen placed her trust in God, she nevertheless harboured a keen interest in astrology. Her personal astrologer, John Dee, became one of her closest advisers, and she would regularly consult him about the most apposite moment to undertake key events, such as her coronation. An astrologer, astronomer, mathematician and philosopher, Dee was one of the most learned men of the day. Close in age to Elizabeth, he had served her sister Mary but had been arrested in 1555 on suspicion of conjuring and witchcraft.

Dee was introduced to Elizabeth by her favourite Robert Dudley soon after she became queen, and before long he was one of her most intimate confidantes. As well as advising the queen, he also provided technical assistance to her adventurers as they planned voyages of discovery across the globe. The queen and her chief adviser, William Cecil, also put Dee's skills to use as a foreign spy. The astrologer would report on intrigues abroad using complex codes, and would sign his letters with the numerals '007'.

The queen became so fascinated with Dee's art that she studied it in detail herself and commissioned a number of astrolabes for her personal use.[50] Always insecure on her throne, she had a particular interest in horoscopes as a means of helping her to root out potential threats and rivals. Dee once had a premonition that Elizabeth would never marry, and it is interesting to speculate whether this became a self-fulfilling prophecy. Devoted to his royal mistress and concerned for her welfare, Dee also advised her on herbs, medicine and diet. Astrology and health were closely interlinked, and the planets were believed to have a direct influence upon the humours of the body. Thus, for example, those born when Saturn was in the ascendant would be prone to melancholy, swarthy complexions and disfiguring skin diseases. Each star sign ruled a particular part of the body – Aries the head, Taurus the neck and throat, Scorpio the genitals, and so on. In order to reach an accurate diagnosis, therefore, the practitioner needed to consult horoscopes indicating the disposition of the heavens when the patient was born, as well as whenever they fell ill.

More covertly, Elizabeth and Dee shared a passion for alchemy: the art of turning base metals into gold through the discovery of a universal elixir known as the 'philosopher's stone'. Elizabeth became so obsessed with this art that she had a suite of private rooms at Hampton Court Palace filled with alchemical equipment and potions. When she was in her late thirties, she was rumoured to have employed another alchemist, from the Netherlands, to find the elixir of youth.

The queen's quest for eternal youth would take other forms too, as the hard-working ladies of her privy chamber knew all too well.

'A thousand eyes see all I do'

E LIZABETH I WAS never alone. She herself admitted that she was
'always surrounded by my Ladies of the Bedchamber and maids
of honour'.[1] It was essential that this unmarried queen should be
accompanied by her ladies at all times in order to avoid any slur on
her reputation.

The queen had two separate groups of attendants: one to serve
her in the public court and the other to attend her during her private
hours. The former included the ladies of the presence chamber,
who were only required to attend 'when the queen's Majesty calleth
for them', which was usually when she granted audiences to ambassadors or other prestigious guests.[2] The maids of honour were in
attendance at other times, such as when the queen progressed in
state to chapel, and they also ran errands for their royal mistress.

The staff of the privy chamber and bedchamber were almost
exclusively female. The only men present were the gentleman and
grooms. The former was an honorary position that required attendance on the queen during court functions. For the early part of the
reign, it was held by John Astley, husband of Elizabeth's beloved
Kat. A later incumbent was Sir Christopher Hatton, who rose to
become one of the queen's closest favourites. The grooms, meanwhile, helped to keep their royal mistress's rooms in order, and a
gentleman usher scrutinised entrants and etiquette. In all, they only
amounted to a handful of male attendants.

Among the female members of Elizabeth's privy chamber staff,
there were three tiers of posts: the ladies of the bedchamber, gentlewomen of the privy chamber and the chamberers. All together,
they numbered about sixteen women. This structure appears to

have been modelled upon the household of her favourite stepmother, Katherine Parr, who influenced so much of Elizabeth's outlook. These ladies received salaries, lodgings, horses and clothing as part of their remuneration, as well as gifts from their royal mistress.

The new queen also employed a group of unsalaried women and a further reserve list 'on call', which meant that the number of staff who attended her in this inner sanctum was higher than it had been during her sister Mary's reign.[3] Even so, it was still far more modest than it had been in Henry VIII's day. And the fact that it was staffed by women meant that, in theory at least, it was largely devoid of the politics and factionalism that had dominated her father's inner sanctum. It more closely resembled the privy chamber of her grandfather, which had acted as a barrier against such concerns.

There was a remarkably low turnover of staff in Elizabeth's privy chamber. Most of the women held office for decades and died in post, rather than resigning or being dismissed. Indeed, during the whole of what would be the longest reign of any of the Tudor monarchs, only twenty-eight women occupied paid posts in the privy chamber. Recruitment was also largely limited to the families of the incumbents – most notably the Careys, Howards, Knollyses and Radcliffes – with daughters inheriting posts from their mothers. This made Elizabeth's privy chamber 'virtually a closed shop' for place-seekers at court.[4]

The ladies who served the queen in her inner sanctum would see the private face that she kept hidden in the public rooms beyond. They would wash her, attend to her makeup and coiffure, dress her, serve her food and drink, and carry out any other task that she saw fit to demand. The most menial servants were the chamberers, who cleaned the queen's apartments, emptied her washbowls and made up her bed. Although Elizabeth chose not to appoint a groom of the stool, Kat Astley, as chief gentlewoman, was keeper of the queen's close-stools and would also attend her royal mistress when she used the new flushing lavatories.

Each of the queen's ladies had specific duties, as well as the general ones associated with their position. For example, her child-hood nurse Blanche Parry acted as librarian, Jane Brussels took care of the queen's ruffs, Mary Radcliffe and Katherine Carey were responsible for jewels, and Lady Carew cared for the queen's French hoods.[5] Mary Scudamore, meanwhile, was in charge of the day books which recorded the vast gifts of clothing given to and by the queen.

At least one of Elizabeth's ladies would sleep in the same room as her, usually upon a truckle bed at the end of the queen's own bed. This meant that as well as being able to run errands at a moment's notice, these ladies also helped to safeguard the royal person. Elizabeth was under constant threat of assassination, particularly after 1570, when Pope Pius V issued a bull of excommunication and encouraged her Catholic subjects to rise against her. Although her guards were male, her women fulfilled an invaluable role with their constant presence and vigilance. As well as carrying out nightly searches of her private apartments, they would taste each dish before it was served to the queen to ensure that it was not poisoned, and would test any perfume that was sent to her as a gift.

By the time she ascended the throne, Elizabeth had grown used to being attended by an entourage of ladies and servants, and she had become an exacting, often capricious, mistress. She expected all of her women to be in constant attendance upon her and to put her needs above any personal concerns. Illness, unless it was very severe or contagious, was no excuse for absence. Neither were domestic circumstances. If any of her ladies fell pregnant, they must return to court as soon as possible after the birth, leaving their offspring to the care of wet-nurses and governesses.

Although Elizabeth herself admitted: 'I am no morning woman' and would only permit her most intimate female servants to see her before she had put on her queenly robes and adornments, she liked to go for early morning walks in the gardens of her palaces still dressed in her night garments.[6] Access to her during these perambulations was strictly limited to a coterie of her most trusted ladies.

As soon as the queen had returned from her private walks to the even greater seclusion of her bedchamber, the ceremony of her enrobing would begin. After she had been washed and dried, it would take at least an hour to dress Elizabeth in the garments that she or her ladies had chosen for that day. It might seem like an unnecessary luxury to be dressed by an array of servants, but the nature of Tudor gowns meant that even if she had wished to, Elizabeth would not have been able to dress by herself. Each layer of clothing had to be carefully fastened into place with pins and laces. As many as a thousand pins could be used to keep every intricate piece of her garment in place, and a pinner was employed to supply them. A man named Robert Carles was enlisted early in the reign and supplied 24,000 pins of varying types and sizes in 1559, including 'great velvet pins', 'medium farthingale pins' and 'small head pins'.[7] He delivered similar numbers every six months for many years afterwards.

Often, the queen's gowns had to be sewn on each day and then the stitches carefully unpicked before she retired at night. Decorative features, such as collars, ruffs and cuffs, would be attached to the queen's smocks in this way and removed every night so that they could be washed and starched separately. Evidence from the few surviving garments of the period reveals that silk or linen thread was used for stitching. This was first drawn through a lump of beeswax to strengthen it and prevent fraying.

As well as sewing their mistress's clothes into place, Elizabeth's ladies would use laces, buttons, hooks, pins, ribbons and aiglets. To complete the luxurious effect, gold or embellished fastenings would sometimes be added. From the very beginning of her reign, Elizabeth cast aside the sober dresses that had defined her pious image during the reigns of her siblings in favour of sumptuous materials and rich colours. That said, black and white were established as 'my colours' (as she told the Spanish ambassador) from early in the reign.[8] The choice was deliberate: white represented purity and black stood for constancy. As the queen's reign progressed, so did her colour palate. Her courtiers would have understood the significance of each shade. Red represented blood and power, yellow the sun and fruitfulness, green denoted youth and hope, while blue represented amity.[9]

The embellishments that were added to the queen's dresses were also laden with symbolism. They included embroidered eyes and ears (such as in the 'Rainbow Portrait') to represent her seeing and hearing everything at court, as well as a bejewelled serpent, which symbolised wisdom. Other emblems favoured by Elizabeth were the pelican (representing piety), spires (pointing in the direction of heaven), and rainbows (representing the celestial). She also wore a shawl embroidered with a spider so lifelike that it gave one visiting ambassador a fright. 'Over her breast, which was bare, she wore a long filigree lace shawl, on which sat a hideous large black spider that looked as if it were natural and alive,' he reported in dismay, hastily adding: 'Many might have been deceived by it.'[10]

As Elizabeth's dresses became ever more ostentatious, so the task of enrobing her became increasingly complicated and time-consuming. Only those at the very highest echelons of society could afford the leisure and accessories involved in donning such elaborate gowns. The complexity of an outfit was therefore as much a symbol of the wearer's status as the rich materials and embellishments from which it was crafted.

The queen's clothes were delivered to her chamber folded and wrapped in the finest linen. The household accounts for 1583 note that Anne Twiste, the queen's laundress, took delivery of 'twelve ells of Holland cloth to our use to fold and carry our clothes in of our great Guarderobe [wardrobe]'.[11] The keeper of Elizabeth's wardrobe was Sir John Fortescue, who was appointed to this distinguished position the year after her accession and served for the remainder of the reign.[12]

Before the chosen gowns and accessories reached the queen, they would be carefully checked for poison. This was perceived to be a very real threat from the very beginning of the reign, given that Elizabeth was viewed as a heretic usurper by most of Catholic Europe, and became more so after she had been excommunicated. Her chief minister, William Cecil, wrote detailed instructions to protect the queen from ingesting or absorbing poison from her gowns, stating that 'we think it very convenient that your Majesty's Apparell and specially all manner of Things that shall touch any Part of your Majesty's Body bare, be circumspectly looked unto; and that no person be permitted to come near it, but such as have the Trust and Charge thereof.' Similarly, no perfume, whether it be for 'Apparell or Sleeves, Gloves or such like . . . shall be . . . presented by any stranger.'[13] It probably fell to Elizabeth's yeoman of the robes, Ralph Hope, to check each garment for poison.[14]

Like all women, Elizabeth wore a smock of linen cloth underneath her other layers of clothing. This was her underwear: neither she nor her contemporaries wore knickers. It provided modesty and, being directly next to her skin, hygiene. Linen is a very cool fibre, which was a blessing in summer but uncomfortable to put on when standing in a draughty room on a cold winter's morning. The queen's ladies therefore warmed her smock by the fire until she was ready to put it on.

The quilted whalebone stays (later known as a corset) would be put on after the smock, followed by a farthingale (a hooped or padded petticoat) and a nightgown (an informal robe) to protect her from the cold while the rest of the process was conducted. One of Elizabeth's favourite nightgowns was made of 'tawny satin' and richly embroidered – a gift from her secretary of state, Sir Francis Walsingham. The queen's ladies would then gently pull linen under-stockings and knitted silk stockings over their mistress's legs. These stockings (or hose) were shorter than the ones worn by men, and were tied in place just below the knee. The dressers would then gently place shoes on Elizabeth's feet and tie them with a 'strong double knot'.

Next, Elizabeth's ladies would turn their attention to her hair. As the sixteenth century progressed, so the rules about ladies' hairstyles were gradually relaxed so that by the time of Elizabeth's accession it was no longer frowned upon for women to wear their hair uncovered. The queen exploited this to the full and began to experiment with ever more elaborate hairstyles. Her typically Tudor auburn hair was considered the height of fashion, and other ladies at court and across the country would try to emulate it with the use of hair dye. Various concoctions were used to achieve the requisite shade, including saffron and sulphur powder – the latter was both eye-wateringly expensive and highly toxic.

Elizabeth was very proud of her long, auburn hair and always displayed it to maximum effect, curled, pinned and adorned with priceless pearls and other jewels. 'She delighted to show her golden coloured hair, wearing a caul and bonnet as they do in Italy,' observed the Scottish ambassador Sir James Melville, adding: 'Her hair was more reddish than yellow, curled in appearance naturally.'[15] The Tudors did not wash their hair very frequently, but would rinse it in cold, herb-scented water from time to time. As part of Elizabeth's daily routine, her ladies would place a piece of material over her shoulders and gently rub her hair with a warm cloth to remove grease and dandruff. They would then use a comb, not a brush, to style it. Combs were used by everyone – men and women, courtiers and commoners – and were often shipped in from overseas. In a single year, from 1567/8, a staggering 90,000 combs were imported into London. As well as making the hair neat and tangle-free, combs were also useful for wheedling out lice.

As her reign progressed Elizabeth favoured wigs over her natural locks. There has been some debate about whether this was to follow the fashion of the day or to conceal her thinning, greying hair. The theory that she was in fact bald by the age of thirty was rooted in a reference by an early twentieth-century biographer, who claimed that from 1564 Elizabeth wore wigs all of the time. This led a contemporary historian to state: 'At thirty she was as bald as an egg.'[16]

There is no reliable evidence to corroborate this. In a portrait of Elizabeth on the frontispiece of a 1569 prayer book, her hair is clearly not a wig; it is strained back from her temples and pushed into a net. A close study of other portraits from the 1560s and 1570s has proved less conclusive as to whether she was wearing a wig. Even if she was, it is entirely possible that she was simply conforming to a fashion that had become popular among members of the elite.

Her coiffure complete, the queen's face and hands would be washed by her ladies. A paste of almonds was sometimes used because it 'scoureth better', and her skin would then be dried with a linen cloth. When Elizabeth came to the throne, the fashion among court ladies was for fresh-faced beauty, with few if any cosmetics applied. The Venetian ambassador wistfully observed the 'fresh' complexions and lack of paint, which formed a welcome contrast to the ladies of his home city whose beauty boxes were crammed full of creams, tinctures, paints and 'even preparations for tinting the teeth and eyelids'.[17]

The queen was then adorned with precious stones around her neck and in her wig. Last of all came the gown itself, which would be carefully unpacked from the linen wrapping and held open at the queen's feet so that she could step into it. Small pins were used to fasten the gown and cuffs into place. The finishing touches were then applied. These, too, could be time-consuming. Setting a starched ruff and pinning the flounce around the edge of the farthingale could take up to an hour.[18] Next there were the accessories: purse, handkerchief, gloves or muff, fan, girdle, and a small case hanging from it which could contain a knife to open and close letters, a seal and other ephemera.

As Elizabeth's reign progressed, fashions became both more complex and more dramatic. The queen set the trend for the striking silhouette of a long, slim waist, stiff, padded sleeves and a wide skirt supported by a farthingale. Ruffs worn around the neck were all the rage too, for both men and women, and became ever more elaborate in the later years of the reign. They were made from fine linen, which was starched so that the pleats were stiff enough to stay in place. From around 1570, the introduction of small heated goffering irons, custom-made by the royal locksmith, helped to make shaping more effective and allowed for more extreme ruff sizes.

It is interesting that now a queen wielded power, women's dress became more elaborate (and expansive) than men's. The reverse had been true during her father's reign, with the imposing male silhouettes created by the many layers of elaborate clothing. Under Elizabeth, women's clothes also began to incorporate elements that had until now been the strict preserve of men. The bodices of rich ladies were fastened with buttons rather than laces, and they took to wearing felt hats rather than hoods or veils. This outraged the more conservative members of society, who complained that it was becoming increasingly difficult to tell the two sexes apart.

At the same time, men were adopting a more elegant stance. In stark contrast to the aggressive masculine pose favoured by Elizabeth's father, the fashion was now to stand with one leg forward, the foot pointed outward, and the other leg slightly bent. Rather than facing square on, the torso should be twisted and the hand placed on the hip. The result was a look of casual elegance and sophistication. Women, meanwhile, were obliged to walk at a more sedate pace and to hold their arms to the front rather than the side, thanks to their increasingly elaborate gowns. Their movements were, by necessity, very deliberate, slow and dignified, and their posture rigidly upright.

Comfort as well as fashion dictated the clothes worn by Elizabeth and her court. The Tudor age witnessed a prolonged period of cold weather known as the Little Ice Age. On average, temperatures were two degrees Celsius colder than today, and there were times when they suddenly plummeted for weeks on end. In June 1529, the papal legate at the court of Elizabeth's father complained: 'Here we are still wearing our winter clothing, and use fire as if it was January.'[19] Another very cold spell occurred during the 1570s, when the summer temperatures were recorded as being far below average.

In order to keep out the ever-present chill, people wore multiple layers of clothing. For members of the royal family and their courtiers, garments made of wool would be concealed beneath richer materials. For example, men wore quilted waistcoats under their doublets and women wore under-petticoats of warm flannel wool. The latter were often dyed in bold colours, which were believed to have 'warming' properties. Scarlet flannel was thought to be particularly effective in warding off both the cold and illness. When Elizabeth fell ill of scarlet fever, her ladies wrapped her in scarlet flannel in a desperate attempt to preserve their mistress's life. The fact that she survived no doubt strengthened the belief in the efficacy of this practice.

The shoes worn by Elizabeth and her courtiers were inspired more by comfort and practicality than high fashion. They were usually flat and tied with ribbons, and were decorated with pinking – which also made the leather more flexible and therefore comfortable to move in. From the mid-1560s, small heels made from cork were added to some shoes, and 'pantobles' or slippers were worn over the shoe to protect it from mud and dirt. 'Buskins' or riding boots were a favourite with the queen herself and featured a slight heel, but purely for the purpose of accommodating the stirrup.

The queen's love of riding had a significant impact upon the fashions of the court. One observer wrote in 1575 that the English, 'when they go abroad riding . . . don their best clothes, contrary to the practice of other nations'.[20] The regularity with which Elizabeth went riding, preferring this mode of transport to a carriage, meant that she and her ladies had special clothing made for such occasions which combined fashion with practicality. This included special riding hoods to keep their hair in place, as well as a safeguard: a riding skirt that fastened at the waist and covered the feet, probably tied to the stirrup with strings. The latter prevented the skirts from flying up, thus preserving the ladies' modesty, and also kept dirt off the underskirts. But it would have been quite dangerous because if the rider fell from the horse they would have been dragged along, connected to the stirrup as they were, rather than falling clear of their mount.

Elizabeth had the same love of clothes as her father, and throughout her reign she issued a series of proclamations that reflected the changing fashions. No fewer than nine Acts of Apparel were passed during her reign. Not surprisingly, one of these (in 1574) made the sumptuary laws apply to women as well as men for the first time. It also ensured that no woman at court could rival the queen's appearance. Her legislation concerned the fashions of her male courtiers, too, in particular the Sumptuary Act of 1562 that expressed concern about the 'monstrous and outrageous greatness' of men's hose. The new fashion for double ruffs was also deemed unsuitable for anyone outside the court.[21]

For the first few months of her reign, Elizabeth had been content to retain John Bridges, the tailor who had served her father and both of her siblings, but he was dismissed in 1559. Likewise, the embroiderer Guillam Brallot undertook a great deal of work for her coronation but appears no more on the record books thereafter. His colleagues William Middleton and David Smith had also worked on the new queen's coronation robes but were evidently more to her liking because she retained them until the 1580s – Middleton embroidering her furnishings and Smith her clothing and accessories. Elizabeth's preference for black may have had something to do with its suitability as a foundation for surface embellishment, which could be stitched and unpicked numerous times without leaving any trace on the fabric. This cleverly created the illusion of an extremely large wardrobe.

Walter Fyshe was employed as the new royal tailor. Although he was highly skilled at making gowns in the traditional English style, which Elizabeth was content to wear as she established her authority during the early years of her reign, when she grew more secure on her throne she wished to indulge her penchant for French and Italian fashions. In 1566, she secretly instructed her chief minister, William Cecil, to write to Sir Henry Norris, her ambassador in Paris, that 'the Queen's Majesty would fain have a tailor that had skill to make her apparel both after the Italian and French manner.'[22] The need for discretion may have been to avoid causing offence to Fyshe, but it is perhaps more likely that the queen was too embarrassed to admit that English tailors were inferior to those on the Continent. Norris apparently failed to find a suitable tailor, however, so a compromise was made. From thenceforth Fyshe made 'toiles' (plain patterns) to Elizabeth's size, and these were then sent across the Channel to be made up in the French style. This process inspired the design of other gowns in the queen's wardrobe. Ideas for fashionable dress were conveyed to her as plain toiles made from buckram (stiff linen cloth) with samples of materials and embroidery for her approval.

As well as making up gowns to the queen's orders, Fyshe and his colleagues were also privately commissioned to fashion clothes and accessories by ambitious courtiers who hoped to win favour by presenting these to her as gifts. This was a surer means of achieving the correct fit because only Elizabeth's personal wardrobe staff would know her exact measurements and preferred cut. One such gift was made in July 1602 by her master of the rolls, Sir Thomas Egerton, who paid the royal mercers a huge sum to acquire silks for a gown to be made by the queen's tailor, embroiderer and 'silkman'. It is likely that this was the dress that Elizabeth wore in the famous 'Rainbow Portrait', painted by Marcus Gheeraerts the Younger later that year.[23]

Elizabeth also received gifts of clothing from overseas, such as in the 1580s when Ivan the Terrible of Russia sent her four timbers of sable, lynx and ermines. These would have been worth a fortune, and the queen was overjoyed when they arrived. Her skinner was set to work preparing the skins for the royal tailor to incorporate into her gowns and accessories.[24]

Walter Fyshe worked very closely with the queen's embroiderer, David Smith, throughout his years of service in the Great Wardrobe. Although they regularly travelled to court for fittings, the majority of their time was spent in the great wardrobe itself. This provided them with the space they needed to craft Elizabeth's increasingly lavish and ostentatious gowns, which comprised many yards of silks and other rich fabrics. Contemporary woodcuts of a tailor's workshop show a large laying-out surface, yardstick, chalk, parchment to note the measurements, shears, irons, pins, needles, thread and a thimble. Tailors often sat cross-legged on the floor to sew, which was presumably for practical reasons but could not have been very comfortable, especially after several hours in that position. Working side by side like this for almost thirty years, Fyshe and Smith became very fond of each other. In his will, which was enacted in 1585, Fyshe left rings 'of gold of forty shillings a piece' to 'Davye Smith, embroiderer'.[25]

The pair that replaced Fyshe and Smith forged an equally close partnership. William Jones (tailor) and John Parr (embroiderer) began their service in Elizabeth's Great Wardrobe in the early 1580s and were so successful that they remained in post for the remainder of her reign and well into the next. This suggests that the community within the great wardrobe was very tightly knit, with men and women who proved their worth serving out their careers there and making close and enduring friendships along the way.

The insular nature of life in the departments at court was intensified by the fact that most tradesmen trained their children up so that they could inherit the business when they retired or died. Thus, in 1594, Adam Bland, the queen's skinner, passed his business to his son Peter. Adam had himself inherited the post from his master, William Jurden, to whom he had been apprenticed.[26] Likewise, Garret

Johnson had been shoemaker to Elizabeth since she was a princess and continued in the role until the 1590s, when his son Peter took over.[27]

Sadly, all but a handful of garments worn by Elizabeth have been lost. But we can still glimpse the magnificence of her wardrobe through the eyes of those who saw it. They include Paul Hentzner, a German visitor to England in 1598, who was granted special access to the Wardrobe Tower at the Tower of London. He describes being shown 'above a hundred pieces of arras [wall hangings] . . . made of gold, silver and silk . . . and immense quantity of bed furniture . . . some of them most richly ornamented with pearl; and some royal dresses so extremely magnificent, as to raise any one's admiration at the sums they must have cost.'[28] Among the many gowns within the wardrobe was the queen's coronation robe which, thanks to being so carefully preserved, was still as dazzling as it had been forty years earlier.

Thanks to the striking and ostentatious image that Elizabeth projected through her clothes, the rumours about the size of her wardrobe were wildly exaggerated. The Venetian Secretary to England claimed that the queen owned 6,000 dresses.[29] Although she boasted a rich array of gowns from all over Europe, the total number of items was around 1,900, including separate parts.[30] She might dress in as sumptuous a style as her father, but she was as naturally thrifty as her grandfather. This was of necessity as well as preference: Henry VIII had spent so lavishly that the royal coffers were virtually empty.

'Make do and mend' could have been Elizabeth's catchphrase. The records show that her gowns were altered many times, and that most of the embellishments, such as embroidery and jewellery, were regularly swapped from one outfit to another.[31] In one six-month period alone from September 1587 to March 1588, William Jones, her tailor, altered no fewer than forty gowns.[32] The queen's ladies were obliged to spend many hours mending any tears, rather than simply discarding the damaged gown or passing it on to someone else. They were assisted by a dedicated silkwoman, who was among the permanent staff of Elizabeth's household. Alice Smith had been silkwoman to the queen's sister Mary, and Elizabeth was content to retain her in that post.[33] The records note that Alice supplied 'all manner of lace, linen, buttons, and loupes garnishments and silk' for the queen's dresses. In 1561, she presented her royal mistress with her first pair of knitted silk stockings.[34] Like other silkwomen, Alice also assisted in the skilled task of washing and starching sleeves and ruffs.

As well as having her gowns mended and altered regularly, Elizabeth also incorporated fabric and jewels that she had inherited from her predecessors. These included a set of white silk and silver buttons belonging to her father, which were used to embellish the sumptuous white gown that she wore in the 'Ditchley' portrait of 1592. The portrait also shows the 'Black Prince's ruby' in her headdress. The jewel (which was technically a spinel, not a ruby proper) was about the size of a small chicken's egg and was immensely valuable. Legend has it that this blood-red stone had been given to Edward III's eldest son, Edward the Black Prince, by Pedro the Cruel, King of Spain, to thank him for helping to restore him to power in 1367. The jewel had stayed in the royal family and had been set into the crown worn by Henry V at Agincourt in 1415. Perhaps in the hope that it would bring him the same luck, Richard III reputedly wore it in his crown at the Battle of Bosworth. Legend has it that the crown fell from the ill-fated king's head as he was overcome by the forces of Elizabeth's grandfather, Henry VII, and was later found under a hawthorn bush – the ruby still intact.[35]

A Dutch woman named Gwillam Boone was employed to starch Elizabeth's linen. The other craftsmen and women involved in creating the royal wardrobe are listed in a bill from 1586 as: 'Blande the Skinner, Sipthorpe farthingale maker, Herne hosier, Garret shoe-maker, Grene coffermaker, Polson locksmith . . . Margaret Skettes hoodmaker'.[36] While the tailor, embroiderer and coffermaker would have had an allocated workspace within the Great Wardrobe, the makers of the smaller items and accessories, such as the queen's hats and shoes, may have used their own workshops and served other customers too.[37]

When a gown had outlived its usefulness, it would be unpicked and remade into dresses for the queen's ladies or acquaintances. Or it might be repurposed as a cushion, seat cover, wall hanging or, as in the notable instance below, an altar cloth. Therefore, even though only one or two of Elizabeth's garments still survive in their original form, it is quite possible that stately homes across the country are littered with furnishings made from her formerly resplendent dresses.

What may be a rare survivor from Elizabeth's wardrobe was recently discovered in a remote village church in Herefordshire. Bacton was the birthplace of the queen's most faithful attendant, Blanche Parry, who had served her since Elizabeth's earliest days. Displayed for many years in a glass case on an interior wall of St Faith's Church in Bacton was an exquisitely embroidered altar cloth made of a white ribbed silk with an additional weft of silver strip thread. The quality of the material makes this a very high-status garment. It is skilfully embroidered with flowers, rowing boats, caterpillars, butterflies, dogs, stags, frogs, squirrels and more fantastical creatures. That it once formed part of a dress is revealed by a small dart in the material. The style dates from the 1590s or very early seventeenth century, and the pattern is almost identical to the bodice of the dress worn by the queen in the famous 'Rainbow Portrait' of around 1600. By the time that it was painted, Blanche had been dead for more than a decade, but it has been surmised that the dress was given to her home church of Bacton after Elizabeth's own death in 1603.[38]

In 1593, Sir John Fortescue, master of the Great Wardrobe, described the queen's clothing as 'royal and princely beseeming her calling, but not sumptuous or excessive.'[39] This is borne out by the household accounts. In the last four years of her reign, Elizabeth spent £9,535 on her wardrobe (just shy of £1 million in today's money), which was one-quarter of the amount that her successor spent each year for the first five years of his reign.[40]

Of course, Elizabeth did not have to buy all of her clothes. She received many gifts of clothing during her long reign, and her courtiers soon realised that these were more appreciated than the traditional presents of money and plate. When Bess of Hardwick and her fourth husband the Earl of Shrewsbury sent a gift of a cloak and safeguard (riding skirt) to her royal mistress, it was so well received that 'if my lord and your ladyship had given 500 pound, in my opinion it would not have been so well taken.'[41]

That the queen never took her lavish wardrobe for granted and guarded it jealously might have had something to do with a painful memory from childhood. After her mother Anne Boleyn's execution in 1536, the regular stream of pretty made-to-measure dresses and caps that Anne had sent her daughter at Hatfield stopped abruptly. Within weeks, the infant princess had started to outgrow all of the dresses and undergarments that she had left, and her lady mistress, Lady Margaret Bryan, had been obliged to write to Thomas Cromwell. 'I beg you to be good to her and hers, and that she may have raiment,' Lady Bryan implored, 'for she has neither gown nor kirtle nor petticoat, nor linen for smocks, nor kerchiefs, sleeves, rails [night dresses], body stitchets [corsets], handkerchiefs, mufflers, nor begins [night caps].' She insisted that she had 'driven off as long as I can, that, by my troth, I cannot drive it any longer'.[42] This humiliating episode evidently had a profound impact upon the young Elizabeth.

As Elizabeth's reign progressed, she appeared at court bedecked in an ever more dazzling array of gems. One observer noted that she would enter the room 'like starlight, thick with jewels'.[43] Elizabeth was particularly fond of pearls because they represented purity, and for these she was prepared to overlook her accustomed thriftiness. In one three-year period alone, from July 1566 to April 1569, she ordered 520 pearls just to trim her partlets and ruffs.[44]

But one of Elizabeth's most cherished possessions was a comparatively simple ring, fashioned from mother-of-pearl and embossed with tiny rubies and diamonds. It opened to reveal two portraits: one of the queen herself, shown in profile; the other of her mother. That Elizabeth cherished such a personal reminder of her mother is perhaps one of the most telling indications of her feelings towards her. A memento that she wore often and kept close to her at other times, it was symbolic of the private sympathy for Anne that she cherished throughout her life.

Elizabeth's ladies would painstakingly care for and catalogue all of the clothes and jewels in the queen's collection. They would also ensure that the former remained as sweet-smelling as possible, despite being unable to wash the outer garments. In 1562 a payment was made to Adam Bland, the queen's skinner, who provided 'one gross of crimson sarsenet bags and viii lb of sweet powder, as well to make sweet our robes and apparel remaining within our wardrobe of robes and also remaining within our Tower of London.' Elizabeth was even more fastidious than her predecessors about keeping her clothes clean, and employed an extra member of staff for the task. In 1583, Robert Pamplin was enlisted as 'brusher of our robes'. In addition, the queen's skinner was required to regularly beat furs to remove dust and pests. Meanwhile, her yeoman of the robes continued to perform the function of airing the clothes on a regular basis. For example, the account books for April 1569 include a payment for coal to be delivered to the Wardrobe Tower to 'air our robes and apparel within our said Tower'.[45]

Despite their best efforts, pests did sometimes take up residence in the queen's clothes. On such occasions, more forceful measures were required. In 1590, eight men were employed for a full day to beat the furs at Windsor Castle, while in 1598 six men spent four full days beating and airing the robes at Whitehall Palace and the Tower of London.[46]

As had been the case in previous reigns, Elizabeth's gowns and accessories were stored in robust coffers and chests, made by the sons of her father's coffer-maker, William Green. They evidently became more elaborate as the reign progressed. An order of 1565 requests a travelling coffer with 'room above to put our hats in, covered with leather, lined with cotton, bound with iron as locks, joints, handles and squires'.[47] The coffer-makers also crafted busks (narrow pieces of wood to shape the bodice) for the queen's dresses.

The high status and value of the royal gowns necessitated strict security. One of the most important and trusted members of her household was the locksmith, who was based at the Great Wardrobe.

Only two men held this post throughout the whole course of Elizabeth's long reign: William Hood and his successor Richard Jeffrey. In 1575, Hood provided 'one great stock lock for our Robes doors at Hampton Court with two keys'. He also supplied 'two new locks with keys . . . for presses in the office of our Robes at our Tower' in 1572.[48]

It was the job of Elizabeth's ladies to maintain lists of the clothes that their mistress required at each palace. With such a bewildering array of garments, and such regular removes, this was a complex enough task, but was made more so by Elizabeth's tendency to change her mind about what she wanted to wear. One eyewitness noted that the preparations for a move from Windsor to Hampton Court had been 'quite dashed', thanks to the carter having to return to Windsor no fewer than three times 'to carry away . . . some part of the stuff of her majesty's wardrobe'. Upon returning to Windsor for the third time, the exasperated servant cried: '"Now I see . . . that the queen is a woman as well as my wife." Which words being overhead by her majesty, who then stood at the window, she said, "What a villain is this?"'[49]

As well as caring for Elizabeth's wardrobe and jewels, her ladies also took charge of any other gifts received by their royal mistress. Some of these required a good deal of looking after, for as well as the various jewels and ornaments with which the queen was routinely presented, she also received a pet dog, a monkey and a parrot in a gilded cage.

Elizabeth's ladies would attend to other aspects of their royal mistress's appearance. Perhaps because of her fondness for sugar, Elizabeth took great care over her dental regime and liked to keep her breath as sweet-smelling as possible. First thing in the morning, she would rinse her mouth out with fresh water fragranced with cinnamon or myrrh, and would chew herbs at intervals during the day. She also used a toothpick to remove any fragments of food after each meal. The queen's long-standing favourite, Robert Dudley, spent a considerable sum on disposable toothpicks, mindful that using knives or fingers to remove food particles was considered the height of bad manners. If bad breath persisted despite these measures, the sufferer was advised to sleep with their mouth open and wear a nightcap with a hole in it, 'through which the vapour will go out'.[50]

It fell to the privy chamber ladies to clean the queen's teeth. They had a range of products at their disposal. Improbable though it sounds, soot was particularly effective at removing stains and it also had deodorising properties. It was sometimes combined with salt, which was similarly abrasive. The ladies also used a concoction of white wine and vinegar boiled up with honey, which they rubbed onto her teeth with fine cloths. The honey might have sweetened Elizabeth's breath but it probably accelerated the damage to her teeth.

Elizabethan recipe books recommend cloves for cleaning teeth because not only did they remove smells, but they also eased pain. Given that the queen regularly suffered from severe tooth decay thanks to her penchant for sugar, it is likely that she took this advice. Her physicians may also have treated her regular bouts of toothache with parsley, marjoram and spurge. The latter contained a particularly toxic sap that when applied to the tooth would burn the nerve endings away – thus permanently numbing the pain.

On one occasion in 1575, however, Elizabeth had such a terrible and prolonged toothache that her doctors advised that the only remedy was to remove the offending tooth. Terrified at the prospect of surgery (which was understandable, given the instruments used), Elizabeth flatly refused. But the pain was so acute that something had to be done. At length, Thomas Aylmer, Bishop of London, came to the rescue. He assured her that the pain of having a tooth drawn was less than she feared. To prove it, he volunteered to have one of the few teeth he had left removed while the queen watched. She agreed and was so much encouraged by his example that 'she did likewise' – much to the relief of her courtiers, who had suffered her ill humour for weeks.[51]

Elizabeth was not an easy patient. Like her father, she perceived illness as a sign of weakness and would rail against her ladies and physicians if they attempted to nurse her, insisting that there was nothing wrong. On one occasion, she ordered some water to be fetched from the Derbyshire town of Buxton, famous for its health-giving springs, so that she might bathe in it and thus ease a persistent pain in her leg. But when the water arrived, she flew into a rage and sent it away again because, by then, a rumour had begun to circulate that she was unwell.[52] Sometimes, though, the queen was so ill that she was forced to retreat to her private chambers and give in to her symptoms. On one such occasion, she hid herself away for three days and was said to be 'very unapt to be dealt with . . . being troubled with an extreme cold and defluxion into her eyes, so as she cannot endure to read any thing.'[53]

Although Elizabeth generally enjoyed better health than the rest of the Tudor monarchs, she periodically suffered from ailments that she kept concealed from the rest of the court. Most of these, such as headaches, stomach pains, aching limbs, breathlessness and insomnia, would flare up at times of stress. She did not always succeed in keeping them private. Early in her reign, the Spanish ambassador predicted that she was 'not likely to have a long life', although this could have been just wishful thinking.[54]

The queen was unusually fastidious about her personal hygiene and bathed more than most: usually once a month 'whether she needed it or no'.[55] She had a specially made 'hip bath' (large enough to sit in but not to lie down) that would travel with her from palace to palace. On other occasions, she would be washed by her ladies with cloths soaked in water from pewter bowls. She was also fond of dabbing herself with perfumed oil of rose and musk, which had also been a favourite of her father's. In addition, she sometimes wore a perfume of her own invention, which was made by boiling up water with sugar and adding sweet marjoram and powder of the herb benjamin. It was described as 'very sweet' by a contemporary.[56]

When, at last, Elizabeth retired to the privacy of her bedchamber at the end of each long day, she would be attended by her ladies. Away from the prying eyes of her courtiers, they would carefully undress her, take off any makeup and unpin her hair. No matter how late the hour, or how tired they or their mistress were, each task would be carefully performed and would take as long as the ceremony of dressing, so that it was often very late into the night when Elizabeth finally laid her head on her pillow. The separation of her public and private persona was as essential to her authority as queen as it was to her vanity as a woman, and only her most trusted ladies were permitted to see both.

15

'I am soft and made of melting snow'

IN THE SUMMER of 1575, Robert Dudley resolved upon one final, spectacular attempt to persuade Elizabeth to marry him. He staged a series of extraordinarily lavish entertainments for her at his Warwickshire home, Kenilworth Castle. These comprised several weeks of feasting, masques and revelry, almost bankrupting his estates in the process. Delighted though she was with it all, when the entertainments at last came to an end, Elizabeth still refused to commit.

It is likely, though, that at the same time that Dudley had been trying to court Elizabeth, he had been secretly bedding Lettice Knollys, whom he had invited to join the festivities. He was also still seeing Douglas Sheffield in secret, and she had borne him a son, Robert, the previous year.

For a time, Elizabeth was blissfully unaware that her favourite was betraying her. When he went to stay with the Earl and Countess of Shrewsbury at Chatsworth House in the summer of 1577, she wrote a light-hearted letter, requiring them to restrict the rich diet which she had heard he had been enjoying. 'Allow him by the day for his meat two ounces of flesh, referring the quality to yourselves, so as you exceed not the quantity, and for his drink the twentieth part of a pint of wine to comfort his stomach,' she prescribed. 'On festival days, as is meet for a man of his quality, we can be content you shall enlarge his diet by allowing unto him for his dinner the shoulder of a wren, and for his supper a leg of the same, besides his ordinary ounces.'[1] That the queen should take the time to write such a frivolous letter when she had so many pressing matters of state to deal with suggests that she was missing her old companion and that his absence had made her heart grow even fonder.

Dudley viewed his separation from Elizabeth rather differently. Although he missed being away from the centre of power, it did enable him to more easily carry on his liaison with Lettice. Their meetings evidently became ever more frequent, and it is possible that Lettice fell pregnant. Certainly, in 1578 the question of marriage was suddenly raised with some urgency. Not one to be put aside (as Douglas had been shortly after the birth of her son), Lettice demanded that Dudley legitimise their union. Fearing the inevitable backlash from his royal mistress, but conscious of the need to safeguard his dynasty, he agreed to a secret ceremony at his country house at Wanstead in Essex. The bride was said to have worn 'a loose gown', which may have been a coded reference to her pregnant state.[2]

It was not long before the secret leaked out at court. The result was explosive. When Elizabeth learned that her despised cousin had stolen the only man she had truly loved, she flew into a jealous rage, boxing Lettice's ears and screaming that 'as but one sun lightened the earth, she would have but one Queen in England'.[3] She then banished this 'flouting wench' from her presence, vowing never to set eyes on her again. Although she eventually forgave Dudley, it was a long time before their relationship regained the intimacy that had defined it for so many years.

Smarting from Dudley's betrayal, Elizabeth was inclined to look more favourably upon her latest foreign suitor, François, Duke of Alençon and Anjou, who was first proposed as a husband for the English queen in the same year that her favourite married Lettice Knollys. Elizabeth was then forty-five and her suitor just twenty-three. Despite the considerable age gap, the pair became very close – aided by the fact that the duke was the only one of the queen's many suitors to court her in person. Perhaps, also, Elizabeth was aware that Anjou represented her last realistic chance of matrimony and of bearing an heir.

The courtship raised the old question of Elizabeth's fertility. An anonymous tract among the Venetian state papers claimed: 'It is impossible to hope for posterity from a woman of the Queen's age, and of so poor and shattered a constitution as hers.'[4] As speculation surrounding Elizabeth's ability to have children with the French duke grew ever more intense, her chief minister William Cecil, who had long favoured a French alliance, took it upon himself to investigate the matter. He had his royal mistress examined by physicians in order to ascertain whether she was still capable of bearing a child, and also made a show of closely interrogating Elizabeth's laundresses and ladies-in-waiting. He recorded his findings in a private memorandum. 'Considering the proportion of her body, having no impediment of smallness in stature, of largeness in body, nor no sickness nor lack of natural functions in those things that properly belong to the procreation of children, but contrariwise by judgment of physicians that know her estate in those things, and by the opinion of women, being more acquainted with Her Majesty's body,' he concluded that there was a high probability 'of her aptness to have children'.[5]

Elizabeth's old favourite, Robert Dudley, who was vehemently opposed to the Anjou match, warned his royal mistress that child-birth at her age was fraught with danger. Given his recent betrayal, the queen was not minded to pay any heed to his words, and when the duke arrived in England in 1579 she seemed instantly captivated. She showered the young duke with affection, calling him her 'frog', and Anjou gave every appearance of returning her love. He presented her with 'a most beautiful and precious diamond, of the value of 5,000 crowns', as proof of his 'love and goodwill'. In return, 'the Queen, on her part, having commanded her lady in waiting to bring her a small jewelled harquebus of a very great price, made Monsieur a present of it.'[6]

The pair were virtually inseparable during Anjou's visit, and Elizabeth lavished every conceivable luxury on her suitor. At Richmond Palace, she appointed him the magnificent bed that had been used for her own birth in 1533. The queen personally supervised the furnishings of his rooms and mischievously told the duke that he might recognise the bed. She was referring to the fact that it had been part of the ransom paid for a former Duke of Alençon, but her remark has been taken as evidence that she and her young suitor had slept together on a previous meeting.

After Anjou's return to France, he and the English queen exchanged numerous gifts and letters. In January 1580, Elizabeth wrote to her 'dearest' duke, assuring him of her unwavering affection and begging him not to heed the 'storm of evil tongues' at court. In a thinly veiled reference to Dudley, she complained of 'those who make the people believe that you are so arrogant and so inconstant that they can easily make us withdraw our favour from our dearest when they have us to themselves'.[7] In another, more playful missive, Elizabeth quipped that she would give a million pounds to see her 'frog' swimming in the Thames again. In 1581, when the prospect of their marriage seemed a distant one, thanks to opposition from Elizabeth's councillors who feared a backlash from Spain, the queen penned a touching poem 'On Monsieur's Departure':

> I grieve and dare not show my discontent;
> I love, and yet am forced to seem to hate;
> I do, yet dare not say I ever meant;
> I seem stark mute, but inwardly do prate . . .
> Some gentler passion slide into my mind,
> For I am soft and made of melting snow . . .
> Or let me live with some more sweet content,
> Or die, and so forget what love e'er meant.

This bitter lament neatly summarises Elizabeth's predicament as queen: to rule effectively, she must forever disguise her private desires behind the public face of monarchy.

The courtship might have made Elizabeth feel young again, but she was also painfully aware that age was creeping up on her. In one letter, she admitted that she had been sleeping badly, disturbed by bad dreams, 'as old women are wont'. She also complained of an 'extreme pain in my throat continually this past fortnight', which had left her feeling frail and vulnerable.[8] In fact, Elizabeth would outlive her young suitor by almost twenty years. In 1583, she privately instructed John Dee to foretell the duke's future. Her astrologer gave the grim prediction that her suitor would commit suicide. The prognosis was inaccurate, but the suddenness of Anjou's death was not: he died of a fever the following year. Even if she had by then abandoned any idea of marrying him, Elizabeth was nevertheless grieved by the duke's passing. Inside the tiny prayer book (two inches by three) that she compiled for her private devotion were two miniatures by Hilliard: one of the queen and the other of Anjou. Elizabeth wore the book about her waist, attached to a jewelled girdle. It remained one of her most precious possessions until her death.

By the beginning of the 1580s, there was no longer any hope that Elizabeth would bear a child to continue the Tudor dynasty. At the same time, the old rumours suddenly resurfaced that Elizabeth had some physical impediment that had made it impossible for her to have sex. Mary, Queen of Scots, spread a rumour that her English rival was 'not like other women' and that even if she had taken a husband, the marriage could never have been consummated. As if to substantiate her claims, Mary added that an ulcer on the queen's leg had dried up at exactly the same time that her periods had ceased.[9]

Even though she had claimed that Elizabeth was physically incapable of having sex, Mary also laughed at the notion that she was the Virgin Queen. In a scandalous conversation that she had with her guardian Bess of Hardwick, Mary attested that the English queen was so insatiable that she had seduced a host of men. Not surprisingly, she claimed that the most frequent visitor to Elizabeth's bed had been Robert Dudley. But she also depicted the queen as a sexual predator, claiming that she had forced Sir Christopher Hatton to have sex with her, had tried to entice the Duke of Alençon into bed by wearing nothing but a chemise, and had kissed his envoy, Simier, taking 'various indecent liberties with him'.[10]

Choosing to ignore such outlandish rumours, Elizabeth was quick to make a virtue of her unmarried state. She even drew comparisons between herself and the Virgin Mary in order to create a semi-divine and iconic image as the Virgin Queen. From the beginning of the reign, her speeches had been littered with references to her being the 'bride' of England and the 'mother' of her people. In 1559, she replied to the House of Commons' petition to marry by telling them to 'reproach me so no more . . . that I have no children: for

everyone of you, and as many as are English, are my children.'
Warming to her theme, on another occasion she declared: 'I assure
you all that though after my death you may have many stepdames,
yet shall you never have any, a more natural mother, than I mean
to be unto you all.'[11]

Two events conspired to strengthen Elizabeth's growing confidence as a female monarch. The first was her triumph over her
longest-standing and most deadly rival. Mary, Queen of Scots'
triumph in bearing a son by Lord Darnley had proved short-lived.
Her second husband had soon proved feckless, cruel and dangerously
unstable. Together with his henchmen, he had brutally murdered
Mary's Italian secretary and confidante, David Rizzio, in full view
of his heavily pregnant wife. Shortly after her son's birth, Mary's
husband was himself murdered. In a bewildering sequence of events,
she eloped with the chief suspect in his murder, James Hepburn,
4th Earl of Bothwell. A coup by the Scottish lords ousted her from
power and she fled south to England, throwing herself on the mercy
of her cousin Elizabeth. This was one of many fatal lapses of judgement on Mary's part. Elizabeth wasted no time in taking the fallen
Scots queen prisoner, and so she remained for almost twenty years.

The rivalry between Elizabeth and Mary was thrown into sharp
relief now that the Scottish queen was on English soil. Although
politically they had every reason to despise each other, their enmity
was altogether more personal. Elizabeth was intensely jealous of
this younger, more beautiful cousin who had a large coterie of male
admirers and had indulged her passions just as much as the English
queen had restricted hers. Yet she was always careful to disguise
her personal feelings behind a mask of exaggerated affection.
Although Mary begged to meet her cousin, Elizabeth always
demurred – afraid, perhaps, that her jealousy would be justified.

The English queen wasted no opportunity to reinforce her superiority. Upon Mary's arrival in England in 1568, she had written to
her cousin, pleading: 'I have nothing in the world, but what I had
on my person when I made my escape.'[12] She therefore begged for
a supply of new clothes, befitting of her status. Triumphant, Elizabeth
chose some of the shabbiest gowns from her own wardrobe. When

an embarrassed Sir Francis Knollys arrived at Carlisle with the garments, he made the excuse that they had been chosen for 'lightness of carriage'. Mary was not to be fooled and maintained a frosty silence. But when she failed to write a letter of thanks to her cousin, the latter had the audacity to berate her for ingratitude and demanded to know how her gifts had been received. A hapless Knollys admitted: 'Her silence argues rather scornful than grateful acceptance.'[13]

Elizabeth enjoyed another, very personal triumph over Mary. The strain of her long captivity in England, during which numerous plots to release her all resulted in failure, began to take their toll on the fallen Queen of Scots. She suffered from rheumatism and a chronic pain in her side, her hair turned prematurely grey, and she put on a considerable amount of weight. Despite spending extraordinary sums on sumptuous clothes and jewels, eager to make the most of her fading looks, she bore little resemblance to the beautiful princess who had been the most desirable bride in Europe just a few years before.

Although she was not subject to the same hardships as her rival, Elizabeth, too, was beginning to lose her looks. In 1581, William Whittell, one of her tailors, was set to work in 'altering, enlarging, new making and lining of thirty pairs of bodies and sleeves' because the queen had put on weight. Her tailors were kept busy with many more alterations during the remainder of that decade. Between September 1587 and April 1589, William Jones altered and enlarged no fewer than 102 of the queen's gowns. Although some of these alterations reflected the change in fashion to wider farthingales and heavily padded sleeves, the references to 'piecing long and wider in the bodies' reveals that Elizabeth's shape was changing too. Even her frugal diet and regular exercise could not prevent a little middle-age spread. A Venetian observer described her as 'very strongly built' in November 1596, when she was sixty-three years old.[14]

The efforts that Elizabeth made to conceal her expanding waistline and other signs of age was more than vanity: any outward sign of infirmity on a sovereign's part undermined the immortal, God-like status that was essential to retaining their power. For Elizabeth, there was an added incentive to maintain her youthful looks as long as possible so that she might still be considered a prize in the international marriage market. One contemporary described her as 'most royally furnished, both for her person and for her train, knowing right well that in pompous ceremonies a secret of government doth much consist, for that the people are naturally both taken and held with exterior shows.'[15]

In November 1582, some fourteen years after her flight to England, Mary wrote a long and embittered letter to her cousin, listing everything that she had suffered at her hands and demanding 'satisfaction before I die, so that all differences between us being settled, my disembodied soul may not be compelled to utter its complaints before God.' Mary shared her laments with anyone who would listen, complaining to the Spanish ambassador of the 'implacable vengeance with which this Queen was treating her'.[16]

There was worse to come. Elizabeth had been at pains to cultivate her rival's son, James, during his mother's captivity. It made diplomatic sense to do so, but there was more to it than that. Deeply embittered by his birth, she seized the opportunity to create a rift between him and his mother. In her favour was the fact that Mary had been a stranger to her son since his earliest infancy, and he had been raised by men known to be hostile to her. Far from him cherishing any loyalty towards his mother, when in 1583 Mary opened negotiations for a joint sovereignty with her son, James sided with Elizabeth and rejected the scheme. The English queen must have derived intense satisfaction from knowing that this son, of whose birth she had been so jealous, had shown more loyalty to her than to his own mother. 'If the half of that good nature had been in his mother that I imagine to be in himself he had not been so soon fatherless,' she could not resist declaring.[17] By July 1586, James had proved this 'good nature' by concluding an alliance with the English queen that brought him an annual pension of £4,000 and all but severed ties with his mother for good.

It may have been this terrible blow that provoked Mary to lend her support to yet another rebellion that was forming in her name. In the summer of 1586, a Catholic gentleman named Anthony

Babington masterminded a plot to assassinate Elizabeth and place Mary on the throne, assisted by Spanish forces. The queen's spymaster, Francis Walsingham, soon heard of it and resolved to lay a trap for the Scottish queen. He did not have to wait for long. On 17 July, Mary wrote to Babington, endorsing his suggestion that the English queen be 'despatched' by a group of noblemen. 'Set the six gentlemen to work,' she urged. The letter was intercepted by Walsingham's spies. Upon receiving it, their master drew a hangman's noose on the page: Mary had effectively signed her own death warrant.

The Scottish queen was tried at Fotheringay Castle that October and found guilty of treason. Yet her cousin flinched from authorising the only punishment fitting for such a crime. Mary was no straightforward traitor: she was an anointed queen and had Tudor blood coursing through her veins. To put her to death would set a shocking and dangerous precedent, not to mention plaguing Elizabeth's conscience more than anything else that she had done. 'What will they now say that for the safety of her life a maiden Queen could be content to spill the blood even of her own kinswoman?' she lamented.[18]

The very public dilemma of what to do with Mary took a private toll on her cousin. Elizabeth still recalled the horror that she had felt at the execution of her mother and stepmother, and she flinched from condemning her kinswoman to the same horrific death. This was the greatest crisis of her reign so far, and Elizabeth, who had always prided herself on her sang-froid, almost broke down under the stress. In desperation, she retreated to Richmond, the palace where she had always found solace, accompanied by just a handful of trusted ladies. It is a sign of how vulnerable she felt that she invited her old favourite, Robert Dudley, to attend her there. This sparked a renewal of an intimacy that they had not enjoyed for many years.

But the queen's councillors followed close behind, plaguing her with demands to mete out the punishment that her cousin deserved. Furious at this interruption to the privacy she so craved, Elizabeth rounded on them. 'I assure you,' she told the astonished delegation, 'if the case stood between her and myself only, if it had pleased God to have made us both milkmaids with pails on our arms, so that the matter should have rested between us two; and that I knew she did and would seek my destruction still, yet could I not consent to her death.'[19] The delegation was dismissed, and the queen retreated to the privacy of her chambers.

But there was to be no escape. Shortly afterwards, a letter arrived from Mary herself. This long and impassioned missive forced Elizabeth to face the terrible reality of having her cousin executed. 'When my enemies have slaked their black thirst for my innocent blood, you will permit my poor desolated servants altogether to carry away my corpse, to bury it in holy ground, with the other Queens of France, my predecessors, especially near the late queen, my mother,' she wrote. She also reminded Elizabeth of their kinship by making reference to Henry VII – 'your grandfather and mine' – and begged that she might be permitted to send 'a jewel and a last adieu to my son'.[20] Statecraft or not, this letter worked the desired effect. Robert Dudley reported that it had 'wrought tears' from his royal mistress, who pleaded that the 'timerousnes of her [own] sex and nature' made the dilemma she faced all the more agonising.[21]

Mary's letter went unanswered and another month dragged by. But with the coming of the new year, Elizabeth finally resolved to take action and reluctantly acknowledged that death was the only option for her cousin. However, she still could not bear the thought of signing the death warrant and having Mary executed in public. She therefore privately instructed her keeper, Amias Paulet, to 'ease her of this burden' by secretly putting Mary to death with poison or some other means. Paulet was horrified at the suggestion and utterly refused to carry it out. With apparently no other option left to her, Elizabeth finally signed her cousin's death warrant on 1 February.

Her councillors did not hesitate. Just one week later, on the morning of 8 February 1587, Mary, Queen of Scots mounted the scaffold in the great hall of Fotheringay Castle. 'Round shoulder'd, of face fat and broad, double chinned and hazel eyed [and with] borrowed hair,' she was barely recognisable as the beautiful woman who had held the world in thrall for so many years.[22] But Mary was determined to triumph even in death. When her ladies took off her outer gown, it revealed an under-dress of scarlet, the colour of martyrs. Mary then proclaimed her status as an anointed queen and referred to her cousin one last time as a fellow sovereign, woman and 'sister'. Having pardoned her executioner, she turned to her ladies and told them to cease their 'whining and weeping'.

But there was no dignity in what followed. When Mary lowered her head onto the block and gave the signal that she was ready for death, the executioner 'struck at her neck' with his axe but missed and instead sliced into the side of her face. 'Lord Jesus, receive my soul,' Mary cried out, at which the executioner again hacked at her neck but still did not sever it, and it was only with the third blow that Mary's head finally fell upon the scaffold. When the executioner stooped to pick it up, it came away in his hands and he was left holding only her wig. Her little dog then scurried from where he had been hiding under her skirts and 'laid itself down betwixt her head and body, and being besmeared with her blood, was caused to be washed, as were other things whereon any blood was.'[23]

Elizabeth reacted to the news of Mary's execution with something like disbelief. William Camden claimed that she was 'in a manner astonished'.[24] The next morning, however, she flew into a rage so fierce that even her courtiers, who had grown used to her frequent outbursts of temper, had never seen the like. One eyewitness recorded that she was in such 'heat and passion' that she screamed out against the execution 'as a thing she never commanded or intended'. She then set about 'casting the burden generally upon them all'.[25]

But Elizabeth also put on a show of extreme sorrow at the death of her cousin. Camden noted: 'She gave her self over to grief, putting her self into mourning weeds, and shedding abundance of tears.' She also retired to the privacy of her apartments more than usual. An ambassador at court observed that she had 'taken to her bed owing to the great grief she suffered through this untoward event.'[26] Undoubtedly, this was intended at least partly for show. The queen was anxious to distance herself from the decision to have Mary executed in order to avoid a backlash from Catholic Europe. She wrote at once to Mary's son, James VI of Scotland, claiming that she was 'overwhelmed' by an 'extreme dolour' because of 'that miserable accident which (far contrary to my meaning) hath befallen . . . I beseech you that as God and many more know, how innocent I am in this case: so you will believe me.'[27] Not taking any chances, she also dispatched a trusted courtier to plead her case with James in person.

The artifice of such hollow assurances was obvious to all. But there was more to Elizabeth's horrified reaction than mere statecraft. In private she experienced genuine horror at having had a fellow queen beheaded – particularly when she learned of the bungled nature of Mary's execution. Imagining the grisly details gave her nightmares for years to come, and she was still tortured by them on her deathbed, when she was said to have whispered Mary's name.

If Elizabeth felt genuine remorse for her cousin's death, however, this did not inspire her to arrange a funeral befitting her rank and status. Some five months after the execution, Mary's corpse still lay rotting in Fotheringay Castle. The summer heat made the already 'noisome' stench intolerable, so that nobody wished to enter the room where it was kept. Finally, at the end of July, Elizabeth gave orders for her cousin's body to be buried at Peterborough Cathedral, which already housed the remains of another beleaguered queen, Catherine of Aragon. Although she decreed that Mary should be accorded full royal honours, the woman whom she chose to represent her as chief mourner was not even the highest-ranking member of her entourage.

It was not long before Elizabeth's enemies started preparing to avenge the Queen of Scots' death. Chief among them was Philip II, who had not been fooled by Elizabeth's show of regret, declaring: 'It is very fine for the Queen of England now to give out that it was done without her wish, the contrary being so clearly the case.'[28] He embarked upon a smear campaign against Elizabeth, determined to discredit the heretical English queen in the eyes of the world. He was inspired by the arrival of a curious visitor in the summer of 1587. A young man going by the name of Arthur Dudley had been shipwrecked off the coast of Spain and conveyed to Philip II's court. He claimed to be the illegitimate child of the English queen and her old favourite, Robert Dudley. His age placed his conception at 1561, which coincided with Elizabeth being bedridden with a mysterious illness that caused her body to swell. The account therefore had an air of authenticity, which was enhanced by the fact that Arthur was able to name a servant who had spirited him away from Hampton Court as soon as he was born and raised him as his own, only confessing the truth on his deathbed in 1583. There is no firm evidence to corroborate the story, but it suited Philip's interests to discredit the English queen, whom he had long since abandoned any hope of marrying, so he made sure that it was repeated far and wide. For that reason, it was given more credence than it perhaps deserves.

But Philip's campaign against Elizabeth took the form of more than mere words. In May 1588, he launched a mighty Armada against England. Although he claimed to be avenging Mary's death, he had long had his sights set upon reclaiming the kingdom that he had seen as rightfully his since his marriage to Mary Tudor. This was the greatest threat that Elizabeth had faced in her reign, and that England had faced since the Norman invasion more than five hundred years before. Once more, Elizabeth retreated to the privacy of Richmond Palace, where she was attended by just a few trusted ladies. But as messengers brought news that the Spanish fleet had been spied in the Channel and was making its way to meet the forces of the Duke of Parma, off the coast of the Netherlands, she was spurred into more decisive action. On 9 August, she travelled to Tilbury, where her land forces had gathered to repel the expected invasion. Ever conscious of the power of image, she instructed her ladies to dress her in a military-inspired outfit with a plumed helmet and steel 'cuirass' or breastplate over a white velvet gown. To ensure that she stood out even more among the crowds of her soldiers, she rode on a white horse and held a gold and silver baton aloft as she addressed them. Her speech has gone down in history as the most brilliant of all her public addresses. Painfully aware that she lacked experience of warfare, she famously assured her troops that although she had 'the body of a weak and feeble woman,' she had 'the heart and stomach of a King, and a King of England too' and vowed to fight alongside them if Parma's troops reached her shores.

In the event, the Armada failed to join forces with Parma, the tactics of the English navy proved superior, and the weather also played a part in vanquishing the attempted Spanish invasion. This was Elizabeth's finest hour. At a stroke, she became the celebrated 'Gloriana' of legend, immortalised in portraits and prose all praising her wisdom, virtue and beauty. Now, at last, her virginity was something to be celebrated: it enhanced her divine status as the Virgin Mary on earth. Her sex, too, was no longer a source of regret, and Elizabeth had the confidence to flaunt her femininity, both in her dress and in her speeches. Even though she was now in her mid-fifties, her gowns became more low-cut and the waists even more cinched, while her features were enhanced by ever thicker layers of makeup. The playwrights and artists were quick to take up the theme. Elizabeth inspired 'Gloriana', 'a most royal queen and empress' to Edmund Spenser, as well as 'Diana', 'Cynthia', 'Astraea' and 'Belphoebe', 'a most virtuous and beautiful lady'. The portraits of her became ever more fantastical, emphasising her ethereal nature as an eternally youthful goddess ruling over her adoring subjects.

Increasingly, it seemed, the private Elizabeth was merging with the public one.

16

'The crooked carcass'

THE DEFEAT OF the Armada had proved a pivotal moment in the development of the so-called 'Cult of Elizabeth', propelling the queen to iconic status in her own lifetime. But the year 1588 was also one of private grief for Elizabeth. Just a few short weeks after her victory over Philip II's fleet, her closest favourite, Robert Dudley, Earl of Leicester, died. He had served her loyally to the end. Although gravely ill during the preparations for the Armada, he had not hesitated to accept the post of 'Lieutenant and Captain-General of the Queen's Armies and Companies' and had walked bare-headed beside Elizabeth's horse as his royal mistress had delivered her famous speech at Tilbury.

Elizabeth was grief-stricken at the loss of the only man whom she had truly loved. That love had endured throughout many trials and tribulations so that, almost fifty years after they had first met, they were as affectionate towards each other as they had been at the start. In 1585, Dudley had given his royal mistress the deliberately intimate gift of a nightgown of tawny velvet lined with carnation unshorn velvet.[1] If he was unable to keep her warm in her bedchamber, then this would help fill his place.

One of the last surviving letters that Elizabeth wrote to her 'Sweet Robin', dated July 1586, reveals the abiding intimacy of their relationship. Setting aside the usual formalities required of her correspondence, she began: 'Rob, I am afraid you will suppose by my wandering writings that a mid-summer moon hath taken large possession of my brains this month, but you must needs take things as they come in my head, though order be left behind me.' Dudley was then in the Netherlands, commanding the troops that his royal mistress had sent to aid the Dutch in their struggle against Spanish authority. That Elizabeth was missing him desperately is evident from her closing line: 'Now will I end that do imagine I talk still with you, and therefore loathly say farewell, ōō, though ever I pray God bless you from all harm and save you from all foes, with my million and legion of thanks for all your pains and cares.' She signed the letter: 'As you know, ever the same. E.R.' 'Ever the same' or 'semper eadem' was Elizabeth's motto, but she and Dudley knew how much more it signified in their relationship. Although they were both now well into their fifties, their feelings towards each other had remained constant.

Dudley had stayed with the queen in the immediate aftermath of the Armada, wishing to be certain that the danger had passed. He had also played a hand in the victory celebrations. One of the last recorded sightings of the pair together was at a palace window, watching a parade staged by his stepson, the Earl of Essex. By now in very poor health, Dudley had taken his leave of Elizabeth. He at least must have known that it would be for the last time.

A few days later, Dudley wrote to Elizabeth from Rycote, the home of Sir Henry Norris and his wife, where he and his royal mistress had spent happier times early in the reign. Referring to himself as 'your poor old servant', he set aside his own discomfort to ask 'what ease of her late pain she finds, being the chiefest thing in the world I do pray for, for her to have good health and long life.' He then thanked her for the medicine that she had sent him, assuring her that it 'amends much better than any other thing that hath been given me.' The brevity of the note indicates not lack of care, but how much the earl was suffering. It ends: 'I humbly kiss your foot. From your old lodging at Rycote, this Thursday morning . . . by Your Majesty's most faithful and obedient servant.'[2]

These were probably the last words ever written by Robert Dudley. Five days later, on 4 September 1588, he breathed his last. Elizabeth was utterly inconsolable. In the days immediately after his death, she kept to her private rooms, unable to face her court or council. It was said that Lord Burghley eventually had the door to her privy bedchamber broken down because he feared his mistress would never come out. The brief note that Dudley had sent her from Rycote now became her most treasured possession. She inscribed it 'His last letter' and kept it in a locked casket by her bed for the rest of her life. Also among her private treasures were the emeralds, diamonds and pearls that he had left her in his will. Elizabeth wore the latter in many of her official portraits, including the famous Armada portrait. For years afterwards if anyone mentioned Dudley's name her eyes filled with tears.

During the later years of Elizabeth's reign, loss became an ever more constant theme. In March 1589, she mourned the passing of a cherished female attendant. Although it is questionable whether the Tudor monarchs were able to have friends in the true sense of the word, Lady Elizabeth Fiennes de Clinton came closest to enjoying that honour with Elizabeth. Born Elizabeth Fitzgerald, she was herself of royal blood, being the great-granddaughter of Edward IV's queen, Elizabeth Woodville. She had inherited the legendary beauty of this scandalous queen and was known as 'Fair Geraldine'. She had been a companion of Princess Elizabeth since childhood, and their friendship had been reignited when Elizabeth Fitzgerald, now Lady Fiennes de Clinton, had joined the queen in waiting at Hatfield in 1558. She had served her faithfully ever since.

The queen was often observed to confide in Lady Clinton, 'in whom she trusted more than all others'.[3] In theory, her service was restricted to the privy chamber, but in reality her influence spread a good deal further. A shrewd political operator, Lady Clinton was employed by the queen on a number of diplomatic errands. For most of her service to Elizabeth, Lady Clinton found herself besieged by petitions from ambitious place-seekers or those who had fallen from favour.[4]

The intimacy between the two women had deepened as the reign progressed. Perhaps Elizabeth felt that Lady Clinton's royal pedigree made it acceptable to treat her as a friend, not just a servant. But Elizabeth also took genuine pleasure in Lady Clinton's company, and they shared both humour and intellect. As well as spending many hours together in the privy chamber, the queen would also attend private supper parties with her away from court.

Lady Clinton's death, at the age of about sixty, left her royal mistress heartbroken. 'Fair Geraldine' had served her faithfully for more than thirty years and the loss of her companionship left a void in Elizabeth's private life that would never be filled. The queen ordered a magnificent funeral to be conducted at Windsor, where her cousin's body was interred in the royal chapel, next to that of her second husband.

A little under a year later, Elizabeth lost her longest-standing and most faithful female attendant, Blanche Parry, who had served the queen for every one of her fifty-seven years. Blanche had been appointed to serve in the three-month-old Elizabeth's newly created household at Hatfield and had remained by her side ever since. In contrast to many of the queen's other ladies, Blanche had been unflinchingly loyal to her royal mistress, sacrificing everything for her interests and refusing to profit from what had become a position of enormous trust and influence. While most of the other women in Elizabeth's privy chamber had left her service – temporarily or permanently – to marry and have children, Blanche remained a spinster throughout her long life. Her loyalty served as a benchmark by which all of Elizabeth's other private attendants were judged.

As well as epitomising the service that the queen expected from her women, Blanche demonstrated the blurring of responsibilities between Elizabeth's private and public attendants. Although her chief role was to attend the queen's person, she became an unofficial secretary to her mistress, drafting and editing Elizabeth's personal correspondence. She also received and read many letters and official papers that arrived for her royal mistress. Wily courtiers took to addressing them directly to Blanche because they knew that she would often append her own comments in favour of the sender before showing them to the queen.[5]

Blanche's constancy and devotion had been a vital stabilising influence for Elizabeth. By the later years of the reign, she was the only person in the queen's life who could remember her mother, Anne Boleyn, and who was able to share her royal mistress's private reminiscences of her childhood. When Blanche's health began to fail, Elizabeth ordered her own apothecary to attend her, and tradition has it that she herself was with her old nurse in her final hours. She died on 12 February 1590. The queen was utterly bereft, and one visitor to court described her 'great sorrow' at the loss of her most faithful servant.

Blanche Parry and Elizabeth Fiennes de Clinton are two rare examples of women who had served the queen's interests ahead of their own. Most of her other private attendants were quick to exploit their positions for personal gain. Sir Walter Ralegh, who had fallen foul of their intrigues, compared the queen's ladies to 'witches' because they were 'capable of doing great harm, but no good'.[6] Elizabeth had made it clear from the beginning of her reign that her ladies must not meddle in political affairs. In so doing, she had attempted to depoliticise the privy chamber and return it to the private domestic retreat that it had been in her grandfather's day. But unlike Henry VII, her actions proved entirely different to her words.

The Tudor court was a tightly knit world in which almost all the occupants were related by ties of blood, marriage or friendship. Elizabeth was quick to appreciate the advantages of controlling her court through her female attendants' networks. These were so extensive that the queen's ladies were able to acquaint her with matters that even her most trusted officials had deliberately concealed from her. They could also listen in on private conversations and gossip in the public court and report everything they had heard back to Elizabeth in the privy chamber. Before long, her ladies were perceived to have so much influence that even the most powerful men at court sought their intervention. As one courtier wryly observed: 'We worshipped no saints, but we prayed to ladies in the Queen's time.'[7]

By far the most influential of Elizabeth's private attendants was Lady Anne Dudley, Countess of Warwick. Anne had been one of Elizabeth's favourite maids of honour even before her marriage to Robert Dudley's brother, Ambrose, Earl of Warwick, in 1565. Now that Anne was a countess, Elizabeth had been obliged to promote her to gentlewoman of the privy chamber. But Anne viewed the post as more than just a sinecure and proved extraordinarily diligent in her duties. Her husband once complained to Sir Francis Walsingham that she had 'spent the chief part of her years both painfully, faithfully, and serviceably' attending the queen in her privy chamber, adding with some resentment that she had not received 'any kind of wage'.[8] But Elizabeth rewarded Lady Anne in other ways, entrusting her with increasingly important matters as the years wore on, which gave her an enormous amount of influence at court. The countess's niece would later claim that her aunt was 'more beloved and in greater favour with the Queen than any other woman in the kingdom.'[9]

A testament to Anne Dudley's influence is the fact that she received more requests for assistance than any other lady of the privy chamber. It was said that she was 'a helper to many petitioners and others in distress', and this is borne out by the contemporary records.[10] Lady Anne's networks extended well beyond the court, and even the kingdom. Having forged close relationships with English ambassadors and envoys, she was regularly informed of international, as well as domestic, matters. Foreign ambassadors were also well aware of her influence, and when she fell ill in the late 1590s, it was reported as far afield as Venice.[11]

Another member of the Dudley family who formed part of Elizabeth's personal entourage was Katherine Hastings, the youngest sister of the queen's late favourite, and wife to Lord Huntingdon. She had been known to Elizabeth since the early years of her reign, but it was not until the 1590s that Katherine became a regular presence in Elizabeth's privy chamber, whether in an official capacity is not clear. As usual, her growing influence was signalled by the number of her friends and relatives who began seeking preferment through her intervention with the queen.

By the end of 1595, Elizabeth had grown so fond of Katherine that she personally shielded her from the distressing news that her husband, who served as Earl President of the Council of the North, had fallen gravely ill in York. When Elizabeth was told of the Earl's death shortly afterwards, she caused a scandal by cutting short a visit away from London so that she could relay the sad tidings to his widow in person. Katherine fell into a state of near-hysteria when her royal mistress broke the news, and the latter was so concerned about her that she paid a 'very private' visit to her the following day, which had 'much comforted her'.[12]

Widowed and childless as she was, Katherine's relationship with the queen became ever closer. Sorry though she was for Lady Huntingdon's loss, Elizabeth might have secretly welcomed the fact that there was now no other draw upon her attention. Before long, Katherine had risen to great prominence at court. Those in attendance on the queen noted that she kept her by her side for many hours of the day. By February 1598, it was reported that: 'Lady Huntingdon is at court and with her Majesty very private twice a day.'[13]

To her credit, Katherine was reluctant to use her influence with the queen to advance the cause of her friends and family. Constantly besieged by petitions from her ladies during her private hours of leisure, it must have made a welcome change to Elizabeth that Lady Huntingdon was apparently content to spend time with her out of loyalty or pleasure, rather than for any more material gain. By the summer of 1600, Katherine had risen so high in her favour that Whyte claimed: 'She governs the Queen, many hours together very private.'[14]

The other women with whom Elizabeth chose to spend her private hours during the later years of her reign showed a similarly selfless loyalty to Lady Huntingdon. The most senior was Katherine Howard, Countess of Nottingham, who had known her royal mistress before she became queen, and had been promoted to first lady of the bedchamber in 1572. Her duties required her to spend many hours with Elizabeth, and her primary role was to oversee her extensive wardrobe. She was also one of a select group of ladies who were entrusted with the care of the royal jewels, including the array of priceless stones, necklaces, bracelets and other items of jewellery that were regularly presented as gifts to the queen. The countess was a generous gift giver herself. Knowing that Elizabeth was fond of animals, she once gave her 'a jewel of gold being a cat and mice playing with her garnished with small diamonds and pearls', as well as a gold greyhound with a diamond-studded collar, and a gold and ruby dolphin.[15]

The friendships that Elizabeth maintained with her closest female attendants reveal a more tender and sympathetic side to her character than the fearsome public displays of authority or temper. Another old companion was Lady Margery Norris, wife of one of her favourite courtiers, Sir Henry Norris. Upon hearing that two of the couple's sons had been killed on campaign in Ireland in 1597, Elizabeth wrote a heartfelt letter of condolence to 'Mine own Crow', urging her: 'Harm not yourself for bootless help, but show a good example to comfort your dolorous yoke-fellow [husband].' She also assured Lady Norris: 'Nature can have stirred no more dolorous affection in you as a Mother for a dear Son, than a gratefulness and memory of his service past, hath wrought in Us his Sovereign.'[16]

Another of Elizabeth's favourite women was Helena Gorges (née Snakenborg), a Swedish lady who had visited England in 1564 as part of the entourage of Princess Cecilia, sister of King Eric of Sweden, one of Elizabeth's many suitors. Helena was then sixteen years old and, with her red hair and pale complexion, resembled a younger version of the English queen. She was completely enthralled by Elizabeth and tried to emulate her in dress and manner. She even copied her signature, underlining the 'H' with the same elaborate flourish that Elizabeth used for her 'E'. Charmed, the queen insisted that the young girl remain behind when her mistress returned to Sweden. Helena had served Elizabeth faithfully ever since.

As she approached old age, the queen increasingly withdrew from the glare of court life to the comforting presence of this small coterie of faithful women. By the time that she turned sixty, a gulf had opened up between her private, trusted attendants and the new generation of maids of honour, whose youthful exuberance was a source of irritation both to Elizabeth and the other older members of her court. Her aged vice chamberlain, Sir Francis Knollys, complained about the boisterous antics of the young ladies of her household, who would often 'frisk and hey about in the next room, to his extreme disquiet at nights.'[17] Elizabeth herself became increasingly intolerant of their silliness and often 'swore out [against] such ungracious, flouting wenches', making them 'cry and bewail in piteous sort'.[18] Her anger was sharpened by the knowledge that she was steadily losing her grip on her privy chamber attendants, as well as by the painful realisation that she was no longer the most desirable woman at court.

But the queen was not willing to relinquish the battle for sexual supremacy quite yet. She appeared at court bedecked in increasingly lavish and brightly coloured gowns, but ordered her ladies to wear only black or white. Not all of them were prepared to acquiesce. Lady Mary Howard was one of the most audacious and disrespectful members of the queen's entourage. One day she appeared at court dressed in an ostentatious gown made from a rich velvet and 'powdered with gold and pearl'. An associate of Sir John Harington recalled the envious looks that were cast her way, not least from the queen, who realised the gown 'exceeded her own'. Intent upon revenge, a few days later the queen ordered a servant to steal the dress from Lady Mary's chamber and bring it to her. Elizabeth was considerably taller than Lady Mary, so the gown was far too short for her. Undeterred, she paraded in it before her ladies, demanding to know 'How they liked her new-fancied suit?' When nobody answered, the queen addressed the question to Lady Mary herself, who resentfully snapped that it was 'too short and ill becoming'. 'Why then,' Elizabeth retorted, 'if it become not me, as being too short, I am minded it shall never become thee, as being too fine; so it fitteth neither well.'[19]

The dress was hastily packed away and Lady Mary never dared to wear it again in the queen's presence. But she deeply resented this humiliating reprimand and became even more insolent towards her royal mistress, refusing to fetch her cloak in time for her customary early morning walk or to carry the 'cup of grace' when the queen dined in private.[20] She was also often absent for meals and prayers. When Elizabeth upbraided her for failing in her duties, Lady Mary 'did vent such unseemly answer as did breed much choler in her mistress'.[21] It is a sign of how much things had changed that a lady should dare to show such disrespect towards her queen. But Mary was by no means the only one of Elizabeth's ladies to flout her authority. It was said that her attendants often laughed at her behind her back for 'trying to play the part of a woman still young'.[22]

Their role in this pretence was critical. In the later years of Elizabeth's reign, her ladies were obliged to spend ever more time applying her makeup and other adornments in order to conceal the marks of age. Although the queen had originally worn wigs that matched her own colouring, these now concealed a head of thinning, grey hair. There is some evidence to suggest that her hair might have started to turn grey when she was still young. A lock of greying red hair preserved at Wilton House is reputed to have been given by Elizabeth to Philip Sidney in 1572, when she was thirty-nine, although another source dates the gift to 1582. Certainly, by 1596, when Elizabeth was in her mid-fifties, her famous copper tresses had faded to grey. In that year, the Bishop of St David's in Wales caused offence in his sermon by referring to the fact that 'time had sowed meal upon her hair'.

From the 1580s, the queen's wigs were fashioned into elaborate ringlets using curling irons specially made by her personal locksmith. These were heated in the fire before being applied to the hair piece. Elizabeth's wigs grew ever more elaborate during the later years of her reign. The fanciful new wigs were made by her 'silk-woman', Dorothy Spekarde, who in 1602 made a payment for 'six heads of hair, twelve yards of hair curl and one hundred devices made of hair'.[23] By the end of her reign, Elizabeth owned more than eighty wigs.

Meanwhile, increasingly thick layers of makeup were applied to maintain the so-called 'mask of youth', as well as to keep up with Italian fashions. Educated as a humanist princess, Elizabeth had always embraced Italian ideals and influences, and it had not taken long for the fresh-faced beauty that typified her early reign to be replaced by the highly painted visage favoured by Italian ladies. As ever, the fashions at court had been quickly replicated by those lower down the social scale. It was 'a rare face if it be not painted', according to a satirical broadside of the period, which poked fun at the lengths that the women of London would go to in their quest for everlasting beauty:

Waters she hath to make her face to shine,
Confections, eke, to clarify her skin;
Lip salve and cloths of a rich scarlet dye . . .
Ointment, wherewith she sprinkles o'er her face,
And lustrifies her beauty's dying grace . . .
Storax and spikenard, she burns in her chamber,
And daubs herself with civet, musk, and amber.[24]

The queen tried to keep her forehead wrinkle-free by having it regularly pasted with curd skimmed off posset, a creamy drink made from milk mixed with sugar, wine or ale. She also used a cleansing lotion made from two newly laid eggs and their shells, burnt alum, powdered sugar, borax and poppy seeds ground with water. It was believed to whiten, smooth and soften the skin.

Once Elizabeth's skin had been cleansed and treated, her entire face, neck and hands were painted with ceruse (a mixture of white lead and vinegar) in order to achieve the palest possible complexion. This was the ideal for well-born ladies because it proved that they lived a life of genteel leisure, as opposed to the women whose skin was coloured by the sun from many hours of working outdoors. To create a dramatic contrast to her pale skin, Elizabeth's lips and cheeks were coloured with a red paste made from beeswax, cochineal and plant dye, and her eyes were lined with kohl.

Although they helped to conceal the ravages of time, some of these concoctions were so toxic that they did more damage to the skin than ageing ever could. Ceruse was particularly corrosive and could cause serious lead poisoning, which not only dried out the skin but could provoke significant hair loss. One contemporary observed with some distaste: 'Those women who use it about their faces, do quickly become withered and grey headed, because this doth so mightily dry up the natural moisture of their flesh.'[25] Mercury and antimony were also used in cosmetics. Both are extremely harmful metals with side effects that range from irritability, mood swings, headaches and insomnia, to more serious respiratory problems and organ damage. It is interesting to speculate whether Elizabeth's notoriously fiery (or 'mercurial') temper may have been caused by her makeup.

Elizabeth, though, was so desperate to maintain her ageless visage that she continued to have these toxic substances pasted onto her face each day. Only a handful of her most private attendants saw what lay beneath. It is also possible that the attack of smallpox she had suffered in 1562 had left her skin pockmarked, so the thick layers of makeup could have been as much to cover this up as to preserve the illusion of youth. The ladies of the court were quick to flatter their mistress by imitation, so the use of makeup and wigs increased in the later years of the reign.

When Elizabeth retired to the privacy of her bedchamber every evening, her ladies would remove her dark red wig, jewels and other accessories, and would wipe off the thick makeup that covered her face, bosom and hands. To do so, they might have used some of the highly perfumed soap that had become popular among the fashionable elite in London during the closing years of the sixteenth century. Stripped of her queenly adornments, Elizabeth would become the private woman once more.

The queen had always revelled in the flattery of her courtiers, but although it had been freely given in the past, she was now obliged to seek it out. Anxious not to be outshone by her ladies, she once asked a visiting French nobleman what he thought of them. He immediately protested that he was unable to 'judge stars in the presence of the sun'.[26] Elizabeth was greatly satisfied, for the tactful visitor had neatly defined the role that she had created for the women at her court. But even when she was dressed and adorned to her magnificent best, the queen could no longer eclipse the youthful beauty of her maids of honour.

Neither could she rein in their behaviour. Her grip on the affairs of court was loosening, and during the 1590s the formerly strict moral standards began to seriously decay. The younger generation of ladies at court were frustrated by what they perceived to be the queen's old-fashioned attitudes, and they were unwilling to make the sacrifices of their elder colleagues in order to serve her faithfully. The incidents of scandals, elopements and secret pregnancies grew ever more frequent as the years passed. 'The talk in London is all of the Queen's maids that were,' reported one visitor to court, who went on to reveal that although Elizabeth Southwell had absented herself from the privy chamber on account of a 'lameness in her leg', the real reason was that she had fallen pregnant by a 'Mr Vavisor'.[27]

Elizabeth ('Bess') Throckmorton caused an even greater scandal during the 1590s. Bess had entered the queen's service as a gentlewoman of the privy chamber in 1584, at the age of nineteen. Intelligent, witty and forthright, Bess was a great beauty and had an exquisite sense of style. Among her many admirers was the celebrated adventurer, Sir Walter Ralegh, who had gained renown for his expeditions to the 'New World'. He was also a great favourite with the queen. Although he was twenty-one years younger than his royal mistress, Ralegh showered her with romantic poems and letters, all praising her beauty. Elizabeth was delighted by his attentions and returned them in full, to the scandal of the court. In December 1584, a foreign visitor was astonished to see the obvious intimacy that existed between the pair and described how Elizabeth had pointed 'with her finger at his [Ralegh's] face, that there was a smut on it, and was going to wipe it off with her handkerchief; but before she could he wiped it off himself.'[28]

But as far as Ralegh was concerned, all of this was for show. In private, he flirted with the queen's ladies and bedded several of them. His position as captain of the gentleman pensioners gave him the ideal opportunity because he was sworn to protect them and had a key to their private chambers. He was always careful to keep any liaisons from the queen in order to maintain the pretence that she was the sole object of his devotion. But when Bess Throckmorton caught his eye, he was so smitten that he abandoned his accustomed discretion – with catastrophic results.

Their furtive encounters in the hidden corners of the royal palaces came to an abrupt end when, in July 1591, Bess realised that she was pregnant. In panic, she fled to her lover and begged him to marry her. Fearing exposure, Ralegh complied and they were married in a secret ceremony. The new wife of the queen's favourite continued with her duties in the privy chamber, concealing her growing belly. At the end of February 1592, by which time she was eight months pregnant, she begged leave of absence and went to the house of her brother Arthur, who had enlisted the services of a midwife. On 29 March, she gave birth to a son. Four weeks later, Bess returned to her service at court as if nothing had happened.

But in the tightly knit world of the Tudor court, no secret could be long concealed. That summer, the scandal broke. Upon discovering the scale of Bess's betrayal, Elizabeth's fury knew no bounds. 'If you have . . . anything to do with Sir Walter Ralegh, or any love to make to Mrs Throckmorton,' reported the courtier Sir Edward Stafford, 'at the Tower tomorrow you may speak with them.'[29] Having committed her favourite and his secret wife to that dread fortress, the queen waited, seething, until she had decided what to do with them.

Ralegh desperately tried to clamour his way back to favour by sending urgent messages to the queen – his 'nymph' and 'goddess' – assuring her of his undying love and bitterly lamenting that he had been 'left behind her in a dark Prison all alone', where he could no longer gaze upon her 'fair hair' and 'pure cheeks'.[30] Bess, on the other hand, showed no remorse but instead seemed to revel in the fact that her marriage to the most eligible bachelor at court was no longer a secret. She signed all of the letters that she wrote from the Tower 'Elizabeth Ralegh', which infuriated her royal mistress even more.

Although the queen soon forgave her favourite, she was too deeply embittered against Bess, who had been one of her closest attendants, to allow her her freedom. Even when Bess's infant son died in October 1592, Elizabeth showed no sympathy, and it was not until two months later that she finally granted her release. But she made it clear that Bess would never be allowed back into the privy chamber, so she was obliged to retreat to her husband's estates in Wiltshire.

Shocking though it was, Bess Throckmorton's transgression was by no means an isolated incident. As the 1590s progressed, the sexual scandals at court came thick and fast. In 1598, another of the queen's ladies, Elizabeth Vernon, fell pregnant by the Earl of Southampton, one of the most notorious rakes at court. Although she attempted to conceal her 'grave condition' for as long as possible, her increasing girth caused tongues to wag. Sir John Chamberlain, a notorious gossip, slyly observed: 'Some say that she hath taken a venue [a thrust, in fencing terms] under the girdle, and swells upon it,' adding: 'yet she complains not of foul play but says the Earl of Southampton will justify it.'[31] When news of his mistress's pregnancy reached the earl, he reluctantly agreed to marry her. It was not long before the queen found out. She was so incensed at having been deceived yet again that she refused to go to chapel (which caused a scandal in itself) and instead kept to the privacy of her chambers, 'grievously offended'.[32] Soon afterwards, Elizabeth consigned the earl and his new wife to Fleet prison. Although she eventually allowed them their freedom, they were banished from her presence ever after.

Elizabeth Vernon's betrayal had made the queen more resentful than ever before of any of her ladies who dared to have affairs or marry in secret. Her punishments, even for minor misdemeanours, became progressively more severe during the closing years of her reign. Harington noticed that she 'doth not now bear with such composed spirit as she was wont; but . . . seemeth more forward than commonly she used to bear herself towards her women.'[33] Robert Dudley's illegitimate son was exiled from court for kissing a lady of the household, and two of the queen's other ladies were dealt 'words and blows of anger' for spying on the Earl of Essex as he played sports.[34] A short while later, when the queen suspected Lady Mary Howard of having an affair with Essex, she lashed out in fury at all her maids, reducing them to tears. 'She frowns on all the ladies,' remarked Sir John Harington.[35]

By now, Essex had replaced Ralegh as the queen's chief favourite. The son of Elizabeth's despised rival Lettice Knollys by her first husband Walter Devereux, he was thirty years younger than his royal mistress but gave every appearance of being passionately in love with her. Elizabeth was seduced by his darkly handsome looks and swaggering self-confidence, which enabled him to take greater liberties with her than anyone else dared. Painfully aware that age had ravished her looks, Elizabeth was fiercely possessive of his attentions. But Essex had already proved as false as Elizabeth's other favourites. In 1590, he had incurred the queen's wrath by marrying in secret Frances Walsingham, daughter of the secretary of state. Typically, Elizabeth had been more ready to forgive him than his new wife, and she remained jealously watchful of any other women at court who paid him attention.

When the earl, who fancied himself as an adventurer, prepared to embark upon an expedition to Cadiz in May 1596, his royal mistress sent him a private note to wish him well. Her concern for her favourite was obvious. She prayed that God would protect Essex 'with His benign hand [and] He will shadow you so, as all harm may light beside you.' Although he had not yet sailed, she longed for his return, which she said would 'make you better, and me gladder,' and ended with a plaintive wish that she could be with him.[36]

While Essex skilfully maintained the charade of courtly love when he was with the queen, all the time he was secretly mocking her. After the notorious incident when he had burst into her bedchamber and seen her 'unadorned', he derided her as 'an old woman . . . no less crooked in mind than in carcass.' This greatly amused the queen's young attendants, 'whom he had deluded in love matters'.[37] Lady Mary Howard grew ever more flirtatious, knowing that it drove her royal mistress to distraction. She took great care over her appearance, which one courtier shrewdly noted was 'done more to win the earl, than her mistress' good will'. Essex encouraged Mary's attention by showing her 'much favour and marks of love'.[38]

Even those who remained loyal to the queen admitted that her appearance had started to deteriorate. Sir John Harington noticed that his godmother was 'much disfavoured, and unattired', and that she was surviving on the plainest of food, such as manchet bread and chicory pottage, having no stomach for the richer dishes on offer. She had lost the few pounds gained during middle age and was now so painfully thin that her godson was grieved to see her wasting away. 'Thou seest my bodily meat doth not suit me well,' she told him sadly. 'I have eaten but one ill tasted cake since yesternight.'[39]

Others were less kind. The fading of Elizabeth's looks was reported by all of the visiting ambassadors so that before long she was the laughing stock of Europe. Giovanni Carlo Scaramelli, the waspish Venetian envoy, scornfully observed that the woman who had once been such a leader of fashion was now sadly out of touch: 'Her skirts were much fuller and began lower down than is the fashion in France,' he reported, adding: 'her hair is of a light colour never made by nature'.[40] Reporting on his visit to court in 1597, during which he had been admitted to the queen's privy chamber, the French ambassador de Maisse sniggered that the English queen was 'strangely attired' in an elaborately decorated dress that was so low-cut that 'one could see the whole of her bosom', which he added was 'somewhat wrinkled'. Worse still, Elizabeth 'often opened this dress and one could see all her belly, and even to her navel.' To be fair, Elizabeth had been continuing to adhere to Italian fashions, which were for low-cut necklines and even bared breasts. A contemporary manual advised ladies: 'Your garments must be so worn always, that your white paps may be seen.'[41] Whether this advice was intended for ladies of Elizabeth's age is another matter.

De Maisse went on to report that Elizabeth's hair was covered by a 'great reddish-coloured wig, with a great number of spangles of gold and silver, and hanging down over her forehead some pearls, but of no great worth.' Meanwhile, her face 'appears very aged . . . and her teeth are very yellow and unequal, compared with what they were formerly, and on the left side less than on the right. Many of them are missing so that one cannot understand her easily when she speaks quickly.'[42]

In desperation Elizabeth tried to maintain the illusion that she was still the most desirable woman in Europe. 'She speaks of her beauty as often as she can,' remarked John Chapman, a former servant of Lord Burghley. But he saw through the queen's attempt to 'dazzle' her subjects by her ever more outrageously ostentatious clothes, so that by 'those accidental ornaments [they] would not so easily discern the marks of age and decay of natural beauty.' She put on a similar performance for de Maisse. 'By chance approaching a door and wishing to raise the tapestry that hung before it, she said to me laughing that she was as big as a door, meaning that she was tall,' he reported. She also made a show of drawing off one of her gloves so that he might see her hand, 'which is very long and more than mine by more than three broad fingers,' de Maisse observed. But the plan backfired because he added: 'It was formerly very beautiful, but it is now very thin.' Lorenzo Priuli, the Venetian ambassador in France, was more brutal, describing Elizabeth as being of an 'advanced age and repulsive physical nature'.[43]

But if the queen's artifice failed to deceive distinguished visitors to court, those of a more humble status were more easily blinded by the magnificence of her apparel and the gorgeousness of her surroundings. The Swiss tourist Thomas Platter was one such. Reflecting on his visit to Nonsuch in 1599, he described the English queen as: 'Most lavishly attired in a gown of pure white satin, gold-embroidered, with a whole bird of paradise for panache, set forward on her head studded with costly jewels, [she] wore a string of huge round pearls about her neck and elegant gloves over which were drawn costly rings. In short she was most gorgeously apparelled, and although she was already seventy-four, was very youthful still in appearance, seeming no more than twenty years of age. She had a dignified and regal bearing.'[44]

In the queen's favour was the fact she remained in good health, despite the occasional bout of illness – such as during de Maisse's visit in 1597, when she claimed to have been 'very ill with a gathering on the right side of her face'. She assured the ambassador that 'she did not remember ever to have been so ill before'. He suspected that this was merely an excuse for not seeing him earlier, however, and observed: 'I should never have thought [it] seeing her eyes and face.'[45]

De Maisse was right to be suspicious. Even now, in what was considered old age, Elizabeth was physically agile and still had some of the restless energy that had characterised her youth. A visiting ambassador from Württemberg in March 1595 was amazed that during one of his audiences with the queen, 'She stood for longer than a full hour by the clock conversing with me, which is astonishing for a Queen of such eminence and of such great age.'[46] In 1599, when she was in her mid-sixties, Elizabeth surprised the Spanish ambassador with her sprightliness at the dance. 'The head of the Church of England and Ireland was to be seen in her old age dancing three or four galliards,' he reported.[47] The galliard was a particularly energetic dance, requiring frequent leaps, jumps and hops, so it was impressive that Elizabeth could carry it off with such aplomb. She was still performing it in 1602, at the age of almost seventy, when she honoured the Duke of Nevers by dancing it twice with him. That same year, another foreign visitor saw the queen walking in her garden at Oatlands and was astonished by her agility. 'Her Royal Majesty passed us several times,' he recalled, 'walking as freely as if she had been only eighteen years old.'[48]

For all her physical agility, there are hints that Elizabeth had started to lose her formidable mental capacity. Like her father, she became increasingly paranoid as age and infirmity overtook her. Even though it had been easily defeated by the royal forces, the Earl of Essex's rebellion in 1601 had seriously destabilised her and more than ever she sought sanctuary in her private apartments. 'These troubles waste her much,' reported Sir John Harington. 'Every new message from the city doth disturb her . . . the many evil plots and designs have overcome all her Highness' sweet temper.' Although weakened by stress and lack of food, the restless energy that the queen had displayed throughout her life still remained. Harington described how she 'walked fastly to and fro' when in a fury against Essex, and reported: 'She walks much in her privy chamber, and stamps with her feet at ill news, and thrusts her rusty sword at times into the arras in great rage . . . the dangers are over, and yet she always keeps a sword by her table.'[49] Another (perhaps more truthful) account describes the ageing monarch as 'very feeble and tottering on account of her illness,' but the author admits that she was nevertheless 'adorned and bedecked right royally'.[50]

'The court was very much neglected, and in effect the people were generally weary of an old woman's government,' reported another courtier.[51] In ever greater numbers, her subjects flocked north to James VI, King of Scotland, anxious to ingratiate themselves with the queen's likely successor. As Camden noted: 'They adored him as the sun rising, and neglected her as now ready to set.'[52] Elizabeth was well aware of this and was tormented that 'the question of the succession every day rudely sounded in their ears'.[53]

The loss of her subjects' love hastened Elizabeth's decline. Lamenting that she was now but a 'crooked old woman', one day in her privy chamber she called for a looking glass for the first time in twenty years. Upon seeing her face 'lean and full of wrinkles', she 'fell presently into exclaiming against those which had so much commended her, and took it so offensively, that some which before had flattered her, durst not come into her sight.' Thereafter, the queen was observed to be 'extreme oppressed' and fell into a deep melancholy.[54]

Privacy had always been Elizabeth's solace, and she now all but withdrew from court, closeting herself away in her privy chamber with just a few favoured ladies for company. 'She has suddenly withdrawn into herself,' observed Scaramelli, 'she who was wont to live so gaily, especially in these last years of her life.' He added: 'Her days seemed numerous indeed but not now she allows grief to overcome her strength.'[55]

In late 1602, Sir John Harington paid a visit to court and found his godmother had become 'a lady shut up in a chamber from her subjects and most of her servants, and seldom seen but on holy days.' He was shocked by her 'pitiable state' and confided to his wife: 'My royal godmother, and this state's natural mother, doth now bear show of human infirmity, too fast for that evil which we shall get by her death, and too slow for that good which she shall get by her releasement from pains and misery.'[56]

Harington tried to cheer his royal mistress by sitting with her in the privy chamber and reading some verses that he had written in her honour. Although she listened politely, as soon as he had finished she told him: 'When thou dost feel creeping time at thy gate, these fooleries will please thee less; I am past my relish for such matters.'[57] Even her favourite cousin, Sir Robert Carey, could not raise her spirits. Observing that during their conversation she had 'fetched not so few as forty or fifty great sighs . . . I used the best words I could to persuade her from this melancholy humour; but I found by her it was too deep rooted in her heart, and hardly to be removed'.[58]

In January 1603, the queen left the court in Whitehall on the advice of her trusted old astrologer John Dee, and moved to her favourite palace of Richmond, to which she could 'best trust her sickly old age'.[59] She was accompanied only by a small entourage of ladies. They included the Countess of Warwick, who by now had served Elizabeth for more than forty years and represented a treasured link with her heyday as 'Gloriana', the ageless Virgin Queen. Perhaps it was for this reason that the queen sought the countess's company above all others during her final illness. The countess's niece, Lady Anne Clifford, recalled how she would accompany her aunt to the palace, but would be obliged to wait for hours outside the queen's privy chamber as the countess attended her royal mistress, often staying with her until 'very late'.[60]

Elizabeth, like her grandfather, had often retreated to Richmond when she felt the need for privacy and peace, and it had always revived her spirits. But this time, it soon became obvious to the women who accompanied her that she would never leave. In parallel with Henry VII, the first Tudor monarch, Elizabeth, the last of her house, had chosen this private and comfortable palace as her final resting place.

As the days passed, she continued to slip into a steady decline. Ever mistress of her fate, the queen refused to lie down in her bed or to take any food for three days and nights, instead 'holding her finger almost continually in her mouth, with her eyes open and fixed upon the ground, where she sat on cushions without rising or resting herself, and was greatly emaciated by her long watching and fasting.' She angrily dismissed the ministrations of her physicians, and those around her began to suspect that she had simply decided to die. 'The Queen grew worse, because she would be so, none about her being able to persuade her to go to bed,' recalled an exasperated Sir Robert Carey. 'It seems she might have lived if she would have used means,' another visitor concurred, 'but she would not be persuaded, and princes must not be forced.'[61]

In her weakened state, Elizabeth succumbed to mental torments. The old feelings of guilt over Mary, Queen of Scots resurfaced, and she was observed to 'shed many tears and sighs, manifesting her innocence that she never gave consent to the death of that Queen'.[62] This sparked a fresh bout of paranoia, which drove Elizabeth into even deeper seclusion. One courtier reported that she 'rests ill at nights, forbears to use the air in the day, and abstains more than usual from her meat, resisting physic, and is suspicious of some about her as ill-affected.'[63]

When in late February news was brought to the queen that her old servant, Katherine Howard, Countess of Nottingham, had died, it served as a painful reminder – as if she needed one – of her own mortality. 'The Queen loved the Countess well, and hath much lamented her death, remaining ever since in deep melancholy that she must die herself, and complaineth much of many infirmities wherewith she seemeth suddenly to be overtaken,' observed Anthony Rivers. In her grief, Elizabeth sought even greater privacy: 'The Queen for many days has not left her chamber . . . they say that the reason for this is her sorrow for the death of the Countess,' observed Scaramelli.[64]

Racked by sorrow and weakened by lack of food and sleep, the queen presented a sorrowful sight to the few courtiers who were permitted to visit her. Among them was the Countess of Nottingham's widower, Charles Howard, the Lord High Admiral. Perhaps softened by pity, Elizabeth heeded his entreaties that she must retire to her bed. As soon as she did so, her life slipped rapidly away. The corridors of the palace echoed with 'great weeping and lamentation' as the queen's ladies 'passed to and fro, and perceived there was no hope that Her Majesty should escape.'[65]

Shortly after taking to her bed, Elizabeth was seized by a 'defluxion in the throat', which left her unable to speak and 'like a dead person'. The glands of her neck were enlarged and her breathing became laboured. Modern medical analysis suggests that she was suffering from bronchopneumonia, which, in a weakened or aged person, is rapidly followed by pneumonia and often proves fatal.[66]

Four days later, Scaramelli reported: 'Her Majesty's life is absolutely despaired of, even if she be not already dead.'[67] On 23 March, however, Elizabeth suddenly rallied. With tears streaming down her cheeks, she exhorted her ministers to care for the peace of the realm. When the Lord High Admiral asked her if the King of Scots should be her heir, she lifted her thin, wasted hand up to her head and slowly drew a circle around it to indicate a crown.[68]

That evening, everyone but the queen's ladies departed. They watched over her as she drifted between waking and sleeping. Between two and three o'clock the following morning, their royal mistress breathed her last, slipping from life 'easily like a ripe apple from the tree'.[69]

In their haste to pay homage to the new king, Elizabeth's former subjects seemed to have forgotten all about her. For days after her death, her corpse lay at Richmond, hastily wrapped in a cerecloth in a 'very ill' fashion.[70] The late queen had left instructions to her ladies that her body should be afforded the same privacy in death that it had been in life. Scaramelli reported: 'The body of the late Queen, by her own orders, has neither been opened, nor indeed seen by any living soul, save by three of her ladies.'[71]

These ladies, who included the Countess of Warwick and Helena Snakenborg, watched over Elizabeth's corpse as it was carefully placed in a lead coffin and taken under cover of darkness from Richmond to Whitehall Palace by barge in a sombre, torchlit procession. Upon arrival, it was carried into a withdrawing chamber and placed upon a bed of state, 'certain ladies continually attending it'.[72]

Elizabeth's most trusted ladies proceeded to watch over her corpse day and night for several weeks, her successor apparently being in no hurry to arrange a funeral. While the rest of the court clamoured to meet their new king, these ladies did not flinch from their duty. They would admit nobody else into that gloomy chamber, determined to preserve their mistress's privacy to the end.[73]

'Such lack of good order'

T HE DEATH OF Elizabeth I represented more than just the end of the Tudor dynasty. It was the end of a court life to which England had become accustomed, with its clear – if interlinked – distinction between the public and private life of the monarch.

The accession of the new Stuart king had been eagerly anticipated by his English subjects after almost half a century of being under the authority of queens. But James soon proved a disappointment. The Venetian ambassador echoed the views of many when he scornfully observed that 'from his [the king's] dress he would have been taken for the meanest of courtiers'. Others agreed that, in sharp contrast to the late queen, James lacked 'great majesty' and 'solemnities'.[1]

His wife made no better impression. In July 1603, the Venetian secretary to England reported to the Doge that Queen Anne, who lacked Elizabeth's sense of style, had even plundered the late queen's wardrobe. For 'though she declared that she would never wear cast clothes, still it was found that art could not devise anything more costly and gorgeous, and so the Court dressmakers are at work altering these old robes, for nothing new could surpass them.'[2]

James might have been the long-awaited king, but he hardly cut a very manly figure. His skin was remarkably white and soft, and his beard was 'sparse'. Physically weak and uncoordinated, 'his walk was ever circular' and he had a disconcerting habit of 'fiddling about his codpiece'. Upon his arrival at the court in London, James already had his arm in a sling thanks to falling from his horse. He also complained of having been 'very ill' with a heavy cold ever since coming to England. One eyewitness noted with some distaste that the king's tongue seemed too large for his mouth, which made his already broad Scottish accent even harder to understand. It also 'made him drink very uncomely, as if eating his drink, which came out into the cup of each side his mouth.'[3]

James's 'unmanly' nature extended to his private life, which, though shocking, he took little care to disguise from his courtiers. Although he had fathered five children by Anne of Denmark, their marriage was one of politics, not passion. They lived separate lives at court, and it was noted that they did not 'converse' together. Instead, James surrounded himself with a succession of beautiful young men, each of whom was rapidly promoted to exalted positions at court, and then just as rapidly dropped when a younger, more attractive man came along. That the queen who had been lauded for her virginity should be succeeded by a sexual deviant was too much for some of James's new subjects to bear.

The Jacobean court also presented a stark contrast to the dazzling pageantry, culture and refinement that had been the hallmark of the Tudors. Early in the new reign, a disapproving Sir John Harington described the 'beastly delights' that the new king and his courtiers 'wallowed in'. 'The entertainment and show went forward, and most of the presenters went backward, or fell down; wine did so occupy their upper chambers,' he wrote. One of the actresses was so drunk that she could not remember her lines; another 'left the court in a staggering condition,' and was found 'sick and spewing in the lower hall'.[4]

In the summer of 1607, King Christian IV of Denmark, brother of the new queen, paid a visit to England and embarked upon a 'drunken and orgiastic progress' with James around a series of great houses and palaces close to London. By the time that they reached Theobalds House in Hertfordshire, their excesses had reached fever pitch. One particularly drunken evening ended with the Danish king being smeared in jelly and cream before collapsing in a stupor and being carried off to bed.[5]

The free-flowing wine soon sparked a climate of general excess and immorality. Flirtations and illicit affairs had long been a feature of court life, but they now emerged – brazenly – from the shadows.

Suddenly the court was filled with a shockingly large number of prostitutes, pimps and procuresses. They included the notorious 'Dame of Pleasure', Lady Grisby, the beautiful and highly expensive courtesan Venetia Stanley, and the 'young mignon of Sir Pexall Brockas . . . whom he had entertained and abused since she was twelve years old'.[6] Even official court employees, such as laundresses, were known to supplement their income by selling sexual favours.

Far from providing the same strict controlling influence that Elizabeth I and her Tudor forebears had wielded, James embraced all of the excess and licentiousness that his court had to offer. Those who had been familiar with the Elizabethan court were appalled by the contrast. Lady Anne Clifford reported that 'all the ladies about the Court had gotten such ill names that it was grown a scandalous place.' She also noted that the new fashion for plunging necklines served to 'burn men's souls in sensual hot desires'.[7] Sir John Harington agreed: 'I have much marvelled at these strange pageantries, and they do bring to my remembrance what passed of this sort in our Queen's days . . . I never did see such lack of good order, discretion, and sobriety, as I have now done.'[8]

Neither was the privy chamber the private retreat that it had been for most of the Tudor period. James deprived its staff of their traditional roles of attending his person and serving his meals, which made attendance there a good deal less prestigious than it had been under his predecessors. Instead, the new king made the bedchamber his inner sanctum. Its structure and personnel closely mirrored that of the Tudor privy chamber, with a groom of the stool, gentlemen, grooms and so on. The apartments were also very similar to the old privy chamber and comprised the bedchamber itself, a with-drawing chamber, privy galleries and lodgings, a library, privy closet and bathroom.

James staffed his bedchamber with a coterie of favoured 'minions': men such as Robert Carr, whom the king had fallen in love with early in his reign and immediately appointed as a gentleman of the bedchamber. Before long, his inner sanctum was almost entirely staffed by handsome young favourites, who were imbued with a great deal of political power and held sway in the public rooms beyond. At a stroke, this dramatically reduced the influence of the Privy Council. It also blurred the boundaries between the king's private and public worlds, which was typical of James's approach to his rule. Rather than indulging in drunken excesses, sexual debauchery and other personal pleasures behind closed doors, he did so in full view of the court and encouraged his close attendants to do the same. His character and habits, with all their flaws, were as visible to courtiers and ambassadors as they were to his most intimate servants.

As his reign progressed, the new king made no secret of his impatience to be away from court altogether. He fell asleep during plays and other court entertainments, mocked the endeavours of artists and explorers, showed no interest in any of the refined pursuits at which his predecessors had excelled, and was generally ill-mannered and uncouth. Bored of the ceremonial that governed his palaces, the new king spent all the time he could in humble hunting lodges far from London. 'The King, in spite of all the heroic virtues ascribed to him when he left Scotland and inculcated by him in his books, seems to have sunk into a lethargy of pleasures and will not take heed of matters of state,' observed the Venetian envoy Scaramelli. 'He remits everything to the Council, and spends his time in the house alone, or in the country at the chase.'[9]

It was not long before there was a widespread dissatisfaction with the new Stuart dynasty among everyone except the dwindling number of favourites and sycophants who hung about the court. The fact that James lived so much of his increasingly self-indulgent life on a public stage took away the mystique of monarchy that had been the hallmark of the Tudors. This would prove disastrous for the Stuart regime – which, by the time of James's death, already looked dangerously unstable. It now became obvious that the private lives of the Tudors, just as much as their public displays of majesty, had been the key to their success.

ACKNOWLEDGEMENTS

I have once again benefitted hugely from the support of the team at Hodder & Stoughton, in particular my editor, Maddy Price, whose advice and enthusiasm have been utterly invaluable. I am also indebted to Rupert Lancaster, Rebecca Mundy, Caitriona Horne and Juliet Brightmore, all of whom have been a joy to work with. My agent Julian Alexander has, as ever, provided both inspiration and sage advice throughout.

I am also indebted to Historic Royal Palaces, in particular Michael Day, John Barnes, Lucy Worsley, Wendy Hitchmough and Sebastian Edwards, for enabling me to undertake some of the research as part of my role there. Eleri Lynn, curator of the dress collection, has been extremely generous in sharing her research for her forthcoming book, *Tudor Fashion: Dress at Court 1485-1603*. I am very grateful to Marc Meltonville, an expert on historic food and a member of the Historic Kitchens team at Hampton Court Palace, for imparting his considerable knowledge on the subject. I would also like to thank my colleagues at Bishop Grosseteste University in Lincoln and the Heritage Education Trust for their continued support.

I have been fortunate to receive the advice of numerous other experts on the period, including Alison Weir, Nicola Tallis and Josephine Watkinson. I am indebted to Dr Tim Cutler, honorary curator of the physic garden at the Worshipful Company of Barbers, for sharing the secrets of Henry VIII's medicine cabinet with me, and to Dr Julian Nash for providing a modern physician's view of the king's ulcerated leg and resulting health complaints.

The picture section has been considerably enhanced thanks to the generosity of the Duke of Buccleuch, Historic Royal Palaces, the National Archives and Hever Castle. I am also indebted to John Walkley for championing me so energetically in my home village and for organising such a wonderful Tudor event last year.

This is the first of my books to form the subject of a television series, and I have hugely enjoyed working with the production team at Like A Shot, in particular Danny O'Brien, Bruce Burgess, Henry Scott, Steve Gillham, Sam Brolan, Matt Green and Frankie Darvell-White. I am also very grateful to Ella Sullivan for enduring anti-social hours and freezing temperatures in order to facilitate the filming.

The continued support of my family and friends has meant a huge amount. Their encouragement, enthusiasm and practical help have sustained me at least as much, if not more, than the inordinate amount of coffee and cake that I have consumed during the writing process. My friends Stephen Kuhrt, Cheryl Floyd, Honor Gay and Maura and Howard Davies have been amazing in their unstinting support and enthusiasm. I would also like to give particular thanks to my parents, Joan and John Borman, my sister Jayne, my parents-in-law Joy and John Ashworth, my daughter Eleanor and stepdaughters Lucy and Lottie, and my husband Tom. In researching and writing about the lives that the Tudors led behind closed doors, I became something of a recluse myself, and for bearing with me throughout that time I offer my heartfelt thanks.

AUTHOR'S NOTE

All spelling and punctuation has been modernised for ease of reference.

The titles of court departments (Privy Chamber, Great Wardrobe, etc.) are capitalised, but the rooms themselves and the officers serving within them are written in lower case.

ABBREVIATIONS

BL MS	British Library Manuscript
CSPD	*Calendar of State Papers, Domestic Series*
CSPF	*Calendar of State Papers, Foreign Series*
CSPS	*Calendar of State Papers, Spanish*
CSPV	*Calendar of State Papers, Venetian*
Hall, *Chronicle*	Hall, Edward, *Chronicle; containing the History of England, during the reign of Henry the fourth and the succeeding monarchs, to the end of the reign of Henry VIII*
HMC	Historical Manuscripts Commission
LP Henry VIII	*Letters and Papers, Foreign and Domestic, of the Reign of Henry VIII, 1509–47*
TNA	The National Archives

BIBLIOGRAPHY

Primary sources

A Collection of Ordinances and Regulations for the Government of the Royal Household, Made in Divers Reigns: From King Edward III to King William and Queen Mary (London, 1790).

Adams, S. and Rodríguez-Salgado, M.J., 'The Count of Feria's Dispatch to Philip II of 14 November 1558', *Camden Miscellany*, XXVIII (London, 1984).

Akrigg, G.P.V., *Jacobean Pageant: Or, the Court of King James I* (London, 1962).

Arber, E. (ed.), *John Knox, First Blast of the Trumpet against the Monstrous Regiment of Women* (London, 1878).

Bacon, F., *The Historie of the Raigne of King Henry the Seventh* (London, 1622).

Bain, J., Mackie, J.D., et al. (eds), *Calendar of the State Papers Relating to Scotland and Mary, Queen of Scots, 1547–1603*, Vols I–XIII, Part ii (Edinburgh, 1898–1969).

Becket, T. and De Hondt, P.A., *Instructions Given by King Henry the Seventh, to His Embassadors, When He intended to Marry the Young Queen of Naples: Together with the Answers of the Embassadors* (London, 1761).

Bell, J., *Queen Elizabeth and a Swedish Princess: Being an Account of the visit of Princess Cecilia of Sweden to England in 1565* (London, 1926).

Bergenroth, G.A., et al., *State Papers of King Henry the Eighth* (London, 1830–52).

Birch, T., *Memoirs of the Reign of Queen Elizabeth from the year 1581 till her Death*, 2 vols (London, 1754).

Borde, A., *The Fyrst Boke of the Introduction of Knowledge* (London, 1542).

Bourdeille, P. de, Seigneur de Brantôme, *The Lives of Gallant Ladies* (London, 1965).

Boyle, J. (ed.), *Memoirs of the Life of Robert Carey . . . Written by Himself* (London, 1759).

Brewer, J.S. and Bullen, W. (eds), *Calendar of the Carew Manuscripts, preserved in the Archiepiscopal Library at Lambeth, 1515–1603*, 4 vols (London, 1867–70).

Brewer, J.S., et al. (eds), *Letters and Papers, Foreign and Domestic, of the Reign of Henry VIII, 1509–47*, 21 vols and 2 vols addenda (London, 1862–1932).

Brown, R. (trans. and ed.), *Four years at the court of Henry VIII: Selection of despatches written by the Venetian Ambassador, Sebastian Giustinian, and addressed to the Signory of Venice, January 12th 1515, to July 12th 1519*, 2 vols (London, 1854).

Brown, R., et al. (eds), *Calendar of State Papers and Manuscripts, Relating to English Affairs, Existing in the Archives and Collections of Venice*, Vols IV–IX (London, 1871–97).

Bruce, J. (ed.), Hayward, J. (eds), *Annals of the First Four Years of the Reign of Queen Elizabeth*, Camden Society, Old Series, VII (London, 1840).

Butts, H., *Diets Drye Dinner* (1599).

Camden, W., *The Historie of the Most Renowned and Victorious Princesse Elizabeth, late Queene of England* (London, 1630).

Cavendish, G., *The Life of Cardinal Wolsey*, 2 vols (London, 1825).

Cerovski, J.S. (ed.), *Sir Robert Naunton, Fragmentia Regalia or Observations on Queen Elizabeth Her Times and Favourites* (London and Toronto, 1985).

Clifford, D.J.H. (ed.), *The Diaries of Lady Anne Clifford* (Stroud, 1992).

Clifford, H., *The Life of Jane Dormer, Duchess of Feria* (London, 1887).

Collins, A. (ed.), *Letters and Memorials of State, in the reigns of Queen Mary, Queen Elizabeth, etc . . . Written and collected by Sir Henry Sidney, etc*, 2 vols (London, 1746).

Collins, A.J. (ed.), *Jewels and Plate of Queen Elizabeth I: The Inventory of 1574* (London, 1955).

Craik, G.L., *The Romance of the Peerage, or Curiosities of Family History*, Vols I–IV (London, 1849).

Edward, E., *The Life of Sir Walter Ralegh. Based on Contemporary Documents . . . Together with his Letters*, 2 vols (London, 1868).

Ellis, H. (ed.), *Original Letters Illustrative of English History, Including Numerous Royal Letters*, 3rd series, Vols II–IV (London, 1846).

Elyot, T., *The Boke named the Governour* (London, 1531).

Elyot, T., *The Castel of Helth* (London, 1534).

Falkus, C. (ed.), *The Private Lives of the Tudor Monarchs* (London, 1974).

Feuillerat, A. (ed.), *Documents relating to the revels at court in the time of King Edward VI and Queen Mary* (London, 1914).

Feuillerat, A. (ed.), *Documents relating to the revels at court in the time of Queen Elizabeth* (London, 1914).

Fitzherbert, J., *The Book of Husbandry* (London, 1533).

Fortescue, J., *The Governance of England*, ed. Plummer, C. (Oxford, 1885).

Foxe, J., *The Acts and Monuments of John Foxe*, 3 vols (London, 1853–5).

Francis Steuart, A. (ed.), *Sir James Melville: Memoirs of His Own Life, 1549–93* (London, 1929).

Froude, J.A. (ed.), *The Pilgrim: A Dialogue of the Life and Actions of King Henry VIII, by William Thomas, Clerk of the Council to Edward VI* (London, 1861).

Guillemeau, J., *The Happie Deliverie of Women* (London, 1612).

Hall, E., *Chronicle; containing the History of England, during the reign of Henry the fourth and the succeeding monarchs, to the end of the reign of Henry VIII, in which are particularly described the manners and customs of those periods* (London, 1809).

Halliwell, J.O. (ed.), *The Private Diary of John Dee*, Camden Society, Vol. XIX (London, 1842).

Harington, Sir J., *Nugae Antiquae: Being a Miscellaneous Collection of Original Papers in Prose and Verse: Written in the Reigns of Henry VIII, Queen Mary, Elizabeth, King James, etc* (London, 1779).

Harrison, G.B., *The Letters of Queen Elizabeth* (London, 1935).

Harrison, G.B. and Jones, R.A., *André Hurault de Maisse, A Journal of all that was accomplished by Monsieur de Maisse, ambassador in England from King Henri IV to Queen Elizabeth, 1597* (London, 1931).

Haynes, A., *Collection of State Papers Relating to Affairs in the Reigns of King Henry VIII, King Edward VI, Queen Mary and Queen Elizabeth, From the Year 1542 to 1570 . . . Left by William Cecil, Lord Burghley . . . at Hatfield House* (London, 1740).

Hays, D. (ed. and trans.), *The Anglica historia of Polydore Vergil, A.D. 1485–1537* (London, 1950).

Hearne, T., *Syllogue Epistolarum* (London, 1716).

Heath, J.B., 'An Account of Materials Furnished for the use of Queen Anne Boleyn, and the Princess Elizabeth, by William Loke, The King's Mercer, between the 20th January 1535 and the 27th April, 1536', *Miscellanies of the Philobiblon Society*, Vol. VII (London, 1862–3).

Hentzner, P., *Travels in England during the Reign of Queen Elizabeth* (London, 1889).

Historical Manuscripts Commission, *Calendar of the Manuscripts of the Most Honourable the Marquess of Bath, preserved at Longleat, Wiltshire, 1533–1659*, Vol. V (London, 1980).

Historical Manuscripts Commission, *Report on the Manuscripts of Lord De L'Isle & Dudley, preserved at Penshurst Place*, Vols I and II (London, 1925).

Historical Manuscripts Commission, *The Manuscripts of His Grace the Duke of Rutland, preserved at Belvoir Castle*, Vol. I (London, 1888).

Historical Manuscripts Commission, *Calendar of the Manuscripts of the Marquis of Salisbury, preserved at Hatfield House, Herts*, Vols I–XV (London, 1883–1930).

Hoby, Sir T., *The Book of the Courtier, From the Italian of Count Baldessare Castiglione, 1561* (London, 1900).

Holinshed, R., *Chronicles of England, Scotland and Ireland*, Vol. VI (London, 1587).

Hume, M.A.S. (ed.), *Calendar of Letters and State Papers relating to English Affairs, preserved principally in the Archives of Simancas, Elizabeth I*, 4 vols (London, 1892–9).

Hume, M.A.S. (ed. and trans.), *Chronicle of King Henry VIII of England . . . written in Spanish by an unknown hand* (London, 1889).

Hume, M.A.S., Tyler, R., et al. (eds), *Calendar of Letters, Despatches, and State Papers, relating to the Negotiations between England and Spain, preserved in the Archives at Simancas and Elsewhere, 1547–1558* (London, 1912–54).

James, H. (ed.), *Facsimiles of National Manuscripts from William the Conqueror to Queen Anne*, 2 vols (Southampton, 1865).

Jones, M.K. and Underwood, M.G., *The King's Mother: Lady Margaret Beaufort, Countess of Richmond and Derby* (Cambridge, 1992).

Jordan, W.K. (ed.), *The Chronicle and Political Papers of King Edward VI*, 2 vols (London, 1966).

Kempe, W., *The Education of Children in Learning* (London, 1583).

Klarwill, V von (ed.), *Queen Elizabeth and some Foreigners* (London, 1928).

Lababnoff, A. (ed.), *Lettres, Instructions et Memoires de Marie Stuart, Reine d'Ecosse*, 7 vols (London, 1844).

Laing, D. (ed.), *Notes of Ben Jonson's Conversations with William Drummond of Hawthornden*, Vol. I (London, 1842).

Leed, D., 'Ye Shall Have It Cleane: Textile Cleaning Techniques in Renaissance Europe', in Netherton, R. and Owen-Crocker, G., *Medieval Clothing and Textiles*, Vol. II, (Woodbridge, 2006).

Lerer, S., *Courtly Letters in the Age of Henry VIII: Literary Culture and the Arts of Deceit* (Cambridge University Press, 1997).

Letts, M. (ed.), 'The Travels of Leo of Rozmital', *Hakluyt Society*, 2nd series, Vol. CVIII (London, 1957).

Loades, D.M. (ed.), *Elizabeth I: The Golden Reign of Gloriana – English Monarchs: Treasures from the Archives* (Richmond, 2003).

Manning, C.R., 'State Papers Relating to the Custody of the Princess Elizabeth at Woodstock', *Norfolk Archaeology*, IV (Norwich, 1855).

Marcus, L.S., Mueller, J. and Rose, M.B., *Elizabeth I: Collected Works* (Chicago and London, 2002).

McClure, N.E., *The Letters and Epigrams of Sir John Harington* (London, 1930).

Merriman, R.B. (ed.), *Life and letters of Thomas Cromwell*, 2 vols (Oxford, 1902).

Moulton, T., *This is the Myrrour or Glasse of Helth* (London, *c.*1539).

Murdin, W., *A Collection of State Papers Relating to Affairs in the Reign of Queen Elizabeth, 1571–96 . . . Left by William Cecil Lord Burghley . . . at Hatfield House* (London, 1759).

Myers, A.R., *The Household of Edward IV: The Black Book and the Ordnance of 1478* (Manchester, 1959).

Noailles, A. de, *Ambassades de Monsieur de Noailles en Angleterre* (Leyden, 1763).

Nichols, J., *The Progresses and Public Processions of Queen Elizabeth*, 3 vols (London, 1823).

Nichols, J.G. (ed.), *The Diary of Henry Machyn: Citizen and Merchant-Taylor of London, from AD 1550 to AD 1563* (London, 1848).

Nichols, J.G. (ed.), *The Chronicle of Queen Jane and of Two Years of Queen Mary*, Camden Society, Vol. 48 (London, 1850).

Nichols, J.G. (ed.), *Literary remains of King Edward the Sixth*, 2 vols (London, 1857).

Nicolas, N.H. (ed.), *The Privy Purse Expenses of Henry VIII* (London, 1827).

Nicolas, N.H. (ed.), *Privy Purse Expenses of Elizabeth of York: Wardrobe Accounts of Edward the Fourth* (London, 1830).

Norton, E., *The Anne Boleyn Papers* (Stroud, 2013).

Penn, T., *Winter King: The Dawn of Tudor England* (London, 2011).

Perry, M., *The Word of a Prince* (London, 1990).

Prescott, A.L. (ed.), *The Early Modern Englishwoman: A Facsimile Library of Essential Works, Series I, Printed Writings, 1500–1640, Part 2, Vol. 5, Elizabeth and Mary Tudor* (Aldershot, 2001).

Pryor, F., *Elizabeth I: Her Life in Letters* (California, 2003).

Read, C. and Plummer, E. (eds), *Elizabeth of England: Certain Observations concerning the Life and Reign of Queen Elizabeth by John Chapman* (Philadelphia, 1951).

Record Commission, *State Papers of the Reign of Henry VIII*, 11 vols (London, 1830–52).

Rigg, J.M. (ed.), *Calendar of State Papers, Relating to English Affairs, Preserved*

Principally at Rome, in the Vatican Archives and Library, 1558–71 and 1572–78, 2 vols (London, 1916 and 1926).

Rhodes, H., *The Book of Nurture* (London, 1577).

Rye, W.B. (ed.), *England as seen by Foreigners in the days of Elizabeth and James the First* (London, 1865).

Sawyer, E. (ed.), *Memorials of Affairs of State in the Reigns of Queen Elizabeth and King James I, Collected (chiefly) from the Original Papers of the Right Honourable Sir Ralph Winwood*, Vol. I (London, 1725).

Seaton, E., *Queen Elizabeth and a Swedish Princess, Being an Account of the visit of Princess Cecilia of Sweden to England in 1565 From the original Manuscript of James Bell* (London, 1926).

Skelton, J., *Magnificence* (London, c.1532).

Sneyd, C.A. (ed.), *A Relation, or Rather a True Account of the Island of England . . . about the year 1500* (Camden Society, 1847).

St Clare Byrne, M., *The Lisle Letters*, 6 vols (Chicago and London, 1981).

Stevenson, J. (ed.), *The Life of Jane Dormer, Duchess of Feria, by Henry Clifford: Transcribed from the Ancient Manuscript in the possession of the Lord Dormer* (London, 1887).

Stevenson, J., et al. (eds), *Calendar of State Papers, Foreign Series, of the Reign of Elizabeth I, 1558–1591* (London, 1863–1969).

Stow, J., *A Survey of London written in the year 1598*, ed. Morley, H. (Stroud, 1994).

Strangford, Viscount, 'Household Expenses of the Princess Elizabeth during her Residence at Hatfield, October 1, 1551 to September 30, 1552', Camden *Miscellany*, Vol. II (London, 1853).

Strype, J., *Ecclesiastical Memorials, Relating chiefly to Religion, and the Reformation of it . . . under King Henry VIII, King Edward VI and Queen Mary I*, 3 vols (Oxford, 1822).

Stubbes, P., *The Anatomie of Abuses* (London, 1583).

Taylor, J., *In Praise of Cleane Linen* (London, 1624).

The Union of the Red Rose and the White By a Marriage Between King Henry VII and a Daughter of King Edward IV (Huntingdon Library, University of California).

Thoms, W.J. (ed.), *Anecdotes and Traditions, Illustrative of Early English History and Literature*, Camden Society (London, 1850).

Traherne, J.M. (ed.), *Stradling Correspondence: A Series of Letters Written in the Reign of Queen Elizabeth* (London, 1840).

Turnbull, W.B., *Calendar of State Papers, Foreign Series, of the Reign of Edward VI*, (London, 1861).

Tytler, P.F., *England under the Reigns of Edward VI and Mary, Illustrated in a Series of Original Letters*, 2 vols (London, 1839).

Vaughan, W., *Natural and Artificial Directions for Health* (London, 1600).

Weldon, Sir A., *The Court and Character of King James* (London, 1650).

Wernham, R.B., *List and Analysis of State Papers Foreign Series, Elizabeth I, Preserved in the Public Record Office, June 1591–December 1596* (London, 1980–2000).

Williams, C.H. (ed.), *English Historical Documents*, Vols V and V(A) (London, 1967, 2011).

Wood, M.A.E., *Letters of Royal and Illustrious Ladies of Great Britain*, 3 vols (London, 1846).

Wright, T., *Queen Elizabeth and her Times, A Series of Original Letters, Selected from the Inedited Private Correspondence of the Lord Treasurer Burghley, the Earl of Leicester, the Secretaries Walsingham and Smith, Sir Christopher Hatton, etc*, 2 vols (London, 1838).

Wriothesley, C., *A Chronicle of England During the Reigns of the Tudors, From A.D. 1485 to 1559*, ed. Hamilton, W.D., 2 vols, Camden Society, 2nd series (London, 1875–7).

Wyatt, G., *Extracts from the Life of the Virtuous, Christian and Renowned Queen Anne Boleyn*, in Singer, S.W. (ed.), Cavendish, G., 'The Life of Cardinal Wolsey' (London, 1827).

Yorke, P. (ed.), *Miscellaneous State Papers: From 1501 to 1726*, Vol. I (London, 1778).

Secondary sources

Adams, S., 'Eliza Enthroned? The Court and its Politics', in Haigh, C., (ed.), *The Reign of Elizabeth I* (London, 1984).

Anglo, S., *Spectacle and Pageantry and Early Tudor Policy* (Oxford, 1997).

Arnold, J., 'Lost from Her Majesties back': items of clothing and jewels lost or given away by Queen Elizabeth I between 1561–1585, entered in one of the day books kept for the records of the Wardrobes of Robes* (Costume Society, 1980).

Arnold, J., *Patterns of Fashion: The Cut and Construction of Clothes for Men and Women c.1560–1620* (London, 1985).

Arnold, J., *Queen Elizabeth's Wardrobe Unlock'd* (Leeds, 1988).

Ashdown, D.M., *Ladies-in-Waiting* (London, 1976).

Baldwin Smith, L., *A Tudor Tragedy: The Life and Times of Catherine Howard* (London, 1961).

Baldwin Smith, L., *Henry VIII: The Mask of Royalty* (London, 1971).

Ballard, G., *Memoirs of Several Ladies of Great Britain who have been celebrated for their writings or skill in the learned languages, arts and sciences* (Detroit, 1985).

Bassnett, S., *Elizabeth I: A Feminist Perspective* (Oxford and New York, 1988).

Beer, A., *Bess: The Life of Lady Ralegh, Wife to Sir Walter* (London, 2005).

Betteridge, T. and Riehl, A. (eds), *Tudor Court Culture* (New Jersey, 2010).

Bolland, C. and Cooper, T., *The Real Tudors: Kings and Queens Rediscovered* (London, 2014).

Bradford, C.A., *Blanche Parry, Queen Elizabeth's Gentlewoman* (London, 1935).

Bradford, C.A., *Helena, Marchioness of Northampton* (London, 1936).

Bradford, G., *Elizabethan Women* (New York, 1969).

Brayshay, M., *Land, Travel and Communications in Tudor and Stuart England: Achieving a Joined-up Realm* (Liverpool, 2014).

Brears, P., *All the King's Cooks: The Tudor Kitchens of King Henry VIII at Hampton Court Palace* (London, 1999).

Brears, P., Black, M., Corbishley, G., Renfrew, J. and Stead, J., *A Taste of History: 10,000 Years of Food in Britain* (London, 1993).

Brewer, C., *The Death of Kings: A Medical History of the Kings and Queens of England* (London, 2004).

Brooke, X. and Crombie, D., *Henry VIII Revealed: Holbein's Portrait and its Legacy* (London, 2003).

Bruce, M.L., *Anne Boleyn* (London, 1972).

Burton, E., *The Elizabethans at Home* (London, 1970).

Burton, E., *The Early Tudors at Home* (London, 1976).

Camden, C., *The Elizabethan Woman* (New York, 1975).

Carleton Williams, C., *Bess of Hardwick* (Bath, 1959).

Cawthorne, N., *Sex Lives of the Kings and Queens of England* (London, 2012).

Chalmers, C.R. and Chaloner, E.J., '500 Years Later: Henry VIII, Leg Ulcers and the Course of History', *Journal of the Society of Medicine*, Vol. 102 (2009), pp. 513–17.

Chamberlain, F., *The Private Character of Queen Elizabeth* (London, 1921).

Chapman, H.W., *Two Tudor Portraits: Henry Howard, Earl of Surrey and Lady Katherine Grey* (London, 1960).

Chapman, H.W., *Anne Boleyn* (London, 1974).

Cooper, T., *Elizabeth I and Her People* (London, 2013).

Classen, C., Howes, D. and Synnott, A., *Aroma: The Cultural History of Smell* (London and New York, 1994).

Cockayne, G.E. (ed.), *The Complete Peerage of England, Scotland, Ireland, Great Britain and the United Kingdom*, 12 vols (London, 1910–59).

Cowen Orlin, L., *Locating Privacy in Tudor London* (Oxford, 2007).

Crawford, P., *Blood, Bodies and Families in Early Modern England* (Harlow, 2004).

Cressy, D., *Birth, Marriage and Death: Ritual, Religion, and the Life-Cycle in Tudor and Stuart England* (Oxford, 1997).

Cruickshanks, E. (ed.), *The Stuart Courts* (Stroud, 2000).

Davey, R., *The Sisters of Lady Jane Grey and their Wicked Grandfather* (London, 1911).

Delaney, J., Lupton, M.J. and Toth, E., *The Curse: A Cultural History of Menstruation* (Illinois, 1988).

Denny, J., *Katherine Howard: A Tudor Conspiracy* (London, 2005).

Doran, S., *Elizabeth: The Exhibition at the National Maritime Museum* (London, 2003).

Doran, S., *The Tudor Chronicles* (London, 2008).

Dovey, Z., *An Elizabethan Progress: The Queen's Journey into East Anglia, 1578* (Sutton, 1999).

Duby, G. (ed.), *A History of Private Life – Volume II: Revelations of the Medieval World* (Harvard, 1988).

Dunlop, I., *Palaces and Progresses of Elizabeth I* (London, 1962).

Dunn, J., *Elizabeth and Mary: Cousins, Rivals, Queens* (New York, 2004).

Dutton, R., *English Court Life: From Henry VII to George II* (London, 1963).

Eccles, A., *Obstetrics and Gynaecology in Tudor and Stuart England* (London, 1982).

Elias, N., *The History of Manners* (Oxford, 1983).

Erickson, C., *Great Harry* (London, 1980).

Erickson, C., *Mistress Anne* (New York, 1984).

Erickson, C., *The First Elizabeth* (London, 1999).

Erickson, C., *Bloody Mary* (London, 2001).

Fraser, A., *Mary, Queen of Scots* (London, 1994).

Fraser, A., *The Six Wives of Henry VIII* (London, 1996).

Friedmann, P., *Anne Boleyn: A Chapter of English History*, 2 vols (London, 1884).

Frye, S., *Elizabeth I: The Competition for Representation* (New York and Oxford University Press, 1993).

Frye, S., *Maids and Mistresses, Cousins and Queens: Women's Alliances in Early Modern England* (New York and Oxford University Press, 1999).

Gairdner, J., 'Mary and Anne Boleyn', *English Historical Review*, Vol. 8 (London, 1893).

Gent, L. and Llewellyn, N. (eds), *Renaissance Bodies: The Human Figure in English Culture c.1540–1660* (London, 1990).

Glasheen, J., *The Secret People of the Palaces: The Royal Household from the Plantagenets to Queen Victoria* (London, 1998).

Goodman, R., *How to be a Tudor: A Dawn-to-Dusk Guide to Everyday Life* (London, 2015).

Graves, J., *A Brief Memoir of the Lady Elizabeth Fitzgerald, Known as the Fair Geraldine* (Dublin, 1874).

Gristwood, S., *Arbella* (London, 2003).

Gristwood, S., *Elizabeth & Leicester* (London, 2007).

Groom, S., *At the King's Table: Royal Dining Through the Ages* (London, 2013).

Groom, S., Dolman, B., Fitch, R. and Meltonville, M., *The Taste of the Fire: The Story of the Tudor Kitchens at Hampton Court Palace* (Historic Royal Palaces, 2007).

Gross, P.M., *Jane the Quene, Third Consort of King Henry VIII* (Lewiston, Queenston and Lampeter, 1999).

Guy, J., *'My Heart is My Own': The Life of Mary, Queen of Scots* (London, 2004).

Guy, J.A., *Tudor England* (Oxford, 1988).

Haigh, C. (ed.), *Elizabeth I* (London and New York, 1988).

Haynes, A., *Sex in Elizabethan England* (Stroud, 1997).

Hayward, M., *Dress at the Court of Henry VIII* (Leeds, 2007).

Hayward, M. and Ward, P. (eds), *The Inventory of King Henry VIII: Textiles and Dress*, Vol. II (London, 2012).

Heisch, A., 'Elizabeth I and the Persistence of Patriarchy', *Feminist Review*, Part IV (London, 1980).

Herman, E., *Sex with Kings* (New York, 2004).

Hibbert, C., *Elizabeth I: A Personal History of the Virgin Queen* (London, 1992).

Holles, G., *Memorials of the Holles Family, 1493–1656* Camden Society, 3rd series, Vol. IV (London, 1937).

Hopkins, L., *Queen Elizabeth I and her Court* (London and New York, 1990).

Howe, B., *A Galaxy of Governesses* (London, 1954).

Hume, M., *The Courtships of Queen Elizabeth: A History of the Various Negotiations for her Marriage* (London, 1904).

Hume, M., *Two English Queens and Philip* (London, 1908).

Hurren, T.E., 'Cultures of the Body, Medical Regimen, and Physic at the Tudor Court', in Betteridge, T. and Lipscomb, S. (eds), *Henry VIII and the Court: Art, Politics and Performance* (Farnham, 2013), pp. 65–89.

Hurren, E., 'King Henry VIII's Medical World' (unpublished article for Historic Royal Palaces, 2009).

Hurstfield, J., *The Queen's Wards: Wardship and Marriage under Elizabeth I* (London, 1958).

Hutchinson, R., *Young Henry: The Rise of Henry VIII* (London, 2011).

Ives, E., *Anne Boleyn* (Oxford, 1986).

Ives, E., *The Life and Death of Anne Boleyn: 'The Most Happy'* (Oxford, 2004).

Ives, E., *Lady Jane Grey: A Tudor Mystery* (Chichester, 2009).

James, S.E., *Catherine Parr: Henry VIII's Last Love* (Stroud, 2008).

Jenkins, E., *Elizabeth the Great* (London, 1965).

Johnson, L., 'All the King's Fools: Mirth & Medicine' (unpublished research for Historic Royal Palaces, September 2011).

Johnson, P., *Elizabeth I: A Study in Power and Intellect* (London, 1974).

Kenny, R.W., *Elizabeth's Admiral: The Political Career of Charles Howard, Earl of Nottingham, 1536–1624* (Baltimore and London, 1990).

Lever, T., *The Herberts of Wilton* (London, 1967).

Levin, C., *The Heart and Stomach of a King: Elizabeth I and the Politics of Sex and Power* (Philadelphia, 1994).

Levin, C. and Watson, J., *Ambiguous Realities: Women in the Middle Ages and Renaissance* (Detroit, 1987).

Levine, M., *The Early Elizabethan Succession Question* (California, 1966).

Licence, A., *In Bed with the Tudors: The Sex Lives of a Dynasty from Elizabeth of York to Elizabeth I* (Stroud, 2013).

Licence, A., *The Six Wives and Many Mistresses of Henry VIII: The Women's Stories* (Stroud, 2015).

Lipscomb, S., 'All the King's Fools', in *History Today*, Vol. 61, issue 8 (August 2011).

Lloyd Williams, N., *Tudor London Visited* (London, 1991).

Loades, D., *The Tudor Court* (London, 1986).

Loades, D., *Mary Tudor: A Life* (Oxford, 1989).

Loades, D., *Henry VIII and His Queens* (Sutton, 2000).

Loades, D., *Intrigue and Treason: The Tudor Court 1547–1558* (Harlow, 2004).

Loades, D., *Henry VIII* (Stroud, 2011).

Longford, E. (ed.), *The Oxford Book of Royal Anecdotes* (Oxford, 1989).

Lovell, M.S., *Bess of Hardwick: First Lady of Chatsworth, 1527–1608* (London, 2005).

Lynn, E., *Tudor Fashion: Dress at Court 1485–1603* (to be published by Yale University Press in 2017).

Mackay, L., *Inside the Tudor Court: Henry VIII and his Six Wives through the Eyes of the Spanish Ambassador* (Stroud, 2014).

Mackie, J.D., *The Later Tudors* (London, 1952).

Madden, F., *Privy Purse Expenses of the Princess Mary* (London, 1831).

Marshall, R.K., *Queen Mary's Women: Female Relatives, Servants, Friends and Enemies of Mary, Queen of Scots* (Edinburgh, 2006).

Martienssen, A., *Queen Katherine Parr* (London, 1975).

McCaffrey, W.T., *Elizabeth I* (London, 1993).

Medvei, V.C., 'The Illness and Death of Mary Tudor', *Journal of the Royal Society of Medicine*, Vol. 80, no. 12 (December 1987).

Merton, C., 'The Women who Served Queen Mary and Queen Elizabeth: Ladies, Gentlewomen and Maids of the Privy Chamber, 1553–1603' (Cambridge PhD thesis, 1992).

Meyer, G.J., *The Tudors: The Complete Story of England's Most Notorious Dynasty* (New York, 2010).

Montagu, W., *Court and Society from Elizabeth to Anne*, 2 vols (London, 1864).

Mortimer, I., *The Time Traveller's Guide to Elizabethan England* (London, 2012).

Murphy, J., 'The Illusion of Decline: The Privy Chamber, 1547–1558', in Starkey, D. (ed.), *The English Court: From the Wars of the Roses to the Civil War* (Longman, 1987).

Neale, J.E., 'The Sayings of Queen Elizabeth', *History*, Vol. X (October, 1925).

Neale, J.E., *Queen Elizabeth I* (London, 1998).

Norton, E., *Anne of Cleves: Henry VIII's Discarded Bride* (Stroud, 2009).

Norton, E., *Jane Seymour: Henry VIII's True Love* (Stroud, 2009).

Notestein, W., 'The English Woman, 1580–1650', in Plumb, J.H. (ed.), *Studies in Social History: A Tribute to G.M. Trevelyan* (London, 1958).

Pasmore, S., *The Life and Times of Queen Elizabeth I at Richmond Palace* (Richmond Local History Society, 2003).

Pelling, M., 'Appearance and Reality: Barber-Surgeons, the Body, and Disease in Early Modern London', in Beier, L. and Finlay, R. (eds), *London 1500–1700: The Making of the Metropolis* (London and New York, 1986), pp. 82–112.

Percival, R. and A., *The Court of Elizabeth the First* (London, 1976).

Plowden, A., *Marriage with My Kingdom: The Courtships of Elizabeth I* (London, 1977).

Plowden, A., *Two Queens in One Isle: The Deadly Relationship between Elizabeth I and Mary, Queen of Scots* (Sutton, 1999).

Plowden, A., *Tudor Women: Queens and Commoners* (Sutton, 2002).

Porter, L., *Mary Tudor: The First Queen* (London, 2007).

Prescott, H.F.M., *Mary Tudor* (London, 1952).

Redworth, G., 'Matters Impertinent to Women: Male and Female Monarchy under Philip and Mary', *English Historical Review*, Vol. 40, no. 4 (December 1997).

Rex, R.A.W., *The Tudors* (Stroud, 2002).

Reynolds, A., *In Fine Style: The Art of Tudor and Stuart Fashion* (Royal Collection Trust, 2013).

Richards, J.M., '"To Promote a Woman to Beare Rule": Talking of Queens in Mid-Tudor England', *Sixteenth Century Journal*, Vol. 28, no. 1 (1997).

Richards, J.M., 'Love and a Female Monarch: The Case of Elizabeth Tudor', *Journal of British Studies*, Vol. 38 (April 1999).

Richardson, A., *Famous Ladies of the English Court* (London, 1899).

Richardson, R.E., *Mistress Blanche: Queen Elizabeth I's Confidante* (Herefordshire, 2007).

Ridley, J., *Elizabeth I: The Shrewdness of Virtue* (New York, 1987).

Ridley, J.G., *Henry VIII* (London, 1984).

Rowse, A.L., 'The Coronation of Queen Elizabeth I', *History Today*, Vol. 3 (May 1953).

Rowse, A.L., *The England of Elizabeth* (MacMillan, 1953).

Russell, J.G., *The Field of the Cloth of Gold: Men and Manners in 1520* (London, 1969).

Scarisbrick, J.J., *Henry VIII* (London, 1968).

Seymour, W., *Ordeal by Ambition: An English Family in the Shadow of the Tudors* (London, 1972).

Sim, A., *Food & Feast in Tudor England* (Stroud, 2005).

Sim, A., *Pleasures & Pastimes in Tudor England* (Stroud, 2009).

Sitwell, E., *The Queens and the Hive* (London, 1991).

Skidmore, C., *Edward VI: The Lost King of England* (London, 2007).

Skidmore, C., *Death and the Virgin: Elizabeth, Dudley and the Mysterious Fate of Amy Robsart* (London, 2010).

Skidmore, C., *The Rise of the Tudors: The Family That Changed English History* (New York, 2013).

Smith, V., *Clean: A History of Personal Hygiene and Purity* (Oxford, 2007).

Smither, L.J., 'Elizabeth I: A Psychological Profile', *Sixteenth Century Journal*, Vol. XV (London, 1984).

Somerset, A., *Ladies-in-Waiting: From the Tudors to the Present Day* (London, 1984).

Somerset, A., *Elizabeth I* (London, 1991).

Souden, D., *The Royal Palaces of London* (London, 2008).

Souden, D. and Worsley, L., *The Story of Hampton Court Palace* (London, 2015).

Southworth, J., *Fools and Jesters at the English Court* (Stroud, 2003).

Starkey, D., 'Representation through Intimacy: A Study in the Symbolism of Monarchy and Court Office in Early Modern England', in Lewis, I. (ed.), *Symbols and Sentiments, Cross-Cultural Studies in Symbolism* (London, 1977), pp. 187–224.

Starkey, D., 'Intimacy and Innovation: The Rise of the Privy Chamber, 1485–1547', in Starkey, D., et al. (eds), *The English Court from the Wars of the Roses to the Civil War* (London, 1987).

Starkey, D., *Elizabeth: Apprenticeship* (London, 2001).

Starkey, D., *The Reign of Henry VIII: Personalities and Politics* (London, 2002).

Starkey, D., *Six Wives: The Queens of Henry VIII* (London, 2003).

Starkey, D., et al. (eds), *The English Court: From the Wars of the Roses to the Civil War* (London and New York, 1987).

Stewart, A., *The Cradle King: A Life of James VI & I* (London, 2003).

Stone, L., *The Family, Sex and Marriage in England, 1500–1800* (London, 1977).

Strickland, A., *Lives of the Queens of England*, Vols II and III (London, 1851).

Strickland, A., *The Life of Queen Elizabeth* (London, 1910).

Stride, P. and Lopes Floro, K., 'Henry VIII, McLeod Syndrome and Jacquetta's Curse', Royal College of Physicians (Edinburgh, 2013).

Strong, R., *Tudor and Jacobean Portraits*, 2 vols (London, 1969).

Strong, R., *The Cult of Elizabeth: Elizabethan Portraiture and Pageantry* (London, 1977).

Strong, R., *Gloriana: The Portraits of Queen Elizabeth I* (London, 1987).

Thirsk, J., *Food in Early Modern England* (London, 2007).

Thurley, S., *The Royal Palaces of Tudor England: Architecture and Court Life 1460–1547* (New Haven and London, 1993).

Thurley, S., *Whitehall Palace: An Architectural History of the Royal Apartments, 1240–1698* (New Haven and London, 1999).

Thurley, S., *Hampton Court: A Social and Architectural History* (New Haven and London, 2003).

Tremlett, G., *Catherine of Aragon: Henry's Spanish Queen* (London, 2010).

Warnicke, R.M., *The Rise and Fall of Anne Boleyn* (Cambridge University Press, 1991).

Warnicke, R.M., *The Marrying of Anne of Cleves: Royal Protocol in Early Modern England* (Cambridge University Press, 2000).

Watkins, S., *In Public and Private: Elizabeth I and her World* (London, 1998).

Watkinson, J.F., 'The Painted Lips of Queen Elizabeth I', unpublished MA thesis, University of Bristol (September 2015).

Waugh, M.A., 'Venereal Disease in Sixteenth Century England', *Medical History*, Vol. 17 (Cambridge, 1973).

Weir, A., *The Six Wives of Henry VIII* (London, 1991).

Weir, A., *Children of England: The Heirs of King Henry VIII, 1547–1558* (London, 1996).

Weir, A., *The Life of Elizabeth* (New York, 1998).

Weir, A., *Henry VIII: King and Court* (London, 2001).

Weir, A., *Mary, Queen of Scots and the Murder of Lord Darnley* (London, 2003).

Weir, A., *Mary Boleyn: 'The Great and Infamous Whore'* (London, 2011).

Weir, A., *Elizabeth of York: The First Tudor Queen* (London, 2013).

Wiesener, L., *The Youth of Queen Elizabeth, 1533–1558*, 2 vols (London, 1879).

Wilkinson, J., *The Early Loves of Anne Boleyn* (Stroud, 2009).

Williams, C. (ed. and trans.), *Thomas Platter's Travels in England, 1599* (London, 1937).

Williams, N., *Powder and Paint: A History of the Englishwoman's Toilet, Elizabeth I– Elizabeth II* (London, 1957).

Williams, N., *Henry VIII and his Court* (London, 1971).

Williams, N., *Elizabeth, Queen of England* (London, 1984).

Williams, P.I., *The Later Tudors: England 1547–1603* (Oxford, 1995).

Williamson, G.C., *Lady Anne Clifford, Countess of Dorset, Pembroke & Montgomery, 1590–1676: Her life, Letters and Work* (Wakefield, 1967).

Wilson, D., *Sweet Robin: A Biography of Robert Dudley, Earl of Leicester, 1533–1588* (London, 1981).

Wilson, D., *In the Lion's Court: Power, Ambition and Sudden Death in the Reign of Henry VIII* (London, 2002).

Wilson, V.A., *Queen Elizabeth's Maids of Honour and Ladies of the Privy Chamber* (London, 1922).

Wilson, V.A., *Society Women of Shakespeare's Time* (London, 1924).

Wright, L., *Clean and Decent: The History of the Bath and Loo, and of Sundry Habits, Fashions and Accessories of the Toilet principally in Great Britain, France and America* (London, 1980).

Wright, P., 'A Change in Direction: The Ramifications of a Female Household, 1558–1603', Starkey, D. (ed.), *The English Court: From the Wars of the Roses to the Civil War* (Longman, 1987).

NOTES

PREFACE

1. Williams, C. (ed. and trans.), *Thomas Platter's Travels in England, 1599* (London, 1937), p. 192.
2. Camden, W., *The Historie of the Most Renowned and Victorious Princesse Elizabeth, late Queene of England* (London, 1630), p. 172.

INTRODUCTION 'THE PUBLIC SELF AND THE PRIVATE'

1. Pryor, F., *Elizabeth I: Her Life in Letters* (Los Angeles, 2003).

CHAPTER 1 'INFINITELY SUSPICIOUS'

1. Penn, T., *Winter King: The Dawn of Tudor England* (London, 2011), p. 11.
2. Bacon, F., *The Historie of the Raigne of King Henry The Seventh* (1622).
3. Williams, C.H. (ed.), *English Historical Documents*, Vol. V: *1485–1558* (London, 1967), p. 387.
4. Penn, *Winter King*, p. 7.
5. Williams (ed.), *English Historical Documents*, Vol. V, p. 387.
6. Castiglione, B., *The Book of the Courtier*, trans. Bull G. (Harmondsworth, 1976), p. 63.
7. Falkus, C. (ed.), *The Private Lives of the Tudor Monarchs* (London, 1974), pp. 14–17.
8. Williams, N., *Henry VIII and His Court* (London, 1971), p. 16.
9. The household accounts for December 1487, for example, record that the king's four footmen each received a gown of crimson lined with black fur, a doublet of black velvet, a jacket of crimson velvet, and a red bonnet. Lynn, *Tudor Fashion*.
10. Myers, A.R. (ed.), *The Household of Edward IV: The Black Book and the Ordinance of 1478* (Manchester, 1959), p. 117.
11. Lynn, *Tudor Fashion*.

12. Fortescue, J., *The Governance of England*, ed. C. Plummer (Oxford, 1885), p. 125.

13. Letts, M. (ed.), 'The Travels of Leo of Rozmital', *Hakluyt Society*, 2nd series, Vol. CVIII (1957), p. 45.

14. Thomas, A.H. and Thornley, I.D., *The Great Chronicle of London* (London, 1938), p. 215; Fortescue, *Governance of England*, pp. 352–3.

15. Lynn, *Tudor Fashion*.

16. Sneyd, C.A. (ed.), *A Relation, or Rather a True Account of the Island of England . . . about the year 1500* (Camden Society, 1847), p. 46.

17. Lynn, *Tudor Fashion*.

18. Henry VII's average expenditure through his reign was around £1,899 every two years – almost £1 million in today's money. Lynn, *Tudor Fashion*.

19. Lynn, *Tudor Fashion*.

20. Lynn, *Tudor Fashion*.

21. The building and its contents were destroyed in the Great Fire of London in 1666, and its functions were absorbed by various other departments of the royal household.

22. *Calendar of the Patent Rolls 1485–94* (HMSO, London, 1914), p. 26. See also McSheffrey, S., *A Remarrying Widow: Law and Legal Records in Late Medieval London* (Concordia University, 2011). Curteys held the post until 1493, when he was succeeded by Sir Robert Lytton. Upon the latter's death in 1505, Andrew Windsor inherited the position.

23. *CSPV*, Vol. I, *1202–1509*, p. 298.

24. More, T., *A Rueful Lamentation* (1503).

25. *CSPV*, Vol. I, *1202–1509*, pp. 141–59.

26. Hays, D. (ed. and trans.), *The Anglica historia of Polydore Vergil, A.D. 1485–1537* (London, 1950), p. 559.

27. Weir, A., *Elizabeth of York: The First Tudor Queen* (London, 2013), p. 167.

28. *CSPV*, Vol. I, *1202–1509*, p. 158.

29. Weir, *Elizabeth of York*, p. 178.

30. The papal dispensation was granted in March, and Pope Innocent VIII formally validated his legate's authorisation in July.

31. Licence, A., *In Bed with the Tudors: The Sex Lives of a Dynasty from Elizabeth of York to Elizabeth I* (Stroud, 2013), p. 103.

32. Apricots would not have been served at Henry VII's wedding feast, however, because they did not arrive in England until the 1520s.

33. Hall, *Chronicle*, p. 425.

34. Souden, D., *The Royal Palaces of London* (London, 2008), p. 27.

35. Williams (ed. and trans.), *Thomas Platter's Travels*, p. 202.

36. The discovery of Henry and Elizabeth's bed is one of the most significant finds of modern times. In 2010, a historic bed expert and restorer saw the ornately carved bed on an auctioneer's website. It had been discovered in Chester, where it lay dismantled outside a hotel that was being renovated. Research by historians, supported by DNA analysis, has made a convincing case that it was commissioned by Henry's stepfather, Thomas Stanley, first Earl of Derby, for a visit by the royal couple to his seat of Lathom House in Cheshire and the hunting lodge of Knowsley.

37. Weir, *Elizabeth of York*, p. 186.

38. Penn, *Winter King*, p. 21.

39. *CSPV*, Vol. I, 1202–1509, p. 158.

40. Bacon, *Historie of the Raigne of King Henry The Seventh*.

41. Culpeper, N., *The Compleat Midwives Practice* (London, 1658), p. 67; Riverius, L., *The Practice of Physick* (London, 1655), p. 503. See also, Crawford, P., *Blood, Bodies and Families in Early Modern England* (Harlow, 2004), p. 59.

42. *CSPS, Mary I 1554–8*, Vol. XIII, p. 166.

43. Lynn, *Tudor Fashion*.

44. *A Collection of Ordinances and Regulations for the Government of the Royal Household* (London, 1790), pp. 125–6.

45. Weir, A., *Henry VIII: King and Court* (London, 2001), p. 137; *Collection of Ordinances and Regulations*, pp. 125–6.

46. *Collection of Ordinances and Regulations*, pp. 125–6.

47. Hall, *Chronicle*.

48. Licence, *In Bed with the Tudors*, p. 103.

49. Williams (ed.), *English Historical Documents*, Vol. V, p. 1046.

CHAPTER 2 'NOT ADMITTING ANY NEAR APPROACH'

1. Some historians place it as early as 1487 or 1488, while others argue that it was between 1499 and 1502.

2. Licence, *In Bed with the Tudors*, p. 138.

3. See Nicolas, N.H. (ed.), *Privy Purse Expenses of Elizabeth of York; Wardrobe Accounts of Edward the Fourth: With a Memoir of Elizabeth of York, and Noted* (London, 1830).

4. Weir, *Elizabeth of York*, pp. 213, 267.

5. Penn, *Winter King*, p. 101.

6. Penn, *Winter King*, p. 98.

7. *CSPS*, Vol. I, no. 205; Jones, M.K. and Underwood, M.G., *The King's Mother:*

Lady Margaret Beaufort, Countess of Richmond and Derby (Cambridge, 1992), pp. 67–70, 73–4.

8. Penn, *Winter King*, p. 101.
9. Falkus (ed.), *Private Lives*, p. 16.
10. Lynn, *Tudor Fashion*.
11. Starkey, D., 'Intimacy and Innovation: The Rise of the Privy Chamber, 1485–1547', in Starkey, D., et al. (eds), *The English Court from the Wars of the Roses to the Civil War* (London, 1987), p. 76.
12. Weir, *Henry VIII*, pp. 40–1.
13. Starkey, D., 'Representation through Intimacy. A study in the symbolism of monarchy and court office in early modern England', in Lewis, I. (ed.), *Symbols and Sentiments, Cross-Cultural Studies in Symbolism* (London, 1977), p. 203.
14. Starkey, D., 'Intimacy and Innovation: The Rise of the Privy Chamber, 1485–1547', in Starkey, et al. (eds), *English Court*, p. 74.
15. Starkey, 'Representation through Intimacy', p. 204.
16. Hales, J.W. and Furnival, F.J., *Bishop Percy's Folio Manuscript: Ballads and Romances* (London, 1868), p. 179.
17. Starkey, 'Representation through Intimacy', p. 212.
18. *CSPV*, Vol. I, *1202–1509*, pp. 263–4.
19. *CSPS*, Vol. I, no. 210.
20. Edwards, A.S.G., *Skelton: The Critical Heritage* (1981), p. 44.
21. Skelton, J., *Speculum Principis*, reproduced in Salter, F.M. (ed.), *Speculum*, Vol. IX, no. 1 (January 1934), pp. 25–37.
22. Penn, *Winter King*, p. 109.
23. Penn, *Winter King*, p. 110.
24. Falkus (ed.), *Private Lives*, pp. 11–12.
25. Brewer, C., *The Death of Kings: A Medical History of the Kings and Queens of England* (London, 2004).
26. Falkus (ed.), *Private Lives*, pp. 11–12.
27. Licence, *In Bed with the Tudors*, p. 52.
28. Licence, *In Bed with the Tudors*, p. 52.
29. Thurley, S., *The Royal Palaces of Tudor England* (New Haven and London, 1993), p. 140.
30. Hall, p. 494.
31. Weir, *Elizabeth of York*, p. 374.
32. Penn, *Winter King*, p. 64.
33. *LP Henry VIII*, Vol. IV, Part iii, no. 5773.
34. Penn, *Winter King*, p. 64.

35. Penn, *Winter King*, pp. 66–7.
36. Licence, *In Bed with the Tudors*, p. 54.
37. Falkus (ed.), *Private Lives*, pp. 12–13.

CHAPTER 3 'CLOSETED AWAY LIKE A GIRL'

1. Penn, *Winter King*, p. 96.
2. More, T., *A Rueful Lamentation* (London, 1503).
3. Falkus (ed.), *Private Lives*, p. 19.
4. Penn, *Winter King*, p. 141.
5. *The Union of the Red Rose and the White By a Marriage Between King Henry VII and a Daughter of King Edward IV* (Huntingdon Library, University of California).
6. Penn, *Winter King*, p. 113.
7. *CSPV*, Vol. I, 1202–1509, p. 306.
8. Williams, (ed.), *English Historical Documents*, Vol. V, p. 387.
9. The wranglings over the dowry were still going on in July 1506, when Henry instructed his ambassador to Spain to demand the payment of the portion that was still due or he 'would send the Princess home'. *CSPV*, Vol. I, 1202–1509, p. 324.
10. *CSPV*, Vol. I, 1202–1509, p. 303.
11. Becket, T. and De Hondt, P.A., *Instructions Given by King Henry the Seventh, to His Embassadors, When He intended to Marry the Young Queen of Naples: Together with the Answers of the Embassadors* (London, 1761).
12. *CSPV*, Vol. I, 1202–1509, pp. 303, 309.
13. Brewer, *The Death of Kings*, p. 110.
14. Licence, *In Bed with the Tudors*, p. 65.
15. Penn, *Winter King*, pp. 178–9.
16. Penn, *Winter King*, p. 179.
17. *CSPS*, Vol. I, no. 398.
18. *CSPS*, Vol. I, no. 552.
19. Penn, *Winter King*, p. 321.
20. Weir, *Henry VIII*, p. 98.
21. Penn, *Winter King*, p. 309.
22. *CSPS*, Vol. I, nos. 551, 553; *CSPS* supplement to Vols I and II, no. 23.
23. Penn, *Winter King*, pp. 311, 317.
24. Penn, *Winter King*, p. 298.
25. Penn, *Winter King*, p. 319.
26. Penn, *Winter King*, p. 317.

27. Penn, *Winter King*, pp. 349–50.
28. Norton, E., *The Anne Boleyn Papers* (Stroud, 2013), pp. 105–6.
29. Brewer, *The Death of Kings*, p. 111.
30. *CSPS* supplement to Vols I and II, no. 4.
31. Williams (ed. and trans.), *Thomas Platter's Travels*, p. 202.
32. Penn, *Winter King*, p. 342.

CHAPTER 4 'THEIR BUSINESS IS IN MANY SECRETS'

1. Weir, *Henry VIII*, pp. 1–2, 19.
2. These measurements were taken from Henry's armour of 1515, which survives in the collection of the Royal Armouries. The waist was actually thirty-five inches, but about four inches should be deducted to allow for the layers of padding and dress between metal and skin. Lynn, *Tudor Fashion*.
3. Weir, *Henry VIII*, p. 2; Williams (ed.), *English Historical Documents*, Vol. V, pp. 388–91.
4. Williams (ed.), *English Historical Documents*, Vol. V, p. 389; Weir, *Henry VIII*, p. 3.
5. Falkus (ed.), *Private Lives*, p. 20.
6. Licence, *In Bed with the Tudors*, p. 76.
7. It must have been satisfying for Compton when, in 1521, he received orders to arrest the Duke of Buckingham. Although there is no evidence, beyond gossip, that Compton and Anne were guilty of adultery, in 1523 Henry's groom took the unusual step of bequeathing land to her in his will. He also directed his executors to include Anne in the prayers for his kin.
8. Licence, *In Bed with the Tudors*, p. 76.
9. Weir, *Henry VIII*, p. 140.
10. Vaughan, W., *Natural and Artificial Directions for Health* (London, 1600), p. 47; Licence, *In Bed with the Tudors*, pp. 111–12.
11. Vicary, T., *A Profitable Treatise of the Anatomie of Mans Bodie* (London, 1577).
12. Reynolds, A., *In Fine Style: The Art of Tudor and Stuart Fashion* (Royal Collection Trust, 2013), p. 123.
13. *LP Henry VIII*, Vol. II, no. 4568.
14. Although she was no longer his mistress, the king made sure that Bessie would live out her days in comfort. A statute was passed granting her property worth £200 a year for life out of her husband's lands. Even as late as 1532, the king gave her a lavish New Year's gift of a gilt goblet with a cover

weighing over thirty-five ounces. Bessie and Gilbert had an apparently settled married life. She bore him three children, Elizabeth, George and Robert. After Gilbert's death in 1530, Bessie married Edward, 9th Baron Clinton, and bore him three children too. She briefly returned to court during Henry's short-lived marriage to Anne of Cleves, but died later that year.

15. Souden, *Royal Palaces of London*, p. 139.
16. Williams, *Henry VIII and His Court*, p. 20.
17. Hayward, M. and Ward, P. (eds), *The Inventory of King Henry VIII: Textiles and Dress*, Vol. II (London, 2012), p. 4.
18. A detailed analysis of Henry's tapestry collection is provided by Thomas Campbell in Hayward and Ward (eds.), *The Inventory of King Henry VIII*, Vol. II, pp. 9–65.
19. Hayward and Ward (eds), *The Inventory of King Henry VIII*, Vol. II, p. 341.
20. Thurley, S., *Whitehall Palace: An Architectural History of the Royal Apartments, 1240–1698* (New Haven and London, 1999), p. 65.
21. Weir, *Henry VIII*, p. 51.
22. *LP Henry VIII*, Vol. I, Part I, nos. 474, 734.
23. Starkey, 'Representation through Intimacy', p. 212.
24. Weir, *Henry VIII*, p. 96.
25. Weir, *Henry VIII*, p. 97.
26. Weir, *Henry VIII*, p. 97.
27. Weir, *Henry VIII*, pp. 99–100.
28. *Collection of Ordinances and Regulations*, pp. 154–9.
29. *Collection of Ordinances and Regulations*, pp. 154–9.

CHAPTER 5 'LAY HANDS UPON HIS ROYAL PERSON'

1. *LP Henry VIII*, Vol. III, Part i, p. 350.
2. Weir, *Henry VIII*, p. 107.
3. Weir, *Henry VIII*, p. 54.
4. 'Ordinances for the Household made at Eltham in the XVII year of King Henry VIII in 1526', in *Collection of Ordinances and Regulations*, p. 156.
5. Arnold, J., *Queen Elizabeth's Wardrobe Unlock'd* (Leeds, 1988), p. 22.
6. 'Ordinances for the Household made at Eltham in the XVII year of King Henry VIII in 1526', in *Collection of Ordinances and Regulations*, pp. 155–6.
7. *CSPV*, Vol. II, *1509–1519*, pp. 556–65; Castiglione, *Book of the Courtier*, p. 125. See also: Lynn, *Tudor Fashion*.
8. Lynn, *Tudor Fashion*. Although Henry had been quick to replace his father's tailor, he was content to retain his embroiderer, William More, who

continued in this post until 1518, when he was succeeded by two more Williams: Mortimer and Ibgrave. Hilton, meanwhile, evidently impressed his royal master because he remained in this post until his death in the late 1520s. He was followed by John Malte, who also served until his death in 1545, and then by John Bridges who dressed the king for the last two years of his reign and was tailor to all three of his successors.

9. See for example: Alcega, J. De, *Libro de Geometria practica y traca* (Book of Geometry, Practice and Patterns) (1580).

10. Hayward, M., *Dress at the Court of Henry VIII* (Leeds, 2007), p. 345.

11. Hayward and Ward (eds), *The Inventory of King Henry VIII*, Vol. II, p. 81.

12. *CSPV*, Vol. II, *1509–1519*, pp. 556–65; Castiglione, *Book of the Courtier*, p. 125. See also: Lynn, *Tudor Fashion*.

13. The hat was acquired by Historic Royal Palaces thanks to the vision and assiduity of the curator of its Royal Ceremonial Dress Collection, Eleri Lynn. I am greatly indebted to Eleri for giving me permission to tell its story in this book. She tells it herself – more extensively – in her own book, *Tudor Fashion: Dress at Court 1485–1603*.

14. 'Ordinances for the Household made at Eltham in the XVII year of King Henry VIII in 1526', in *Collection of Ordinances and Regulations*, pp. 157–8.

15. Lynn, *Tudor Fashion*.

16. Johnson, L., 'All the King's Fools: Mirth & Medicine' (unpublished research for Historic Royal Palaces, September 2011).

17. This had significantly enhanced the status and prestige of the surgical profession, and encouraged new advances by fostering greater consultation between its members.

18. I am indebted to Dr Tim Cutler, Honorary Curator of the Physic Garden at the Worshipful Company of Barbers, for generously sharing his knowledge and expertise on the herbal remedies employed by the Tudors.

19. Borde, A., *The Fyrst Boke of the Introduction of Knowledge* (1542).

20. I am indebted to Marc Meltonville, an expert on historic food and a member of the Historic Kitchens Team at Hampton Court Palace, for sharing his knowledge on the subject.

21. Forks had been introduced from Italy during Henry's reign, but until the reign of Elizabeth they were used mainly for serving rather than eating.

22. Hayward and Ward (eds), *The Inventory of King Henry VIII*, Vol. II, p. 205.

23. Hayward and Ward (eds), *The Inventory of King Henry VIII*, Vol. II, p. 204.

24. Lynn, *Tudor Fashion*.

25. Sim, A., *Food & Feast in Tudor England* (Stroud, 2005), p. 32; Weir, *Henry VIII*, p. 60.

26. An important reason for the predominance of men in the royal kitchens is that they were more costly to employ. It therefore enhanced the status of the royal household. This was replicated in grand households throughout the kingdom.

27. 'Ordinances for the Household made at Eltham in the XVII year of King Henry VIII in 1526', in *Collection of Ordinances and Regulations*, p. 158; Brears, P., *All the King's Cooks: The Tudor Kitchens of King Henry VIII at Hampton Court Palace* (London, 1999), p. 142.

28. Sim, *Food & Feast in Tudor England*.

29. Pottage was a cross between porridge and stew. It consisted of vegetables and occasionally meat, with oats or barley to thicken it. Although pottage was the staple diet of the lower classes, it was also served at court and could be enhanced with almonds, spices and wine.

30. Although this time was quite consistent at court, with its brightly (and expensively) lit rooms, for ordinary people supper times would vary according to the time of year so that it could be eaten in daylight. In August it would be a short early evening break so as not to interrupt the harvest.

31. Hurren, T.E., 'Cultures of the Body, Medical Regimen, and Physic at the Tudor Court', in Betteridge, T. and Lipscomb, S. (eds), *Henry VIII and the Court: Art, Politics and Performance* (Farnham, 2013), p. 67.

32. Sim, *Food and Feast in Tudor England*, pp. 121–2.

33. Markham, G., *The English Housewife* (London, 1615). Cited in Sim, *Food & Feast in Tudor England*, p. 12.

34. Sim, *Food and Feast in Tudor England*, p. 37.

35. Weir, *Henry VIII*, p. 68.

36. So solidly were these conduit houses built that they still survive today, on the outskirts of what is now New Malden in Surrey.

37. Borde, *The Fyrst Boke of the Introduction of Knowledge*.

38. Weir, *Henry VIII*, p. 55.

39. Weir, *Henry VIII*, p. 55.

40. Barclay, A., *The Ship of Fools* (1509).

41. Hayward and Ward (eds), *The Inventory of King Henry VIII*, Vol. II, p. 297.

42. Hayward and Ward (eds), *The Inventory of King Henry VIII*, Vol. II, p. 103.

43. Moulton, T., *This is the Myrrour or Glasse of Helth* (London, c.1539).

44. Lynn, *Tudor Fashion*.

45. Classen, Howes and Synnott, *Aroma*, p. 71.

46. Shakespeare, W., *The Merry Wives of Windsor*, Act III, scene v.

47. Taylor, J., *In Praise of Cleane Linen* (1624).

48. Lynn, *Tudor Fashion*.

49. Lynn, *Tudor Fashion*.
50. Lynn, *Tudor Fashion*.
51. 'Ordinances for the Household made at Eltham in the XVII year of King Henry VIII in 1526', in *Collection of Ordinances and Regulations*, p. 215; Lynn, *Tudor Fashion*. Anne was well rewarded for her services, and in 1546 she was granted the Vine Garden and the Mill Bank at Westminster.
52. Lynn, *Tudor Fashion*.
53. Lynn, *Tudor Fashion*.
54. I am indebted to Ruth Goodman's intensive research into this subject, which has included trying out this method of keeping clean – with surprisingly positive results. *How To Be a Tudor* (London, 2015), pp. 17–27.
55. Elyot, T., *The Castel of Helth* (London, 1534).
56. *Collection of Ordinances and Regulations*, p. 156.
57. *Collection of Ordinances and Regulations*, pp. 121–2. The Eltham Ordinances changed this routine slightly by omitting the sprinkling of holy water.
58. Weir, *Henry VIII*, p. 84.

CHAPTER 6 'SHE EXCELLED THEM ALL'

1. Watson, F. (ed.), *Vives and the Renascence Education of Women* (New York, 1912), p. 133.
2. Porter, L., *Mary Tudor: The First Queen* (London, 2007), p. 29.
3. *LP Henry VIII*, Vol. XVII, no. 1153.
4. Goodman, *How To Be a Tudor*, p. 197.
5. Elyot, T., *The Boke named the Governour* (London, 1531).
6. Lynn, *Tudor Fashion*; Thurley, *Royal Palaces of Tudor England*, p. 141.
7. Goodman, *How To Be a Tudor*, p. 205.
8. *LP Henry VIII*, Vol. I, Part iii, pp. xxxvii–xxxviii.
9. Southworth, J., *Fools and Jesters at the English Court* (Stroud, 2003), p. 83. 'Goose' was probably Henry's nickname for his fool.
10. The 's' was first added to the end of his surname by Thomas Nashe to create a pun in his play *Summer's Last Will and Testament* (1592).
11. Lipscomb, S., 'All the King's Fools', in *History Today*, Vol. 61, issue 8 (August 2011).
12. Southworth, *Fools and Jesters*, p. 9.
13. Elizabeth I's seventeenth-century biographer, William Camden, claimed that Anne was born in 1507, as did other sources of that time. But this would have made her no more than six years old when she entered Margaret of Austria's service in 1513 – an impossibly young age.

14. Ashdown, D.M., *Ladies-in-Waiting* (London, 1976), pp. 23–4.
15. Strickland, A., *Lives of the Queens of England* (London, 1851), Vol. II, p. 572.
16. *CSPV*, Vol. IV, p. 365.
17. Lynn, *Tudor Fashion*.
18. In reality, this was little more than a second nail growing on the side of one of her fingers. Anne was so self-conscious about it that she took to wearing long-hanging oversleeves, which instantly became fashionable among court ladies.
19. Wyatt, G., 'Extracts from the Life of the Virtuous, Christian and Renowned Queen Anne Boleyn', in Singer, S.W. (ed.), *The Life of Cardinal Wolsey* by George Cavendish (London, 1827), p. 424.
20. Wyatt, *Extracts*, p. 441.
21. By the time of his resignation, Compton had become so great a magnate thanks to the offices he had been given by the king that he may have been content to relinquish the post of groom.
22. *Collection of Ordinances and Regulations*, pp. 154–9.
23. Starkey, 'Representation through Intimacy', p. 213.
24. 'Ordinances for the Household made at Eltham in the XVII year of King Henry VIII in 1526', in *Collection of Ordinances and Regulations*, pp. 154, 157.
25. *Collection of Ordinances and Regulations*, p. 154.
26. *LP Henry VIII*, Vol. IV, no. 3218; Falkus (ed.), *Private Lives*, pp. 21–33.
27. *Letters and Papers of Henry VIII*, Vol. IV, Part II i, p. 1468; Falkus (ed.), *Private Lives*, pp. 21–33.
28. Nicolas, N.H., ed., *The Privy Purse Expenses of Henry VIII* (London, 1827), p. 223.
29. Anne's double chin may have in fact been due to swollen glands. Historians have speculated that she suffered from a glandular condition, which could explain her later medical problems.
30. Cavendish, G., *The Life of Cardinal Wolsey*, Vol. I (London, 1825), p. 67.
31. Lynn, *Tudor Fashion*.
32. Ives, E.W., *Anne Boleyn* (Oxford, 1986), pp. 173–5.
33. *Leviticus* chapter 20, verse 21.
34. Starkey, 'Representation through Intimacy', p. 194.
35. *CSPV*, Vol. IV, p. 287.
36. Hayward and Ward (eds), *The Inventory of King Henry VIII*, Vol. II, p. 178.
37. One of these has recently been discovered by archaeologists at Hampton Court Palace and will be the subject of a major excavation.
38. Weir, *Henry VIII*, p. 307.
39. Starkey, 'Representation through Intimacy', p. 207.

40. Starkey, 'Representation through Intimacy', p. 206.
41. *LP Henry VIII*, Vol. VI, no. 923.
42. *LP Henry VIII*, Vol. IV, no. 4005.
43. *LP Henry VIII*, Vol. V, no. 1377, pp. 589–99.
44. *LP Henry VIII*, Vol. VI, no. 351.
45. Anne's new subjects were quick to follow suit. In preparation for a visit by the royal couple soon after the Queen's coronation, the owners of Kimberley House in Norfolk commissioned a luxurious valance in white silk with applied black velvet cut into various patterns, such as honeysuckle and acorns, and the entwined 'HA' that was found throughout the royal palaces. The valance is a rare survivor from the Tudor period and is now part of the Burrell Collection.
46. After Anne's fall, Henry ordered all traces of her to be removed from court – including these initials at Hampton Court. In their haste, the royal carpenters missed one of them, which can still be seen in the Great Hall today.
47. *LP Henry VIII*, Vol. VI, Part ii, nos. 1018, 1054.
48. *LP Henry VIII*, Vol. VI, Part ii, nos. 1018, 1054.
49. *LP Henry VIII*, Vol. VI, Part ii, no. 1089.
50. BL Harley MS 283, fo.75. Letter from Chapuys to the Emperor Charles V.
51. Latymer, W., *Chronickille of Anne Bulleyne*. Latymer was Anne's earliest biographer.
52. Strickland, A.,*The Life of Queen Elizabeth* (London, 1910), Vol. II, p. 651.
53. Weir, A., *The Six Wives of Henry VIII* (London, 1991), p. 258.

CHAPTER 7 'A THIN, OLD AND VICIOUS HACK'

1. Licence, *In Bed with the Tudors*, p. 148.
2. Licence, *In Bed with the Tudors*, p. 149.
3. *LP Henry VIII*, Vol. IX, no. 568.
4. *LP Henry VIII*, Vol. X, no. 901.
5. *LP Henry VIII*, Vol. VII, Part ii, no. 1257.
6. Starkey, D., *Six Wives: The Queens of Henry VIII* (London, 2004), p. 584.
7. Weir, *Six Wives of Henry VIII*, p. 345; *LP Henry VIII*, Vol. X, no. 1069.
8. *LP Henry VIII*, Vol. XI, no. 29.
9. Norton, *Anne Boleyn Papers*, p. 297.
10. Weir, *Six Wives of Henry VIII*, p. 293.
11. *LP Henry VIII*, Vol. X, p. 51.
12. *LP Henry VIII*, Vol. X, p. 102.

13. *LP Henry VIII*, Vol. XII, Part i, no. 1068.
14. *CSPS*, Vol. V, Part ii, nos. 1536–8, p. 84.
15. Alison Weir provides a compelling and detailed analysis of the case against Anne in *The Lady in the Tower* (London, 2009), proving that the vast majority of the allegations must have been false.
16. Falkus (ed.), *Private Lives*, p. 34.
17. *LP Henry VIII*, Vol. X, no. 876.
18. Lynn, *Tudor Fashion*.
19. Thurley, *Royal Palaces of Tudor England*, p. 143.
20. *LP Henry VIII*, Vol. XII, Part ii, no. 77.
21. Licence, *In Bed with the Tudors*, pp. 160–1.
22. *LP Henry VIII*, Vol. XI, no. 203.
23. Whalebone is not a bone as such, but the cartilage from the mouth of the baleen whale. It can be split vertically into strong but pliable strips, and has the advantage of moulding slightly to the shape of the body as it heats up with the body's own warmth. Lynn, *Tudor Fashion*.
24. Byrne, M. St Clare (ed.), *The Lisle Letters: An Abridgement* (Chicago, 1981), p. 206.
25. Starkey, 'Representation through Intimacy', p. 212.
26. *LP Henry VIII*, Vol. XIII, Part i, no. 1313.
27. Williams (ed. and trans.), *Thomas Platter's Travels*, p. 202.
28. Hume, M.A.S. (ed. and trans.), *Chronicle of King Henry VIII of England: being a contemporary record of some of the principal events of the reigns of Henry VIII and Edward VI written in Spanish by an unknown hand* (London, 1889), p. 73.
29. Licence, *In Bed with the Tudors*, p. 165.
30. Merriman, R.B. (ed.), *Life and Letters of Thomas Cromwell*, Vol. II (Oxford, 1902) p. 96.
31. *LP Henry VIII*, Vol. XII, Part ii, no. 972.
32. *LP Henry VIII*, Vol. XIII, Part i, no. 647.
33. *LP Henry VIII*, Vol. XII, Part ii, no. 1023.
34. Licence, *In Bed with the Tudors*, p. 166.
35. *LP Henry VIII*, Vol. XII, Part ii, no. 1004.
36. Hayward, *Dress at the Court of Henry VIII*, p. 210.
37. Thurley, *Royal Palaces of Tudor England*, p. 141.
38. Skidmore, C., *Edward VI: The Lost King of England* (London, 2007), p. 24.
39. Skidmore, *Edward VI*, pp. 37–8.
40. *Edward's Chronicle*, reproduced in Falkus (ed.), *Private Lives*, pp. 53–74.
41. Sybil Penn later attended Edward's sister, Elizabeth, and remained in her

household after she ascended the throne in 1558. Four years later, she nursed the queen through smallpox at Hampton Court but caught the disease herself and died shortly afterwards. She is reputed to haunt the palace to this day, and there have been several sightings of a 'grey lady' walking through the royal apartments.

42. Wood, M.A.E., *Letters of Royal and Illustrious Ladies of Great Britain*, Vol. III (London, 1846), p. 112.

43. *LP Henry VIII*, Vol. XIV, Part ii, no. 12.

44. Hayward and Ward (eds), *The Inventory of King Henry VIII*, Vol. II, p. 92.

CHAPTER 8 'TRUE CARNAL COPULATION'

1. *LP Henry VIII*, Vol. XIII, Part i, no. 995.

2. Weir, *Henry VIII*, p. 400.

3. Chalmers, C.R. and Chaloner, E.J., '500 Years Later: Henry VIII, Leg Ulcers and the Course of History', *Journal of the Society of Medicine*, Vol. 102 (2009), pp. 513–17.

4. Hayward and Ward (eds), *The Inventory of King Henry VIII*, Vol. II, p. 77.

5. Lynn, *Tudor Fashion*; St Clare Byrne, M. (ed.), *The Lisle Letters*, ed., p. 252; *LP Henry VIII*, Vol. XV, no. 23, pp. 1–19.

6. Licence, *In Bed with the Tudors*, p. 178.

7. Hume (ed. and trans.), *Chronicle of King Henry VIII of England*, pp. 91–2.

8. Weir, *Henry VIII*, p. 457.

9. Hurren, 'Cultures of the Body', p. 67.

10. Hume (ed. and trans.), *Chronicle of King Henry VIII of England*, p. 108.

11. *LP Henry VIII*, Vol. XIV, Part ii, no. 153.

12. Merriman (ed.), *Life and Letters of Thomas Cromwell*, Vol. II, pp. 270–1.

13. Falkus (ed.), *Private Lives*, p. 41.

14. Falkus (ed.), *Private Lives*, p. 41.

15. Falkus (ed.), *Private Lives*, p. 42.

16. Falkus (ed.), *Private Lives*, pp. 45–6.

17. Merriman (ed.), *Life and Letters of Thomas Cromwell*, Vol. II, p. 271; Strype, J., *Ecclesiastical Memorials, Relating Chiefly to Religion, and the Reformation of it . . . under King Henry VIII, King Edward VI and Queen Mary I* (Oxford, 1822), pp. 555–6.

18. Starkey, D., *The Reign of Henry VIII: Personalities and Politics* (London, 2002), pp. 101–2.

19. Strype, *Ecclesiastical Memorials*, Vol. I, Part ii, p. 462.

20. BL Cotton MS Titus B i.

21. Starkey, *The Reign of Henry VIII*, pp. 98–9.
22. *LP Henry VIII*, Vol. XV, no. 825.
23. Licence, *In Bed with the Tudors*, pp. 184–5.
24. Licence, *In Bed with the Tudors*, p. 186.
25. Lynn, *Tudor Fashion*; Weir, *Six Wives of Henry VIII*, p. 413.
26. Wood, *Letters of Royal and Illustrious Ladies*, Vol. III, p. 161.
27. *LP Henry VIII*, Vol. XVI, Part i, no. 12.
28. Starkey, D., *Six Wives: The Queens of Henry VIII* (London, 2004), p. 651.
29. Hume (ed. and trans.), *Chronicle of King Henry VIII of England*, p. 77.
30. Hayward and Ward (eds), *The Inventory of King Henry VIII*, Vol. II, p. 297.
31. *LP Henry VIII*, Vol. XVI, pp. 282–9.
32. Weir, *Henry VIII*, p. 449.
33. *LP Henry VIII*, Vol. XVI, no. 325.
34. Johnson, 'All the King's Fools'.
35. *HMC, Bath*, Vol. II (London, 1907), p. 10.
36. Weir, *Henry VIII*, p. 452; Glasheen, J., *The Secret People of the Palaces: The Royal Household from the Plantagenets to Queen Victoria* (London, 1998), p. 23.
37. Weir, *Henry VIII*, p. 452.
38. Weir, *Henry VIII*, p. 453.
39. *LP Henry VIII*, Vol. XVI, no. 1325. Heneage had been promoted to the position of groom of the stool after the spectacular fall from grace of his master, Henry Norris, in 1536.
40. Bergenroth, G.A., et al., *State Papers of King Henry the Eighth* (London, 1830–52), Vol. I, p. 695.
41. Starkey, *Six Wives*, p. 683.
42. Lynn, *Tudor Fashion*.
43. *LP Henry VIII*, Vol. XVI, no. 1489; Vol. XVIII, Part i, no. 224; Lynn, *Tudor Fashion*.
44. *LP Henry VIII*, Vol. XVIII, Part i, no. 904.

CHAPTER 9 'KINGS AND EMPERORS ALL BE BUT MORTAL'

1. The numbers had in fact been rising steadily throughout the previous decade so that by 1539 the privy chamber staff had almost doubled in size to twenty-eight.
2. The Bayne Tower still survives today, although it is not accessible to visitors.
3. Weir, *Henry VIII*, pp. 445–6.
4. Skidmore, *Edward VI*, p. 27.

5. Elyot, *The Boke named the Governour*.

6. Licence, *In Bed with the Tudors*, p. 196.

7. Weir, *Henry VIII*, p. 457.

8. Weir, *Henry VIII*, p. 457.

9. Weir, *Six Wives of Henry VIII*, p. 493.

10. Licence, *In Bed with the Tudors*, p. 196.

11. Hayward and Ward (eds), *The Inventory of King Henry VIII*, Vol. II, p. 80.

12. Five of these caps were among the possessions that were sent to the Tower Wardrobe from Katherine's home, Sudeley Castle, in April 1550, some eighteen months after her death. Hayward and Ward (eds), *The Inventory of King Henry VIII*, Vol. II, p. 95.

13. Hayward and Ward (eds), *The Inventory of King Henry VIII*, Vol. II, pp. 95–6.

14. Martienssen, A., *Queen Katherine Parr* (London, 1975), p. 190.

15. Lynn, *Tudor Fashion*.

16. Hayward and Ward (eds), *The Inventory of King Henry VIII*, Vol. II, p. 341.

17. Falkus (ed.), *Private Lives*, p. 46.

18. Weir, *Henry VIII* p. 468.

19. Weir, *Henry VIII* p. 470.

20. Lynn, *Tudor Fashion*.

21. *LP Henry VIII*, Vol. XXI, Part I, no. 136.

22. Lynn, *Tudor Fashion*.

23. *LP Henry VIII*, Vol. XIX, Part i, no. 864.

24. Pollnitz, A., 'Humanism and Court Culture in the Education of Tudor Royal Children', in Betteridge, T. and Riehl, A., *Tudor Court Culture* (New Jersey, 2010), p. 47.

25. Goodman, *How To Be a Tudor*, p. 108.

26. Skidmore, *Edward VI*, p. 22.

27. Skidmore, *Edward VI*, pp. 33–4.

28. Perry, M., *The Word of a Prince* (London, 1990), pp. 30–1. The original letter is held at the British Library: Cotton MS C X f.235.

29. An excellent analysis of the two conditions, and their relation to Henry VIII, is provided by Stride, P. and Lopes Floro, K., 'Henry VIII, McLeod Syndrome and Jacquetta's Curse', Royal College of Physicians (Edinburgh, 2013).

30. The measurement for Henry's waist was actually fifty-four inches, but four inches should be allowed for the clothing that he wore underneath the armour.

31. Weir, *Henry VIII*, p. 493.

32. Hayward and Ward (eds), *The Inventory of King Henry VIII*, Vol. II, p. 105.

33. Starkey, 'Representation through Intimacy', p. 207.
34. *LP Henry VIII*, Addenda, Vol. I, Part ii, no. 1794.
35. Hayward and Ward (eds), *The Inventory of King Henry VIII*, Vol. II, p. 84.
36. *LP Henry VIII*, Vol. XXI, Part I, no. 1383 (item 96), pp. 663–97.
37. Weir, *Henry VIII*, p. 497.
38. *LP Henry VIII*, Vol. XXI, Part ii, no. 605.
39. Weir, *Henry VIII*, pp. 500–1.
40. Weir, *Henry VIII* p. 502.
41. Russell, J.G., *The Field of the Cloth of Gold: Men and Manners in 1520* (London, 1969), p. 218.

CHAPTER 10 'BEING YET BUT A CHILD'

1. Starkey, 'Representation through Intimacy', p. 205.
2. Thurley, *Royal Palaces of Tudor England*, p. 173.
3. Lynn, *Tudor Fashion*.
4. Hayward and Ward (eds), *The Inventory of King Henry VIII*, Vol. II, p. 96.
5. Lynn, *Tudor Fashion*.
6. Hayward and Ward (eds), *The Inventory of King Henry VIII*, Vol. II, pp. 96–7.
7. Classen, Howes and Synnott, *Aroma*, p. 65.
8. Nichols, J.G. (ed.), *Literary Remains of King Edward the Sixth* (1857), Vol. I, pp. xliv–xlv.
9. Skidmore, *Edward VI*, p. 197.
10. Perry, M., *The Word of a Prince* (London, 1990), p. 45; Haynes, A., *Collection of State Papers Relating to Affairs in the Reigns of King Henry VIII, King Edward VI, Queen Mary and Queen Elizabeth, From the Year 1542 to 1570 . . . Left by William Cecil, Lord Burghley . . . at Hatfield House* (London, 1740), p. 61.
11. Weir, *Six Wives of Henry VIII*, p. 544; Martienssen, *Queen Katherine Parr*, p. 233.
12. Seymour purchased the wardship for £2,000, although he only ever paid £500 of this.
13. Haynes, *Collection of State Papers*, p. 99.
14. Haynes, *Collection of State Papers*, p. 99.
15. Marcus, L.S., Mueller, J. and Rose, M.B., *Elizabeth I: Collected Works* (Chicago and London, 2002), p. 30.
16. *CSPD, Edward VI*, p. 92.
17. Haynes, p. 96.
18. Haynes, p. 96.
19. Licence, *In Bed with the Tudors*, pp. 199–200.

20. TNA SP 10/2 no. 25.
21. Chamberlain, F., *The Private Character of Queen Elizabeth* (London, 1921), p. 9; BM Cotton MS Otho C X fo.236v.
22. *CSPD, Edward VI*, p. 49.
23. Haynes, pp. 103–4.
24. *CSPD, Edward VI*, p. 91.
25. *CSPD, Edward VI*, p. 91; Haynes, p. 100.
26. Haynes, pp. 70, 98; Marcus, Mueller and Rose, *Elizabeth I*, pp. 23–4.
27. Haynes, pp. 96–7.
28. *CSPD, Edward VI*, p. 92.
29. Haynes, pp. 99–101.
30. Haynes, p. 102.
31. Falkus (ed.), *Private Lives*, p. 97. In Greek mythology, Hippolyta was a virtuous but forceful woman, whereas Phaedra wreaked havoc by falling in love with a man who was not her husband.
32. Falkus (ed.), *Private Lives*, p. 76.
33. *CSPS, 1550–1552*, p. 63.
34. Falkus (ed.), *Private Lives*, p. 57.
35. Falkus (ed.), *Private Lives*, p. 54.
36. Falkus (ed.), *Private Lives*, p. 92.
37. Skidmore, *Edward VI*, p. 227.
38. Murphy, J., 'The Illusion of Decline: The Privy Chamber, 1547–1558', in Starkey, et al. (eds), *English Court*, p. 129.
39. Skidmore, *Edward VI*, p. 228.
40. *CSPV, 1534–1554*, pp. 535–6.
41. Skidmore, *Edward VI*, p. 240.
42. Falkus (ed.), *Private Lives*, p. 57.
43. Skidmore, *Edward VI*, pp. 196–7.
44. Aylmer, J., *A Harbour for Faithful Subjects* (1559); quoted in Lynn, *Tudor Fashion*.
45. Hayward, *Dress at the Court of Henry VIII*, p. 213.
46. Falkus (ed.), *Private Lives*, p. 63.
47. Skidmore, *Edward VI*, p. 241.
48. Skidmore, *Edward VI*, p. 241.
49. *CSPS, 1553*, p. 3.
50. Skidmore, *Edward VI*, p. 247.
51. Skidmore, *Edward VI*, pp. 250, 254.
52. Skidmore, *Edward VI*, p. 255.
53. Skidmore, *Edward VI*, p. 260.

CHAPTER II 'THINKING MYSELF TO BE WITH CHILD'

1. Somerset, A., *Elizabeth I* (London, 1991), p. 71.
2. *CSPV, 1556–7*, Vol. VI, Part ii, p. 1054.
3. Wriothesley, C., *A Chronicle of England During the Reigns of the Tudors, From A.D. 1485 to 1559*, ed. Hamilton, W.D., Camden Society, 2nd series, Vol. II (London, 1877), p. 93.
4. Lynn, *Tudor Fashion*.
5. Falkus (ed.), *Private Lives*, p. 76.
6. *CSPS*, Vol. XIII, *Mary 1554–8*, p. 6.
7. Knox, J., *First Blast of the Trumpet Against the Monstrous Regiment of Women*, first published 1558 (New York, 1972), pp. 9–10.
8. *CSPS, Mary I 1554–8*, Vol. XIII, p. 61.
9. Hayward and Ward (eds), *The Inventory of King Henry VIII*, Vol. II, p. 155, p. 179 and *Dress at the Court of Henry VIII*, Vol. II (London, 2012), p. 179.
10. *CSPS*, Vol. XIII, p. 31.
11. Porter, *Mary Tudor*, p. 350.
12. Plowden, A., *Tudor Women: Queens and Commoners* (Sutton, 2002), p. 138.
13. Davis, J.C., *Pursuit of Power: Venetian Ambassadors' Reports on Spain, Turkey, and France in the Age of Philip II 1560–1600* (New York, 1970), pp. 81–2.
14. Hayward and Ward (eds), *The Inventory of King Henry VIII*, Vol. II, p. 155.
15. *CSPV*, Vol. VII, p. 601.
16. As queen, Elizabeth was always suspicious of her ambitious and scheming cousin, and twice imprisoned her in the Tower.
17. *CSPD, Mary*, pp. 53–4.
18. Nichols, J.G. (ed.), *The Chronicle of Queen Jane and of Two Years of Queen Mary*, Camden Society, Vol. 48 (London, 1850), pp. 70–1.
19. John Elder's letter describing the arrival and marriage of King Philip, his triumphal entry into London, the legation of Cardinal Pole, & C.
20. John Elder's letter.
21. *CSPV*, Vol. VI, Part ii, p. 1055.
22. *CSPV*, Vol. VI, Part ii, p. 1055.
23. Porter, *Mary Tudor*, p. 319.
24. *CSPS*, Vol. XIII, p. 2.
25. John Elder's letter describing the arrival and marriage of King Philip, his triumphal entry into London, the legation of Cardinal Pole, & C.
26. John Elder's letter.
27. John Elder's letter. See also: Wriothesley, *A Chronicle*, p. 120.

28. BM Cotton MS Vespasian Fiii fo.23.
29. Porter, *Mary Tudor*, p. 325; *CSPS, Elizabeth 1554–8*, Vol. XIII, pp. 2–3.
30. Porter, *Mary Tudor*, p. 307.
31. *CSPS, Mary I 1554–8*, Vol. XIII, p. 28.
32. *CSPS, Elizabeth 1554–8*, Vol. XIII, pp. 2–3, 6, 13.
33. Licence, *In Bed with the Tudors*, p. 215.
34. Thurley, *Royal Palaces of Tudor England*, p. 160.
35. Foxe, *Book of Martyrs*, quoted in Falkus (ed.), *Private Lives*, p. 83.
36. An excellent summary of the various theories to explain Mary's symptoms is provided by Medvei, C.V., 'The illness and death of Mary Tudor', *Journal of the Royal Society of Medicine*, Vol. 80, No. 12 (December 1987). See also: Erickson, C., *Bloody Mary* (London, 2001), pp. 127–8; Brewer, *The Death of Kings*.
37. Nichols, J.G. (ed.), *The Diary of Henry Machyn: Citizen and Merchant-Taylor of London, from AD 1550 to AD 1563* (London, 1848), p. 76; *CSPS, Mary I 1554–8*, Vol. XIII, p. 124.
38. *CSPS, Mary I 1554–8*, Vol. XIII, pp. 51, 226.
39. HMC, *Rutland*, Vol. I, pp. 310–11.
40. Foxe, *Acts and Monuments*, Vol. VIII, pp. 619–21.
41. Nichols (ed.), *Diary of Henry Machyn*, pp. 79–90.
42. Foxe, *Book of Martyrs*, quoted in Falkus (ed.), *Private Lives*, p. 83.
43. *CSPF, Mary I*, pp. 165–6.
44. Foxe, *Book of Martyrs*, quoted in Falkus (ed.), *Private Lives*, p. 83.
45. Foxe, *Book of Martyrs*, quoted in Falkus (ed.), *Private Lives*, p. 81.
46. Foxe, *Book of Martyrs*, quoted in Falkus (ed.), *Private Lives*, p. 81.
47. *CSPS*, Vol. XIII, p. 176.
48. Foxe, *Book of Martyrs*, quoted in Falkus (ed.), *Private Lives*, p. 81.
49. *CSPF, Mary I*, p. 172.
50. *CSPV*, Vol. VI ii, p. 1059.
51. *CSPS, Mary I 1554–8*, Vol. XIII, p. 224.
52. *CSPS, Mary I 1554–8*, p. 174.
53. HMC, *Rutland*, Vol. I, pp. 310–11; *CSPS, Mary I 1554–8*, Vol. XIII, p. 250.
54. Foxe, *Book of Martyrs*, quoted in Falkus (ed.), *Private Lives*, pp. 83–4.
55. *CSPS, Elizabeth 1558–67*, Vol. I, p. 9.
56. *CSPV*, Vol. VI, Part i, p. 558.
57. A useful list of Mary's household staff throughout her life is provided in Loades, D., *Mary Tudor: A Life* (Oxford, 1989), Appendix 1.
58. Porter, *Mary Tudor*, p. 387.
59. *CSPV, 1556–7*, Vol. VI, Part ii, p. 1054.

60. *CSPV*, Vol. VI, Part ii, p. 1060.
61. Loades, *Mary Tudor*, p. 189.
62. *CSPV*, Vol. VI, Part ii, p. 1060.
63. Camden, *Historie of the Most Renowned and Victorious Princesse Elizabeth*, p. 8. Camden mistook Mary's age: she was forty-one.
64. *CSPV*, Vol. VI, Part i, p. 201; *CSPS, Mary I 1554–8*, Vol. XIII, p. 416; *CSPS, Elizabeth 1558–67*, Vol. I, p. 34; Erickson, *Bloody Mary*, p. 481.
65. *CSPS, Mary I 1554–8*, Vol. XIII, p. 438.
66. Falkus (ed.), *Private Lives*, pp. 84–5.
67. Adams, S. and Rodríguez-Salgado, M.J., 'The Count of Feria's Dispatch to Philip II of 14 November 1558', *Camden Miscellany*, Vol. XXVIII (London, 1984), p. 328.

CHAPTER 12 'WE HIGHLY COMMEND THE SINGLE LIFE'

1. Hibbert, C., *Elizabeth I: A Personal History of the Virgin Queen* (London, 1992), p. 67.
2. Haigh, C. (ed.), *Elizabeth I* (London and New York, 1988), p. 20.
3. Pryor, *Elizabeth I*, p. 31; HMC, *Salisbury*, Vol. I, p. 158.
4. Crawford, *Blood, Bodies and Families*, p. 59.
5. Erickson, C., *The First Elizabeth* (London, 1999), p. 71.
6. Somerset, *Elizabeth I*, p. 90; Plowden, *Tudor Women*, p. 154; *CSPD, Mary I*, no. 753.
7. Francis Steuart, A. (ed.), *Sir James Melville: Memoirs of His Own Life, 1549–93* (London, 1929), p. 94; *CSPV*, Vol. VII, p. 594; Levin, C., *The Heart and Stomach of a King: Elizabeth I and the Politics of Sex and Power* (Philadelphia, 1994), p. 172.
8. Weir, A., *The Life of Elizabeth* (New York, 1998), p. 46.
9. *Calendar of Letters and State Papers relating to English Affairs preserved principally in the Archives of Simancas*, Vol. III, p. 252; Somerset, *Elizabeth I*, p. 96.
10. Weir, *Life of Elizabeth*, p. 47.
11. Collins, A. (ed.), *Letters and Memorials of State, in the reigns of Queen Mary, Queen Elizabeth, etc . . . Written and collected by Sir Henry Sidney, etc*, Vol. II (London, 1746), pp. 200–3.
12. Harington, *Nugae Antiquae*, pp. 123–4.
13. Klarwill, V. von (ed.), *Queen Elizabeth and Some Foreigners* (London, 1928), pp. 113–15.
14. Skidmore, C., *Death and the Virgin: Elizabeth, Dudley and the Mysterious Fate of Amy Robsart* (London, 2010), pp. 381–2.

15. Wilson, V.A., *Queen Elizabeth's Maids of Honour and Ladies of the Privy Chamber* (London, 1922), p. 25.
16. *CSPF, Elizabeth 1560–1*, p. 10.
17. Lynn, *Tudor Fashion.*
18. Watkins, S., *In Public and Private: Elizabeth I and her World* (London, 1998), p. 162.
19. Weir, *Life of Elizabeth*, p. 51; Cowen Orlin, L., *Locating Privacy in Tudor London* (Oxford, 2007), p. 231.
20. *CSPF, Elizabeth 1562*, pp. 217–24.
21. *CSPF, Elizabeth 1560–1*, p. 173.
22. Falkus (ed.), *Private Lives*, p. 98.
23. Falkus (ed.), *Private Lives*, pp. 99–100.
24. Henry VIII had excluded his elder sister's descendants from the succession, but this fact was largely disregarded by Mary's supporters.
25. Robert Dudley was Elizabeth's master of the horse.
26. Gristwood, S., *Elizabeth and Leicester* (London, 2007), p. 158.
27. Francis Steuart (ed.), *Sir James Melville*, p. 91.
28. *CSP, Scotland 1563–69*, Vol. II, p. 49.
29. Falkus (ed.), *Private Lives*, p. 103.
30. Falkus (ed.), *Private Lives*, pp. 102–3.
31. Falkus (ed.), *Private Lives*, p. 104.
32. Francis Steuart (ed.), *Sir James Melville*, pp. 95–7.
33. *CSPF, Elizabeth 1566–68*, p. 45.
34. *CSPS, Elizabeth 1558–67*, Vol. I, p. 562.
35. Jenkins, E., *Elizabeth the Great* (London, 1965), pp. 76–7.
36. *CSPS, Elizabeth 1558–67*, Vol. I, p. 63.
37. Weir, *Life of Elizabeth*, p. 47; Jenkins, *Elizabeth the Great*, p. 77.
38. Camden, *Historie of the Most Renowned and Victorious Princesse Elizabeth*, p. 9.
39. *CSPV, Elizabeth 1558–80*, Vol. VII, p. 105.
40. Gristwood, *Elizabeth & Leicester*, pp. 132–3.
41. Lynn, *Tudor Fashion.*
42. Lynn, *Tudor Fashion.*
43. Jenkins, *Elizabeth the Great*, p. 123.
44. Erickson, *The First Elizabeth*, p. 262; Somerset, *Elizabeth I*, p. 101; Johnson, P., *Elizabeth I: A Study in Power and Intellect* (London, 1974), p. 115; Weir, *Life of Elizabeth*, pp. 48–9; Laing, D. (ed.), *Notes of Ben Jonson's Conversations with William Drummond of Hawthornden*, Vol. I (London, 1842), p. 23.
45. Marcus, Mueller and Rose, *Elizabeth I*, p. 157; Weir, *Life of Elizabeth*, p. 48; HMC, *Salisbury*, Vol. II, p. 245.

46. Haigh (ed.), *Elizabeth I*, p. 22.

47. Jenkins, *Elizabeth the Great*, pp. 141–2.

48. Alison Weir provides an excellent assessment of this theory, which was put forward by Michael Bloch, in *Elizabeth the Queen*, p. 49.

49. Smither, L.J., 'Elizabeth I: A Psychological Profile', *Sixteenth Century Journal*, Vol. XV (London, 1984), pp. 71–2.

50. Eccles, A., *Obstetrics and Gynaecology in Tudor and Stuart England* (London, 1982), pp. 26–7.

51. Frye, S., *Elizabeth I: The Competition for Representation* (New York and Oxford, 1993), p. 12.

52. Loades, D.M., *The Tudor Court* (Oxford, 2003), p. 119.

CHAPTER 13 'SHE SELDOM PARTAKES BEFORE STRANGERS'

1. *CSPV*, Vol. VII, p. 659.

2. Somerset, *Elizabeth I*, p. 65; Nichols (ed.), *Diary of Henry Machyn*, p. 263.

3. Boyle, J. (ed.), *Memoirs of the Life of Robert Carey . . . Written by Himself* (London, 1759), p. 73n.

4. Birch, T., *Memoirs of the Reign of Queen Elizabeth from the year 1581 till her Death*, Vol. II (London, 1754), pp. 120–1.

5. Harrison, G.B. and Jones, R.A., *Andre Hurault de Maisse, A Journal of all that was accomplished by Monsieur de Maisse, ambassador in England from King Henri IV to Queen Elizabeth, 1597* (London, 1931), pp. 23–4.

6. Williams (ed. and trans.), *Thomas Platter's Travels*, p. 192.

7. Watkins, *In Public and Private*, p. 59.

8. Rye, W.B. (ed.), *England as seen by Foreigners in the days of Elizabeth and James the First* (London, 1865), Vol. II, p. 18.

9. Rye (ed.), *England as seen by Foreigners*, Vol. II, p. 18.

10. Williams (ed. and trans.), *Thomas Platter's Travels*, p. 202.

11. Souden, D. and Worsley, L., *The Story of Hampton Court Palace* (London, 2015), p. 57.

12. Watkins, *In Public and Private*, p. 59.

13. Watkins, *In Public and Private*, p. 67.

14. Smith, V., *Clean: A History of Personal Hygiene and Purity* (Oxford, 2007), p. 190.

15. Watkins, *In Public and Private*, pp. 58–9.

16. Harrison and Jones, *Andre Hurault de Maisse*, pp. 23–4.

17. Watkins, *In Public and Private*, p. 58.

18. Watkins, *In Public and Private*, pp. 72–3.

19. Watkins, *In Public and Private*, pp. 57–8.
20. Classen, Howes and Synnott, *Aroma*, p. 65.
21. Goodman, *How To Be a Tudor*, p. 30.
22. Thurley, *Royal Palaces of Tudor England*, p. 173.
23. Thurley, *Royal Palaces of Tudor England*, p. 75.
24. Falkus (ed.), *Private Lives*, p. 124.
25. Falkus (ed.), *Private Lives*, p. 125.
26. Rye (ed.), *England as seen by Foreigners*, Vol. III, p. 107.
27. Williams (ed. and trans.), *Thomas Platter's Travels*, p. 192.
28. Watkins, *In Public and Private*, p. 51.
29. Smith, *Clean*, p. 190.
30. Thurley, *Royal Palaces of Tudor England*, p. 160.
31. Watkins, *In Public and Private*, p. 182.
32. Sim, *Food & Feast in Tudor England*, p. 155.
33. Sim, *Food & Feast in Tudor England*, p. 13.
34. Buttes, H., *Diets Drie Dinner* (1599).
35. Rye (ed.), *England as seen by Foreigners*, Vol. II, p. 109.
36. Hayward and Ward (eds), *The Inventory of King Henry VIII*, Vol. II, p. 179.
37. Watkins, *In Public and in Private*, p. 50.
38. Harrison and Jones, *Andre Hurault de Maisse*, p. 95.
39. Gosson, S., *Schoole of Abuse, containing a pleasant invective against Poets, Pipers, Plaiers, Jesters and such like Caterpillars of the Commonwealth* (London, 1579).
40. Cardano, G., *Liber De Ludo Aleae* (1564). The title is translated as: 'Book on Games of Chance'.
41. Williams (ed. and trans.), *Thomas Platter's Travels*, p. 202.
42. Arnold, *Queen Elizabeth's Wardrobe Unlock'd*, p. 105; Lynn, *Tudor Fashion*.
43. Southworth, *Fools and Jesters*, p. 145.
44. Lynn, *Tudor Fashion*.
45. Doran, S., *Elizabeth: The Exhibition at the National Maritime Museum* (London, 2003).
46. *CSPS*, Vol. I, p. 465.
47. His contemporary, Arthur Throckmorton, financed his visit to court in 1583 by selling land and borrowing his brother's legacy. He was still paying interest many years later. Lynn, *Tudor Fashion*.
48. Falkus (ed.), *Private Lives*, p. 100.
49. Falkus (ed.), *Private Lives*, pp. 100–1.
50. An astrolabe is an ancient astronomical device for solving problems relating to time and the position of the sun and stars in the sky.

CHAPTER 14 'A THOUSAND EYES SEE ALL I DO'

1. Weir, *Elizabeth*, p. 51.
2. TNA LC 2/4 (3) fos.104–5.
3. Wright, P., 'A Change in Direction: The Ramifications of a Female Household, 1558–1603', in Starkey, et al. (eds), *English Court*, p. 151.
4. Wright, 'A Change in Direction', p. 158.
5. Lynn, *Tudor Fashion*.
6. Merton, C., 'The Women who Served Queen Mary and Queen Elizabeth: Ladies, Gentlewomen and Maids of the Privy Chamber, 1553–1603' (Cambridge PhD thesis, 1992), p. 64.
7. The great number of pins found in archaeological excavations at Hampton Court testifies to the sheer volume of pins delivered, worn and regularly lost at the palace. Lynn, *Tudor Fashion*.
8. *CSPS, 1558–67*, Vol. I, p. 368.
9. Lynn, *Tudor Fashion*.
10. Klarwill (ed.), *Queen Elizabeth and Some Foreigners*, p. 394.
11. Lynn, *Tudor Fashion*.
12. From 1589, Fortescue also served as Elizabeth's Chancellor of the Exchequer.
13. Haynes, S., *A Collection of State Papers . . . from 1542 to 1570, Transcribed from original Letters and other authentic memorials left by William Cecill, Lord Burghley* (London, 1740), Vol. I, p. 368; Lynn, *Tudor Fashion*.
14. *Calendar of Patent Rolls 1560–63* (HMSO, London, 1948), p. 3.
15. Falkus (ed.), *Private Lives*, p. 104.
16. Chamberlain, *The Private Character of Queen Elizabeth*, p. 54; Belloc, H., *History of England* (1931), p. 3.
17. Smith, *Clean*, p. 191.
18. Lynn, *Tudor Fashion*.
19. *LP, Henry VIII*, Vol. IV, Part iii, no. 5636.
20. Rye (ed.), *England as seen by Foreigners*, Vol. II, p. 71.
21. Goodman, *How To Be a Tudor*, p. 55.
22. Lynn, *Tudor Fashion*.
23. Lynn, *Tudor Fashion*.
24. Lynn, *Tudor Fashion*.
    Lynn, *Tudor Fashion*.
    Lynn, *Tudor Fashion*.
    eter Johnson continued to create royal shoes well into the reign of James
    Lynn, *Tudor Fashion*.

28. Hentzner, P., *A Journey into England in the Year MDXCVIII* (London, 1757; Reprinted Reading, 1807), p. 20.

29. *CSPV*, 1603–1607, Vol. X (London, 1900), no. 91, pp. 58–72.

30. Lynn, *Tudor Fashion*; Arnold, *Queen Elizabeth's Wardrobe Unlock'd*, p. 174.

31. Lynn, *Tudor Fashion*; Arnold, *Queen Elizabeth's Wardrobe Unlock'd*, p. xiv.

32. Warrant of 3 April 1588, BL, Egerton 2806, fo.227.

33. Alice married in the early 1560s and changed her name to Montague. In the early 1580s, a Roger Montague appears in the accounts, which may have been her husband or son entering her trade. Arnold, *Queen Elizabeth's Wardrobe Unlock'd*, p. 219.

34. Lynn, *Tudor Fashion*.

35. The stone continued to adorn the crowns of the kings and queens of England during the Tudor and Stuart dynasties, and it was only saved from destruction by Oliver Cromwell (who had the rest of the crown jewels melted down) thanks to a secret Royalist sympathiser, who bought it for the paltry sum of £4 before the crown was sent to the furnace. He carefully preserved it until Charles II's restoration in 1660, when it was restored to its place at the front of the king's new state crown. It is still part of the royal regalia today and is set in the Imperial State Crown.

36. Lynn, *Tudor Fashion*.

37. Arnold, *Queen Elizabeth's Wardrobe Unlock'd*, p. 179.

38. Eleri Lynn provides a detailed analysis of how Tudor royal garments were repurposed, and it is thanks to her efforts that the Bacton altar cloth has been identified. She tells its fascinating story in her new book, *Tudor Fashion: Dress at Court 1485–1603* (to be published by Yale University Press in 2017). Eleri also arranged the loan of the altar cloth to Historic Royal Palaces, where it will be conserved and displayed as part of the Royal Ceremonial Dress Collection.

39. D'Ewes, S., *The Journals of all the Parliaments during the Reign of Queen Elizabeth both of the House of Lords and House of Commons Collected by Sir Simonds D'Ewes of Stow-Hall in the County of Suffolk* (Shannon, 1682), p. 473.

40. Arnold, *Queen Elizabeth's Wardrobe Unlock'd*, p. 1.

41. Quoted in Lynn, *Tudor Fashion*.

42. *LP Henry VIII*, Vol. XI, p. 190.

43. Jenkins, *Elizabeth the Great*, p. 317.

44. Lynn, *Tudor Fashion*.

45. Lynn, *Tudor Fashion*; Arnold, *Queen Elizabeth's Wardrobe Unlock'd*, p. 234; BL Egerton 2806, f.15.

46. Lynn, *Tudor Fashion*.

47. TNA LC5/33, fo.150.
48. Presses were the specialist cases in which clothing was folded and kept. Lynn, *Tudor Fashion*.
49. Birch, *Memoirs of the Reign of Queen Elizabeth*, Vol. I, p. 155.
50. Weir, *Henry VIII*, p. 56.
51. Burton, E., *The Elizabethans at Home* (London, 1970), pp. 164–5.
52. HMC, *Salisbury*, Vol. II, p. 159.
53. BM Cotton MS Galba C IX fo.128.
54. Hibbert, *Elizabeth I*, p. 109.
55. Classen, Howes and Synnott, *Aroma*, p. 71.
56. Williams, N., *Powder and Paint: A History of the Englishwoman's Toilet, Elizabeth I– Elizabeth II* (London, 1957), pp. 27–8.

CHAPTER 15 'I AM SOFT AND MADE OF MELTING SNOW'

1. Falkus (ed.), *Private Lives*, pp. 108–9.
2. HMC, *Bath*, Vol. V, p. 206. If Lettice was pregnant at the time of their marriage, then she either miscarried or the child did not survive, because there is no mention of it in the sources. Their only recorded child, Denbigh, was born in 1581 but died three years later.
3. *CSPD, Elizabeth 1580–1625 Addenda*, p. 137.
4. *CSPV, Elizabeth 1558–80*, Vol. VII, p. 601.
5. Marcus, Mueller and Rose, *Elizabeth I*, p. 157.
6. *CSPV, Elizabeth 1558–80*, Vol. VII, p. 611.
7. Falkus (ed.), *Private Lives*, pp. 109–10.
8. Falkus (ed.), *Private Lives*, p. 109.
9. Murdin, W., *A Collection of State Papers Relating to Affairs in the Reign of Queen Elizabeth, 1571–96 . . . Left by William Cecil Lord Burghley . . . at Hatfield House* (London, 1759), p. 558; *CSP, Scotland 1584–5*, Vol. VII, p. 5.
10. Murdin, *A Collection of State Papers*, p. 559; *CSP, Scotland 1584–5*, Vol. VII, p. 5.
11. Marcus, Mueller and Rose, *Elizabeth I*, p. 168; Heisch, A., 'Elizabeth I and the Persistence of Patriarchy', *Feminist Review*, Part IV (London, 1980), p. 50.
12. Pryor, *Elizabeth I*, p. 51.
13. *CSP, Scotland 1563–69*, Vol. II, p. 430.
14. Arnold, *Queen Elizabeth's Wardrobe Unlock'd*, pp. 1–2; *CSPV*, Vol. IX, p. 239.
15. Merton, 'The Women who Served Queen Mary and Queen Elizabeth', p. 106.

16. Williams, N., *Elizabeth I, Queen of England* (London, 1967), p. 256; *CSPF, Elizabeth 1581–82*, p. 589; *CSPS, Elizabeth 1580–86*, Vol. III, p. 495.

17. HMC, *Salisbury*, Vol. XIII, pp. 254–5, 309.

18. Perry, M., *The Word of a Prince* (London, 1990), p. 273.

19. Marcus, Mueller and Rose, *Elizabeth I*, pp. 186–8, 199–202; Chamberlain, *Sayings*, pp. 240–3.

20. Strickland, *Life of Queen Elizabeth*, p. 476.

21. Strickland, *Life of Queen Elizabeth*, p. 477.

22. Ballard, G., *Memoirs of Several Ladies of Great Britain who have been celebrated for their writings or skill in the learned languages, arts and sciences* (Detroit, 1985), p. 175.

23. Longford, E. (ed.), *The Oxford Book of Royal Anecdotes* (Oxford, 1989), p. 244. The dog died soon afterwards, apparently from pining for his dead mistress.

24. Camden, *Historie of the Most Renowned and Victorious Princesse Elizabeth*, p. 115.

25. BM Lansdowne MS 1236 fo.32.

26. Camden, *Historie of the Most Renowned and Victorious Princesse Elizabeth*, p. 115; *CSPV*, VIII, p. 256.

27. Falkus (ed.), *Private Lives*, pp. 115–16.

28. Weir, *Life of Elizabeth*, p. 381.

CHAPTER 16 'THE CROOKED CARCASS'

1. Lynn, *Tudor Fashion*.

2. Above the word 'poor', Dudley added the symbol that the Queen used to denote his nickname of 'Eyes' – 'ōō'. Dudley's last letter to Elizabeth is now preserved in The National Archives. SP 12/215 fo.65.

3. Somerset, A., *Ladies-in-Waiting: From the Tudors to the present day* (London, 1984), p. 71.

4. See for example: BM Additional MS 12,506, fos.47, 72; 12,507 fo.131.

5. See for example: Richardson, R.E., *Mistress Blanche: Queen Elizabeth I's Confidante* (Herefordshire, 2007), p. 78.

6. Ashdown, *Ladies-in-Waiting*, p. 60.

7. Weir, *Life of Elizabeth*, p. 260.

8. Merton, 'The Women who Served Queen Mary and Queen Elizabeth', pp. 54–5.

9. Williamson, C., *Lady Anne Clifford, Countess of Dorset, Pembroke and Montgomery 1590–1676* (Wakefield, 1967), p. 37.

10. Merton, 'The Women who Served Queen Mary and Queen Elizabeth', pp. 168, 171, 180, 194, 197; SP 46/125 fo.236. For other examples of Lady Warwick's influence at court, see: BM Additional MS 27,401 fo.21; 12,406 fos.41, 80; Lansdowne MS 128 fo.12; HMC, *Salisbury*, Vol. IV, p. 199; Vol. V, pp. 53, 444, 481; Vol. VI, p. 402; Vol. IX, p. 21; Vol. X, pp. 86, 319; Vol. XIV, pp. 16–17.

11. Merton, 'The Women who Served Queen Mary and Queen Elizabeth', pp. 165, 168.

12. HMC, *De L'Isle and Dudley*, Vol. II, pp. 203–5.

13. HMC, *De L'Isle and Dudley*, Vol. II, p. 314.

14. HMC, *De L'Isle and Dudley*, Vol. II, p. 472.

15. Wilson, *Queen Elizabeth's Maids of Honour*, p. 133.

16. Harrison, G.B., *The Letters of Queen Elizabeth* (London, 1935), p. 268; Pasmore, S., *The Life and Times of Queen Elizabeth I at Richmond Palace* (Richmond Local History Society, 2003), p. 56.

17. Thoms, W.J. (ed.), *Anecdotes and Traditions, Illustrative of Early English History and Literature*, Camden Society (London, 1850), pp. 70–1.

18. Haigh (ed.), *Elizabeth I*, p. 98.

19. Harington, *Nugae Antiquae*, p. 125.

20. The 'Grace Cup' or 'Loving Cup' was a silver bowl or tankard with two handles that was traditionally passed round the table after grace had been said.

21. Harington, *Nugae Antiquae*, p. 125.

22. Hibbert, *Elizabeth I*, p. 253.

23. Jenkins, *Elizabeth the Great*, p. 296.

24. Smith, *Clean*, p. 192.

25. Camden, C., *The Elizabethan Woman* (New York, 1975), p. 178.

26. Wilson, *Queen Elizabeth's Maids of Honour*, p. 3.

27. HMC, *Salisbury*, Vol. IV, p. 153. Elizabeth Southwell was the granddaughter of Elizabeth's friend, the Countess of Nottingham.

28. Klarwill (ed.), *Queen Elizabeth and Some Foreigners*, p. 336.

29. Birch, *Memoirs of the Reign of Queen Elizabeth*, Vol. I, p. 79.

30. Murdin, *A Collection of State Papers*, p. 657.

31. Chamberlain, *Letters*, p. 44.

32. *CSPD, Elizabeth 1598–1601*, p. 97.

33. Somerset, *Elizabeth I*, pp. 552–3.

34. HMC, *De L'Isle and Dudley*, Vol. II, p. 265.

35. Harington, *Nugae Antiquae*, p. 90.

36. Falkus (ed.), *Private Lives*, p. 117.

37. Camden, *Historie of the Most Renowned and Victorious Princesse Elizabeth*, p. 172.

38. Falkus (ed.), *Private Lives*, pp. 119–20.

39. Falkus (ed.), *Private Lives*, pp. 122–3.

40. Harington, *Nugae Antiquae*, p. 90; Perry, M., *The Word of a Prince* (London, 1990), p. 316; *CSPV*, Vol. IX, pp. 531–2.

41. Smith, *Clean*, p. 192.

42. Harrison and Jones, *Andre Hurault de Maisse*, pp. 25–6, 36–9, 55.

43. Rye (ed.), *England as seen by Foreigners*, Vol. III pp. 104–5; Pasmore, *The Life and Times of Queen Elizabeth I*, p. 9; *CSPV*, Vol. VII, p. 628; Harrison and Jones, *Andre Hurault de Maisse*, pp. 55–6.

44. Williams (ed. and trans.), *Thomas Platter's Travels*, p. 192.

45. Harrison and Jones, *Andre Hurault de Maisse*, pp. 23–4.

46. Klarwill (ed.), *Queen Elizabeth and Some Foreigners*, p. 394.

47. Goodman, *How To Be a Tudor*, p. 205.

48. Arnold, *Queen Elizabeth's Wardrobe Unlock'd*, p. 12.

49. Harington, *Nugae Antiquae*, p. 90; Falkus (ed.), *Private Lives*, p. 124.

50. Watkins, *In Public and Private*, p. 75.

51. Weir, *Life of Elizabeth*, p. 470.

52. Camden, *Historie of the Most Renowned and Victorious Princesse Elizabeth*, p. 222.

53. *CSPD, Elizabeth 1580–1625*, Addenda, p. 407.

54. Nichols, *Progresses*, Vol. III, p. 612; Merton, 'The Women who Served Queen Mary and Queen Elizabeth', p. 90.

55. *CSPD, Elizabeth 1601–03*, p. 301; Gristwood, S., *Arbella* (London, 2003), p. 188; *CSPV*, Vol. VII, p. 554.

56. Falkus (ed.), *Private Lives*, p. 122.

57. Weir, *Life of Elizabeth*, p. 480; Haigh (ed.), *Elizabeth I*, p. 166; Harington, *Nugae Antiquae*, p. 96.

58. Harington, *Nugae Antiquae*, p. 96; Boyle (ed.), *Memoirs of the Life of Robert Carey*, pp. 137–8.

59. Bassnett, S., *Elizabeth I: A Feminist Perspective* (Oxford and New York, 1988), p. 258.

60. Bassnett, *Elizabeth I*, p. 149.

61. Merton, 'The Women who Served Queen Mary and Queen Elizabeth', p. 90; Birch, *Memoirs of the Reign of Queen Elizabeth*, Vol. II, pp. 506–7; Boyle (ed.), *Memoirs of the Life of Robert Carey*, p. 140; Pasmore, *The Life and Times of Queen Elizabeth I*, p. 65.

62. Boyle (ed.), *Memoirs of the Life of Robert Carey*, p. 137.

63. *CSPD, Elizabeth 1601–3*, pp. 298, 301; *CSPV*, Vol. IX, p. 554; HMC, *Salisbury*, Vol. XII, p. 670.

64. *CSPD, Elizabeth 1601–3*, pp. 298, 301; *CSPV*, Vol. IX, p. 554. See also: HMC, *Salisbury*, Vol. XII, p. 670.

65. *CSPD, Elizabeth 1601–3*, p. 303.

66. Brewer, *The Death of Kings*, p. 151.

67. *CSPD, Elizabeth 1601–3*, p. 302.

68. Read, C. and Plummer, E. (eds), *Elizabeth of England: Certain observations concerning the life and reign of Queen Elizabeth by John Chapman* (Philadelphia, 1951), p. 99; Kenny, R.W., *Elizabeth's Admiral: The Political Career of Charles Howard, Earl of Nottingham, 1536–1624* (Baltimore and London, 1990), p. 257.

69. Bruce, J. (ed.), *The Diary of John Manningham*, Camden Society (London, 1868), entry for 23 March 1603.

70. Somerset, *Elizabeth I*, p. 569; Bruce (ed.), *Diary of John Manningham*, p. 159.

71. Johnson, *Elizabeth I*, p. 438.

72. Clifford, D.J.H. (ed.), *The Diaries of Lady Anne Clifford* (Stroud, 1992), p. 21.

73. Clifford (ed.), *Diaries of Lady Anne Clifford*, p. 21.

EPILOGUE 'SUCH LACK OF GOOD ORDER'

1. Stewart, A., *The Cradle King: A Life of James VI & I* (London, 2003), pp. 171–2.

2. *CSPV*, Vol. X, *1603–1607* (London, 1900), pp. 58–72.

3. Weldon, Sir A., *The Court and Character of King James* (London, 1650), p. 178.

4. Harington, *Nugae Antiquae*, Vol. I (London, 1804), pp. 348–51.

5. Thurley, S., *Hampton Court: A Social and Architectural History* (New Haven and London, 2003), p. 109.

6. Akrigg, G.P.V., *Jacobean Pageant: Or, the Court of King James I* (London, 1962), p. 241.

7. Akrigg, *Jacobean Pageant*, p. 242.

8. Harington, *Nugae Antiquae*, Vol. I, pp. 351–2.[AS ABOVE]

9. Stewart, *Cradle King*, p. 175.

INDEX

Addington, Thomas 209

Alcaraz, Dr 57

Aldrich, Robert 172

Amadas, Elizabeth 82, 152

Amadas, Robert (Master of the Jewel House) 82

Androgen Insensitivity Syndrome 292–3

Anne of Cleves (1515-57)
  betrothal and marriage to Henry 178–81, 183–4
  description of 180
  disastrous wedding night 184–5
  attempts to please Henry 186
  lack of accomplishments 187
  marriage annulled 188–9
  rewarded for her compliance 189
  hopes to revive association with Henry 203
  comment on Katherine Howard's lack of children 206

Anne of Denmark 373, 374

Anne of York 31, 52

apothecaries see physicians, apothecaries and barber-surgeons

Apparel, Acts of 104, 224, 324

Armada 348–9, 350, 351

Arthur, King 30

Arthur Plantagenet 43, 65

Arthur, Tudor (1486-1502)
  birth 34–5
  given his own household 35–6
  education 36
  character and description 40, 42
  marriage to Catherine of Aragon 54–8, 72
  death 58–60

Ascham, Roger 235

Ashridge 253

Astley, John 233

Astley, Katherine 'Kat' Champernowne (c1502-65)
  involvement in Seymour's infatuation with Elizabeth 228–30, 232–4, 235
  committed to the Tower 234–5
  protests at treatment of Elizabeth by queen's guards 253–4
  concerned at Elizabeth's relationship with Dudley 277
  involvement in King of Sweden's proposed marriage to Elizabeth 280
  appointed keeper of the queen's close-stools 316

astrology, astrologers 110, 155–6, 240–1, 313–14, 339

Audley, Thomas, Lord Chancellor 176

Ayala, Pedro de 50

Aylmer, Thomas, Bishop of London 333

Babington, Anthony 343–4
Bacon, Francis 26, 27
Bacton, Herefordshire 329
Badoer, Andrea (Venetian
  Amabassador) 79, 85
Ball (dog) 16
Banister, John 242
barber-surgeons *see* physicians,
  apothecaries and barber-surgeons
barbers and hairdressers 11, 100, 108,
  221, 320–1
Barbour, Piers 65
Barclay, Alexander 121
Barnes, Cecily 248
Bassano family 187
Baynard's Castle 9, 17, 57, 61
Beaufort, Lady Margaret (1443-1509)
  character and description 6, 40–1
  weeps at her sons coronation 6
  clothes, jewellery and table linen
    15–16
  marriage of eldest daughter to
    Henry VII 18
  Elizabeth of York placed in her
    household 19, 20
  compiles Book of the Royal
    Household 30–1
  attends Elizabeth's confinements 41,
    62
  benefactor of Cambridge University
    52
  believes her son is dying 72
  death of her son Henry 75, 77
  death 77
Beaulieu Abbey 49
Becon, Thomas 271
beds and bedding 23, 24–6, 130–2, 174,
  189, 192, 215, 297, 298, 299, 338
birthing chamber 30–2, 156–7,
  170–1

Bland, Adam (skinner) 326, 331
Bland, Peter (skinner) 326
Blande (a skinner) 328
Bletchingley Manor, Surrey 189
Blount, Elizabeth 'Bessie' 87, 92–3
Blount, William, 4th Baron
  Mountjoy 53
Bodmin Moor 49
Boleyn, Anne (c1504-36)
  turbulent affair with Henry 4,
    146–50, 152–3
  appointed to household of Henry's
    sister Mary 133, 142
  takes part in a masque as
    'Perseverance' 134
  birth and education 142
  character and description 142–4,
    148, 150, 293
  receives luxury gifts from Henry
    147–8, 152
  influence at court 149–50
  triumphant visit to Calais 152–3
  marriage to Henry 153
  pregnancies, miscarriages and
    childbirth 153–7, 158–9, 160, 161–2
  prevented from breastfeeding
    Elizabeth 158
  involvement in Elizabeth's weaning
    159–60
  evidence against 162, 163–4
  arrest and trial 164–5
  execution 165, 274
  name banned from court 212–13
  appoints female court jester 249
Boleyn, Elizabeth, Countess of
  Wiltshire 80, 99, 133
Boleyn, George 133, 163
Boleyn, Mary 133–4, 144
Boleyn, Sir Thomas, 1st Earl of
  Wiltshire 99, 133, 142, 144

Book of Common Prayer (1549 & 1552) 236, 312

Book of the Courtier (Castiglione) 103

Book of the Excellent Fortunes of Henry Duke of York and his Parents' (1500) 62

Book of Nurture (c1452) 47

Boone, Gwilliam 328

Borde, Andrew ('Merry Andrew') 112, 121, 205, 214

Bosworth, Battle of (1495) 5, 15, 18

Boulogne, siege of (1544) 107–8

Bowge of Court (Skelton) 52–3

Brallot, Guillam (embroiderer) 324

Brandon, Charles, Duke of Suffolk 70–1, 136, 210, 239

Brandon, Henry 210, 239

Brantôme, Pierre de 143

Bray, Sir Reynolds 40

Braybrooke, James 65

Brellont, Guillaume 213

Brereton, William 151, 163

Bridges, John (tailor) 324

Bridges, Master (Lieutenant of the Tower) 255

Bristowe, Nicholas 107–8, 196

Browne, Anne 70–1

Brussels, Jane 316–17

Bryan, Francis 98

Bryan, Lady Margaret 91, 159, 168, 176, 201, 330

Bucer, Martin 239–40

Buckingham, Edward Stafford, 3rd Duke 82, 98

Bulmer, Joan 193

Burbage, James 310

Burgh, Sir Edward 204

Butts, Sir William 171, 172, 185, 196

Buxton, Derbyshire 334

Caedano, Hieronymus 240–1

Calais 152, 165

Cambridge University 52, 109

Camden, William 268, 288, 346, 368

Campeggio, Cardinal Lorenzo 149

Canterbury Cathedral 81

Capel, Giles 70

Carew, Elizabeth Norwich, Lady 317

Carey, Catherine 134, 317

Carey family 316

Carey, Henry, 1st Baron Hunsdon 134

Carey, Sir Robert 369, 370

Carey, William 133

Carles, Lancelot de 142

Carles, Robert 318

Caroz, Luis 81

Casimir, Duke of 288

Castel of Helth (Elyot) 305

Castiglione, Baldassare 103

Castillon, Louis Perreau, Sieur de 177

Catherine of Aragon (1485-1536) 247

  marriage to Arthur 55–8

  death of Arthur 58–9

  as potential bride for her father-in-law 66–7

  betrothal and marriage to Henry 68, 71–2, 79–80

  health of 68–9

  household 80

  pregnancies and childbirth 80–7, 90–2, 139, 149

  piety of 83, 122, 148

  ignores Henry's affairs 134

  practices her dance steps 139

  expenditure on clothes 148

  marriage annulled 149, 150–1, 153

  banishment from court 150–1

  continues to make Henry's shirts 150

  refuses to give Anne her jewels 152

  death of 162

Catherine de Valois 6

Cecil, Richard 103

Cecil, Robert 291

Cecil, William, Lord Burleigh
(1520-98)
  rise to prominence 103
  nicknamed 'Sir Spirit' 276
  possible involvement in Amy
    Robsart's death 278
  involved in Elizabeth's matrimonial
    negotiations 280
  in Elizabeth's bedchamber with
    Dudley 283
  employs John Dee as a foreign spy
    313
  writes instructions to protect
    Elizabeth from ingesting or
    absorbing poison in her gowns
    319–20
  instructed to find a skilled tailor 325
  assured that Elizabeth can still bear
    children 338
  orders door to Elizabeth's privy
    bedchamber broken down 351–2

Cecilia, Princess 357

Cecily of York 31

Chamberlain, Sir John 364

Chambers, Lady Elizabeth 228

Chapman, John 366

Chapuys, Eustace 122, 152, 153, 155,
  159, 160, 162, 166, 167, 205

Charles, Duc d'Angoulême 287

Charles IX, King of France 290

Charles V 149, 153, 162, 251, 259, 265, 270

Cheke, Sir John 210, 239

Chelsea Manor, London 226, 227–8,
  230, 235

Chenies Manor, Buckinghamshire
  192

Chertsey Abbey, Surrey 75

Cheshunt, Hertfordshire 230–1

Cheyney, Sir Thomas 216

Christian IV, King of Denmark 374

Christina, Duchess of Milan 178

Civiltie of Childhood (Erasmus) 202

Clarence, George Plantagenet, 1st
  Duke 91

Clarencieux, Susan 248

Claude of France 133, 142

cleanliness *see* sanitation, washing
  and cleanliness

Clifford, Lady Anne 370, 375

clothes 136
  accessories 127, 322, 325
  Anne of Cleves wardrobe 186
  for babies and children 91, 174
  care and cleaning 16, 102, 125–9, 186,
    331
  Catherine Howard's wardrobe 190,
    195–6
  checked for poison 319–20
  depicted in paintings 102, 143, 168–9,
    181–2, 223–4, 235, 318, 325, 328
  during pregnancy 169
  Edward VI's wardrobe 209, 223–4
  effect on posture and movement
    322–3
  Elizabeth I's wardrobe 208–9, 235–6,
    246–7, 284, 317–32, 342, 366, 367, 373
  fashionable 55, 103, 143, 167, 180,
    252–3, 366
  furs 95, 126, 216–17, 218, 331
  Garter Robes 79, 196
  given as gifts 19, 29–30, 38, 107, 114,
    141, 165, 188, 190, 246, 325–6,
    329–30
  given to Mary Stuart 341–2
  hats 107–8
  Henry VIII's wardrobe 103–8, 178,
    216–17, 220–1

Henry VII's wardrobe 15, 16
importance of 164
inventories 95, 96, 102, 107, 166–7,
    168, 176, 196, 206, 221, 332
Lady Jane Grey's apparel 244
Jane Seymour's wardrobe 166–7
jewellery 15, 47, 50, 55, 61, 328
Katherine Parr's wardrobe 206–7,
    208–9, 217–18
legislation concerning 104, 224,
    324
as mark of status 13–14, 15, 153
Mary Tudor's wardrobe 208–9,
    246–7, 253, 266
mourning 72
production of 14–15, 16, 38, 105–7,
    167, 327–9
queen's wardrobe 17
recycling of 329
servants in charge of 102–3
shoes 207, 323, 326–7
storage of 17–18, 331–2
sums spent on 14, 15, 329
tailors and embroiderers 14–15, 95,
    105, 106, 127, 167, 206–7, 324–7
Thomas Cromwell's attire 196
undergarments 15, 23, 102, 104, 330
weddings 55, 183–4, 257–8
wigs 321, 322, 359
worn by Anne Boleyn at her
    execution 165
worn by Katherine Howard at her
    execution 197
see also textiles
Cobbe, Marjory 33
Coldharbour manor house 19
The Comfort of Lovers (Hawes) 73
Company of Barbers and Surgeons
    109
Compton, Edmund 96

Compton, Sir William 61, 82, 96–7,
    144–5
Conway, Sir Hugh 65
Coombe Hill 120, 199
Cooper, Jane ('Jane Fool') 249–50
Cornwallis, Mrs (cook) 114
Cox, Richard 209–10
Cranmer, Thomas, Archbishop of
    Canterbury 150, 171, 194, 219
Cromwell, Thomas (1485-1540) 149, 152
    gathers evidence against Anne 162,
        163–4
    told of Elizabeth's eating habits 168
    learns of Edward's progress 176
    involvement in Anne of Cleves
        marriage 179, 180, 184, 186
    asked to provide clothes for
        Elizabeth 330
Culpeper, Nicholas 27, 193, 194, 195,
    197
Culpeper, Thomas 192
Cumnor Place, Oxfordshire 277
Curteys, Peter 18
Cutte (spaniel) 105

Darnley, Henry Stuart, Lord 285, 341
Dean's House 256
Dee, John 313–14, 339, 369
Delft, François van der 218
Denny, Sir Anthony 186, 216, 219, 221,
    230
Denton, Elizabeth 43, 61, 91
Denys, Hugh 47, 65, 75
Dereham, Francis 187, 188, 193, 195,
    197
Deryck, Dionisia 291
Devereux, Robert, 2nd Earl of Essex
    (1565-1601)
    witnesses Elizabeth in her privy
        apartments 1–2, 365

barred from entering the privy
chamber 295
parade staged by 351
as queen's favourite 364
mocks Elizabeth behind her back
365
secretly marries Frances
Walsingham 365
defeat of his rebellion 368
Devereux, Walter, 1st Earl of Essex
287, 364
Domus Magnificence (upstairs household) 11, 12
Domus Providencie (below stairs
household) 11, 12
Dormer, Jane 231, 248
Douglas, Mary, Countess of Lennox
254
Dudley, Ambrose, Earl of Warwick
354
Dudley, Anne, Countess of Warwick
354–5, 370, 372
Dudley, Arthur 347–8
Dudley, Edmund 71, 79
Dudley, Guildford 244, 253
Dudley, John, Duke of
Northumberland 237, 242
Dudley, Robert, Earl of Leicester
(1532-88)
friendship with Edward VI 210,
238
relationship with Elizabeth I 210,
238, 274, 276–80, 283, 286–7, 336,
338, 344
death of his wife Amy Robsart
277–8
as possible husband for Mary Stuart
281–5
in Elizabeth's bedchamber with
Cecil 283

liaison with Lettice Knollys 286–7,
336, 337
affair with Douglas Sheffield 287,
336
patronage of troupe of actors 310,
311
retains a fool 310
stages series of lavish entertainments 336
witnesses Elizabeth's reaction to
Mary Stuart's letter 345
death of 350–2
illegitimate son exiled from court
364

Edmund Tudor (1499-1500) 51, 64
The Education of a Christian Woman
(Vives) 134–5
Edward the Black Prince 328
Edward the Confessor 24
Edward III 6, 10, 19
Edward IV 5, 9, 12, 13, 14, 18, 20, 38,
53
Edward V 18
Edward VI (1537-53)
death of 4, 243
birth and christening 171–2
childhood and education 173–6, 201,
209, 210–11, 238–9
household size and cost 175–6,
209–12, 237–8
relationship with his half-sisters 175,
237
health of 196, 240–3
taught social rules and behaviours
201–3
love of rich clothes and possessions
209, 223–5
character and description 211, 222,
236, 237, 241

reveres his mother's memory
211–12
childhood possessions 212
coronation 220, 223
religious beliefs and reforms 222–3,
236–7
fond of music and sport 225, 239
reaction to Katherine's marriage to
Seymour 226
keeps a journal 239
reaction to illness and deaths of
friends 239–40
disinclined to marry 240
interested in astronomy and
astrology 240–1
tries to secure line of succession
242
Egerton, Sir Thomas 325
Elizabeth I (1533-1603)
character and description 1, 271–2,
292–3, 342–3, 360, 365–8
never forgives Robert Devereux for
his untimely intrusion 1–2
desire for privacy 3, 279, 295, 302–3,
369, 371
sexual health and virginity 4, 279,
280, 287–93, 338, 340
birth and childhood 157, 168, 175
considered a bastard 165
demoted to rank of 'Lady' 167–8
attends Edward's christening 171
taught social rules and behaviours
202–3
education of 209, 210, 228
relationship with Katherine Parr
209, 213–14, 227
wears her mother's pendant in
family portrait 212–13
Thomas Seymour's dalliance with
227, 228–31, 232–5

rumours concerning illegitimate
children 231, 291
portraits of 235, 249, 318, 325, 328,
352
transforms her image 235–6
relationship with her half-brother
Edward 237
health of 253–4, 280, 292, 323, 333–4,
367
committed to the Tower 254–5
writes placatory letter to Mary 254
Gardiner's plot to execute her 255
Mary Tudor's antipathy towards
261–2, 263, 265–6
Philip of Spain's dalliance with
263–4, 265–6
as possible bride for Philip of Spain
263, 289–90
acknowledged as Mary's successor
to the throne 269–70
disinclined to marry 272–5, 282
flirtatious nature 272, 366–7
rejects several suitors 272, 280–1,
337–9
relationship with Robert Dudley
276–80, 283, 286–7
suggests that Robert Dudley should
marry Mary, Queen of Scots
281–5
attempts to beguile Sir James
Melville 283–5
jealousy of Mary Stuart 284–6
rumoured to be a man 290–1
court of 294–6
as user and embellisher of palaces
296–302
sensitive to unpleasant aromas
300–2
consumption of food and drink
302–7

covert affection for her mother 304–5

eating and drinking habits 305–7, 365

enjoys physical exercise, reading, playing cards and embroidery 307–8

love of dancing, music and theatre 308–11, 367–8

as skilled needlewoman 308

religious beliefs 311–13

fascinated by astrology and alchemy 313–14

female attendants 315–22, 352–9, 361–4

enrobing ceremony 317–20

excommunicated by the Pope 317

wears wigs 321, 322, 359

dental regime 332–3

personal hygiene 334–5, 360–1

makes a virtue of her unmarried state 340–1

imprisons and humiliates Mary Stuart 341–2

suffers from middle-age spread 342–3

relationship with Mary Stuart's son James 343

reluctantly agrees to execution of Mary Stuart 344–7

Philip's smear campaigns against 347–8

success against the Spanish Armada 348–9

Tilbury speech 348–9

celebrated as 'Gloriana' 349, 370

grief-stricken at death of Dudley 350–2

mourns the loss of close female attendants 352–4

irritated at youthful female attendants 357–8

insolence of female attendants towards 358–9

thick layers of makeup used by 359–61

punishes female transgressors 362–4

fading looks noted and reported by many 365–7

decline and paranoia in old age 368–72

guilt at Mary Stuart's death 370–1

death of 371–2, 373

Elizabeth Tilney, Countess of Surrey 52

Elizabeth Tudor (1492-95) 44, 64

Elizabeth of Valois 240

Elizabeth of York (1466-1503)

character and description 18–19, 50

lineage 18, 19

marriage to Henry VII 19–22

placed in her mother-in-law's household 19, 20

receives gifts from Henry 19, 26, 29–30, 38, 39

bedding ceremony 22–6, 28

pregnancies and childbirth 26–35, 37–9, 41–2, 43–4, 50, 51, 60, 61–3

given her own chambers 28

churching ceremony 35, 42

influence on Arthur's education 36, 53

coronation 37

makes and presents gifts to Henry 38

female attendants and household 39–40, 43

death of children 44, 51, 59–60

marriage of Arthur to Catherine 55

death and burial 63–4

makes improvements at Greenwich Palace 80
Eltham Ordinances (1526) 144–6
Eltham Palace 9, 43, 51, 53, 61, 69, 83
Elyot, Sir Thomas 129, 137, 305
Empson, Sir Richard 69, 71, 79
entertainments 151, 159
  court jesters 8, 140–2, 225, 249–50, 309–10
  dancing 139, 150, 210, 308–9
  Jacobean 374
  masques 134, 250
  music 176, 208, 225, 250, 284–5, 308
  Revels 222
  theatre 139–40, 225, 250, 310–11
Erasmus, Desiderius 52, 53–4, 79, 140, 141, 201, 202, 210
Eric XIV, King of Sweden 280–1, 357
Esher 170
Exeter 49

Fagolo, Paolo 252
The Family of Henry VIII (painting) 212–13
Famous Imposters (Stoker) 291
Ferdinand of Aragon 24, 68, 71, 73, 81
Feria, Gômez Suárez de Figueroa y Córdoba, 1st Duke of 270, 288
Fetherstone, Dr Richard 135
Field of the Cloth of Gold (1520) 118, 134, 219
Fiennes de Clinton, Lady Elizabeth ('Fair Geraldine') 278, 352–3
Fisher, Bishop John 40, 76
Fisher, John 219
Fitzpatrick, Barnaby 210, 238
Fitzroy, Henry, Duke of Richmond and Somerset 93, 135–6, 167
Fitzwalter, Elizabeth Stafford, Countess of Sussex 82

Fitzwilliam, William 99
Flodden Field, Battle of (1513) 85
food and drink
  ale and wine 23, 116–17, 120, 305, 307
  cheese 117, 304
  for children 160, 168
  confectionary and sweet treats 114, 306
  cost and quantity 250
  during pregnancy 28, 81, 83
  Elizabethan period 302–7
  feasts and banquets 21–2, 136, 304
  fish 118
  health-giving properties 115–16
  humanist views on 305
  infected with listeriosis 86
  keeping, preparing and cooking 115, 119–21
  meals of the day 112–18, 122, 303–4
  meat 114, 115, 116, 305
  salad, fruit and vegetables 117, 304, 306–7
  snacks 114, 115
  utensils 304
Fortescue, Sir John 13, 319, 329
Fotheringay Castle, Northamptonshire 344, 345–6, 347
Fox, Nicholas 68
Fox, Richard, Bishop of Winchester 75
Foxe, John 262, 263, 265
Francis I, King of France 106, 133, 134, 152, 172, 287
François, Duke of Alençon and Anjou 290, 337–9, 340
Fyrst Boke of the Introduction of Knowledge (Borde) 112, 214
Fyshe, Walter (tailor) 325–6

Gage, Sir John 139

gambling 7–8, 62, 138, 187, 225, 250
Gardiner, Stephen 217, 255, 258
Garret (shoemaker) 328
Gates, Sir John 238
George, Lord Tailboys of Kyme (Lincolnshire) 93
Gesner, Conrad 224
Gheeraerts the Younger, Marcus 325
Ginzam, Alexander 240
Giovanni de' Gigli 26
Giustinian, Sebastian 92, 103, 122
Glasebury, Henry 40
Glastonbury, Somerset 49
The Globe theatre 310
Glover, William 156
Gómez de Fuensalida, Don Gutierre 73–4
Gómez de Silva, Ruy 257, 258, 259, 263
Goose, John (court jester) 140
Gorges, Helena Snakenborg 357, 372
Gosson, Stephen 308
The Governance of England (Fortescue) 13
Great Wardrobe 17–18
Green, William (coffer-maker) 331
Greenwich Palace see Palace of Placentia
Grene (coffermaker) 328
Grenier, Pasquier 16
Grey, Henry, 1st Duke of Suffolk 228
Grey, Lady Jane 228, 232, 240, 242, 243–4, 253
Grimaldi bank 74
Grindal, William 228
Grisby, Lady ('Dame of Pleasure') 375
Guildford, Henry 51, 63, 99
Guildford, Sir Richard 51

hairdressers see barbers and hair-dressers
Hall, Edward 56, 183, 215, 219
Hampton Court 165, 191, 195, 206, 234, 263, 280
  Bayne Tower (secret lodgings) 198–9, 215
  Chapel Court 174
  chapel of 171
  Edward VI's private suite of rooms 174
  Elizabeth I's possessions at 297
  fresh water supply 120
  Great Hall 120, 155
  Great Watching Chamber 120
  Henry's bedchamber at 174
  Henry's embroidered chair at 213
  Jewel House at 137, 199
  Katherine Parr's suite of rooms 208
  kitchens 118–21, 174
  landing stage at 302
  larders 120
  library 297
  Paradise Chamber 297
  plan of 200
  privy garden 297–8
  remodelled and extended 94, 169, 173–4, 198–9
  sporting facilities 137, 151
  steam baths installed 124
  suite of rooms filled with alchemical equipment 314
  toilet arrangements and Great House of Easement 129–30
  washing facilities 174, 199
Harcourt, Mistress 61
Hardwick, Bess of 340
Harington, Sir John 296, 302, 305, 358, 365, 368, 374, 375
Harris, Anne (laundress) 128

Harris, Richard (royal fruiterer) 117

Hastings, Anne 82

Hastings, George, 1st Earl of
Huntingdon 82

Hastings, Henry, 3rd Earl of
Huntingdon 355–6

Hastings, Lady Katherine, Countess
of Huntingdon 355–6

Hatfield House, Hertfordshire 235,
269, 352, 353

Hatton, Sir Christopher 276, 340

Havering Palace, Havering-atte-
Bower (Greater London) 174

Hawes, Stephen 73

Heneage, Thomas 152, 195

Henry III 24

Henry IV 8

Henry IV, King of France 295

Henry, Lord Hastings 210

Henry Tudor (1511) 83–4

Henry V 6, 10, 328

Henry VI 5, 8, 13

Henry VII (1457-1509)
weeps at death of Arthur 3
prospective brides for 4, 66–8
gains the throne 5–6
birth and exile 6
character and description 6–8, 26–7,
50, 66, 68
household accounts 7–8
inherits suite of palaces 8–10
household structure and members
10–13, 45–9, 73
daily routine 101
pageantry and ceremony 10–11
apparel 13–16, 17–18
fondness for tapestries 16–17
marriage to Elizabeth 18–22
presents gifts to Elizabeth 19, 26,
29–30, 38, 39

legitimation of kingship 20
bedding ceremony 22–6, 28
insecurities and paranoia 45, 49, 69,
73, 76
correspondence with his mother 54
failing eyesight 54
secures bride for Arthur 54–5
death and burial of Elizabeth 63–4,
65–6
health 64–5, 68, 72–6
keeps a watchful eye on his son
Henry 69–70, 71, 74
death and burial 75–7

Henry VIII (1491-1547)
dalliances and infidelities 4, 82–3,
86–8, 90, 92–3, 133–4, 149, 155, 185
turbulent affair with Anne Boleyn
4, 146–50, 152–3
birth, childhood and education 42,
43, 51–4
character and description 43, 70, 74,
78–9, 104, 181–2, 191, 205, 293
attends his brother's wedding to
Catherine 55, 57
grief at death of his mother 63–4
betrothal and marriage to
Catherine of Aragon 68, 71–2,
79–80
cosseted and restricted by his father
69–70, 74
created Prince of Wales 69
passion for sport, entertainment,
drinking and women 71, 101, 122,
130, 136, 137–8, 139–42, 181
grief at death of his son Henry 84
health of 86, 163, 177–8, 181–3, 185,
191, 192, 206, 214–17
commissions several new palaces
93–4
illegitimate children 93, 134, 135–6

extravagance of 94–6, 327

household structure and members 97–100, 101–3, 169–70

love of clothes and jewels 103–8, 178, 206, 216–18

examined by his physicians 108–12, 205

shaved by his barber 108

meals of the day 112–18

piety of 122–3

bathing, personal hygiene and toilet arrangements 123–5, 126, 129–30, 182

bedding routine 130–2

annulment of his marriage to Catherine 149, 150–1

marries Anne Boleyn 153

infatuated by Jane Seymour 160–1, 162–3

distaste for Anne Boleyn 161–2

jousting accident 162, 166, 177–8, 181

sexual prowess 166, 185, 189, 190–1

remodels Hampton Court 169

organises care and education of his son 173–6

reveres memory of Jane Seymour 173

betrothal and marriage to Anne of Cleves 178–81, 183–4

deeply disappointed in Anne of Cleves 180, 181, 184–5

marries Katherine Howard 188, 189–90

commissions new tapestries 194–5

learns of Catherine Howard's infidelities 194–6

commissions secret lodgings in his palaces 198–201

introduces suites of secret lodgings 198–201

courtship and marriage to Katherine Parr 203, 205–6, 217

commissions suite of lodgings for Katherine Parr at Hampton Court 208

commissions portrait of his family 212

death and burial 218–19, 220

Hentzner, Paul 327

Hepburn, James, 4th Earl of Bothwell 341

Herne (hosier) 328

Hever Castle 99, 189

Heywood, John 249

Hildegard of Bingen 88

Hill, Richard (sergeant of the cellar) 138

Hilliard, Nicholas 308, 340

Hilton, William 106

Historia Animalum (Gesner) 224

Hoby, Lady Elizabeth 208

Holbein, Hans 143, 147–8, 168–9, 201, 299–300

Hood, William (locksmith) 332

Hope, Ralph 320

Horenbout, Lucas 96

Howard, Agnes Tilney, Dowager Duchess of Norfolk 187, 188, 193, 194

Howard, Charles 190, 371

Howard, Elizabeth *see* Boleyn, Elizabeth, Countess of Wiltshire

Howard family 316

Howard, Katherine (1523-42)
courted by Henry 187, 188

sexual experience and affairs 187–8, 192–6

receives gifts from Henry 188, 190

character and description 189–90

marriage to Henry 189

possible pregnancy and miscarriage 191–2
imprisonment and execution 196–7, 274
Howard, Katherine, Countess of Nottingham 278, 356, 371
Howard, Lady Mary 358–9, 364, 365
Howard, Thomas, 2nd Duke of Norfolk 52, 99, 133
Howard, Thomas, 3rd Duke of Norfolk 52, 152, 162, 166, 188, 218, 277
Huick, Dr 288
Humphrey, Duke of Gloucester 8
Hunsdon House (Hertfordshire) 150, 174
Hurault, André, Sieur de Maisse 295–6, 308, 366–7
Hussey, William 70

Ibgrave, William 252
In Praise of Cleane Linen (17th century verse) 126
In Praise of Folly (Erasmus) 140
infant mortality 44, 51
Ippolyta the Tartaryan (dwarf) 309, 310
Isabella of Castile 24, 66, 247
Isabella of Portugal 251
Ivan IV the Terrible 326

James IV of Scotland 45, 85
James VI & I 286, 341, 343, 347, 368, 373–6
Jane the Fool *see* Cooper, Jane
Jane, Lady Lisle 208
Jane, Lady (cousin of Katherine Parr) 208
Jasper, Earl of Pembroke 6
Jasper, Stephen 14, 106

Jeffrey, Richard (locksmith) 332
jewellery 240
  Anne Boleyn's jewels 148, 152, 153
  Anne of Cleves' jewels 183, 186, 189
  availability for portrait painters 102
  Black Prince's Ruby 328
  Catherine of Aragon's jewels 55, 85, 152
  crown jewels 94, 223
  Edward VI's jewels 223, 224
  Elizabeth I's jewels 235, 236, 309, 318–19, 320, 328, 330–1, 332, 338, 352, 356
  given to the Duke of Anjou 338
  Henry VIII's jewels 50, 107, 108, 178, 183
  Katherine Howard's jewels 190, 195
  Katherine Parr's jewels 205, 207, 217
  Mary Tudor's jewels 270
  recycling of 165, 223
  responsibility for 47, 61, 317, 327, 331, 356
  storage of 11, 105, 199
  sums spent on 15
Joan (Elizabeth of York's gentle-woman) 51
Joanna, Queen of Naples 67
John of Gaunt 6
Johnson, Garret (shoemaker) 326–7
Jones, William (tailor) 326, 327, 342
Jonson, Ben 290, 291, 293
Jurden, William (skinner) 326

Katherine Tudor (1503) 62–3
Keble, Thomas 291
Kimbolton Castle 162
king's evil (scrofula) 49, 123
Kingston, Sir William 136
Knollys family 316
Knollys, Lettice 286–7, 336, 337, 364

Knollys, Sir Francis 342, 357
Knox, John 247
Kyvet, Thomas 70

Langton, Elizabeth (silkwoman) 15
Langton, Thomas 15
Langues, Jehan 178
Lascelles, Mary 194
laundries, launderesses 91, 102, 125–8, 266, 289, 291, 338
Le Doux, Piero 114
Leicester's Men 310, 311
Leland, John 216
Lewis, Master 51
libraries 123
Linacre, Thomas 135
Lippomano, Hieronimo 273
London Grey Friars 42
Longueville, Duc de 87
Lord Chamberlain's Men 310
Lorraine, Francis I, Duke of 188
Louis XII 86, 133
Lovekyn, George 14
Lovell, Thomas 20
Love's Labour's Lost (Shakespeare) 309, 310
Lucretia the Tumbler (court jester) 249–50
Ludlow castle 58–9, 135
Luxembourg, François de 41

Machyn, Henry 262
Maisse, Sieur de *see* Hurault, André, Sieur de Maisse
Malt, Isabel 264–5
Margaret of Anjou 8
Margaret of Austria 142
Margaret of Burgundy 45
Margaret of Savoy 67
Margaret Tudor (1489-1541)

birth 42
childhood 43, 51
attends her brother's wedding festivities 57
grief at mother's death 63
protests at alliance between Scotland and France 85
Marillac, Charles de 181, 191, 216
Markye, John 297
Marney, Sir Henry 61, 69
Mary Stuart, Queen of Scots (1542-87) 240, 264
character and description 281–2
Robert Dudley proposed as her husband 281–5
Elizabeth's jealousy of 284–6
marries Lord Darnley 285
pregnancy and childbirth 285–6
spreads rumours concerning Elizabeth's sexual impediments 340
given clothes by Elizabeth 341–2
imprisoned by Elizabeth 341–4
health of 342
execution and burial 345–7
Mary Tudor (1496-1533)
birth 44
childhood 51
grief at mother's death 63
as wife of Louis XII 87, 133
marries Charles Brandon 136
deportment in dancing 139
Mary Tudor (Queen) (1516-58)
phantom pregnancies 3, 259–65, 267–9
birth and childhood 90–1, 98
household 91, 248
education 134–5
relationship with Jane Seymour 167
attends Edward's christening 171

as regular visitor to her half-brother
  Edward 175
relationship with Katherine Parr
  204, 227
affronted by marriage of Katherine
  Parr to Thomas Seymour 226–7
proclaimed queen 244
character and description 245–7,
  256–7, 267
lack of style 246–7, 257
difficulties of accession 248
favourite companions 249–50
love of feasting and revelry 250–1
commitment to the 'old religion'
  251
marriage to Philip of Spain 251–2,
  255–8
commits her half-sister Elizabeth to
  the Tower 253–5
orders executions of Lady Jane
  Grey and her husband 253
horrified at plot to execute
  Elizabeth 255
health of 256, 259–60, 268
antipathy towards Elizabeth 261–2,
  263, 265–6
distressed at Philip's departures for
  the Continent 265–7
confirms crown to go to Elizabeth
  269–70
death of 269–70
Marzen, Francis 65
Massy, Alice 62
Matsys, Cornelius 181, 216
Maximilian I 67, 74
medicines and potions
  against plague 110
  antidote to noisome smells 300–1
  blood-letting 111, 112
  for constipation 182

for contraception 187–8
in cosmetics 360–2
for dental hygiene 332–3
for eyes 54
herbs 110–11, 112, 124, 300–1
holistic approach 111–12
for impotence 190–1
personal hygiene 208
in pregnancy 28, 32–3, 38
for quinsy and tonsilitis 65
for sweating sickness 75
wounds and ulcers 111, 214
Melville, Sir James 273, 283–5, 286,
  287–8, 291, 321
Memo, Dionysius 135
The Merry Wives of Windsor
  (Shakespeare) 126
Michiel, Giovanni 256, 266, 267
Middleton, William (embroiderer)
  324
midwives 33–4, 62, 157, 236–7
Monarcho (court jester) 309
More, Sir Thomas 53, 64, 79, 124
More, William 14
Moreton, William 14
Mortimer, Margaret 70–1
Morton, Margaret 193
Mother Jack (Edward's nurse) 175
Moulton, Thomas 123

Najera, Juan Esteban, Duke of 207
Nashe, Thomas 141
National Library of Wales 63
Nevers, Charles Gonzaga, Duke of
  368
Neville, Edward 99
Neville, John, 3rd Baron Latimer 204
New Hall, Essex 227
Nonsuch Palace 94, 296, 300, 303, 367
Norfolk, Dukes of see Howard family

Norris, Sir Henry 145, 151–2, 163, 325, 351, 357
Norris, Lady Margaret 357
North, Edward, 1st Baron 264
Nunziata, Toto del 199

Oatlands Palace, Surrey 218
Ormond, Thomas Butler, 7th Earl 53
Overcourt House, Cotswolds 290–1
Owen, Dr 243
Oxford University 52, 109, 152

Pace, Richard 101
Pagula, William 88
Palace of Placentia (formerly 'Bella Court'), Greenwich 59, 265, 267
  backgammon set at 309
  Catherine of Aragon at 68, 92
  Christmas and New Year celebrations at 37, 87, 218, 310
  death of Edward at 242
  dining room at 298
  entertainments at 90
  Henry VII at 74
  hunting and tennis equipment stored at 105, 137
  improvements to 8–9, 80
  jousting at 162, 164
  personal and valuable possessions kept at 199
  privy bridge at 302
  royal confinements and births at 42, 81, 90, 92, 155, 158
  sports facilities at 151
  stool chamber at 129
  weddings at 80, 183–4
Pamplin, Robert 331
Paris, John de 106
Parma, Alexander Farnese, Duke of 348

Parr, Anne 207
Parr, John (embroiderer) 326
Parr, Katherine (1512-48)
  character and description 203–5
  courtship and marriage to Henry 203, 205–6, 217
  relationship with step children 204, 208–9, 212–14, 226–7, 228–9, 531
  receives gifts from Henry 206, 217–18
  receives gifts from Elizabeth 308
  wardrobe of 206–7
  household structure and members 207–8
  given a suite of rooms at Hampton Court 208
  acts as regent for Henry 213–14
  at Henry's deathbed 218
  marries Thomas Seymour 226–7
  retires to her manor at Chelsea 226, 227–8
  learns of Seymour's visits to Elizabeth 229–30
  pregnancy and childbirth 229, 231–2
  death and burial 232
Parr, Maud Green 203–4
Parron, William 62
Parry, Blanche 316, 329, 353–4
Parry, Thomas 233, 234, 235
Patch see Sexton
Paulet, Amias 345
Pedro the Cruel, King of Spain 328
Pendred, Mrs (wet-nurse) 158
Penn, Sybil 175
Penny (a barber) 108
Percy, Henry, 6th Earl of Northumberland 144
Perrers, Alice 19
personal hygiene see sanitation, washing and cleanliness

Peterborough Cathedral 162
Philip the Handsome, King of
  Castile 64
Philip II, King of Spain (1527-98) 286,
  288
  description of 251-2
  portrait of 251
  marriage to Mary Tudor 252, 257-8
  arrival in England 255-6
  first meetings with Mary 256-9
  amuses himself with Elizabeth
    263-4
  Elizabeth I as possible bride for 263,
    289-90
  returns to the Continent 265-8
  refuses to return to Mary's
    deathbed 269, 270
  embarks on smear campaign
    against Elizabeth 347-8
  failure of his Armada 348-9
Philip IV the Fair, King of France 66
physicians, apothecaries and
  barber-surgeons 108-12, 166, 182,
  243, 264
Pius V, Pope 317
Placentia, Palace of (Greenwich) 42
Platter, Thomas 296, 303, 367
Pole, Katherine 91
Pole, Margaret, Countess of
  Salisbury 91
Pole, Reginald, Archbishop of
  Canterbury 211, 259, 266
Pole, Sir Reginald 35-6
Pole, Sir Richard 59
Polson (locksmith) 328
Popincourt, Jane 86-7
potions see medicines and potions
Poyntz, Elizabeth 84
pregnancy
  diet 28, 81, 83

medicines and potions 28, 32-3, 38
  rituals and precautions 29
  signs of 38
  cravings 154, 167
Priuli, Lorenzo 367
privy bridges 302
Privy Chamber 192
  changes initiated by Edward
    Seymour 221
  council meetings held in 302
  daily rituals 101-3
  duties of the gentlemen 97-8, 198,
    218
  Edward VI's changes to 237-8
  Elizabeth I's female attendants
    315-22, 352-9, 361-4
  enhancement of prestige 169-70
  esquires of the body 98-9, 221
  functions transferred from presence
    chamber and council chamber 187
  groom of the stool 46-8, 65, 82,
    96-7, 145, 152, 169, 182, 186, 195,
    221, 222, 316
  grooms and pages 99-100, 221
  guard duties 130
  James VI & I's changes to 375-6
  keepers of the great wardrobe
    17-18, 246
  Mary Tudor's appointments 248
  Northumberland's changes to 237-9
  as part of the 'secret lodgings' 199
  personal or private servants 48-9,
    96-100, 199
  progression and access into 294-6
  putting the king to bed 130-2
  structure modelled on French court
    45-6
  at Whitehall 299-300
  Wolsey's reforms 144-6
  see also servants

Privy Council 170, 192, 198, 199, 220, 238, 269, 295
Privy Kitchen 114, 118–21
Propre boke of new Cokerey (1545) 214
Pudsey, Ralph 61
Puebla, Rodrigo de 39, 41, 72

Quadra, Álvaro de la 288
Quirini, Vincenzo 67

Radcliffe family 316
Radcliffe, Mary 317
Ralegh, Sir Walter 300, 362–3
religious festivals (Easter, Christmas, Candlemass etc) 8, 18, 37, 38, 42, 62, 116, 123, 136, 158, 218, 246, 266, 310
religious reforms 236–7
Renard, Simon 251, 261, 264
Rennes Cathedral 18
Rice, Beatrice ap 266
Richard, Duke of Gloucester 5
Richard, Earl of Kent 70
Richard III, Duke of York 5, 6, 14, 15, 18, 20, 328
Richard of Shrewsbury, Duke of York (1473-c1483) 45
Richmond Palace
  built by Henry VII 57–8
  Catherine of Aragon's confinement at 83
  Christmas celebrations at 62
  Duke of Anjou's visit to 338
  Elizabeth's preference for 298, 344, 370
  given to Anne of Cleves 188, 189
  Henry VIII's childhood at 69
  Henry VII's final illnesses and death at 72, 73, 76
  Mary Tudor's confinement at 268
  privy bridge at 302

royal bedchamber at 174
  sophisticated heating and sanitation at 296–7
  steam baths installed 124
Rizzio, David 341
Robsart, Amy 277–8
Rochford, Jane Boleyn, Countess of 193
Rogers, Edward 221
Ros (or Roos) family 47
Rose, Margaret de la 240
Rose Theatre 311
Royal Assent by Commission Act (1542) 197
Royal College of Physicians 109
Rufforth, James 216
Russell, John, 1st Earl of Bedford 192
Russell, John (author) 47
Rutland, Eleanor Paston, Countess of 185
Rutland, Thomas Manners, 1st Earl 172, 186
Rycote Park, Oxfordshire 351

Sadler, Ralph 170
St Albans, Battle of (1455) 5
St David's, Bishop of 359
St Faith's Church, Bacton (Herefordshire) 329
St James's, London 94
St Laurence Priory, Blackmore (Essex) 93
St Paul's Cathedral 9, 55, 57
St Paul's, Dean of 312–13
St Swithin's Priory, Winchester 30
Salerno Regimen (trans. Harington) 305
Salmon, Christopher 243
sanitation, washing and cleanliness
  bathing 123–4, 296, 299

clothes and accessories 102, 125–9
kitchens 120–1
perfumes 124–5, 126–7, 301
personal hygiene 125, 334–5
soap 124, 321, 361
toilet arrangements 129–30, 296, 301–2
Scaramelli, Giovanni Carlo 366, 371, 372
Scheyfe, Jean 242
servants
kitchen staff 118–19, 121
laundresses and seamstresses 127–9
personal 192, 195
relationship with the royal family 138
security of tenure 138–9
water cleaners 120
see also Privy Chamber
sex, sexuality
abstinence during pregnancy 28
after being 'churched' and not before 82
age of consumption 22
bedding ceremony 23–4, 56–7
celibacy vs matrimony 87–8
chasteness of the bride 22–3
contraception 187–8
extra-marital 87–90
female pleasure, necessity and excess 27, 69, 89, 272–3
influencing sex of child 153
male potency 56–7, 164, 166, 190–1
male semen 88–9
menstruation 68–9, 256, 259–60, 288–9, 292
pre-marital 27
sexual organs 89
Sexton (or Patch) (court jester) 8, 142

Seymour, Edward, Duke of Somerset (1500-52) 233
rise to prominence 160
appointed protector during Edward's minority 220
plunders Henry's wardrobe and private treasure 220–1
initiates changes to privy chamber personnel 221
offended by marriage of Katherine to his brother Thomas 226
ousted from power 237
execution of 239
Seymour family 160
Seymour, Jane (1509-37)
character and description 160–1, 167
courted by Henry 162–3
betrothal and marriage to Henry 165–6
receives gifts from Henry 165
pregnancy and childbirth 167, 170–1
death and funeral 172–3
appears in family portrait 212
Seymour, Sir John 160
Seymour, Mary 232
Seymour Place, London 228
Seymour, Thomas (1508-49)
rise to prominence 160
marries Katherine Parr 226
scandalous attentions towards Elizabeth 228–34
pleased at Katherine's pregnancy 231–2
sadness at death of Katherine 232
arrest and imprisonment 234
execution of 235
Seyton, William 162
Sforza, Ludovico, Duke of Milan 49–50
Shakespeare, William 126, 309, 310, 311

Sheen Manor 58
Sheen Palace 10, 38, 43–4, 44
Sheffield, Douglas 287, 336
Sheffield, Robert 336
Shelton, Sir John 168
Shelton, Mary 160
Shenton, William (court jester) 309
Sidney, Sir Henry 243
Sidney, Sir Philip 359
Sidney, William 175–6
Simier, Jean de 340
Simnel, Lambert 5, 50
Sipthorpe (farthingale maker) 328
Skelton, John 51–3
Skettes, Margaret (hoodmaker) 328
Smeaton, Mark 163, 164–5
Smith, Alice (silkwoman) 327–8
Smith, David (embroiderer) 324,
   326
Smith (or Smithson), Elizabeth 289
Smith, William 65
Snape Castle, Yorkshire 204
social rules and behaviours 201–3
Somer, William 'Will' (court jester)
   140–1, 225, 249, 309
Somerset, Charles, Lord Herbert 63,
   75
Somerset Place 17
Soncino, Raimondo da 50
Southwell, Elizabeth 362
Speculum Principis 52
Spekarde, Dorothy (silk-woman) 359
Spenser, Edmund 349
sports
   archery 137
   blood sports 138, 225, 275
   bowling 137, 151
   football 137
   hawking 98, 105, 114, 122, 135, 136,
      137, 210, 225

hunting 101, 114, 122, 130, 137, 150,
   210, 225, 284
jousting 8, 98, 105, 122, 134, 136, 151,
   162
   tennis 8, 98, 122, 137, 151, 225
   weight-lifting 137
Stafford, Sir Edward 363
Stanhope, Sir Michael 221–2, 234
Stanley, Thomas 15
Stoke, Battle of (1487) 5
Stoker, Bram 291
The Story of the Trojan War (tapes-
   tries) 16
Strelley, Frideswide 248
Stuart, Henry, see Lord Darnley
Sudeley Castle, Gloucestershire
   231–2, 233
Summer's Last Will and Testament
   (Nashe) 141
Sumptuary Act (1562) 324
Swynford, Katherine 6
Syemour, Thomas 205
Syon Abbey, Middlesex 196–7

Tailboys, Gilbert 93
Taunton, Somerset 49
Taylor, Robert 51
textiles
   bedding 25–6, 39, 95–6, 299
   carpets 95, 154–5, 300
   cushions 62, 74, 224, 296, 298, 299,
      300
   horse trappings 105
   hunting equipment 105
   table linen 15–16, 113, 115, 298
   tapestries 16–17, 94–5, 156, 170, 194–5,
      224, 297
   see also clothes
Theobalds House, Hertfordshire
   374

This is the Myrrour or Glasse of Helth
(Moulton) 123
Thomas, William 61
Thomasine the Dwarf 309–10
Throckmorton, Arthur 363
Throckmorton, Elizabeth 'Bess' 362–3
Tilbury 348
Tilney, Katherine 193
Titian 251
Tower of London
  celebratory shots fired from 171
  chapel of St John 62
  chapel of St Peter ad Vincula 165,
    197
  executions at 165, 197, 253
  imprisonment in 49, 164, 195, 197,
    253, 254–5
  Queen's Lodgings 62
  royal lodgings at 9
  storage of material possessions in
    17, 331
  Wardrobe Tower 327, 331
  White Tower 9
Treaty of Perpetual Peace (1502) 85
Twiste, Anne 289, 319

Velville, Roland de 7
Vergil, Polydore 7
Vernon, Elizabeth 363–4
Vicary, Thomas 89
Vittoria, Dr 90
Vives, Jean Luis 134

Waldegrave, Edward 246
Wallis Simpson, Duchess of Windsor
  292
Walsingham, Frances 365
Walsingham, Sir Francis 320, 344
Walsingham, Norfolk 85
Warbeck, Perkin 45, 49, 50–1

Warham, William, Archbishop of
  Canterbury 80
Wars of the Roses (1455-87) 5
washing *see* sanitation, washing and
  cleanliness
Wendy, Dr 243
Westminster Abbey 21, 44, 51, 64, 77,
  84
Westminster Palace 21, 24, 37, 41, 61,
  153
Weston, Francis 151
Weston, Richard 65
Whitehall Palace (formerly York
  Place) 264
  apartments converted into a
    kitchen 254
  bedchamber 299
  cock-fighting ring at 138
  Elizabeth I's corpse taken to 372
  extensions to 9–10
  furs kept at 331
  gardens 300
  Henry's private apartments in 218
  jewel house at 199
  laundry at 128
  library 299
  marriages in 166
  plays performed at 310
  privy bridge at 302
  privy chamber, gallery and pres-
    ence chamber 299–300
  queen's closet in 166
  as residence of Archbishop of York
    9
  sauna and bathroom 298–9
  sports complex at 151
  steam baths installed 124
  storage of possessions in 17, 199, 216
  style books at 106
Whittell, William 342

Whyte, Rowland 356
Wilder, Philip van 225
Wilhelm, Duke of Cleves 178
William the Conqueror 9, 10, 30
William II 21
William, Lord Herbert 6
Willoughby, Anthony 57
Willoughby, Katherine, Duchess of
  Suffolk 208, 232
Wilton House, Wiltshire 359
Winchester 29, 30, 164–5
Winchester Cathedral 257
Windsor Castle 10, 94, 220, 278, 298,
  331–2
Wolf Hall, Savernake Forest
  (Wiltshire) 160–1
Wolsey, Thomas (1473-1530)
  entrusted with confinement of
    Bessie Blount 92–3

builds Hampton Court 94
stipulations concerning the
  ceremony of robing 103
horrified at scullions' state of dress
  121
failure of reforms 144–6
fall from power 149, 152
and the King's Great Matter 149
Wolvesey Castle, Winchester 258
Woodstock, Oxfordshire 49, 61
Woodville, Elizabeth 5, 18, 38,
  43–4
Worsop, Lettice 107
Wriothesley, Henry, Earl of
  Southampton 363, 364
Wriothesley, Thomas 72, 204, 217
Wroth, Sir Thomas 225, 243
Wyatt, George 144
Wyatt, Thomas 143–4, 253, 254

ILLUSTRATIONS ACKNOWLEDGEMENTS

© akg-images: 7 above right/Eric Lessing, 9 above right. © Alamy: 3 above right/Heritage Image Partnership Ltd, 11 above left/World History Archive, 12 above left and below left/The Art Archive, 14 centre right/V&A Images. © Bridgeman Images: 1 above left/NPG/Stefano Baldini, 4 below left and below right and 13 above left/Ashmolean Museum University of Oxford, 5 above left/Victoria & Albert Museum London, 8 above/Courtesy of the Worshipful Company of Barbers, 10 above right/NPG, 10 below right/Trustees of the Bedford Estate Woburn Abbey UK, 11 below/Neue Galerie Museumslandschaft Hessen Kassel Germany, 12 above right/Berkeley Castle Gloucestershire UK, 13 above right/Hatfield House Hertfordshire UK, 14 above left/Musée Condé Chantilly France, 15 centre left/Woburn Abbey Bedfordshire UK, 16 above/Burghley House Collection Lincolnshire UK. © The British Library Board: 2 below (Add.45131, f. 54), 3 below (Harley 283, f.75), 6 below (Harley 3469, f.32v), 10 centre left (Cotton Otho C.X, f.235), 16 below (Add.35324, f.38). By kind permission of the Duke of Buccleuch & Queensberry KBE: 8 below, 15 below right. © CSG CIC Glasgow Museums and Libraries Collections: 5 centre right. Photograph courtesy of Hever Castle Kent UK: 1 above right. © Historic Royal Palaces: 5 below, 6 above right, 7 above left and below left, 13 below/photo Claire Collins. © Museum of London: 9 below right. © The National Archives, London: 14 below. © The National Library of Wales/The Vaux Passional, Peniarth MS 482 D f.9r (detail): 2 above. Private Collection: 1 below left. Private Collections/Bridgeman Images:4 above left, 5 above right, 15 above right. Royal Collection Trust © Her Majesty Queen Elizabeth II, 2016/Bridgeman Images: 1 below right, 3 above left and centre left, 4 above right, 7 below right, 9 above left, 12 below right. © Superstock/Fine Art Images: 11 above right. © Victoria and Albert Museum, London: 6 above left, 9 below left.